Borderers

becoming Americans on
the southern frontier

Carla Barringer
Rabinowitz

Haley's
Athol, Massachusetts

© 2018 by Carla Barringer Rabinowitz

Haley's
488 South Main Street
Athol, MA 01331
haley.antique@verizon.net
978.249.9400

Cover image compliments of Pixabay.

The map of Moore County on page 146 is based on a map of early Moore County land patents created by Rassie E. Wicker in 1956 and included in *A History of Moore County, North Carolina, 1747-1847* by Blackwell P. Robinson. The map is used by permission of Moore County Historical Association.

Maps created by Mark Wright.
Proof read by Debra Ellis.

Library of Congress Cataloging-in-Publication Data
Names: Rabinowitz, Carla, author.
Title: Borderers : Becoming Americans on the Southern Frontier / Carla Rabinowitz.
Description: Athol, Massachusetts : Haley's, [2018] | Includes bibliographical references and index.
Identifiers: LCCN 2018043598 | ISBN 9780998273549 (trade pbk.) ISBN 9780998273563 (trade cloth.)
Subjects: LCSH: Bettis family. | Drew family. | Frontier and pioneer life--Southern States. | Southern States--History--18th century. | Southern States--History--19th century. | Southern States--Genealogy.
Classification: LCC CS71.B57 2018 | DDC 929.20973--dc23

LC record available at https://lccn.loc.gov/2018043598

Brandon Barringer   Phil Rabinowitz

for my two greatest supporters, champions, and teachers,
my father, Brandon Barringer,
the family's premier genealogist,
and
my husband, Phil Rabinowitz,
in recognition of their valiant and successful struggle to
tolerate each other

Contents

Photos

Maps

VIRGINIA DREWS

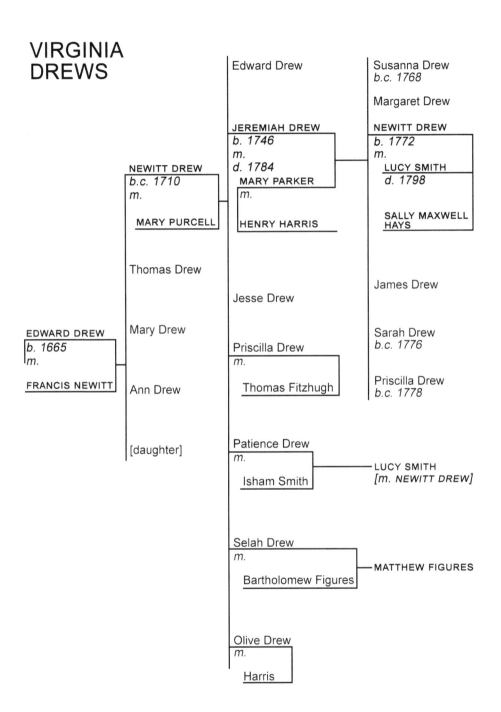

EDWARD DREW
b. 1665
m.
FRANCIS NEWITT

NEWITT DREW
b.c. 1710
m.
MARY PURCELL

Thomas Drew

Mary Drew

Ann Drew

[daughter]

Edward Drew

JEREMIAH DREW
b. 1746
m.
d. 1784
MARY PARKER
m.
HENRY HARRIS

Jesse Drew

Priscilla Drew
m.
Thomas Fitzhugh

Patience Drew
m.
Isham Smith

Selah Drew
m.
Bartholomew Figures

Olive Drew
m.
Harris

Susanna Drew
b.c. 1768

Margaret Drew

NEWITT DREW
b. 1772
m.
LUCY SMITH
d. 1798

SALLY MAXWELL HAYS

James Drew

Sarah Drew
b.c. 1776

Priscilla Drew
b.c. 1778

— **LUCY SMITH**
[m. NEWITT DREW]

— **MATTHEW FIGURES**

TENNESSEE DREWS

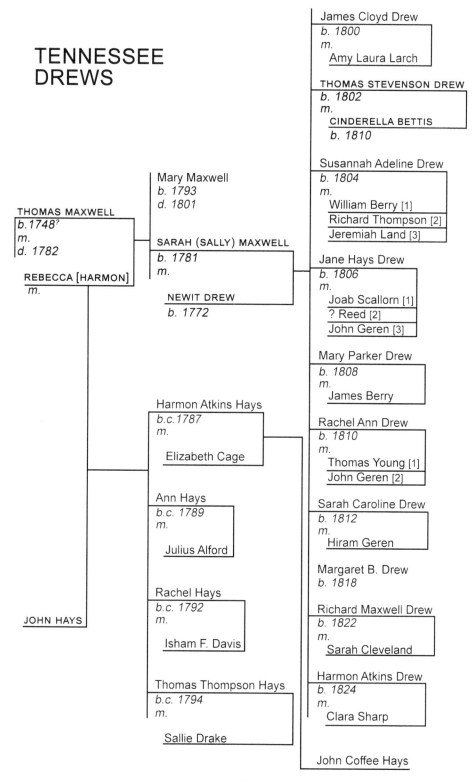

James Cloyd Drew
b. 1800
m.
Amy Laura Larch

THOMAS STEVENSON DREW
b. 1802
m.
CINDERELLA BETTIS
b. 1810

Susannah Adeline Drew
b. 1804
m.
William Berry [1]
Richard Thompson [2]
Jeremiah Land [3]

Jane Hays Drew
b. 1806
m.
Joab Scallorn [1]
? Reed [2]
John Geren [3]

Mary Parker Drew
b. 1808
m.
James Berry

Rachel Ann Drew
b. 1810
m.
Thomas Young [1]
John Geren [2]

Sarah Caroline Drew
b. 1812
m.
Hiram Geren

Margaret B. Drew
b. 1818

Richard Maxwell Drew
b. 1822
m.
Sarah Cleveland

Harmon Atkins Drew
b. 1824
m.
Clara Sharp

John Coffee Hays

Mary Maxwell
b. 1793
d. 1801

SARAH (SALLY) MAXWELL
b. 1781
m.

NEWIT DREW
b. 1772

THOMAS MAXWELL
b.1748?
m.
d. 1782

REBECCA [HARMON]
m.

Harmon Atkins Hays
b.c.1787
m.
Elizabeth Cage

Ann Hays
b.c. 1789
m.
Julius Alford

Rachel Hays
b.c. 1792
m.
Isham F. Davis

Thomas Thompson Hays
b.c. 1794
m.
Sallie Drake

JOHN HAYS

ARKANSAS DREWS

THOMAS S. DREW
b. 1802
m.

CINDERELLA BETTIS
b. 1810

Some spouses and descendants have been omitted for reasons of space.

Samuel Drew
b. 1828
d. 1830

unnamed infant
b. 1830
d. 1830

RANSON DREW
b. 1830

MARY (MOLLIE) DREW
b. 1838
d. 1860

James Drew
b. 1840

Thomas Drew
b. 1842

Bennett Drew?
b. 1843
d. 1850

SAIDEE DREW
b. 1844
m.
GUY CORYELL BENNET

EMMA DREW
b. 1846
m.
? SMITH [1]
WILLIAM MARR [2]

Joseph Drew
b. 1850
m.
Algenora Brimmage [1]
Mattie Williamson [2]

DREW BETTIS
(SON OF THOMAS DREW)
b. 1830
m.
LEANNA ROBINSON

MARTHA BETTIS COOPER
b. 1808

MARTIN BETTIS
b.c. 1835

NORTH CAROLINA BETTISES

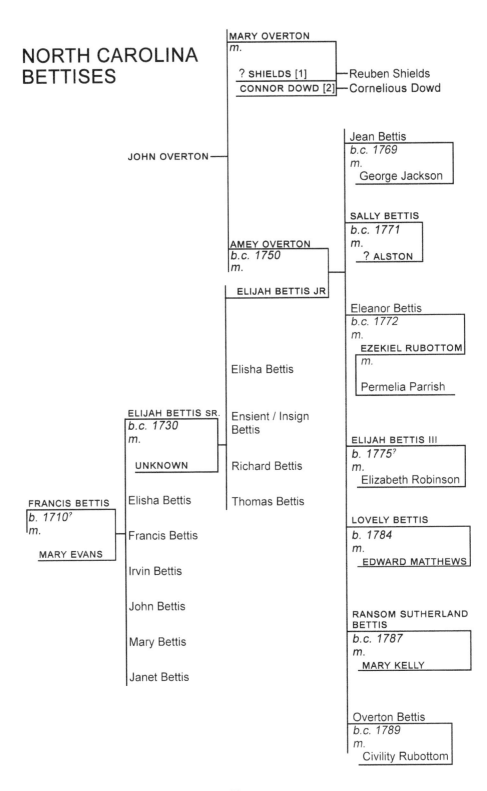

MARY OVERTON
m.

? SHIELDS [1] — Reuben Shields
CONNOR DOWD [2] — Cornelious Dowd

JOHN OVERTON

Jean Bettis
b.c. 1769
m.
George Jackson

SALLY BETTIS
b.c. 1771
m.
? ALSTON

AMEY OVERTON
b.c. 1750
m.

ELIJAH BETTIS JR

Eleanor Bettis
b.c. 1772
m.
EZEKIEL RUBOTTOM
m.
Permelia Parrish

Elisha Bettis

Ensient / Insign
Bettis

ELIJAH BETTIS SR.
b.c. 1730
m.

UNKNOWN

Richard Bettis

ELIJAH BETTIS III
b. 1775?
m.
Elizabeth Robinson

Elisha Bettis

Thomas Bettis

FRANCIS BETTIS
b. 1710?
m.

MARY EVANS

Francis Bettis

LOVELY BETTIS
b. 1784
m.
EDWARD MATTHEWS

Irvin Bettis

John Bettis

RANSOM SUTHERLAND
BETTIS
b.c. 1787
m.
MARY KELLY

Mary Bettis

Janet Bettis

Overton Bettis
b.c. 1789
m.
Civility Rubottom

MISSOURI BETTISES

SALLY BETTIS
b.c. 1771
m.
? ALSTON
- Elijah B. Alston
- Ransom Drew Alston
- Overton B. Alston
- James S. Alston

Eleanor Bettis
b.c. 1772
m.
EZEKIEL RUBOTTOM
m.
Permelia Parrish
— WILLIAM WILEY RUBOTTOM (UNCLE BILLY)
- CIVILITY
  m.
  HILLIARD DORSEY
- Elizabeth
  m.
  Elijah Bettis IV

ELIJAH BETTIS III
b. 1775?
m.
ELIZABETH ROBINSON
- Elijah Bettis IV
- Charnelcy Jean Bettis
- Amey Overton Bettis
  m.
  T.O. MARR
  — WILLIAM MARR
  m.
  EMMA DREW
- Narcissus Bettis

Elijah's known enslaved children
- Elizabeth (Litty) *b.c. 1800*
- Jane (Jenny)
- Charity
- Mahala (Haly)
- Polly
- MARTHA (PATSIE) *b.c. 1808* —
  - DREW BETTIS
    (SON OF THOMAS DREW)
    b. 1830
    m.
    LEANNA ROBINSON
  - MARTIN BETTIS
    b.c. 1835
- Celia

Some spouses and descendants have been omitted for reasons of space.

LOVELY BETTIS
b. 1784
m.
EDWARD MATTHEWS

RANSOM SUTHERLAND BETTIS
b.c. 1787
m.
MARY KELLY
— CINDERELLA BETTIS
b. 1810
m.
THOMAS DREW

Overton Bettis
b.c. 1789
m.
Civility Rubottom

In democratic peoples, new families constantly issue from nothing, others constantly fall into it, and all those who stay on change face; the fabric of time is torn at every moment and the trace of generations is effaced. You easily forget those who preceded you, and you have no idea of those who will follow you. Only those nearest have interest . . . . Thus not only does democracy make every man forget his ancestors, but it hides his descendants from him and separates him from his contemporaries; it constantly leads him back toward himself alone and threatens finally to confine him wholly within the solitude of his own heart.

—Alexis de Tocqueville
Democracy in America

Discovering the Borderers

an introduction by Carla Rabinowitz

In the year 1859, a free man of color named Drew Bettis sailed up the Mississippi and Missouri rivers from Jacksonport, Arkansas, to the Kansas border, an area only recently and temporarily at peace. With him was his mother, Martha Bettis Cooper, the indomitable woman who had finally succeeded in purchasing his freedom twenty years after she herself was freed. It was a dangerous journey. The last major outbreak of violence between Kansas's pro-and anti-slavery settlers had occurred only a year before, and the victorious Free Staters were not always friendly to people of color whether slave or free. But Drew and his mother had no choice. In the hysteria that preceded the Civil War, Arkansas had just passed a law requiring all free people of color to leave the state or face re-enslavement.

When they reached the town of Leavenworth, they disembarked and stayed. Drew Bettis married a woman of Native American descent, tried his hand at the grocery business, and eventually became a farmer. They were joined there by at least two of Martha's sisters and by Martha's second son, Martin, whom she had not seen since her brother carried him to freedom in Canada as a young child. Drew's descendants married the descendants of white and black Kansans, forming a large, close extended family, many of whose members remain in the Leavenworth area today.

Six years later, Drew's white half-sister Saidee Drew made her own journey from her home in Arkansas to Carlinsville, Illinois, to marry the Union Army sutler—an officer in charge of supplying provisions to an army—who had been quartered in her family's home during the war. Her family supported the Confederacy, and two of her brothers had fought in the Confederate Army. Family legend says she was told that if she married the sutler, Guy Bennett, she could never return to Arkansas, and she never did.

Bennett transferred his provisioning skills to the Santa Fe Railroad, then under construction, and the family followed the railroad west. When their daughter Margaret was born in 1873, they were living in Lawrence, Kansas; we have no way of knowing whether Saidee knew of the half-brother living only fifty miles away. As of 2018, Saidee's descendants are scattered across three continents.

Drew Bettis and Saidee Drew were two of at least ten children of Thomas Stevenson Drew, teacher, mailman, lawyer, planter, judge, governor, superintendent of Indian affairs, grocery store clerk, and would-be land speculator. Saidee was my great-grandmother, the daughter of Thomas and his wife, Cinderella Bettis Drew. Drew Bettis was the son of Thomas and his enslaved mistress, then known as Patsie or Martha Bettis, who, in the familiar tangle of black and white relationships within slaveholding families, was Cinderella's first cousin. His descendants are my third cousins.

This is a story about borders, about centuries-long journeys, and about the way those journeys shaped the families who followed those borders. The journeys of Drew and Saidee are part of the two-hundred-year journeys of the Drew and Bettis families, one thread in my own story and a thread in the larger story of who we are as Americans.

* * *

My interest in their story began with a wild goose chase.

When my cousins and I were in our fifties and all but one of our parents were dead, we were finally able to look at each other and ask a question that had not occurred to some of us until then.

4

Why were they so dark? Our family was supposedly German-English from the beginning of North Carolina time—where did the big brown eyes and black curly hair come from? It must have had some connection to our dark-eyed, dark-haired grandmother, Saidee Drew's daughter Margaret Bennett, whose maternal line was the only piece of our ancestry that had not been researched back to its original English or German village. With some free time on my hands, I set out to find the answer.

I never found it. I spent years exploring dead ends and far-fetched theories, but the dark coloring remains as mysterious as ever. Along the way, however, I kept finding other things, fascinating bits of information about my ancestors and their world, things I had never learned from history books, that ended up by turning a fruitless obsession into a story. Picking my way through a complex network of family relationships on the Virginia-North Carolina border, I began to recognize the kinship network that provided one of the first sources of social support in that isolated area. I began to understand the way that members of that network interacted with the free people of color who were their neighbors, occasionally their relatives, and, in that time and place, almost their equals. And then the stroke of lightning: the discovery of the membership list of the Black Creek Baptist Church along with two pairs of religious petitions dealing with the disestablishment of the Episcopal Church in Virginia. In each pair, there was an Episcopalian petition and a much longer and more eloquent Baptist one, the latter containing the signatures of most of the members of the kinship network I had been tracing.

The documents put me on the track of a piece of history I had never been exposed to: the role of the early Virginia Baptists in fighting for, and ultimately securing, the separation of church and state. Somewhat later, searching for Bettises in the North Carolina Piedmont, I discovered instead the rebellion of the Regulators and a renegade Quaker teaching his rebellious neighbors the habits of mind needed for self-government. Then, researching the post-Revolutionary era in North Carolina, I found the Freemasons, helping their members to develop the skills needed to collaborate in business affairs and large-scale community projects and building a network of trust and cooperation that greatly facilitated the development of the new states of the West. Still later, looking at life in Kansas after the Civil War, I became aware of the tireless advocacy of the black veterans who had helped to win the war and who went on to win for themselves the full rights of citizens. Everywhere I looked, I found seeds of the modern United States in the actions of ordinary people and in groups and institutions they formed or joined.

Early in this process, another discovery helped convince me that here was a story worth telling. As the oldest child of the oldest child and the only sibling with an attic, I inherited a small trove of family documents. Among them was a green folder that turned out to contain intriguing scraps of writing by Thomas Drew—drafts of letters and reports, fragments of one excessively long legal brief, and a long letter to his daughter written near the end of his life—all that was left of his papers to be handed down to his descendants. Poring through them, I found clues to a complex and fascinating person— an idealist and a conciliator, irrepressibly hopeful to the end in spite of an endless string of failures. I needed to know what had formed this man—hidden from me by Saidee's flight from Arkansas and by

Margaret's long journey from an Arizona ranch to the gilded precincts of the Philadelphia Main Line—and then to share that knowledge.

In the course of more than a decade of reading and research, I saw certain themes emerging again and again, all of them relevant to the evolution of my ancestors from the barely-civilized inhabitants of a chaotic frontier into American citizens as we recognize ourselves today.

The first theme involves the realization of how different these borderers were, right from the beginning, from the Europeans who were their ancestors, from the European travelers who observed and commented on them, and even from their more civilized countrymen in the coastal cities. The inhabitants of the Virginia and North Carolina backwoods had passed a hinge, a point in history where a path turns, a gate opens, and travelers find themselves in a new and unfamiliar world. At some times, a hinge swings open so slowly and quietly that it can be seen only in retrospect while at other times it opens to the accompaniment of clamor and destruction. The hinge between the old hierarchical world, where a person's status and fate were assigned at birth, and the modern world, where status is acquired at least to some degree by personal achievement, has swung open many times during the past four centuries at different times and in different places. At the dawn of the eighteenth century, it swung open on what was then the American frontier, and everything was different from then on.

Another recurrent theme concerns the slow establishment of what sociologists call "social capital" in the atomized society of the border. The term social capital refers to networks of relationships and shared values that foster trust, encourage cooperation, and enable the building of institutions for the benefit of the group. In the earliest days of the Virginia and North Carolina frontiers, both social capital and social institutions were largely lacking. Then, little by little, networks began to develop, at first between neighbors and relatives, then within church communities, then in increasingly broad networks of communities held together by bonds that supported their members and helped them to build the institutions needed to create a nation. The leading role played by evangelical churches in this process was a revelation for me. Historians of earlier generations have emphasized the culture of individualism that developed on the frontier. But individualism, at least as seen in the stories of the Drew and Bettis families, was at all times in tension with increasingly powerful forces of social connection, forces that helped them not only to survive but to create new and more inclusive communities.

In addition to providing support and structure for their members in a barely-formed society, the evangelical churches accomplished something else: they taught their members skills of citizenship. Quaker meetings and Separate Baptist churches were established, administered, and financed by the members themselves. Points of doctrine and behavior were debated by the members in accordance with rules of decorum they themselves had drawn up, with decisions and unanswered questions referred to quarterly regional meetings. In camp meetings attended by thousands of people, where ministers of several denominations addressed the throngs, attendees argued with each other until the early hours of the morning about the correctness of the teachings they had heard.

Those arguments sharpened both their own powers of debate and their understanding of the arguments of others.

The Masonic lodges that spread across the country after the Revolution taught their members to maintain bonds of fellowship even in the face of disagreement, gave them experience in the arts of collaboration necessary for the establishment of schools and other community institutions, and provided them with access to a continent-spanning network of brothers whose good faith could be relied on in commercial dealings. In the mid nineteenth century, more than seven thousand independent Methodist "classes"— actually somewhat closer to discussion groups—administered and financed by laypeople, met regularly to study Methodist doctrine and support their members in godly living. The skills that Americans acquired in such religious and quasi-religious activities provided one of the foundations for their effective participation as citizens of a republic.

It was not just through institutions that I could trace the evolution of my ancestors into Americans. The conditions of frontier life, in which the energy and skill of its members largely determined a family's survival, bred a self-reliance that overrode the dictates of authority and tradition. Up to the time of the Revolution, however, the backcountry people were dominated by the elites of the coastal cities, who feared their unregulated energy and made an effort to keep them as powerless as possible. After the Revolution, when the Native American peoples to the west had been successfully crushed, the promise of new lands across the mountains unleashed that energy, allowing it to develop in dramatic new ways. The Drews and the

Bettises, formerly obscure yeoman farmers, seized that opportunity, to found churches, build mills, establish ferries, and create towns. Drawing on their experiences in Baptist churches and Masonic lodges, they made themselves into politicians, lawyers, judges, and merchants. As they and hundreds of thousands of others peopled the West, they shifted both the center of power in the American nation and the content of the American character.

The word borderers was used in their own time and later to describe the first permanent settlers in an area newly opened to Europeans. Geographically, the Drews and the Bettises were borderers from the dawn of the eighteenth century to the end of the nineteenth. But they were also borderers in another sense. Again and again, their migrations placed them at the intersection of cultures—the cultures of Native Americans, enslaved Africans, Highland Scots of the upper Cape Fear Valley, Scots-Irish of the Appalachians, and French colonists in the Mississippi Valley. They were shaped by conflicts between Patriots and Loyalists and by conflicts among Anglicans, Quakers, Baptists, Presbyterians, and Freemasons. The necessity of adapting to a complex and constantly changing world gave them the tools they needed to survive and often flourish within that world.

There was also another, much darker, influence on the characters of these borderers and their descendants. It is an influence so all-pervading that although I had written about it repeatedly in this book, it was not until well into the editing process that I thought to name it. That was, of course, the institution of slavery. It was difficult if not impossible for a slaveholder not to have his or her soul deformed at least to some extent by the ownership of human beings. The stories of many of the people in this book and of the society that surrounded them provide evidence of the various forms such deformation could take. In some cases it legitimized sexual abuse or vicious cruelty; in others it sparked self-justifying fantasy or outbreaks of hysterical hatred; in still others it derailed empathy or overrode the impulses of normal human decency. It has cursed our nation since its beginning. As the descendant of slaveholders, I can recognize some of that damage still lurking in my own soul.

Again and again in the course of my research, I also encountered the stories of free people of color, a group trapped between the increasingly rigid boundaries of free and unfree, almost but not quite citizens at the beginning of the American story, almost but not quite slaves just before the Civil War. Their migrations followed the moving border. With each migration they enjoyed, for no more than one generation, a greater degree of freedom and acceptance than in the older society they had left. Throughout this book, these free people will appear in the lives of the Drew and Bettis families, making their way as best they could before the walls closed around them once again.

In order to get to know the people about whom I was writing, I relied on many types of documents: deeds, wills, estate inventories, bills of sale, church records, census records, lawsuits, local histories, records of the United States Bureau of Indian Affairs, colonial and state records of Virginia, North Carolina, and Arkansas, a few scraps of personal correspondence, family histories written by descendants or passed down orally from one generation to another, and the published observations of a series of bemused or appalled foreign travelers. A law degree (unaccompanied by a legal career) enabled me to understand some of the subtleties contained in the legal documents. These records, however, could provide only a partial understanding. In many cases a courthouse fire had destroyed all relevant records for a particular place and time. Census takers sometimes had to guess at ages, literacy status, or the spelling of names, and after their data was collected, it had to be transcribed into neat ledgers, perhaps by people who could not read the original handwriting. Family histories often contain more fantasy than fact.

To flesh out my characters, to give them form as human beings, I have also needed my imagination. That imagination was based on many sources, including personal experience, family history, the work of social historians who have illuminated the lives and societies of similar people, and perhaps a general sense of human nature gleaned from a lifetime of reading. I have tried to be clear about the places where the documents stop and imagination must take over.

In the past three centuries, people have become Americans in many different ways, but seldom by simply stepping off a boat. Dates matter. Places matter. What they were fleeing or seeking, whether they came voluntarily or involuntarily, individually or as part of a community matter as well. But the transformation is almost always a process rather than an event. This book chronicles how that process unfolded for the borderers who were my ancestors. Based on documents, stories, and imagination, the journeys of these two families provide a window into the world of the southern borderers, as America shaped itself around them and formed them into Americans.

Part I
Origins

JAMESTOWN

VIRGINIA

ISLE OF WIGHT
COUNTY

BLACKWATER RIVER

THREE CREEKS
SWAMP

ANGELICO
SWAMP

Drews

ANGELICO
CREEK

SOUTHAMPTON
COUNTY

NORTH CAROLINA

CHESAPEAKE BAY

GREAT DISMAL SWAMP
Original Size

Bettises

ELIZABETH CITY

ALBERMARLE SOUND

1. William Byrd Surveys the Border

Where the southeast corner of Virginia meets the northeast corner of North Carolina lies an expanse of flat, swampy land whose little rivers run south to Albemarle Sound. The Great Dismal Swamp is the most prominent feature of this territory. At the turn of the eighteenth century, the swamp was about three times its present size,[1] the largest of a number of inhospitable boggy places—Flat Swamp, Raccoon Swamp, Nottoway Swamp, and Angelica Swamp, among others. For a long time, the exact location of the border between the colonies of Virginia and North Carolina was unknown, and the few straggling settlers were unencumbered by government of any sort. A small number of the original inhabitants, Nottoway and Nansemond Indians, survived in isolated towns. In 1705, when the colonial authorities officially opened the land south of the Blackwater River for European settlement, two small reservations, one a circle six miles in diameter and the other a square six miles on a side, were set off for the Nottoway Indians. But as their numbers continued to dwindle, piece by piece their land was sold, and in 1825, the reservation was officially eliminated.

By 1725, the swampy border was already sprinkled with cabins and small farms, some of them on fields the Indians had formerly tilled. As settlement spread south and both colonies granted land patents in the border area, it became necessary to determine the precise location of the line that divided those colonies.

In 1728, a Virginia aristocrat, William Byrd II, was appointed as one of the Virginia commissioners in a joint Virginia-North Carolina surveying party whose mission was to fix the location of

the previously undefined boundary. Between them, the two delega-
tions included seven commissioners, four surveyors, and a chaplain.
The Virginia group included twenty additional men, all meticulously listed in the records of the expedition, who did the hard work
of carrying firearms, chains, and surveying instruments, clearing
the way through the thick woods, and looking after the horses and
baggage. The group also included an unknown number of slaves
who waited on the commissioners, carried their baggage, and set up
their tents, but who are given no names and do not exist as far as
Byrd's official report is concerned.

For the first three weeks of their journey, the surveying party did
not go a day without having to wade up to their knees and sometimes
up to their waists for at least a mile through swamp or marsh.
Some local residents wondered aloud whether the party had been
condemned to take part in the expedition as a punishment for crimes.
Others solemnly advised them to make their wills before going on.
One man, whose land bordered the Great Dismal Swamp, told them
a tall tale of a neighbor who had been lost in the swamp and had
escaped only by taking a louse out of his collar and placing it on a
piece of paper. The louse, "having no Eye-lids," turned itself around
until it faced the darkest part of the sky, and the wretched man
followed this improvised compass to the northern end of the swamp.

The passage across the "Dismal" itself, a distance of fifteen miles,
took the surveyors nine days. Knee-deep in water for a good part
of the time, they struggled through thickets of twelve-foot-high
reeds interlaced with brambles that clawed at their legs. The canopy
overhead was too thick for any glimpse of sky. In some places, their
way was blocked by piles of uprooted cedar trees, blown down by

the wind and "horsing" on top of one another. On the eighth day, their food ran out, and some of them began to look hungrily at the expedition's dog. Byrd and his fellow commissioners, meanwhile, rode the sixty-five miles around the north end of the swamp and waited for the rest of the party in comfort.

Byrd's twin *Histories of the Dividing Line Betwixt Virginia and North Carolina*—the first an official account focusing on geography, natural history, and resources and the second a "secret" account focusing on the squabbles between the commissioners—are genial, observant, witty, and unsparing in their scorn for the North Carolina borderers. They were "indolent Wretches" too lazy to clear and fence proper pastures for their cattle and hogs, which were sent off to fend for themselves in the swamps during the winter. The North Carolina men had barely enough ambition to get out of bed, and survived only because of the industry of their wives, who made everything they needed with their own hands. Byrd was merely the first of many aristocratic observers to view the North Carolina settlers with such disdain.

The rivers—where they were navigable at all—ran south to Albemarle Sound, which was blocked by sandbars that made it inaccessible to oceangoing ships. As a result, inhabitants had little access to Atlantic commerce, and manufactured goods were so scarce that even nails were unavailable. Houses were held together with wooden pegs, and doors swung on wooden hinges.[2] One-or two-room affairs built of logs and usually with dirt floors, they were so dirty and vermin-ridden, according to Byrd, that even though hospitality was offered, Byrd and his companions preferred to sleep outside.

We can perhaps detect a note of wry admiration in Byrd's description of the settlers' religious and political beliefs. Byrd and the other commissioners were Anglicans and traveled with a minister who held services and baptized local babies. But he says of the North Carolina settlers "that they are not troubled with Religious Fumes and have the least Superstition of any People living." The settlers were, however, anxious about the possibility that the surveyors might include their land in the territory of Virginia, in which case "they must have submitted to some sort of Order and Government; whereas, in N Carolina, every One does what seems best in his own Eyes."[3]

Not that the surveying party did much to raise the level of civilization in the area. Both commissioners and commoners considered themselves free to molest virtually every woman between the ages of fifteen and fifty with whom they came in contact. The "secret history" records two rapes, numerous attempted rapes, a variety of lesser assaults, and one housewife who barricaded herself in her room with a loaded chamber pot. The womenfolk of the most prosperous and respectable planters were not exempt: some members of the party offered to take "gross Freedoms" with the sister of a local justice. Byrd represents himself as taking no part in these activities and, indeed, as rescuing a number of "damsels" from his importunate companions—a claim that may be met with some skepticism by readers of his other diaries.[4]

Crossing into Isle of Wight County on the Virginia side, the commissioners paid a visit to the town of the Nottoway Indians, hoping to enjoy the legendary hospitality of the Indian women. They were welcomed cordially. The Nottoway women put on all their finery, and the Nottoway men painted themselves and performed dances for the visitors. But, to their disappointment, the visitors were not offered bed partners; apparently there were too many guests for the available women and girls. Some of the commissioners apparently managed to get around this limitation, since Byrd noticed in the morning that their ruffles were stained with the red paint that the Indian women used to decorate their bodies. He estimated the total population of the town at no more than two hundred souls—the largest group of Indians within the territory of Virginia at that time.[5]

In April, the expedition broke off, because warm weather had begun to bring out the rattlesnakes. Recommencing in September, the commissioners reached the westernmost settlers near the location of the Indian Trading Path in Brunswick County. The Carolina commissioners accompanied the expedition for the next fifty miles and then went home, stating that they didn't think any further surveying would be necessary for "an age or two."[6] The Virginians continued the survey, finally coming within sight of the Blue Ridge Mountains, a distance of 241 miles from their starting point, before "the Scantiness of Bread, and the near approach of Winter" persuaded them to turn back toward home.[7]

2. People of the Border

Who were these borderers?

They were a random mixture of small farmers, insolvent debtors, former indentured servants, mixed-race families, and religious dissenters, all of them unable to find a place or a livelihood in William Byrd's Tidewater Virginia. They had come in search of opportunities denied them in the long-settled areas of the Tidewater: the opportunity to live independently, to make their own way, to own their own land, to practice their own faith, or to be treated as equals by their neighbors—to do, as Byrd astutely observed, "what seemed best in their own eyes." The North Carolina historian Jack Temple Kirby describes their culture as "profoundly democratic" and their territory as "a countercultural place, where people removed themselves from disagreeable institutions economic and social."[1]

Elite Virginians of the mid-seventeenth century brought with them a very specific vision of their ideal society, profoundly different from that of the Quakers and Puritans who settled the more northern colonies. Minor gentry, younger sons of aristocratic families, sons of prosperous tradesmen with aristocratic connections, and "distressed Cavaliers" who had lost their fortunes in the English civil war, they dreamed of a land that would afford them the aristocratic status that England denied. Far from exalting the dignity of labor, they sought a society in which they would never have to be defiled by it. Rather than valuing each soul's direct relationship with God, they demanded conformity to the liturgical forms of the Anglican Church. Their ideal commonwealth, like the England they had left, was based on rank and hierarchy, with the authority of both church and state exercised by a small elite served by a large group of laborers with neither dignity nor rights.

William Berkeley, Governor of Virginia on and off for thirty-five years, imagined such a society more clearly than anyone else and did more than anyone else to make it a reality. He actively recruited distressed Cavaliers and ambitious younger sons, and arranged the political institutions of his colony so that power and wealth were concentrated in their hands.[2] He famously thanked God for the absence of free schools and printing presses in Virginia, and he and his successors did their best to ensure that the situation remained unchanged.[3]

The opportunity for wealth presented itself immediately, in the form of the immense profits to be made from the sale of tobacco to European markets. Tobacco cultivation, however, required a large labor force, and the early colonists were not eager to volunteer.

Initially, the local Indians—those few who survived the devastating diseases brought in by Europeans—were pressed into service as indentured servants or wage laborers, or captured and enslaved in so-called "just wars." But the solution was unsatisfactory. Indian men were insubordinate. They ran away. They refused to work in the fields, since agriculture in their world was wholly the province of women. As a result, Indian male captives were commonly either killed or sold south to the sugar plantations of the Caribbean, while captive Indian women remained in slavery in Virginia.[4]

The need for labor was filled at first by English indentured servants. Poor and landless young men and women were recruited, enticed, and sometimes kidnapped to work on Virginia planta-tions. As time went on, convicted criminals were added to the mix.

Three-quarters of the immigrants to Virginia in the seventeenth century came as indentured servants.[5] Of these, at least three-quarters were male, and at least three-quarters were illiterate.[6] On arrival, they worked as virtual slaves for a period of four or sometimes seven years. They could be bought, sold, or savagely punished at the whim of their masters. Before the terms of their indentures were up, more than half of them were dead.

There is still no consensus about the cause of the horrifying death rates among the first generation of settlers, but historian Edmund Morgan suspects typhoid. The water table in the Tidewater was high, and at the time of the early tobacco boom, planters preferred to settle on low land close to the shore, where shallow wells were most vulnerable to contamination. After 1644, life expectancy appears to have increased. Morgan attributes the improvement to the growing presence of orchards, whose fruit, transformed by fermentation, would have provided inhabitants with a relatively safe alternative to the local water.[7]

For a while, there was a reward at the end of the ordeal. If a servant managed to survive his indenture, custom required his master to provide him with food and clothing sufficient to support himself for a year. Before 1660, most former servants eventually acquired small plantations, and some became rich enough to own servants or slaves of their own.[8]

In 1620, the first members of another group arrived in Jamestown: about twenty Africans captured from a Portuguese slave ship bound for the Caribbean.[9] Chattel slavery was as yet unknown in Virginia, and these Africans and the small number who followed them in the first twenty or thirty years were treated in some respects like English indentured servants. As with the English indentured servants, the large majority of Africans arriving on this continent were male. Wills and estate inventories from the period indicate that, on many plantations, the labor force consisted of roughly equal numbers of male Africans and female Indians.[10] Africans, whites, and Indians worked side by side, lived in the same wretched huts, ate the same food, and ran away together when they had the chance. And like the English servants, some of the first Africans gained their freedom, by manumission, self-purchase, or expiration of their term of indenture. Some acquired land and slaves of their own and were treated as respectable property-holders in their communities.[11]

On Virginia's Eastern Shore, a tight-knit community of freed slaves, all of them originally captives from Angola, flourished for two generations during the second half of the seventeenth century. Some members of the community owned both African slaves and white indentured servants, married white women, and interacted with local white planters as social equals.[12] The court records of Northampton and Accomack Counties reveal disputes between black and white neighbors that demonstrate the confidence and assertiveness of these Angolans, and show black men and women verbally abusing whites without any trace of deference. When a white man called John Neene attempted to summon Tony Longo into court to give evidence in a lawsuit, Longo, who was busy getting in his corn crop, replied "Shet of your warrant, have I nothing to do but go to Mr. Walker, go about your business you idle rascal!"[13] Ironically, it was one of these early Angolan immigrants, Anthony Johnson, who first established the legal precedent that gave slaveholders the right to hold their slaves for life.[14]

The surplus of African men, the success of some of them in gaining their freedom, and the shared work experiences of English servants and African and Indian slaves had an entirely predictable consequence: the early appearance of a free, mixed-race or tri-racial population. For our knowledge of the origins of this population, we are indebted to the decades of painstaking research carried out by Paul Heinegg, the author of *Free African Americans of Virginia, North Carolina, and South Carolina*. Tracing free mixed-race families of the colonies back to their earliest roots, Heinegg demonstrates that the large majority of them were not the offspring of black women sexually exploited by white masters but instead the result of consensual liaisons or long-term common-law marriages between white servant women and African men.[15]

Virginia laws against such behavior were severe. White servant women who bore mixed-race children out of wedlock could be publicly whipped, have their terms of servitude extended, and see their children bound out as servants before they were old enough to talk. But no amount of punishment was sufficient to prevent such relationships. Of three hundred free, mixed-race families whose genealogies have been analyzed by Heinegg, more than two-thirds were descended from free white women and free or enslaved black men. Others bore surnames of families of the Tidewater elite, suggesting that their ancestors may have been freed slaves or perhaps blood relatives of those families. By the mid-eighteenth century, "Byrd" was a common surname among free mixed-race families on the Virginia side of the border.

Many of these families remained in poverty on the margins of society. A few, however, became substantial landowners who, like the Angolans of the Eastern Shore, managed to achieve a level of prosperity and social status equal to that of their white neighbors. They appear in the records as "Free Negro," "mulatto," "other free," and eventually "free people of color." Over the course of several generations, some of their descendants married back into the white community until all memory of their African ancestry was erased. Others had no choice but to identify as black. Still others remained caught in a kind of interracial limbo, congregating in communities with others of similar heritage, calling themselves Portuguese or Indian or Melungeon or "Black Dutch," adamantly denying their African ancestry but never fully accepted as white. Among their descendants are hundreds of thousands—possibly millions—of modern "white" Americans.

Two generations after the arrival of the first English and African Virginians, a series of economic and social changes began to affect the lives of small planters and hired laborers, both white and black. Perhaps the most important was the progressive consolidation of land ownership. By 1660, a small group of wealthy families had gained control of all of the levers of power in Virginia—including the Royal Council, which controlled distribution of land. With no trace of shame, they began to distribute unclaimed land in large quantities to themselves and their relatives.[16] People with enough money to transport themselves or others to Virginia, either from Europe or from other colonies, were allowed a "headright" or grant of fifty acres for each person so transported. But the rapaciousness of the wealthy would not be so limited. People with access to capital could buy the headrights of those who lacked resources to make use of them or who died without heirs.[17] In the third quarter of the seventeenth century, the average size of a land patent was 890 acres, and some of the major officeholders owned tens of thousands.[18] William Byrd I, the father of the diarist, amassed an estate of 26,000 acres; by 1739 his son owned 179,000.[19]

Access to ocean transportation was the key to wealth in early Virginia. With hundreds of miles of rivers navigable by oceangoing ships, ownership of riverfront land meant that merchant captains could dock at the owner's wharf, purchase his tobacco crop, and provide him with imported goods to resell to his less fortunate neighbors. By 1665, all of the land along navigable waters was occupied, with large planters claiming the lion's share.[20] The rising class of "great planters" owned not only land and slaves but also ships and warehouses, in addition to holding all major public offices. Small and middling planters had to deal with them, both to sell their tobacco and to purchase their supplies. Great planters' contacts with London banks and merchants allowed them to extend credit to smaller planters, keeping them indebted and dependent.[21] A small planter, by one definition, was one who owned less than three hundred acres, while a middling planter might own up to a thousand. Perhaps sixty to seventy percent of the male population owned no land at all.[22]

By the 1660s, the monopolization of land by great planters had made it difficult or impossible for former indentured servants to acquire land in the settled Tidewater area. They might find work as laborers or tenant farmers, but their only chance for independence and self-sufficiency was to move to the less desirable land of the frontier.[23] In Surry County, the frontier of that era, more than half of the householders in the 1675 tax list were probably newly freed indentured servants, identified as such by listings with a single adult male and no children, servants, or slaves. In addition to economic hardships and exorbitant taxes, they faced the risk of occasional raids by the area's surviving Indians, with little or no protection provided by the Tidewater elite.[24] Resentment of their betters was a constant presence among them, and their betters knew it. And every man of them was armed.

At the same time another process was underway, which, like consolidation of land ownership, increased the rigidity of Virginia society and eliminated opportunities for those on its margins. As economic conditions improved in England, the supply of white indentured servants was drying up. Planters in search of cheap labor increasingly turned to enslaved Africans. As they did, they began to feel increasingly uneasy about the free mixed-race people, who did not fit comfortably into either category, and whose allegiance to the hierarchical order of society seemed even less reliable than that of their white neighbors. That uneasiness was heightened in 1676 by the short-lived upheaval known as Bacon's Rebellion.

Nathaniel Bacon was an ambitious young aristocrat, who considered Governor Berkeley and his associates too common for their positions.[25] Although he had little in common with the struggling borderers, Bacon excelled at exploiting their grievances. When Indian trouble broke out on the Potomac in 1675, he asked Governor Berkeley for a commission to lead the discontented farmers of New Kent County and the south side of the James River in an expedition against the Indians. Fearing, quite reasonably, that Bacon's "Rabble Crue" could turn dangerous, Berkeley refused.

Bacon went ahead anyway. His troops succeeded in killing a number of hostile Indians, and then massacred the friendly ones who had taken the hostile ones captive. This "victory" was followed by a series of feints and maneuvers between Bacon and the governor, ending with open rebellion by Bacon and his army of freedmen and small farmers, both whites and free people of color. As his more affluent followers turned aside to plunder the houses of neighbors who continued to support the beleaguered governor, Bacon went off to capture a band of peaceful Pamunkey Indians, marched them in triumph to Jamestown, burned the town to the ground, and died a month later of the "bloody flux."[26] The rebellion collapsed, and the social order reasserted itself.

Bacon's rebellion had no populist or democratic goals. Indeed, he first attempted to sell his Indian campaigns to Berkeley as a means of redirecting the growing anger of poorer citizens away from the elite. But his rabble of poor white and mixed-race followers threw a serious scare into the Virginia establishment before the uprising was crushed. In the wake of the rebellion, Virginia's lawmakers began to tighten the laws affecting slaves and free people of color with the goals of degrading both groups, encouraging racial contempt, and driving a wedge between poorer whites and all people of African descent. Increasing reliance on slavery as the economic base of the plantation system reinforced this trend, encouraging the passage of ever harsher laws aimed at controlling slaves.[27] A law passed in 1680 imposed a penalty of thirty lashes on any "negro or other slave" who "shall presume to lift up his hand in opposition to any Christian."[28] The law strengthened identification of white servants with their masters, by putting them on a par with those masters in their ability to abuse black slaves without suffering consequences.

Another law, passed in 1691, provided for white mothers of illegitimate mixed-race children to be fined or bound as servants for five years. The children themselves were bound out—sold to the highest bidder for the benefit of the local parish—until the age of thirty. Legitimate mixed-race children, illegitimate white children, and illegitimate mixed-race children of black or mixed-race women were exempt from the penalty, which seems to have been designed to protect the access of white men to the limited supply of white women.[29] In addition, any white person who married a non-white would be banished from Virginia forever. Anyone freeing a slave was required to transport him or her out of the colony within six months of freedom, on penalty of a fine of ten pounds sterling.[30]

The 1705 Black Code, passed as the importation of enslaved Africans was gathering momentum, contained the harshest laws so far. One section defined a mulatto as any person with at least one black great-grandparent,[31] while others barred free people of color from any ecclesiastical, civil, or military office, including service on juries.[32] All livestock belonging to slaves was confiscated and sold for the benefit of the white poor of the local parish, while the rights of white servants were expanded to include "competent" food and lodging and freedom from "immoderate" corporal punishment.[33] At the same time, the code gave white slaveowners the right to apply to the county court for permission to mutilate or dismember disobedient slaves. The penalty for intermarriage was also changed, to six months in prison for the white partner plus a fine of ten pounds.

A minister performing such a marriage was fined ten thousand pounds of tobacco, with half of the fine to go to the informer.[34]

In 1723, a new set of laws forbade the manumission of slaves, except by an act of the governor and his council. Free people of color lost the right to vote, and their right to own guns was severely restricted.[35] The right to bear arms, with the parallel responsibility of serving in the militia, was a badge of free citizenship at least as important as the right to vote. But armed men were harder to control than unarmed ones and harder to subdue when aggrieved. It was safer to divide the potentially aggrieved into "us" and "not us," to discourage them from uniting to address their grievances. Restrictions on gun ownership by free people of color were a pointed reminder of their status as outsiders, permanently suspect and permanently inferior.

On Virginia's southern frontier, however, these laws were enforced only casually, and south of the North Carolina border, they did not apply at all. The availability of unclaimed land on the swampy border, coupled with the increasing difficulties of free blacks and former indentured servants in the more settled Tidewater, provided significant incentives for southward migration from the end of the seventeenth century on.

The more tolerant laws of North Carolina also protected religious dissidents, particularly Society of Friends (Quakers), who suffered ferocious persecution on the Virginia side of the border. The first Quakers arrived in Virginia in 1656, and their numbers increased rapidly after a visit from George Fox, the founder of the sect, in 1672. Many of Fox's early converts belonged to Puritan families who had settled on the northern borders of Isle of Wight and Nansemond counties a generation earlier. That area soon became the center of Quakerism in Virginia.[36]

Sober, industrious, and peaceable, Quakers were nevertheless a threat to Governor Berkeley's Cavalier Utopia. Their belief in the "inner light" and in the equal dignity of all people constituted a direct challenge to the social order. They rejected the spiritual authority of Anglican or any other ministers, establishing in its place a system of authority based on unanimous consent of their own members. They allowed women to preach. Worse still, they rejected the elaborate rituals of deference that supported the hierarchical society of seventeenth-century Virginia. They would not bow or remove their hats to those of higher rank. They addressed everyone with the familiar "thee," usually reserved for children and servants, rather than the respectful "you," and refused to address anyone as "master," "mister," "sir," or "mistress."[37]

Their most radical refusals stemmed from their determination to separate their religion from any state control. Believing that their Truth owed no allegiance to the machinery of the state, they refused to apply for licenses for their meetings or for exemptions from penalties for not attending Anglican services. They would not take oaths, following Jesus's injunction not to swear. They refused to pay any tax designed to support the established church or to pay the salaries of its ministers. These refusals were reinforced by the admonishments of the Virginia Yearly Meeting[38]

Because the authority of Virginia's Anglican Church and that of the colony's governmental institutions were inextricably intertwined, this Quaker defiance gave rise to savage persecution. No sooner had the first Quakers arrived in Virginia than they were officially banished from the colony. Shipmasters who transported Quakers into the colony were fined one hundred pounds and required to remove the offending persons immediately. Missionaries were imprisoned, and both male and female missionaries were publicly whipped.[39] People who persisted in holding or attending Quaker meetings were subjected to imprisonment or ruinous fines. Even being "loving to Quakers" became a crime.[40]

Quaker meetings kept meticulous records of the "sufferings" of their members, itemizing the value of goods taken in each case and the hardships endured by their families as a result. The testimony of Thomas Jordan provides a famous example. In 1701, Jordan was imprisoned for ten months "for Refusing to swear according to their wills & agt the Command of Christ." The sheriff took away his three servants and two feather beds—the family's most valuable possessions—and "left my wife in a Distressed Condition with A young Child sucking at her brests that to help her selfe the Child did burst Itselfe with Crying."[41] In 1723 Robert Jordan was sentenced to a year in prison for refusing to pay clerical tithes but freed after three weeks as a result of repeated personal appeals to the governor. He was rearrested in 1727 and held for fifteen weeks. In 1748, the law governing tithes was passed again, but by then the authorities were becoming used to the peculiarities of Quakers, and imprisonment was increasingly rare.[42]

South of the North Carolina border, on the other hand, the laws provided for full religious toleration.[43] The Quaker missionary William Edmundson made the first few converts when he visited the counties of Pasquotank and Perquimans on Albemarle Sound in 1672. He found there people of "no religion, for they came and sat down in the meeting smoking their pipes." Evidently his preaching was successful, for when Fox himself visited the area five years later, he found Friends there "finely settled" with "no room for the priests."[44] Fox's journal provides a reminder of the land these people inhabited: "much of it plashy, and pretty full of great bogs and swamps; so that we were commonly wet to the knees, and lay abroad a-nights in the woods by a fire: saving one of the nights we got to a poor house at Summertown [Somerton] and lay by the fire."[45]

In Pasquotank and Perquimans counties, immediately south of the Great Dismal Swamp, Quakers quickly became the dominant sect. Quaker meetings established by the early missionaries evolved into a distinctive mini society, a tightly knit community with its own strict rules of dress, speech, and behavior. The most familiar of these is the Quaker tradition of plain dress, sober in color and severely simple in design. There were also rules about sexual behavior, proper speech, use of liquor, and business ethics.[46] Quakers could be disowned by their meetings for "deviating from the truth; keeping liquor in the home; fighting; asking high interest on loans; being seen in the street while a meeting was in progress;" and for marrying out of the faith.[47]

These Quaker meetings provide an early example of the small communities and associations that sustained their members amid the individualistic chaos of frontier life. Edmundson's "people of no religion" may have scorned traditional authority, but they may also have yearned for the structure and security that these tight-knit communities provided. A Quaker meeting served as a kind of extended family, monitoring the behavior of its members, resolving disputes, reconciling conflicts, and expelling those who strayed and would not apologize. The firm behavioral rules provided by these meetings reinforced the perception of Quakers as people whose integrity could be trusted. Their strong social networks gave them the ability to collaborate effectively to achieve their goals. Together, the rules and the networks most likely contributed to the dominance of Quakers in North Carolina politics at the beginning of the eighteenth century.[48]

The Virginia persecutions, coupled with North Carolina tolerance, drove many Virginia Quakers south across the border.[49] But some stayed put. Based on a careful reading of the journals of Quaker missionaries or "traveling Friends," the Quaker historian Stephen Weeks found that Quaker meetings flourished in the counties just north of the Virginia border, collectively known as the Southside, for much of the eighteenth century. In 1727, the traveling Friend Samuel Bownas found meetings in numerous Virginia communities, with nine meeting houses having been erected in the past twenty-two years and old ones enlarged to up to four times their former capacity.[50] Parochial reports from 1725 show an unusually small percentage of Anglican communicants in the Upper Parish of Isle of Wight County, with only a "small proportion" of families attending church at all.[51]

Even at their peak, it is doubtful that Quakers ever amounted to more than ten percent of the population of Isle of Wight, particularly in the southern part that later became Southampton County.[52] But surnames found in early Quaker records remained common in Isle of Wight and Southampton counties throughout the eighteenth century, and families with such surnames remained closely associated and intermarried with each other. The significance of those relationships will become apparent in Part Two, when we look at the membership list of the Black Creek Baptist Church.

Although the Quakers disappear early on from the family histories chronicled here, they had a significant influence on the society in which those families lived, and on the nation coming into being around them. Their determined egalitarianism, their system of governance based on the consent of members, and their insistence on freedom of conscience helped set a pattern for that emerging nation. The freedom of religion that is such a central feature of the American Constitution, the freedom to practice one's religion even in ways that offend the dominant group, is a prize that has had to be fought for again and again: by Baptists in the late eighteenth century, by Mormons in the nineteenth, and by Jehovah's Witnesses in the twentieth. At the dawn of the eighteenth century, the Quakers led the way.

Still another group of settlers had begun appearing along the border at the time of William Byrd's explorations. Some were sons of large families whose fathers' holdings were not enough to provide each of them with an adequate homestead. The terrible death rates of the first decades of settlement had dropped, and families with six, ten, or even a dozen adult children were not uncommon. A planter father might spend his whole life amassing enough land to provide each of his sons with a two-hundred-acre plantation, the minimum needed to support a family in reasonable comfort. As time went on, monopolization of land by the great planters made that goal difficult or impossible.

Other settlers were small planters displaced by the ruthless imperatives of the tobacco economy. Tobacco culture stripped and exhausted the land. A planter needed to clear new fields every few years as the old ones wore out. But if his plantation was too small, there might be no new fields to clear and no chance of acquiring any in the long-settled areas. The boom-and-bust tobacco cycle made the problems worse. When tobacco prices were high, planters went heavily into debt to purchase slaves to grow more. The resulting overproduction led to cyclical crashes in the price. When such a crash occurred, planters rushed to plant even more tobacco in order to earn enough money to pay their debts.

As in every such crisis, the people who went under were the improvident, the unlucky, and the small planters who lacked reserves with which to pay. Some were sustained by small loans from more fortunate neighbors and relatives, but many lost their land to larger planters with the resources to buy them out.[53] Reduced to the status of tenant farmers or hired laborers, they had to work for years to save enough to acquire small new plantations at the edge of the wilderness. Edward Drew, the first of my ancestors to appear in this narrative, may have been one such debtor.

Part II

Creating Communities on the

Virginia Frontier

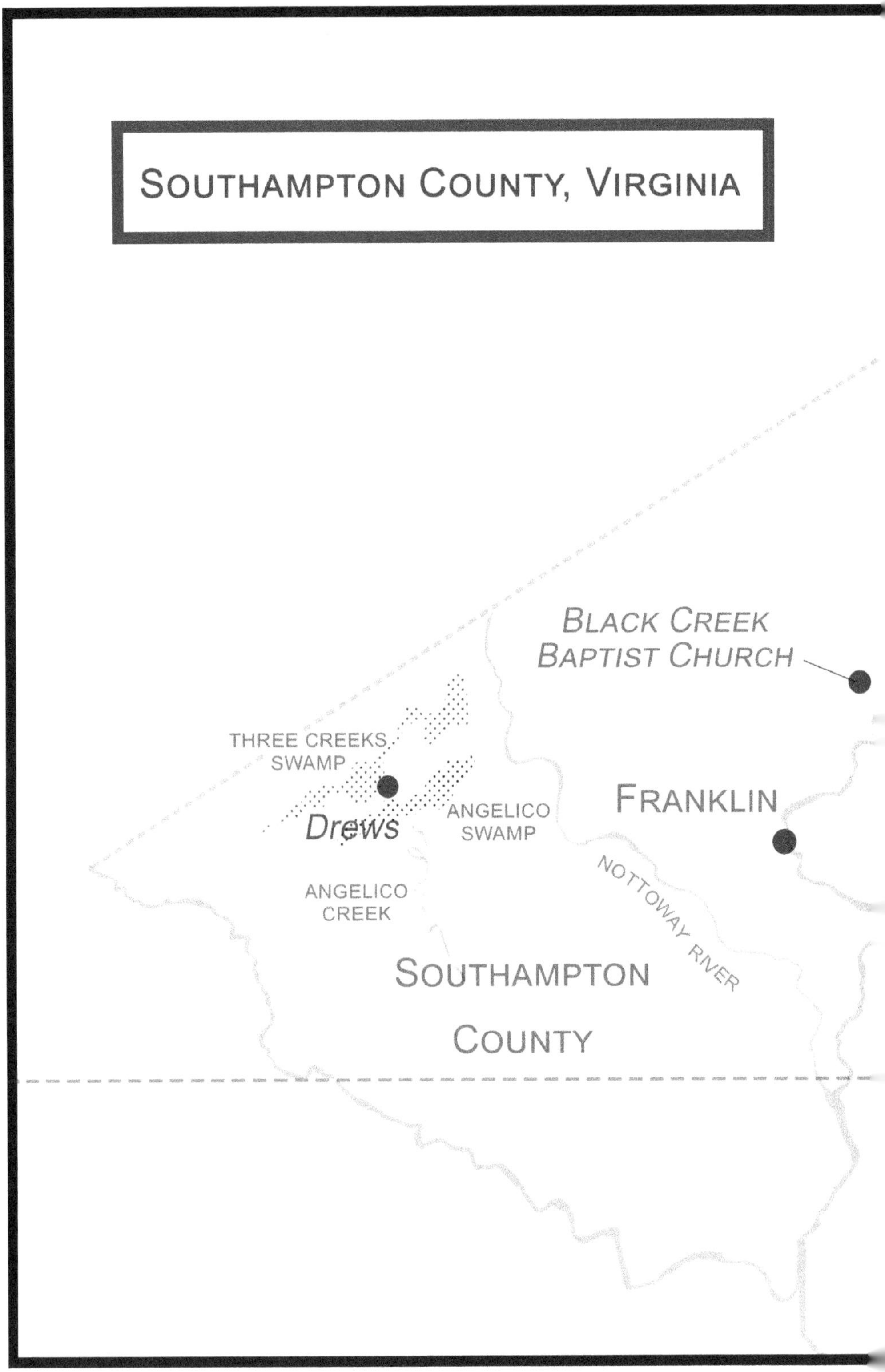

SOUTHAMPTON COUNTY, VIRGINIA

BLACK CREEK
BAPTIST CHURCH

THREE CREEKS
SWAMP

FRANKLIN

Drews

ANGELICO
SWAMP

ANGELICO
CREEK

NOTTOWAY RIVER

SOUTHAMPTON

COUNTY

ISLE OF WIGHT
COUNTY

BLACKWATER RIVER

VIRGINIA
NORTH CAROLINA

3. Around Angelica Swamp

Edward Drew's name first appears in Isle of Wight County records in 1727 on a land patent for ninety acres. A year before William Byrd II and his fellow commissioners were so hospitably entertained by the Nottoway Indians, the Drew family and a few others were already clearing and planting land a few miles to the west of the Nottoway town. On one map of the county as it was in 1730, the land where these families settled is marked as still uninhabited; the frontier is drawn to the north, at the Nottoway River.[1]

In 1660, Edward's father, Richard Drew, was living in Surry County, then a poor frontier area with an unusually large percentage of former indentured servants.[2] Richard, or perhaps his father, most likely came to Virginia in the first half of the century, an indentured servant like three-quarters of his Virginia contemporaries. Whatever his origin, by 1660 he was one of Surry County's more prosperous citizens. Although he could not sign his own name, he provided at least a minimal education for his sons. His 1679 will divided his land between his three sons and his surviving wife, leaving four hundred acres to Edward.[3] But Edward was ultimately unable to keep any of it.

The cyclical crises of the tobacco economy may have been to blame. Rising prices in the years between 1713 and 1720 led inexorably to overproduction, which led, in turn, to a crash in 1720.[4] Edward may have been an early victim of that oncoming crash. In 1719, when he was nearly sixty, he sold his four hundred acres to his cousin William Drew for the nominal price of five shillings, the same price he would have paid for fifty acres of uncleared frontier land.[5] He may have been deeply in debt to William and unable to repay the debt with money or tobacco. Or perhaps his land was simply worn out and worthless. At some point after the sale, he and some of his neighbors moved south to the far edge of the settled area and purchased land on the borders of Angelica Swamp, known in the twenty-first century as Angelico Swamp. It is a measure of his fall from prosperity that he was unable to afford an education for his children. His son Newitt, born in the first decade of the eighteenth century[6] and named after his mother, Frances Newitt, was illiterate like his grandparents.

The settlers called themselves planters; we would call them yeoman farmers. Their lands surrounded Angelica Swamp, between Three Creeks on the north and Flat Swamp on the south. Besides Drew, the names on the patents are Edward Harris, Edward Harris Jr., Amos Harris, Timothy Thorp, and Thomas Purcell. James and Nathaniel Ridley were already there. On the north and south sides of Three Creeks and the south bank of the Nottoway River lived the large family of Thomas Newsom. The descendants of these families continued to be part of the Drews' story until the end of the century.

They left us no letters, and their lives did not allow them the luxury of diaries. Their border community was not even interesting enough for any traveler except William Byrd II to comment on. Any information we have about them comes from court documents or from the writings of historians who have studied similar communities. From their wills and deeds, we can learn something about their social relationships and the structure of their community. Their estate inventories tell us about the material conditions of their lives. For a few individuals there are county court records, and later on church records, that illuminate their role in the community. Taken together, these fragmentary records can help us to construct a picture of their lives.

Today Angelica Creek runs under Highway 58 2.7 miles west of the little town of Capron. North of the highway, it parallels Three Creeks Road before running into the larger Three Creeks system. Angelica Swamp lies just south of the highway, a large swampy area fed by numerous smaller branches. According to a color-coded map of United States stream and river names created by Derek Watkins in 2011,[7] the words "swamp" and "creek" are interchangeable in that corner of Virginia—a linguistic quirk that says something about the character of the landscape. An examination of later deeds suggests that the Drew land probably lay on the northwest side of the swamp.

Patented land was cheap, but it was not free. Men who could not earn headrights by paying for the transportation of others paid a small fee of five shillings for each fifty-acre parcel, plus an annual quitrent. The prospective owner had to find an unclaimed piece of land with the right acreage, pay the county surveyor to have it surveyed, and then pay someone else to have the deed recorded.[8] Because settlers sought to delay payment of these fees for as long as possible, they frequently occupied and planted their land for several years before applying for a patent.[9]

The Angelica Swamp settlers, then, were families with some resources. Most of the men could sign their own names, a task that fewer than half the men of Isle of Wight had mastered.[10] (Most women were illiterate; Governor Berkeley's horror of public education persisted well into the nineteenth century.) They owned livestock and farm equipment. They had grown or growing sons as well as a few enslaved workers to help with the backbreaking task of clearing the land. And they had neighbors. With few social institutions to support them, the borderers created a community out of what they had.

Early Virginians did not settle in compact New England-style towns but rather in widely scattered plantations. Groups of from ten to twenty planter families would coalesce into neighborhoods, connected by traditions of gift-giving and by small loans and bartering transactions. The small loans were critical. In a frontier world without banks and without the dubious assistance of the wealthy merchant-planters of the Chesapeake shore, a loan from a neighbor or brother-in-law might be the only form of credit available.[11] Over time, these neighborhoods would evolve into kinship networks, as members of neighboring families married each other, witnessed each other's wills, and appointed each other as guardians of their children. In this way they served another essential function, that of the protection of children. Mortality rates were still astonishingly high, and the kinship networks provided a system of support for the orphans. The importance of extended families is reflected in naming patterns: typically, children in each family were named after the parents and siblings of their own parents, reinforcing the closeness of their connection.

Many Angelica Swamp settlers were related to each other before they arrived in the area. As time went on, the neighborhood evolved into what the historian David Hackett Fischer calls a "cousinage," a densely interrelated network that persisted for the rest of the century. This kinship network continued to provide support as its members migrated farther towards the frontier. Seventy years later, grandchildren of the original Angelica Swamp settlers were still playing important roles in each other's lives.

Angelica Swamp was one of a multitude of small swamps and swamp-like creeks, miniature cousins of the Great Dismal to the east. Between the swamps were pocosins, an Algonquian word meaning "swamp on a hill"—flat stretches of high boggy ground from which water drained down into the surrounding swamps and creeks. In and around the swamps grew huge ancient cypress trees, some of them large enough for a man to walk upright through a felled hollow trunk. In some places Atlantic white cedars, sixty to seventy feet tall, grew so close together that it was difficult to walk between them.[12] On the sandy high ground were stands of longleaf pines, the northernmost extension of the great coastal pine belt that once stretched all the way to Florida and Louisiana. The narrow, steep-banked local rivers often flooded with such violence that bridges were washed away.[13] Forests and swamps teemed with wildlife—beavers, otters, muskrats and minks, as well as deer, foxes, raccoons, wild turkeys "of an incridible bigness," pheasants, partridges, and pigeons.[14] Snakes infested the pocosins—canebrake rattlers, cottonmouth moccasins, copperheads, and many others less dangerous. They came out of hibernation in the spring and remained active until fall.

And yet, wild as it seemed, the land had been occupied for three thousand years. Its former inhabitants developed a hoe-and-fire culture that allowed a small population to maintain itself indefinitely. Lacking metal tools, they girdled trees or felled them by setting small fires around their bases until they were burned through. Fallen trees were heaped up and re-burned, fertilizing the soil with their ashes. Corn and tobacco were planted in hills between the stumps and cultivated with hoes. Beans were planted around the corn, their vines climbing the stalks. Peas of various kinds grew between the rows, along with squash, pumpkins, potatoes, and melons. The interplanting of beans, peas, and corn returned nitrogen to the soil, maintaining the fertility of each field for several years before it was abandoned.

The Europeans who replaced these Indians learned from them. They, too, felled trees, heaped them and burned them, and planted corn, tobacco, beans, and peas among the stumps. Although slash and burn agriculture has a bad sound to modern ears, the system made ecological sense.[15] It minimized erosion and economized on scarce labor in addition to maintaining the fertility of the soil. But instead of moving on every few years like the Indians, the settlers aimed to acquire tracts large enough to move their fields repeatedly within their own boundaries, leaving about thirty years for the forest to return to each field before it was once again felled, burned, and replanted.

They also raised hogs—thousands of hogs. In moving to the border area, a region without water transportation, the settlers had removed themselves from the tobacco economy. While the wills of the early inhabitants of the Chesapeake shore often list debts or legacies to be paid in tobacco rather than cash, tobacco is almost never mentioned in the wills of the borderers, and their estate inventories seldom contain more than very small amounts. Instead, they relied on crops that could get themselves to market. Packs of hogs roamed at large in the woods and swamps, feeding on the abundant mast of the forest and on the seeds of the longleaf pines.

After a few generations, they reverted to their ancestral traits, fleet and lean, with large bones and bristly coats.[16] Hogs roamed free in the streets of Franklin, the area's main market town, until the mid-nineteenth century. In the 1730s, according to one estimate, up to fifty thousand hogs a year were driven north through Isle of Wight County to the slaughterhouses of Suffolk and Smithfield.[17]

The area's isolation from Atlantic commerce resulted in an economy similar to that of the Eastern Shore seventy-five years earlier: an absence of large plantations, a high proportion of small households without slaves or servants, and a reliance on diversified agriculture. Far from any commercial center, the settlers had to supply most of their own needs. Every house had a loom and at least one spinning wheel and often three or four specialized wheels for different fibers. Each farm had at least a few cattle, sheep, and geese in addition to its hogs. After the first generation, most could also boast an orchard whose peaches or apples were distilled into the county's increasingly famous brandy. Tar, turpentine, and pitch— collectively known as naval stores—were extracted from the longleaf pines.[18] When roads improved in mid century, corn and naval supplies could be transported south to Albemarle Sound and from there to the sea routes to the West Indies.[19]

Up to the middle of the eighteenth century, the houses of the Angelica Swamp settlers would have seemed hopelessly poor by our standards. The typical home of a middling planter in that era— someone who, like the Drews, owned between three hundred and a thousand acres—was a hall-and-parlor house of sixteen by twenty feet with two rooms on the ground floor, one or two chimneys, and a loft or sometimes two or three small rooms above.[20] Walls were made of clapboards over a light frame and rested on logs laid directly on the ground or on posts set into holes.[21] Most houses were surrounded by clusters of outbuildings: a separate kitchen, to reduce the danger of fire and the discomfort of overheating in the summer; smaller huts for slaves and servants; a smoke house; and perhaps a washhouse or a still. The house of a middling planter would have a plank floor, perhaps a brick chimney, a front door that opened directly into the main room, and a partition between that room—the hall—and the parlor. The house of a poorer planter was the same size but with a dirt floor, a chimney made of sticks and mud, a single room on the ground floor and perhaps a sleeping loft. Adapted for an economy where tobacco and corn wore out the soil within a few years, these houses were designed to be abandoned.[22]

Family life was not separate from work. The central activity of every member of the family was the production of the goods needed for survival. Spinning, weaving, candle-making, preservation of meat, preparation of herbal medicines—all were carried out in the house's main room or in the yard or outbuildings that surrounded it. If a planter owned slaves, he and his sons worked alongside them in the endless round of clearing, burning, planting, and harvesting. His daughters worked from early childhood in the vegetable and herb gardens near the house. Bathing was virtually unknown; the interiors of those houses must have had a special redolence.

The wills and estate inventories of these borderers provide us with an additional glimpse of their lives. The first thing one notices is the total absence not only of luxury goods but even of what we would consider the most basic necessities. In the 1690s along the

Chesapeake shore we find inventories for houses of eight or ten rooms containing looking glasses, carpets, imported furniture, china tea sets, and silver plate by the pound. The wills of their inhabitants specifically dispose of silver tankards, bowls, candlesticks, and spoons; swords; silk clothing; and gold and silver jewelry.[23] By contrast, few inventories from the border area mention imported goods or luxuries of any kind. In the first generation of settlement, the typical planter owned three or four beds, a spinning wheel, a loom, a table, and two or three chests. The beds were the most valuable items: not beds as we know them, but mattresses stuffed with feathers that had taken years to accumulate. In homes with no beds or only one, family members slept on piles of straw in the loft or jostled for space on the dirt floor nearest the fireplace. Only about half of the estate inventories from this period contain chairs; in the others, family members sat on chests to eat, or stood, or squatted against the wall.

The first luxury one acquired, after the chairs, was a case of knives and forks, objects so valuable they were always itemized separately. As a planter grew richer, his parlor might boast of a looking glass and a candlestick. If the family really prospered, there might be a china tea set, and occasionally even a chamber pot.

By far the richest people in the Angelica Swamp neighborhood, and the only ones with connections to the Chesapeake gentry, were the brothers James and Nathaniel Ridley. Nathaniel, who died in 1753, owned six plantations and a mill. His houses contained walnut furniture, table linen, silver spoons, books, a fiddle, and not one but three chamber pots.[24]

The Ridley brothers were members of a tiny group of the area's richest citizens, who assumed most of the positions of power when the county of Southampton was established in 1749. The county court, consisting of fourteen justices of the peace who served for life once appointed, was the only governmental authority on the local level. It settled disputes, enforced the laws, managed the county's finances, appointed public officials and militia officers, maintained the tax rolls, and provided for the construction and maintenance of roads and bridges. James and Nathaniel Ridley and their half-brother Albridgton Jones were among the first group of justices. Six of the justices, including Nathaniel Ridley and Jones, also served on the vestry of the parish church, an organization with the power to police the moral behavior of the citizens. Eight of the nine people appointed as militia officers were also justices, including both Ridley brothers.[25]

The real wealth of these citizens, like that of other Virginians, lay in their ownership of human beings. The number of enslaved people in Virginia grew dramatically after 1700, from thirteen percent of the total population in 1700 to more than forty percent in 1750. The yeoman farmers of the border participated in this trade along with the great planters of the Chesapeake shore.[26]

Most of the Angelica Swamp settlers owned between one and six slaves. Edward Drew was the exception. When he died in 1745, at the advanced age of eighty-five, he owned twenty-four, far more than would have been needed to cultivate his two moderate-sized tracts of land. It is likely that, like many middling planters, he rented many of them out to poorer neighbors. In his will, the enslaved people are carefully assigned by name, to his son Newitt, his daughter Mary (born about 1715), and one each to a dozen grandchildren. There is no effort to keep families together, no recognition even of the existence of families. The future "increase" of enslaved women are bequeathed separately: the mother to one heir, the first child to another, and the second to yet another.[27] Although whites and blacks still worked alongside each other in clearing and cultivating the fields, the status of these enslaved people was by then something less than human.

Edward's two plantations both went to Newitt. His older son Thomas, who had moved to North Carolina at least fifteen years earlier, was largely excluded from the will. Thomas's daughter Mary (born about 1729) received one slave like the rest of her cousins. But her four brothers were not mentioned at all, and her father, Thomas, got almost nothing. Perhaps there was an unacceptable second marriage or a long-term liaison that produced four illegitimate sons. Twelve years later, Thomas divided his own land among his sons by deed of gift rather than by will.[28] This arrangement gave the recipients more protection than a will, since a will could have been challenged by another heir. Mary's descendants have been exhaustively researched by family genealogists, but the children of her brothers disappear from the records.

A grim sort of patriarch, this Edward Drew: estranged from his oldest son, grandfather to children he refused to acknowledge, and blind to the humanity of the people he owned. But if the African slaves did not seem human to their owners, there were other people of African descent in the neighborhood, defiantly insisting on their own humanity.

4. The Neighbors

Southampton County's free people of color were the children and grandchildren of white, African, and Indian slaves and servants and of relationships between African men and free white women. Some families had been free since the mid-seventeenth century while others had appeared on the scene more recently, a result of the interracial liaisons and common-law marriages that the most punitive of Virginia laws could not prevent. In Virginia's shifting and increasingly divided racial landscape, free people of color occupied a particularly unstable border. But in the hardscrabble, more or less egalitarian society of the early Southside, they found a place where, for about one generation, they could still be treated as normal citizens—albeit citizens who could not vote, serve on juries, nor marry whom they liked.

The extraordinary research efforts of Paul Heinegg have produced a list of more than 275 free people of color who spent at least part of their lives in the part of Isle of Wight County south of the Blackwater River, later Southampton County, during the eighteenth century.[1] The total is undoubtedly understated, since it includes only people whose names appear on legal documents— wills, deeds, guardianships, tax lists, records of court cases and the binding out of children. A close look at Heinegg's data provides us with a sense of the lives of these people, and, occasionally, a fascinating portrait of an individual.

Most of them were poor. Only one in ten owned land in Isle of Wight or Southampton counties at any point in their lives, and of these, only two owned more than two hundred acres. The rest survived as tenant farmers, hired laborers, or household servants. Although birth dates are usually not available, many seem to have been unable to establish independent households, even as tenant farmers, until they were in their forties. Severely limited in their choice of marriage partners, these families quickly formed a kinship network, with smaller networks within it. Children of landowning mixed-race families married people from families of similar status; children of the poor, if they married at all, married other poor. But for families at this level of society, kinship networks were often inadequate to protect their children.

The extent of their poverty is reflected in the number of their legitimate and illegitimate children who were bound out—sold as indentured servants to the highest bidder, and serving to the age of twenty-one—because their mothers could not support them. Binding out, in these cases, was not a punishment for illegitimacy, since under Virginia law only white women were punished for having illegitimate mixed-race children. Instead, it was a way of making sure that the parish did not have to bear the expense of raising the child. The fathers of these children may have been slaves, who were legally unable to support their children, or white men who had no interest in doing so. Heinegg's list shows thirty-eight women whose children were bound out and well over sixty children bound, often as young as one or two years old. The daughters of landowning families of color were as likely to see their children bound out as the daughters of hired laborers.

It comes as a shock to many modern readers to learn that some free people of color owned slaves. But, in fact, slave ownership among the tiny group of prosperous free African-Americans was common throughout the South from the time of the first captured Africans right up to the end of the Civil War.[2] In order to succeed economically in a slave society, free people of color made use of whatever tools were available to them without questioning the justice of the system any more than their white neighbors did.

Contributing to their acceptance of the system was the enormous gap between the newly enslaved Africans and the light-skinned mixed-race people whose families had been free and thoroughly acculturated for a generation or more. The world had changed from a century earlier, when the first Angolans formed a tight community and provided support to one another whether free or slave. Although white society was beginning to see people of African descent more and more as a single group, those people did not necessarily feel any kinship with each other. In spite of the increasingly restrictive laws and the increasingly close connection between slavery and racial contempt, the free people of color fought to see themselves, and to be seen by others, as members of a society divided not into white and black but into slave and free. Within the limitations imposed on them, they sought to act as much as possible as free people and to take advantage of whatever means of economic survival their society afforded to the free. One of the rights of the free was to claim property in the enslaved.

Across the social and economic gap between the free people of color and their white neighbors, there were still common-law and even legal marriages. Because interracial marriage had been punishable in Virginia since 1691, the parties often moved south across the North Carolina line to avoid prosecution. Among the Angelica Swamp neighbors, one such marriage is clearly demonstrated by the records: that of Moses Newsom, the oldest son of the Drews' neighbor Thomas Newsom.[3] Moses married a woman of African descent called Judah, and their children appear in the North Carolina records as "free negroes." The couple was evidently accepted by the white Newsom family. Several years after the marriage, Thomas Newsom and his wife, Elizabeth, deeded to Moses "for the love Thomas owes his son . . . the land whereon he now lives."[4] There are also hints of one or more mixed marriages in the extended Harris family, based on the similarity of given names between white and mixed-race sibling groups on opposite sides of the border.[5]

Some mixed-race people arrived on the Virginia border with money in their pockets. James Brooks Jr., born in York County around 1707, was one. He, his brother William, and his sister Mary were the children of an enslaved man named James Brooks Sr. who was himself the son of a white servant man named Richard Brooks and an enslaved woman known as Black Betty.[6]

The mother of James, William, and Mary is a mystery. She was definitely free and from a reasonably prosperous family, and her relationship with the slave James was long-term. By the time James Jr. and William were in their mid twenties, they were not only free and literate,[7] but James Jr. had enough money to purchase their father, with enough left over to buy land. When William died in 1789, he was one of the minority of Southampton decedents whose modest inventory included both a punch bowl and a book.[8]

The most likely explanation is that their mother was the daughter of a man rich enough to provide for her and even to pay for the education of her sons in spite of the fact that their father was a slave. If that picture is accurate, James Jr. and his siblings, like many other people of mixed race, would have experienced both sides of the line between free and slave. On their mother's side, they would come from a group of people deeply conscious of their status and privileges as free citizens and intent on preserving them. On their father's side, they would have been exposed to the degradation of slavery. The tensions inherent in this background throw their story into high relief.

In 1742, William Brooks patented 190 acres on the south side of the Nottoway River, a few miles to the north of Angelica Swamp,[9] and in 1746 James Brooks Jr. patented 200 acres on the north side of the Meherrin, perhaps five miles to the south.[10] James Jr. was assertive and more than a little combative. He loaned out substantial sums of money to both white and black neighbors and sued to collect the debts. Two of his debtors and one neighbor, Thomas Taborn, sued him at various times for trespass, assault, and battery. William Brooks was also involved in at least three lawsuits, in one case as a plaintiff against a white defendant.[11] These lawsuits raise an interesting issue. The statutes of 1723 and 1744 forbade any free person of color, "forasmuch as they are people of such base and corrupt natures, that the credit of their testimony cannot be certainly depended upon," from testifying for or against a white defendant in any case.[12] But in some cases the mixed-race plaintiffs had no white witnesses to testify on their behalf, and they won anyway. The court may simply have ignored that particular provision of the law, as Virginia courts sometimes did with racial laws when a free person of color was known and respected in the neighborhood.

In fact, there was a perfect free-for-all of lawsuits in the years between 1747 and 1758 among the small group of relatively well-off people of color. At the center of the melée was a white man named William Bynum.

Members of the Bynum family had served on juries with Edward Drew and his father in seventeenth-century Surry County, and in 1747, William Bynum, or a younger relative with the same name, married Edward Drew's granddaughter. Bynum was a co-defendant with Thomas Taborn, the richest mixed-race landowner south of the Blackwater River, in a 1752 suit for debt.[13] He was also a friend of the mixed-race Joseph Allen, who had settled south of the Nottoway in the early 1740s.[14]

The Allen family, like the Brookses, had migrated from York County, where they and their friend John Byrd had already gotten themselves into trouble for acting white. In 1723, Virginia had reinstated a law that had been allowed to lapse in 1705, under which free women of color and white wives of free men of color were subject to a head tax, sometimes called a tithe, while white women were not. At first the law was largely ignored, but after a while it began to be enforced sporadically, county by county. It was being enforced in York County in 1735, for in that year Joseph Allen and John Byrd were charged with failing to list their wives as titheables, and Joseph's sister Sarah was charged with failing to list herself. The enforcement of the discriminatory law may have been one reason for the two families' move to the far reaches of Isle of Wight, where as yet nobody cared. When Allen died in 1748, Bynum became administrator of his estate and guardian of the three minor heirs.[15]

It was a bad choice. Bynum was a quarrelsome man and in constant financial trouble. Between 1749 and 1760, he was sued for debt no fewer than sixteen times, and he almost always either lost the case or acknowledged the debt. In the majority of cases, he didn't even bother to show up. And the sums were large: twenty-nine, forty-six, or fifty-four pounds at a time when the entire estate of a planter with a slave and some livestock might be valued at fifty. In 1751, Bynum was summoned into court for his failure to file an account of the Allen estate, a summons that set off a long, long series of delays.[16] It wasn't until 1757 that the Allen family finally got the attention of the court, and by then the case had been continued at least ten times. In April of 1754, another suit was filed against him by members of the same family, and that suit, too, was continued over and over until the court finally lost patience in 1757.[17]

Two months after the filing of the second suit, on June 13, 1754, Bynum lashed back at his mixed-race neighbors, bringing suit as an informer against fourteen free people of color for failing to list themselves or their wives as titheables.[18] Among the defendants in those cases were James Brooks Sr., James Brooks Jr., William Brooks, William's daughter Ann Duncan, and William Taborn— the son of Bynum's former co-defendant Thomas Taborn and son-in-law of Joseph Allen, who had trusted Bynum to administer his estate and protect his children. Most of the defendants were Bynum's near neighbors, and nine of the fourteen were landowners, making them among the most prosperous members of Southampton County's mixed-race community.

Three of the defendants initially pled not guilty but changed their pleas when others were convicted. One was acquitted, one case had to be postponed because a witness could not attend, and the case against William Brooks was dropped by agreement. Each of the convicted defendants was fined five hundred pounds of tobacco per titheable, of which Bynum as informer got half. At the going rate of a shilling per ten pounds of tobacco, that came to a pound and five shillings cash per case, out of which Bynum had to pay witness fees that sometimes amounted to half of the total. For all of his time and trouble, he probably ended up with under ten pounds—a small fraction of the money he owed to others.[19]

The Bynum prosecutions raise quite a few questions, and provide more evidence of the complexity of racial status in a mid-century border county. Why, for example, did the defendants think they could get away with not paying the tax? Payment or non-payment was a matter of public record; why did they contest?

Racial identity was clearly at issue, since witnesses were necessary for some of the prosecutions and one defendant was actually acquitted. The cases may have turned on the legal definition of "mulatto." Ann Brooks Duncan, who initially pled not guilty and ultimately said that she "was not informed what answer to make to the plaintiff's action," may have had only one black great-grand-parent and may therefore have considered herself white. Although Virginia law defined a mulatto as anyone with at least one black great-grandparent, that law was enforced only casually in the border counties. The defendants may have hoped that the court, like some others at that time, would base its decisions not on the technicalities of the law but on their appearance, economic status, and community standing. The witnesses may have been needed to give testimony either about those factors or about the remote family history of the people involved.[20]

Assuming that their wives were white, the defendants may also have hoped that the court would ignore the wording of the law that imposed the tax on all wives of free men of color, whatever their race. As with many other laws affecting the ambiguous status of free people of color, that provision was enforced inconsistently, and far more leniently in border areas.

Another detail illustrates the dangers faced even by landowning people of color and the ways in which they made use of the lack of legal clarity to protect themselves. Since 1723, Virginia law had prohibited slaveowners from freeing their slaves except by permission of the legislature in extraordinary circumstances. James Brooks Sr., purchased by his son in 1733, was technically still his son's slave. James Jr., however, did not make that claim publicly until after his father's death, when he challenged his father's will on the grounds that his father belonged to him and was not free to will his own property.[21] But James Sr. had been prosecuted for not paying the tax on a female relative as if he were a free man. It is possible that his family moved to the remote border community specifically to conceal his legal status, perhaps to protect him from being seized and sold in a suit for his son's debts.

The parallel history of the Allen lawsuits, which were ongoing at the time of the Bynum prosecutions, also illuminates the difficulties that free people of color faced in their dealings with the legal system. They were not denied access to the courts, but they were, in this case, treated with considerably less respect than white plaintiffs would have been. Delay and avoidance were Bynum's basic strategies for dealing with lawsuits. He would typically request continuances or would simply fail to show up, receive a default judgment against him, and then return to court with a request for a retrial. But in no case against a white plaintiff was he able to put off judgment for more than six months. The Allen cases, on the other hand, dragged on for three and six years before the court even got annoyed. In September of 1757, the court announced that "... the defendants [Bynum] having stood out all process of contempt without putting in their answers the bill of the plaintiffs [the Allen family] is taken for confessed" and awarded judgment against Bynum in one of the cases and an attachment of his property in the other. But it is not clear that the plaintiffs ever collected. Amazingly, even after the judgment and attachment, the cases were still being continued in April of 1758. In 1760, Bynum was finally ordered to make up his accounts of the Allen estate from the beginning—eleven years earlier[22]—but before he had done so, the case was abated because of his death.

Finally, the Bynum cases cast light on the gradual shift in white attitudes about race in this backwoods community. For reasons we can only guess at, William Bynum suddenly felt free to turn informant against his mixed-race neighbors and former friends, some of whom had put their trust in him. His need for money does not seem like a plausible explanation, given the small amount that he could expect to recover in comparison to the size of his debts. The timing of the event suggests that when the second Allen lawsuit was filed, he simply became exasperated at being harassed by people whom he considered his racial inferiors and decided to remind them of their proper place. But he also seems to have had confidence that his betrayals would not bring down the censure of his white neighbors. His actions suggest that the influx of newly enslaved Africans combined with the increasingly restrictive racial laws had shifted white attitudes, even on the border, towards the assumption that any trace of African descent was justification for racial contempt. It was no longer just a matter of free versus slave. The system of African slavery was by then firmly entrenched, and the free people of color were on the wrong side of the line.

A final intriguing possibility is that Bynum may have felt the need to defend his status in the white community. Even in St. Luke's Parish, where most landowning free people of color were congregated and where the Newsoms and perhaps the Harrises had mixed-race cousins right across the border, only a tiny number of interracial friendships can be inferred from the surviving records. Bynum's relationships with Thomas Taborn and the Allen family were apparently unusual. As racial attitudes hardened, was his own allegiance to the white community somehow in question? Did he perhaps need to demonstrate to his white neighbors and in-laws which side of the line he was on?

The storm of lawsuits continued, with Bynum as a defendant in several cases. James Brooks Jr. went on suing people right up to his death. But the prosecutions marked a change in the economic and social status of the free people of color whose names appear in Heinegg's list. In the twenty-two years between 1732 and 1754, at least thirteen of those people bought or patented land in Isle of Wight County south of the Blackwater River, the area that in 1749 became Southampton County.[23] In the following twenty-five years, only five did. From the first year of the Revolution to the beginning of the nineteenth century, there were only two, and of these, one acquired only ten acres. The majority of people who had already acquired land remained in the county at least until the end of the century. The less fortunate moved on.

It was a pattern repeated in every border county. As the last tracts of unclaimed land were patented, improvements by landowners and continuing migration from more settled areas began to drive up the price. Soon, even long-term residents could no longer provide their children with enough land to support a family. Social stratification increased, and families without substantial capital were forced to move out.[24] Beginning in 1755, there was an accelerating migration of both white and mixed-race families, south across the Meherrin River to what later became Greensville County, Virginia; across the North Carolina border to Northampton County, North Carolina; or west along the Virginia border to Brunswick, Lunenberg, and Mecklenburg counties. In the newer areas there was still cheap land to be had, and some free people of color acquired substantial landholdings and up to half a dozen slaves.[25] On the Isle of Wight border, however, the frontier era was coming to an end.

5. The Birth of Southampton County

The point when mainstream Virginia society caught up with the border can perhaps be located in 1749, when the population of southern Isle of Wight County became large enough for a new county, Southampton, to be carved out south of the Blackwater River. The part of the new county to the south and west of the Nottoway River, including Three Creeks and Angelica Swamp, became St. Luke's Parish while the part to the north and east became Nottoway Parish.

Grandchildren of the original Angelica Swamp settlers reached maturity in an era of increasing prosperity. In 1757, there was already a small port at South Quay on the lower end of the Blackwater River, giving Southampton County access to the growing commerce of Albemarle Sound. By 1777, South Quay had come to occupy a significant position in the Virginia economy.[1] A major part of its trade was in naval stores—tar, pitch, and turpentine harvested from the county's abundant longleaf pines.

In longer-settled areas of Virginia, the hoe-and-fire culture had begun to give way to the cultivation of wheat, previously a luxury good. But wheat culture required iron plows—a technological advance that at first improved agricultural production and then, within two generations, destroyed it utterly. By the end of the century, much of the agricultural land not already worn out by tobacco had been devastated by erosion, with once-fertile fields slashed and scarred by gullies until scarcely an acre of arable land remained.[2] While Virginia's most brilliant aristocrats were busy inventing a nation unlike any the world had ever seen, the economy of their own state was crumbling around them.

In some areas along the border, however, the ancient and sustainable hoe-and-fire system persisted until the end of the nineteenth century. In the last quarter of the eighteenth century, wheat still occupied a small place in Southampton estate inventories in comparison with corn. The scant records of the era reveal an endless round of cutting, heaping, burning, and reburning trees as the fields cycled from worn-out to newer land and back again to the old. Less than half of the land on any given plantation was under cultivation at any one time. Uncultivated land supplied wood for numerous purposes, plus forage for cattle and the ubiquitous free-roaming hogs.[3]

As the agricultural economy of Virginia was beginning its swift decline, the border area was reaching its period of greatest prosperity. In addition to the naval stores and the eternal hogs, Southampton County was becoming known for its peach and apple brandy. Few farms in the county lacked an orchard and a distillery.[4] As yet there were no great fortunes; as with the Eastern Shore in the previous century, limited access to ocean transportation discouraged the growth of large plantations. But many of the middling planters were doing well.

Edward Drew's son Newitt, born about 1715, never learned to read. As a child and young man, he would have worked his father's farm alongside his father's slaves, clearing and planting and tending livestock from dawn to dusk. He and his brother-in-law Abraham Johnson gave many of their children Biblical or religiously-tinged names—Jeremiah, Jesse, Patience, Selah (a word found at the ends of the Psalms and meaning roughly "amen"), and Olive Drew, Micajah and Josiah Johnson—suggesting that the two men had been influenced by the wave of religious fervor known as the Great Awakening, which swept through the colonies in the 1730s and 1740s.

Throughout his life, Newitt's place in the world was defined by the Angelica Swamp kinship network. He maintained close ties not only with Abraham Johnson, one of the poorest members of the cousinage, but with the wealthy Ridley and Jones families as well. He and his wife, Mary, both illiterate, nevertheless managed to provide their sons with the two or three years of education considered sufficient for boys. When he died in 1775 at the age of about sixty, he owned three parcels of land and ten slaves along with eleven leather-bottomed chairs, a looking glass, a desk, two chamber pots and a tea set. A "parcel of books" may have provided the education for his children.[5]

By this time, the members of the Angelica Swamp cousinage had probably moved up from dirt-floored cabins to two- or three- room houses with plank floors and a central hallway, or even the elegant two-over-two "I-houses" that signified prosperity in that era. The houses of many of their neighbors, however, still resembled those of the first settlers. A 1793 will directs the building of such a house for the testator's son: "twenty-eight feet by fifteen with a partition through it one half plank floor and the other half dirt, one brick chimney at each end."[6]

On a dirt road east of Angelica Creek are the ruins of two houses, both probably built in the late eighteenth century and occupied until the mid twentieth. One is a two-story I-house, the other a two-room house with a third room or shed off the back.

Although small by our standards, the one-story house demonstrates the increasing taste for comfort and privacy in that era. It is raised off the ground on brick pillars, with a chimney of brick rather than the wood and mud of more humble houses, and the front door opens not into the main room but into a central corridor lighted by long narrow windows flanking the door. Its first inhabitants probably owned a looking glass and walnut furniture, perhaps even a tea set. Newitt Drew's house was probably much like this one.

Ruined house in Southampton County, Virginia, probably built in the late eighteenth century. With three rooms, plank floors, and a paneled central corridor, it typifies the house in that era of a middling planter with a few slaves.

With the Revolution came a dramatic increase in the opportunity for gain. Although Southampton County men fought in various battles, the county itself was spared the destruction elsewhere wrought by the war. In his history of Southampton County, Thomas Parramore notes a distinct lack of Revolutionary fervor and comments that "the mildness of the regime of the Committee of Safety seems noteworthy." Violations of Revolutionary virtue were not punished, and some citizens refused to accept public office when offered. Parramore suspects Quaker influence in the lack of fervor, but it also seems possible that this community of borderers and outsiders had less allegiance than others to the cause championed by the Chesapeake aristocrats.[7]

Some contemporary observers felt that the inhabitants were less interested in supporting the patriotic cause than in making money from it. They were probably right in the case of Jeremiah Drew, born in 1746 and the only son of Newitt to survive the Revolution. Jeremiah was an ambitious and assertive man, a type not unknown among the children of pious parents. In 1769, at the age of only twenty-three, he was recorded as serving on a grand jury, a position reserved for men of more wisdom and dignity than those selected for an ordinary jury.[8] In 1778, he was recommended as "a fit person to act as Ensign of Militia."[9]

On April 9, 1772, the twenty-five-year-old Jeremiah stood before the justices of the peace, as a specially appointed jury of his neighbors and relatives presented their report on a suit that he had brought against his father Newitt. The suit asked the justices to assess the damages that he would owe his father and two other neighbors for building a grist mill and dam that would flood parts of their properties. The jury included two members of the Angelica Swamp Harris family, Jeremiah's uncle Abraham Johnson, and Thomas Fitzhugh, who was or would soon become his brother-in-law.[10] Outside in the spring sunshine, women gossiped, and men drank, played dice, and bargained over the price of horses. There may even have been a cockfight going on. The courthouse was a focus of community life, and what was happening inside was not an adversarial proceeding but something more in the nature of a community project. The mill would enrich the neighborhood as a whole, providing planter families with a convenient means for grinding their corn and perhaps even making wheat crops economically viable. It had other benefits as well: less than a year after construction began, a group of neighbors filed a petition to build a road over the dam.[11] In the years preceding the Revolution, the services of millers were considered so important that they were exempt from military service and even from jury duty.[12] Although there is no record that he actually served in the Revolution, Jeremiah is listed as a "Patriot" by the Daughters of the American Revolution—for selling brandy to the troops.[13]

Perhaps because of the mill, Jeremiah was the first family member in three generations to rise above the rank of common planter. He married into a prosperous family: his father-in-law owned fifteen slaves, a Delft plate, and one of the county's few two-wheeled carriages or "riding chairs."[14] By the time Jeremiah died in 1784, he too owned a riding chair, along with eight horses and thirteen slaves.[15] Enslaved men worked in his mill and tended the still where fruit from his orchards was processed into brandy. Since only slaves over the age of sixteen appear on the tax lists, we can assume that the total enslaved population of Jeremiah's household was in the neighborhood of two dozen. This was enough to qualify him for gentry status: by that time, the conventional definition of a planter involved the ownership of at least twenty slaves.[16] Roughly thirteen percent of the taxpayers in Southampton County—slightly more in St. Luke's Parish—met that criterion.

Jeremiah's children received no Biblical names. His oldest son was not even named in the traditional way, for a member of one of his parents' families, but instead was called James, perhaps after Jeremiah's rich friend James Ridley. In contrast with their grandparents, Mary Parker Drew and her children would not have been constantly occupied with chores necessary for the family's survival. Cloth—silk and linen for the family, coarse "oznaburg" for the slaves—could be purchased rather than made at home. Slave dressmakers sewed the family's clothes; enslaved women were responsible for cooking, cleaning, and other household chores. Mary would have supervised the household, cut and distributed cloth for the clothing of family and slaves, maintained household accounts, done some spinning and fine sewing, and looked after the education of her children, but there would also have been ample time in her day for exchanging visits with the wives of neighboring planters. Like other women in wealthy Southern families, she was probably an alien in her own kitchen.[17] Her children, tended by slaves, had time to play after their lessons were done.

John Ferdinand Dalziel Smyth, a young Englishman who traveled through Virginia and North Carolina on the eve of the Revolution, left us a description of the men of the "second degree of rank," a category that would have included Jeremiah:

> . . . generous, friendly, and hospitable in the extreme; but mixed
> with such an appearance of rudeness, ferocity, and haughtiness,
> which is in fact only a want of polish, occasioned by their
> deficiencies in education, and in knowledge of mankind, as well

as by their general intercourse with slaves, over whom they are accustomed to exercise an harsh and absolute command. They are all excessively attached to every species of sport, gaming, and dissipation, particularly horse-racing, and that most barbarous of all diversions, that peculiar species of cruelty, cock-fighting.[18]

Southampton County estate inventories from the last quarter of the eighteenth century reveal the emergence of an increasingly stratified society in what was no longer a border area. While there are still inventories without knives or forks, others list elegant walnut furniture, china tea sets, and fine table linen. Punch bowls and coffee pots show up in the estates of a few genial hosts, and, at the upper reaches of luxury, a riding chair like Jeremiah's.[19] The inventories also show that most of what was needed for daily life continued to be produced at home. Farming was still diversified, with a variety of crops and livestock appearing in every estate. Most families owned spinning wheels and carpentry and coopering tools, along with barrels of pork and the apparatus for processing it. Copper kettles and stills were becoming frequent. To keep their complex enterprises running, the yeoman farmers depended on an enslaved labor force, but in contrast to settlers of the first generation, they no longer worked alongside their slaves. By the end of the eighteenth century, the increasingly rigid conventions of their society had made manual labor degrading.[20]

Another indication of the increasing wealth of the county's richest residents was the growing popularity of thoroughbred racehorses. In 1784, Major Thomas Ridley owned eight pedigreed stud horses. Another horse, named Medley, was purchased by a neighbor for a hundred thousand pounds of tobacco.[21]

Despite increasing inequality and growing class divisions within their society, a few free people of color managed to maintain a place. They were concentrated in St. Luke's Parish, in the same part of the county as Angelica Swamp. At least one mixed-race family, that of Elisha Melton, maintained close ties with several of its white neighbors. Randolph Newsom, a nephew of the white Moses Newsom who married an African-American woman, acted as security for the marriage of Elisha's son Randolph Melton. When Elisha's daughter Ann bore an illegitimate daughter, Elisha transferred a piece of land to another white neighbor in trust for the child.[22]

Another free person of color profited handsomely from the emergence of the new elite. Peter Fagan, originally a slave, was freed in North Carolina, where manumission was still legal, by an uncle of Jeremiah's wife Mary Parker Drew, and later amassed a comfortable fortune as a dancing-master. In the parlors of the Ridley and Jones families, furniture was moved aside, and siblings and cousins lined up facing each other as Peter Fagan, in knee breeches and a powdered wig, led them through the intricate motions of minuets and country dances. Dancing was a crucial social skill for the Virginia gentry, both a bonding ritual and an opportunity for self-display in the endless competition to marry well.[23] The popularity of Peter Fagan's dance classes suggests that there were many families in Southampton who aspired to gentry status. Before Jeremiah's early death, his own young children may have attended. In the fine tradition of Virginia gentry, quite a few parents neglected to pay their bills, and Fagan sued several of them for substantial sums. His son Peter Jr. eventually took over the school and by 1797 had acquired two slaves and a riding chair of his own.[24]

Jeremiah Drew's good fortune was short-lived. He died in 1784 at the age of thirty-eight having outlived two brothers, both of whom also died in their thirties. He left six children: two sons, James and Newit; four daughters, Susannah, Sarah, Priscilla, and Peggy; and two wards, Newit and Joshua Claud.[25] Randolph Newsom, his wife's cousin, was named as one of his executors and later on as guardian of his second son, Newit.[26] His wife, Mary, remarried Henry Harris, whose relationship to the Edward Harris of Angelica Swamp is unknown. Remarriage was usually quick in that era, and marriage to a wealthy widow was the main way for a poor man like Henry, who owned four slaves but no land, to rise in the world. They had one child, Nancy, but by 1795, both Mary and Henry had also died,[27] and Mary's seven children were scattered among relatives and guardians across St. Luke's Parish.

6. The Quakers Press On

A few miles north of Angelica Swamp near a small tributary of the Blackwater River, Virginia's religious revolution was gathering steam.

The Quakers had led the way nearly a century earlier. Their long struggle with the values and conventions of their society may have kept their sect small and marginal, but that struggle had important consequences. Isle of Wight County was one of the first strongholds of the Virginia Quakers and the one where their influence was felt the longest.

A key feature of Quaker governance was the creation of small, tightly-knit, egalitarian communities, reinforced by an extraordinary level of social control and organized into an elaborate structure of monthly, quarterly and yearly meetings. The Friends' Yearly Meeting for each state had the responsibility of deciding on matters of Quaker doctrine after propounding questions to the local monthly meetings and receiving their responses. Monthly meetings in each locality made sure those decisions were applied.

The most obvious level of control involved rules about dress, speech, and deportment. Quakers were forbidden any sort of frivolous or stylish clothing; they were warned against "striped and flowered stuffs" and against "faulds in their coats or any other unnecessary fashions." Frolicking, fiddling, and dancing were banned. Quakers were admonished for breaches of these rules and were expected to present their meetings with statements of contrition. Habitual offenders, or those whose contrition was held not to be sincere enough, could be disowned by their meetings, as could anyone who married out of meeting.[1]

A vexing question at mid century was the growing fashion for wigs among men of middling status. In 1752, one of the North Carolina meetings advised that " ... no Friend wear a WIG but such as apply themselves to the Monthly Meeting giving their reason for so Doing which shall be Adjudged of by the same Meeting." Faced with opposition to this decision, the meeting referred the question to the North Carolina Yearly Meeting, which responded, "after several disputes and conferences,"" ... that no person wearing a wig shall be dealt with so as to amount to a denial [i.e., disownment] for that offense only."[2]

Personal relationships were also monitored. In 1785 at the Rich Square Monthly Meeting of Northampton County, North Carolina, a complaint was brought against a woman for "not using her husband well and for not attending to her business at home." A committee was appointed to reconcile the parties but reported to the next meeting "that they had not that satisfaction they desired, things seemed much out of order." The woman was later disowned. So was Mary Elliot, for the offense of "absenting herself from our meetings also for deviating from our well known principles of plainness of speech and dress."[3] The restrictions on dress and behavior increased cohesion among the members of Quaker meetings even as they drove out those who refused to conform. Far more significant, however, were the religious principles that Quakers drew from their close reading of the Bible.

Their rejection of any state control of their religion and their refusal to pay taxes to support the established church have already been mentioned. Also setting them apart was their refusal to bear arms, to participate in militia musters or in any activity of war, or to pay any tax whose purpose was to support such activity. During the Revolution, the Virginia Yearly Meeting even ordered its members to refuse Continental currency.[4] Such refusals made them intensely unpopular without sparing them from the abuses of the British army. But the principle that eventually separated them entirely from the larger society was their evolving opposition to the institution of slavery, on which that society was founded.

The opposition developed slowly. By the end of the seventeenth century, some Quakers had already begun to speak out against the ownership of slaves. But between 1722 and 1764, the Virginia Yearly Meeting went no further than to inquire whether "all Friends [were] clear of being concerned in the importation of slaves or purchasing them for sale" and whether they used their own slaves "as fellow creatures," restrained them from vice, and instructed them in the principles of Christianity. It was not until the visit of the anti-slavery missionary John Griffith in 1765 that the issue of slavery began to arouse any fervor. The practice, said Griffith, "is as contrary to the spirit of Christianity as light is to darkness." The Yearly Meeting responded by proposing a ban on purchase of slaves, to be discussed and reported on by the monthly and quarterly Meetings. A year later it was reported that "Friends are divided in their sentiments," and the matter was left for further consideration.[5]

From that time on, the anti-slavery movement gathered strength with astonishing speed. By 1772, some of the monthly meetings were passing resolutions barring the future purchase of slaves, and a few Quakers had been disowned for violating that rule. The

Virginia Yearly Meeting waffled, instructing the monthly meetings that members should be disowned if they purchased slaves "with no other view but their own benefit and convenience." But only a year later, the meeting

> most earnestly recommend[ed] to all who continue to withhold
> from any their just right to freedom . . . to clear their hands of this
> iniquity, by executing manumissions for all those held by them in
> slavery who are arrived at full age, and also for those who may yet
> be in their minority—to take place when the females attain the
> age of eighteen, and the males twenty-one years.[6]

By the middle of the Revolution, the Yearly Meeting was urging the monthly meetings to "admonish" and "labor with" those Friends who still owned slaves.

An example of what it felt like to be "labored with" is provided in the journal of the Quaker Hugh Judge, who visited North Carolina in 1784. Invited to dinner at the home of a woman Friend whose husband was not a Quaker, he "had some friendly conversation with [the husband] concerning his holding a black man in bondage." The host was reluctant to emancipate his slave, and Judge and the man's wife "labored with him till late bed-time." Early the next morning, Judge had a deed of manumission written, and when the host came in for breakfast, presented it to him. "After a pause"—during which we can imagine the man's thoughts—"it was proposed that he should sign it, which he did."[7]

The passion of the Quakers focused on the issue of emancipation. But other groups were coming to the fore in their society with equal or greater passions. In the battle for religious freedom, the banner had passed to the Baptists.

7. What the Baptists Achieved

The decade of the 1760s, which saw the rise of a gentry class in Southampton County and the dramatic turnaround in Quaker doctrine regarding slavery, also witnessed an explosion of religious populism. At some level, populism and prosperity were connected. The small and middling planters of the Piedmont and border had carved their plantations out of the wilderness by their own efforts with no help from the great planters of the Tidewater. With or without enslaved labor, they had managed to raise themselves above bare subsistence and had reason to be confident in their independence. Elaborate rituals based on rank had less and less appeal for them. The services of the Anglican Church, designed to display the power and wealth of the gentry and offering little in the way of spiritual comfort to the common person, must have seemed increasingly irrelevant.[1]

As early as 1739, the Methodist evangelist George Whitefield was preaching in Virginia. His message borrowed a good deal from the Quaker model, but with a difference that gave his preaching a far wider appeal. Like the Quakers, Whitefield challenged the authority of the clerical establishment and insisted on the necessity of a direct connection between the individual soul and God. But unlike nearly all Quaker missionaries, he preached to blacks and whites as spiritual equals and praised the fervent emotional responses of the enslaved people. Preaching in houses and in fields, he sought to inspire ecstatic religious experience. Worshippers at his meetings wept, cried out, and occasionally fainted. Before long, other itinerant evangelists were preaching to mass meetings of whites and blacks, throwing fear into the hearts of the powerful. But it was not until the arrival of the Separate Baptist preacher Shubal Stearns in 1754 that the battle lines were really drawn.[2]

The Separate Baptists, a rebellious offshoot of the Regular Baptists, experienced their greatest success in southern border areas like Southampton County.[3] They were distinguished from the Regular Baptists of their era by their relatively moderate Calvinism, under which an individual was free to choose whether or not to be saved rather than predestined for salvation or damnation. While the worship of Regular Baptists was decorous and restrained, Separate Baptists, like Whitefield and his followers, welcomed the passionate expressiveness of slaves, an expressiveness that served as a model for the whites and gave them permission to worship in a similar way. They offered their members a supportive community, in which the humblest were respected.[4] Black and white worshippers participated together in the emotionally charged "nine rites": baptism, the Lord's Supper, the love feast, the laying on of hands, foot washing, anointing the sick, the right hand of fellowship, the kiss of charity, and dedicating children. Their worship was loud and fervent, an ecstatic release in which distinctions between master and slave were momentarily erased. Uneducated men, and sometimes even women, were encouraged to preach.[5] Although the two streams of Virginia Baptists ultimately merged in 1787, the worship experiences of the early Separate Baptists continued to have a profound effect on the Southern Baptists over the next two centuries.[6]

Like Quakers, Baptists rejected any state authority over their faith. They refused to apply for licenses for their preaching, or to pay tithes to support the Anglican clergy.[7] While by 1750 the Anglican establishment had more or less come to tolerate the peaceful Quakers, Baptists terrified them. The Baptists, at first mostly poor and uneducated, challenged not only the social hierarchy but also the most sacred rituals of aristocratic Virginia: dancing, gambling, drinking, horse-racing, and the use of violence to settle disputes. Like Quakers, they rejected the culture of deference to social superiors and preached instead a voluntary, egalitarian community where the only authority was that of the membership as a whole.[8] The membership of the early churches was always mixed, with black members sometimes in the majority and often preaching to whites.[9] Worst of all, their numbers were growing like wildfire, and beginning to attract some of the prosperous and educated.[10]

Baptist Historian Lewis Peyton Little provides a list of pre-Revolutionary Baptist churches in Virginia along with their counties and dates of establishment.[11] The list shows two churches at the northern end of the Shenandoah Valley in the 1750s, then ten more in the northern corner of the state by 1768, then another twenty by 1771, and twenty-seven more by 1776, the wave rushing south through the Piedmont following the flood tide of immigration from the north. Another stream of Baptist evangelism began in Pittsylvania County, then the westernmost settled area of the southern border, and spread eastward along the border to Isle of Wight. The list shows not a single Baptist church in the long-settled Tidewater counties during the pre-Revolutionary era.

The Anglican establishment responded with persecutions that equaled or surpassed anything visited upon Quakers at the beginning of the century. The world of the Virginia gentry was shifting and rearranging itself as they watched, as the Enlightenment ideal of the autonomous individual began to challenge the culture of deference and hierarchy. More than a few reacted with violence. In the early 1770s, Baptist preachers were attacked in their pulpits, pulled from their houses, horsewhipped, beaten, kicked, and brutalized by mobs. Jailed, they preached through the bars of their windows, although men outside slashed at their hands with knives or rode their horses into crowds of listeners.[12] It was not until the passage of the Virginia Declaration of Rights at the outset of the Revolution that Baptists and other dissenters received some legal relief. The radical Article 16 of that Declaration, stating that "all men are equally entitled to the free exercise of religion, according to the dictates of conscience," was drafted by a young lawyer named James Madison, who had previously defended imprisoned preachers.

The fine words of Article 16 did not protect an eloquent young preacher named David Barrow. The Barrow family were friends of the Drews; the signatures of David and his brother John appear on several documents along with Jeremiah's. They were members of the same generation as Jeremiah—but David Barrow's ambitions were entirely different.

Born in 1753 in Brunswick County, which shared a border with St. Luke's Parish until 1781, Barrow began preaching at the age of eighteen. He was ordained in 1774, when he was twenty-one years old, and became the first minister of the Mill Swamp Baptist Church in Isle of Wight. By the end of the same year, he was also helping to organize the Black Creek Baptist Church in Southampton County.[13]

In 1778, he was invited to preach at the Shoulder Hill Baptist Church in Nansemond County. No sooner had he begun the service than a "gang of well-dressed men," about twenty in number, came up to the stage that had been erected under some trees and interrupted the hymn with an obscene song. They grabbed Barrow and his companion and plunged them into the mud of the Nansemond River, holding Barrow under water so long that he almost drowned. Letting him up to breathe, they asked him if he believed, to which he replied "I believe you mean to drown me." The assailants drove the two preachers from the property in their wet clothes and threatened the owner with retaliation if they returned. Barrow and his companion did return, and continued to preach.[14]

The Black Creek Baptist Church, located in the northwest corner of Southampton County, was a kinship network before it was a church. Southampton County wills written before its founding show future church members living next to each other, marrying each other, and acting as each other's witnesses and executors. Within the congregation, a secondary network consisted of people with Isle of Wight Quaker surnames.[15] It is likely that the Black Creek Church was established in a Quaker neighborhood, since a Quaker meeting was founded some years earlier near the same little creek and continued in existence for over two centuries. Barrow himself may have had Quaker relatives; there were Quaker Barrows in Perquimans County, just south of the North Carolina border.

Some of the families represented in the congregation were very large, with many members who were neither Quakers nor Baptists. But the influence of kinfolk was profound. Historian Jewel Spangler, who has analyzed the social history of the Black

Creek Church, observes that "over eighty percent of free members had family names that appeared more than once on membership lists through 1790." Once the first member of a kinship network decided for the Baptists, his or her relatives were likely to follow, building the base that the church needed in order to flourish. In this way, early church members created the nucleus of a community, based on intimate personal relationships and on each member's responsibility to the full community for living in a way consistent with Baptist teachings.[16]

The influence of this small community and the respect in which it began to be held can be seen in the fact that although its members were, on average, poorer than other white Southampton County residents, several of their names can be found on lists of people selected for grand juries. They were also frequently appointed by the justices as guardians for orphans.[17] In spite of Barrow's defiance of the established church, he was quickly recognized as a man of standing: in 1781, he was recommended as a justice of the peace, and a year later he was recommended for the post of magistrate. He appears to have first assumed office as a justice in 1784.[18]

Quaker theology was based on belief in the perfectibility of man and in a loving God whose goodness created an "inner light" within every human soul. The possibility of salvation was open to everyone, through each person's own efforts. By contrast, most Regular Baptists were strict Calvinists. They believed in the total depravity of man, the acceptance of the literal words of the Scriptures as the sole authority, and the election of a chosen few, predestined for salvation since the beginning of time while the rest of humanity was damned. Quakers sat in silence, waiting for God to speak to them, while even Regular Baptist services were characterized by passionate preaching and emotional response. The Black Creek Baptist Church was Regular Baptist.[19] The frequency with which the old Quaker surnames of Isle of Wight County appear on its membership lists is testimony to the irrelevance of theology.

What the two faiths shared was an emphasis on the direct connection between the individual soul and God and a fierce opposition to any state control of individual conscience. Both offered believers a self-governing egalitarian community that supported its members, arbitrated their disputes, and prescribed the rules of behavior by which they lived. Both appealed to the independent and self-reliant spirit of the borderers. But Baptist churches offered a far more powerful emotional experience, a cathartic release from the losses and labors and casual brutality of daily life, as well as a more lenient set of behavioral rules. And Baptists allowed their members to keep their slaves.

Like all other eighteenth-century Virginia Baptist churches,[20] the Black Creek Baptist Church had both black and white members. Fifteen of the members were enslaved, and another three had been recently freed. The names of free and slave, black and white, are mixed randomly on the earliest membership list. More than two thirds of the enslaved people belonged to other church members: Lankford's Humphrey, Gray's Lyn, Everett's David, Wright's Jacob, Simmons's Daniel.

Like other Baptist churches, the Black Creek congregation considered complaints by slaves against their masters, and on at least two different occasions actually excommunicated white members for "using Barbarity toward their Slaves."[21] Any member could complain against any other, and if the congregation found the complaint justified, the wrongdoer was expected to show contrition and the complainant, forgiveness. But for all their anti-authoritarian fervor, Baptists left the social structure of their communities essentially unchanged. Spangler points out that slaves were expected to maintain their subordinate position and could be disciplined by a congregation for treating free people with disrespect.[22] Baptists provided their Quaker converts with a familiar context and a familiar set of beliefs about the individual's relationship with God, while allowing them to slip free of the strictures about slavery and pacifism that had separated them from the broader society. In the birth throes of the new nation, Baptists allowed their converts to redefine themselves as full members of that nation and of the slaveholding society in which they lived.

The sleep of conscience, however, was less profound at some moments than at others. The first few years of American independence witnessed a moment of transporting idealism in which anything seemed possible. Perhaps, after the devastation of the war, a new and truly just society could be created. Perhaps the ringing words of the Declaration of Independence could actually be taken seriously.

In 1782, the Virginia Assembly passed a law that, for the first time in sixty years, allowed slaveholders to emancipate their slaves. Immediately upon its passage, a group of Southampton citizens with the surnames of old Isle of Wight Quaker families—Jones, Butler, Pretlow, Eley, and entire tribes of Densons and Rickses—freed their slaves.[23] In 1784, David Barrow did the same. In November of 1786, the Black Creek Church deliberated and formally declared that slavery was "unrighteous"—the only Virginia Baptist church ever to do so.[24] The previous year and again in 1790, the Baptist General Committee, with Barrow as a delegate, considered the question of slavery and found it to be "a violent deprivation of the rights of nature."[25] While Barrow was undoubtedly a man of principle and courage, it is reasonable to assume that the large number of Quaker descendants or relatives among his church's members also had some influence on his decisions.

The real energies of the Baptists were focused on freedom of conscience and on the absolute separation of church and state. In 1784, as morality and social order seemed to be disintegrating on all sides, the Virginia Assembly sought to shore them up with a bill providing for state support for "Teachers of the Christian Religion." All Christian denominations were included; the individual taxpayer could decide which church he wanted to support. Initially the bill gained wide support, but during the legislative recess, James Madison and the Baptists set out to organize resistance. And they were infinitely better organized than their adversaries.

Madison wrote and circulated his famous "Memorial and Remonstrance," a powerful, closely reasoned document that argued that religion is by its very nature "wholly exempt" from the authority of the state. The General Committee of Virginia Baptists sent out word to local churches to prepare their own petitions, and when the Assembly reconvened, it was confronted with more than eighty petitions against the bill, containing more than ten thousand signatures altogether. On the pro-assessment side, there were only eleven, with a thousand signatures.[26] The bill was defeated handily, and in its place Madison secured the passage of the Virginia Statute for Religious Freedom, written years earlier by Thomas Jefferson.

David Barrow's name leads the list of the Southampton petitioners.[27] Of the next fourteen names, twelve are Black Creek Church members, and of these, five bear Quaker surnames. There are at least ten more Quaker names among the next thirty-seven. After that, the signature collectors seem to have branched out to their relatives and neighbors, finally winding up on the other side of the county with Randolph Newsom, later the guardian of Jeremiah's young son Newit, and Randolph's friend and neighbor Elisha Melton. Oddly enough Elisha, the only free person of color to sign either petition, also added his name to the much briefer list of signatures on the petition favoring the bill, even though as a free person of color he was legally barred from voting.

It is worth noting that the objection of the Baptists was not merely to being taxed for the support of other denominations but also to any state aid or entanglement whatsoever with their own. Baptist historians are not shy about claiming credit for the First Amendment to the United States Constitution[28]—and they have a point.

Not content with their initial victory, Virginia Baptists continued to petition the Assembly on a variety of subjects. The final showdown came in 1799 when, after a decade-long battle, the Assembly finally passed a bill championed by the Baptists, which required that all of the property of the Virginia Episcopal Church— property purchased with taxes imposed on Virginia residents—be sold and the money "be apportioned to the support of the Poor in each county."

The controversy over that bill gave rise to petitions from Southampton and other counties as early as 1790. This time the struggle was much more fierce, and the lists of signatures on the Southampton County petitions much longer. Once again names of Black Creek Church members and their relatives top the Baptist list, although Barrow's name is absent, and once again the first page of the list is full of Quaker surnames, most of them shared with Black Creek members. Further down on the Baptist petition are descendants of nearly all the original Angelica Swamp settlers as well as several families connected with them. Randolph Newsom's firm signature is there as well.

Not all families were united in their views. The Episcopalian petition was signed by a majority of Randolph Newsom's male relatives, including several of his brothers. It also bore the signatures of several friends and relatives of the Drews, including Jeremiah's brother-in-law Thomas Fitzhugh, with whom his son James was then living, and a Henry Harris who may have been the stepfather of Jeremiah's children. The petitions give us a picture of a deeply divided community, with Jeremiah's younger son Newit, eighteen years old and already living with his guardian Randolph, squarely on the fault line.

The language of the Episcopalian petitions is that of an older world—the ceremonious, deferential language with which aristocratic Virginians would formerly have addressed the king. The signers apologize in a well-bred manner for bothering the honorable members of the Assembly, speak in terms of duty and of social order, and predict the destruction of all faith and morality should the Baptist petitions be successful. The 1785 signers, who describe themselves as "the most respectable part of [the county], if property or liberality of sentiments can make it deserve that appellation," would never have made such a fuss, but "finding an opposition [to the assessment bill] which could scarcely have been expected, they can no longer withhold their sentiments." In the 1790 petition, we can sense more anxiety. A great number of people

> ... have appeared to change their religious tenets; and are at this time shifting and changing from one religious society to another so that there is no society that appears fixed and stable amongst us. [T]hus by continually creating and abolishing institutions, we shall be reduced to such a state of fluctuation and uncertainty, that there can be no dependence whatever on any thing of a publick nature, and in the end it must destroy all faith and confidence between men and men."

The Baptist petitions, on the other hand, speak of rights, in the vigorous language of the young republic. The language of the 1785 Southampton document, identical to those from several other counties, echoes the ringing cadences of a Baptist sermon.

> Certain it is, that the blessed Author of our Religion supported and Maintained his Gospel in the World for several hundred Years, not only without the Aid of civil Power, but against all the Powers of the Earth ... Nor was it better for the Church when Constantine first established Christianity by human Laws, tho there was Rest awhile from Persecution.

It closes with a confident assertion:

> [I]f such Tax is against the Spirit of the Gospel ... and if against the Bill of Rights; which your petitioners believe: they Trust the Wisdom and Uprightness of your honorable House, will leave them entirely free in Matters of Religion, & the Manner of Supporting its Ministers.

The 1790 Baptist petition begins with a paean to the Revolution, and to

> the boldest Heroes, whose Bosoms swelled with Philanthropy
> and glowed with patriotic zeal, who in a manly manner . . . dared
> the most threatening Attempts of the British Court.

It argues that the property of the established church, paid for by a tax on the people at large, "consequently remains to their Right, whatever changes may have taken place in their religious sentiments."

It is the modern world that we hear speaking in these petitions. The United States, still just barely born, is announcing itself in ringing tones, with its assertion of freedom of conscience as a right established by the people themselves through the Constitution they had created. It is no surprise that this was the world young Newit chose.

Listen. Can you hear the hinge swing?

8. Newit Drew Comes of Age

Those who have lived through this kind of historical moment know how brief it is. Only three members of the Black Creek Church followed Barrow's example and freed all of their slaves.[1] In 1787, Barrow's wife Sarah and some supporters attempted to deny communion to those who did not, but their attempts were unsuccessful.[2] By 1793, the Baptist General Convention had already backtracked and decided to dismiss the subject, "as it belongs to the legislative body."[3]

In 1797, Barrow gave up the struggle and moved to Kentucky with his family, informing his parishioners in a "circular letter" that Southampton County was too poor for him to settle his debts and support his family without either "speculation" or slave ownership. Many other antislavery Baptists made the same choice, seeking a new world free from the wickedness and corruption of the old.

That new world, however, was also attractive to Baptist slaveholders. In the newly settled regions where society was still evolving, the struggle between pro-slavery and anti-slavery factions was more violent. As Barrow and others preached their anti-slavery doctrine from their pulpits, Kentucky Baptists abandoned their cherished doctrines of consensus and community and attempted instead to destroy their opponents. In 1805, some members of the North District Baptist Association mounted a direct attack on Barrow for "preaching the doctrine of emancipation to the hurt and injury of the feelings of the brotherhood." He was tried in 1806 and expelled from the association.[4]

Barrow's status as a religious hero and survivor of the early persecutions made the battle all the more bitter. Emboldened by their victory, the pro-slavery members of the Baptist Association began investigating members of his churches, while other churches started purging their anti-slavery members. Barrow and some of his friends formed a small Baptist emancipationist association, the Baptized Licking-Locust Association, Friends to Humanity, whose members publicly denounced their former colleagues. But immediately after his death in 1819, the Friends to Humanity collapsed, and many of its members returned to their former churches. Once again, the anti-slavery minority gave up the struggle and moved west.[5]

The appearance of a large number of newly freed slaves, dark-skinned, illiterate, and impoverished, coincided with a further decline in the status of Southampton County's long-free people of color. Tax lists for St. Luke's Parish for the years 1782 to 1787, compiled by Paul Heinegg, show a puzzling pattern. In the first two years of the period, hardly any free colored family was without at least one horse, and the average number of cattle per household was over five. By 1787, the last year when cattle were counted, only about half of the householders in this category owned a horse, and the number of cattle had also dropped by half. Even the most solid householders saw their livestock diminish in this way, and several found themselves unable to maintain an independent household at all. In 1800 and 1810, half of the households of these long-free families were still unable to afford a horse. The vast majority of newly freed slaves, most of them in Nottoway Parish, never reached that level. Further south in Greensville County, where many free people of color had moved before the Revolution, the more prosperous families kept their horses and maintained the size of their cattle herds. Their prosperity, however, was tenuous: some families moved in and out of slave ownership while in others the children of the original settlers found themselves unable to maintain their parents' standard of living.[6]

The economic decline of these families reflects the almost immediate backlash against the egalitarian idealism of the Revolution. Although the new constitutions of most southern states granted the right to vote to all free males, subject to property qualifications, those grants were quickly rescinded. In many cases, free people of color were forbidden to enter the state at all, and newly emancipated slaves were required to leave or face reenslavement. In 1793, Virginia began requiring them to register at the local courthouse and to provide proof of their freedom.[7]

This economic decline also paralleled a decline in the status of all people of color, free or enslaved, within Baptist churches. In the early records of the Black Creek Baptist Church, the names of enslaved people and the newly freed were mixed in randomly on the lists of members. The church's 1793 rules of order stated that all "free male members," including the freed slaves Benjamin Blackhead and Sam Blackman, had the right to participate in the governance of the church. But in 1800, after Barrow's departure for Kentucky, his former church in Mill Swamp got a bit queasy about this level of equality and changed its own rules to read "free born members." By 1805, the Black Creek membership lists were segregated, with free and enslaved black women listed together. In 1818, a new membership list moved Blackhead and Blackman from the list of "free male members" and listed them instead with enslaved men.[8] Eventually many members of these families migrated, like the anti-slavery Baptists, to the free states of Ohio, Indiana, and Illinois. A large majority of Virginia Quakers, finding it impossible to continue living in a slave society, did the same.[9]

Jeremiah Drew's second son, Newit (spelled without his grandfather's second T), was twelve when his father died in 1784. By 1790, when he was eighteen, he was living with his guardian Randolph Newsom.[10] The move may have marked a significant change in young Newit's life. Although we have no record of Jeremiah's religious affiliation, we do know that Randolph was a Baptist and would have rejected dancing, gambling, and other activities that served to distinguish the Virginia gentry. He was also either a skilled carpenter in his own right or the owner of a carpentry workshop, specializing in the prime status symbol of the era. The 1781 will of Henry Taylor mentions "my double riding chair now making at Randolph Newsum's,"[11] and Randolph or his workers probably made Jeremiah's riding chair as well.

As Newit grew into adulthood, his relationship with his guardian remained close, and that relationship had a powerful effect on the younger man. At least since 1786, Randolph had been an active member of the Raccoon Swamp Baptist Church, on the western edge of Southampton County just over the Surry County line.[12] The church differed in some respects from the Black Creek Church to the east. While enslaved people represented only nine percent of the Black Creek Church membership,[13] they made up more than a third of the congregation at Raccoon Swamp. There was not a single identifiable free person of color, perhaps because the long-free families did not want to associate themselves too closely with the enslaved. And although the church's membership lists include a scattering of old Angelica Swamp surnames, there is little evidence of the kinship networks that were so important at Black Creek. Interestingly, an early membership list, probably dating from before 1780, includes the small, precise, slightly fussy signature of the same Henry Harris who appears on the Southampton County Episcopalian petition a decade later. If this Henry was indeed Newit's stepfather, he appears to have tailored his convictions to his new social status when he married Mary Parker Drew.

Like the Black Creek Church, the Raccoon Swamp Church can be seen in its minutes[14] defining its own rules and even its beliefs as it went along, with difficult questions of doctrine referred to the Kehukee Baptist Association in North Carolina for clarification. Among the issues considered between 1786 and 1792 were the following:

- Is not the Moral Law, to be considered of use to all Believers?

- Is Election, binding over to Salvation, or Reprobation, to Damnation? Answer: Neither, is Election binding over to salvation, not Reprobation to Damnation, without their secondary causes.

This answer, although murky, seems to make some allowance for free will, a deviation from the strict Calvinism of the Kehukee Association.[15] Another question addressed church decorum.

- Is it reprovable for persons passing about after snuff in the time of Divine service, or not? Answer, it is.

For people who had never before been challenged to think deeply about matters of faith, the deliberations about these questions must have been a mind-expanding experience. But the issue of the morality of slavery never appears in these minutes, and there is no record of a woman or enslaved person being permitted to preach. Like other Virginia Baptist churches, the Raccoon Swamp Church had already moved away from the passionate egalitarianism of the first years and from the early Baptists' outspoken challenges to the racial and gender conventions of their society. Between 1797 and 1802, both the Dover and the Roanoke Baptist Associations, after much debate, recommended to their members that slaves not be allowed a vote on matters affecting the white members of their churches. Across Virginia, white Baptists were also taking steps to restrain the fervent emotionalism of black religious expression.[16]

From 1787 on, Randolph Newsom was one of the small group of white men who directed church affairs. He represented the church at meetings of the Kehukee Association and was frequently appointed to the all-male committees charged with investigating and reconciling conflicts between members. In 1793, he became a deacon as well as one of the three members leading "weekly Prayer meetings for the revival of Religion." Although Newit was never listed as a member of the church, it is clear from his later history that the church and his guardian's role in it made a profound impression on him.

In 1793, Newit married his first cousin Lucy Smith, and two years later, Newit and Randolph together bought out James Drew's interest in Jeremiah's mill.[17] In August of 1797, Newit and Lucy sold their interest in the mill, along with the 298 acres Newit had inherited from his father, to Thomas Ridley, the owner of the eight pedigreed stud horses. One month later, Matthew Figures, a first cousin of both Newit and Lucy, sold his own land in St. Luke's Parish.[18] Tens of thousands of Virginians from the long-settled areas of the state were moving west across the mountains, and the three young cousins planned to join them.

Their reasons are not immediately obvious. Unlike some of his less fortunate neighbors, Newit was not forced off his ancestral land by debt, rising land prices, or an excess of brothers. He still owned the mill that had made his father rich. Unlike the eroded and exhausted lands in many areas of the Tidewater, the land of St. Luke's Parish was still rich and productive. Many of his wealthy relatives and family friends were staying put and growing even wealthier. It is likely that there were other factors, both social and personal, that set him off on his journey.

Unquestionably, he was a restless man. He would not be the last person in his family with that trait. Like millions of his countrymen both then and later, he was forever looking over the next horizon for newer challenges and larger opportunities. A few clues from his later history suggest a strong-willed and difficult personality. Another factor may have been in play as well: a decline in relative social status. Four years after the invention of the cotton gin, at the beginning of the explosive growth of the cotton economy, the society of Southampton County was becoming more and more stratified.[19] Families like the Ridleys and Joneses, the aristocracy of St. Luke's Parish since the days of the first settlement, were establishing large plantations in the Three Creeks area, and in 1797 they were paying unusually high prices for their neighbors' land.[20] Newit's father

Jeremiah had made it into the ranks of the Southampton gentry, but with only three hundred acres, even including the mill, Newit found himself back in the ranks of the middling planters. The contrast with his family's earlier status may have been galling. He may have yearned for a place where he could exercise his talents to their fullest extent, enjoy a status based on his own achievements, and establish himself as a leader in his own community. The still inchoate frontier of Tennessee offered him all those things.[21]

Before they could start off, Lucy died. She was twenty-four years old.[22] Newit's great-grandfather Edward Drew had lived into his eighties, and his grandfathers and great-uncle into their sixties and seventies. Newit's father, mother, stepfather, and two uncles, however, all died in their thirties or early forties, and his wife and his sister Susannah in their twenties. By the time he was forty-five, only two of his six siblings were still alive, and three of his sisters had died childless.[23] Even for that era, the death toll is startling. The connection between mill ponds and malaria was already known, but the connection between typhoid and contaminated water—particularly in areas like Angelica Swamp with high water tables—would not be discovered for another century. It is possible that the mill that was the source of the family's wealth may also have been responsible for their early deaths.

A glimpse of the four sisters that Newit left behind can be found in the will of his sister Susannah (Susan), who died in 1801.[24] Although all four were at that time in their twenties or early thirties, only Peggy was married; the others, orphans with no land of their own, must have been living in the homes of relatives. Susan, however, had had a great friend, a rich widow named

Sally Jones who died in 1798, leaving her a large legacy of two hundred dollars.[25] Whatever was left of that money went to Susan's unmarried sisters. Neither brother is mentioned: Newit was gone, and James may already have been dead.

Like many other migrants, Newit Drew and Matthew Figures set out in the fall, after the harvest was in and the hogs driven to market. The first wagons had passed over the Wilderness Road and through the Cumberland Gap only two years earlier, in 1795.[26] Most emigrants traveled in groups both for safety from robbers and for mutual assistance along the way, and the large majority of them were heading for Kentucky.[27] Newit and Matthew were unusual. Their goal was Tennessee, and as far as can be determined, no neighbors or other family members traveled with them. They most likely followed the Wilderness Road to Knoxville and then to the path known as Avery's Trace, arriving in Wilson County, about twenty miles east of the little village of Nashville, by 1797, to begin another borderer cycle.

Part III

Becoming Citizens in the
Carolina Backcountry

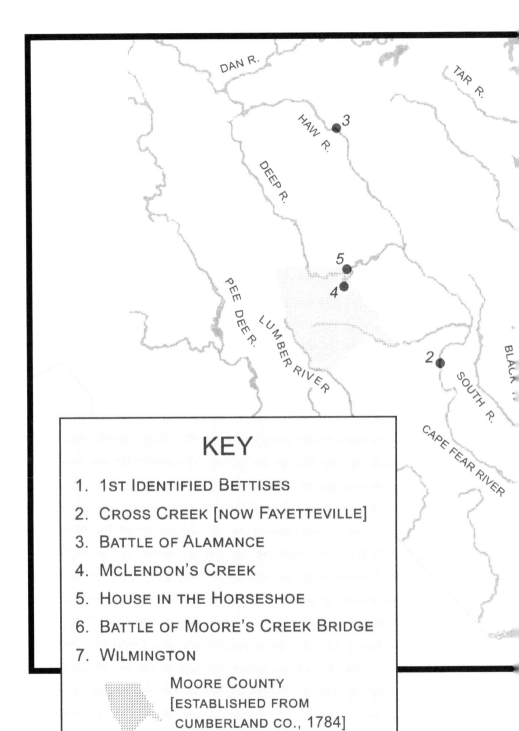

DAN R.

TAR R.

HAW R.

●3

DEEP R.

●5

●4

PEE DEE R.

LUMBER RIVER

●2

BLACK

SOUTH R.

CAPE FEAR RIVER

KEY

1. 1ST IDENTIFIED BETTISES

2. CROSS CREEK [NOW FAYETTEVILLE]

3. BATTLE OF ALAMANCE

4. MCLENDON'S CREEK

5. HOUSE IN THE HORSESHOE

6. BATTLE OF MOORE'S CREEK BRIDGE

7. WILMINGTON

    MOORE COUNTY
    [ESTABLISHED FROM
    CUMBERLAND CO., 1784]

CHOWAN R.

ALBEMARLE SOUND

ROANOKE R.

LAKE
MATTAMUSKEET

NEUSE R.

PAMLICO SOUND

NORTHEAST CAPE FEAR R.

BETTISES, REGULATORS AND
LOYALISTS IN NORTH CAROLINA

LONG BAY

9. The Enterprising Bettises

The inhabitants of Pasquotank and Perquimans counties, just south of the Virginia border between the Great Dismal Swamp and Albemarle Sound, did not fare well in the accounts of their contemporaries. They were the "people of no religion" encountered by the traveling Quakers William Edmundson and Thomas Story, people who knew no better than to smoke their pipes at a meeting for worship. They were the people whose cabins were so filthy that William Byrd preferred to sleep outside. Since North Carolina, in an effort to attract immigrants, protected settlers from debts contracted elsewhere, they also included a large number of insolvent debtors. In the 1680s, Virginia's Governor Thomas Culpeper observed that "Carolina (I meane the North part of it) always was and is the sinke of America, the Refuge of our Renagadoes."[1]

The Reverend John Urmstone, minister of a local parish from 1710 to 1721, described the area as "an obscure corner of the world inhabited by the dregs and gleanings of all other English Colonies."[2] Those "dregs and gleanings" were the same people whom Jack Kirby describes as "profoundly democratic," and of whom Byrd said that "every One does what seems best in his own Eyes." Among them were the first known ancestors of the North Carolina Bettises.

My introduction to the Bettises was an unpublished one-hundred-page manuscript titled *The Bettes: England to America,* completed around 1951 by an elderly woman named Adele Cobb Kerrigan. It is an extraordinary document, an indispensable starting point for Bettis genealogy and the record of a lifetime's dedication to the assembling of her family's history. It is also crammed with errors, some of them absurd, and includes one account of a lengthy interview with a psychic horse. The horse, Lady Wonder, responded to questions by spelling out words with taps of her hoof. When asked, she informed Kerrigan that the first American Bettis had settled in Henrico County, Virginia. She provided no explanation of what drove the family to the swamps of the Albemarle shore, bypassing the still unclaimed land in Isle of Wight and Nansemond Counties. Neither did any other source that I have been able to find.

Francis Bettis was the first of the restless wanderers who will appear in the course of this book, and his wanderings set the pattern for generations of his descendants. He is thought to have been born in Pasquotank Precinct (later Pasquotank County) in the first decade of the eighteenth century. A Thomas and Mary Bettys can be found there between 1715 and 1730, buying and selling small pieces of land, taking fifteen years to accumulate a modest estate of 250 acres. A John Betts Sr. appears as a witness on a will dated 1718 but not on any deeds. Bettis genealogists believe these men to be Francis's father and uncle. The name of "Nobbs Crook Creek" and a reference to "Captain Relfe's tree" on two of these early deeds match up with place names found on later maps, suggesting a location near the narrows of the Pasquotank River just north of present-day Elizabeth City, where a Quaker meeting had been established as early as the late 1600s.[3] Although there is no evidence that the first North Carolina Bettises were Quakers—or, indeed, members of any other religion—several of their in-laws and associates in the next two generations bore the surnames of families who appear in the early Quaker records of Pasquotank and Perquimans Counties.[4] Since Quakers placed great emphasis on schooling for their children, the choice to settle in this area may have been responsible for the fact that all future generations of Bettis men could read and write.

By his late twenties, Francis had set off on his long southwestward migration, moving with the leading edge of settlement down North Carolina's inner coastal plain. Like Edward Drew, he migrated as part of a community, following the same route as the family of his wife, Mary Evans; his Quaker neighbors the Tysons and the Cheeks,[5] and the Swearingen family who joined the group in Edgecomb County. The land through which they traveled had been depopulated for a generation, as a result of the devastating epidemics of the sixteenth and seventeenth centuries and the bloody Tuscarora War, which ended in 1712 with the defeat and emigration of North Carolina's largest remaining tribe. It was part of the vast belt of longleaf pine forest that once stretched from Virginia to Florida and west to the Texas border, a place where the trees were so tall and their lowest branches so high that it was said that you could see for a mile between the trunks. Contemporary travelers described the land beneath the pines as "a universal gloomy shade."[6]

Only scattered patches of this enormous forest remain. To a modern observer, their widely spaced trunks with sparse crowns shading a carpet of grasses and wildflowers have a weird kind of beauty. The longleaf pine flourishes in sandy soil almost bare of nutrients, and its survival depends on fire. For centuries, fire, either started by lightning or deliberately set by native peoples, kept the understory clear of the scrub oak and brush that could smother the pine seedlings. The burning of the underbrush every one to three years on the average also recycled nitrogen and other nutrients to the barren soil, allowing the pine seeds to germinate.[7] This delicately balanced ecosystem nurtured a rich variety of animal life, providing a bountiful food supply for its human inhabitants. The Europeans who replaced those people could profit from it only by destroying it.

As the borderers moved southward through the great forest, they consumed it. Like the Virginians to the north, they girdled the trees to kill them. Unlike the Virginians, they did not cut them down but left them dead, immense, and standing, planting their crops between the enormous trunks. To J. F. D. Smyth,

> . . . a large field in this situation, makes a most singular, striking, and tremendous appearance; it would seem indeed dangerous to walk in it, as the trees are of a prodigious height and magnitude; vast limbs, and branches of enormous size impending in awful ruins, from a great height, sometimes breaking off, and frequently whole trees falling to the ground, with a horrible crash. . .[8]

As in Virginia, the settlers grew tobacco, and those without access to a navigable river raised hogs. And, as in Southampton County, the principal product was naval stores—tar, turpentine, and pitch extracted from the longleaf pines.

The borderers saw no need to conserve resources: there would always be more. They cut V-shaped notches in the trees to extract the turpentine and continued tapping the trees until the trees died. The remaining "lightwood" was converted into tar in a simple homemade kiln. Smyth describes such a kiln, a small-scale operation managed by an individual household:

> They prepare a circular floor of clay, declining a little towards the center; from this is laid a pipe of wood, the upper part of which is even with the floor, and reached ten feet without the circumference; under the end the earth is dug away, and barrels placed to receive the tar as it runs.

Wood was piled in a pyramid in the hole and covered almost entirely with turf, and a fire was lit at the top of the heap. When the fire caught, it was covered as well and burned extremely slowly until all the tar was extracted.[9] The value of the tar could then be increased by boiling or burning it to transform it into pitch.[10] Towards the end of the eighteenth century, much of the production came from large enterprises using enslaved labor. By 1768, sixty percent of all North American exports of tar, pitch, and turpentine came from North Carolina.[11]

The coastal plain is drained by a series of long slow rivers, the Tar, the Neuse, the Cape Fear, and the Pee Dee. These rivers, navigable far upstream, provided transportation to the port cities of Bath, Beaufort, and Wilmington for the tobacco, lumber, and naval stores produced in the interior. Unlike the surrounding pine belt, the river valleys were graced with a rich variety of hardwoods— ash, sycamore, elm, and many species of oak and walnut. Traveling through the area in 1778, the naturalist William Bartram rhapsodized about the many "curious and beautiful flowering and sweet-scented shrubs," among them the beautyberry with its lilac-colored clusters, the witchalder with its feathery blossoms, and the red spikes of the buckeye.[12] At the head of navigation of the rivers, small towns grew up, receiving the products of the interior and sending them on their way to the sea. Tarboro and Cross Creek were two of these towns.

In the early 1730s, as the demand for naval stores rose, Francis Bettis and the Evans family were buying and selling land on the Tar River, near the site of the future Tarboro in Edgecombe

County. Francis's dealings were far more profitable than those of the previous generation of Bettises. In 1732, he acquired a tract of 1400 acres for a price of 70 pounds, or a shilling an acre. Two years later, he sold the same tract to his father- or brother-in-law Charles Evans for 200 pounds, nearly tripling his original investment. In 1749, he patented 660 acres. Eight years later he sold that land for 63 pounds, or nearly two shillings an acre, and he and his family continued their southwestward journey.[13] They had been in Edgecombe County for about 25 years. Four generations of his descendants would follow the same path to self-sufficiency and, in some cases, to wealth.

A number of factors probably contributed to their decision to move on. The pine forests in the Tar River area had been largely tapped out, and the center of production had moved south to the Cape Fear.[14] At the same time, the price of agricultural land was rising as new waves of settlers built houses, cleared fields, and planted orchards. By the mid 1750s, Francis had five grown sons to provide for; it made sense to sell out at a profit and move on to cheaper land. The Bettises followed the fall line, the roughly defined boundary between the eastern Piedmont and the western edge of the coastal plain, southwest to Cumberland County.

When William Bartram first visited the town of Cross Creek, then known as Cambelton and since 1783 as Fayetteville, the town was just laying out its boundaries. By Bartram's estimate, it contained about twenty houses. Francis and his five sons and their relatives were already in the area and buying land.[15] When Bartram returned twenty years later, he found above a thousand houses, many wealthy merchants, and respectable public buildings, a vast resort of inhabitants and travelers, and continual brisk commerce, by wagons, from the back settlements, with large trading boats, to and from Wilmington.[16]

The fact that the Bettises chose to settle near these infant commercial centers at the head of navigation of their respective rivers suggests that, unlike the Southampton settlers, they were not subsistence farmers but connected to the Atlantic commercial economy. The locations suited the enterprising spirit of a family whose later generations would include a significant number of risk-takers and entrepreneurs. Francis's children and grandchildren continued to migrate, south and west down the fall line: to Anson County, North Carolina; to Old Cheraw and Camden in South Carolina; and to Edgefield, South Carolina, on the edge of the ever-shrinking Cherokee territory. From Edgefield many of them moved on, to Georgia and the wilds of Alabama.[17] Of all of Francis's descendants, only one family remained in Cumberland County by the end of the century, in the corner of that county that had by then become Moore: the family of Elijah Bettis Sr., the first of four of that name.

Based on the birth date of 1769 generally given for his oldest grandchild, Elijah Sr. could not have been born later than about 1730. He must have married in Edgecombe County in the late 1740s. The name of his wife has not been clearly established, an unusual gap in the records of a family whose wives and in-laws are otherwise well-documented.

In 1769, a Cumberland County planter named John Overton sold two parcels of land, one of 200 acres and the other of 250, on the muddy, meandering stream known as McLendon's Creek, which flows into the stretch of the Deep River known as the Horseshoe in the northwest corner of the county.[18] It was good land, gently rolling and forested in hardwoods, a few miles north of the barren sandy Pinehills. Although both deeds were made out to Elijah Bettis, it is likely that the buyers were two different Elijahs, father and son. Shortly before the sale, the younger Elijah, then about twenty, had married Amey Overton, whom Bettis family tradition identifies as John's daughter. No documents tie her directly to him, but she named one of her sons Overton Bettis, and he in turn named his son John Overton Bettis.

Although John Overton is said to have had several other daughters, only Mary Overton Shields Dowd can be definitely identified. Mary was a rich young widow when she married an illiterate Scots-Irish peddler named Connor Dowd, who at that time was operating an "ordinary" (pub) in her father's house.[19] With the five hundred acres that Mary brought him on her marriage, Dowd began the construction of a manufacturing empire. Within ten years, he had a tavern, "a manufacturing and mercantile business of considerable importance . . . Saw, Grist and Bolting Mills on Deep River," a tanyard, a bark house and bark mill (to produce the products needed for his tanning operation), a distillery, a store, and eleven slaves. Imprisoned and exiled during the Revolution for his Loyalist sympathies, he later estimated the total value of his former property at thirteen thousand pounds.[20]

The tracts that Overton sold to the two Elijahs were separated by about ten miles, one adjoining Overton's land near the mouth of McLendon's Creek and the other far upstream near Richland Creek and the Old Stage Road. A comparison of the names appearing on a map of old land patents[21] with the neighbors of two Elijah Bettises in the 1790 and 1800 censuses indicates that the elder Elijah settled on the plot next to Overton, near the Deep River, along with his son Elisha, who eventually inherited the land. Amey Overton and young Elijah settled on the upstream parcel. Before and after the Overton purchases, the two Elijahs followed the example of their father and grandfather Francis—and of most early settlers on any given border—by patenting other pieces of land. Between the two of them, they patented eight separate parcels, a total of fourteen hundred acres, in the period from 1768 to 1774.[22]

Joel McLendon's cabin, built around 1760, stands on the high ground above the creek that bears his name. It is a one-room structure with an impressive stone chimney and a single window at the opposite end. Like other still-standing houses of the

Joel McLendon's cabin, built around 1760

eighteenth-century Carolina border, it reveals the striking difference between the construction methods of the North Carolina backwoods and those of Virginians of a generation earlier. Rather than an impermanent frame structure with sills resting directly on the ground, it is constructed of the insect- and disease-resistant heartwood of large logs, carefully squared off and held together with complicated dovetail joints. It includes a puncheon floor, made of split logs planed and finished on one side, and is raised off the ground on large stones. McLendon's cabin, however simple, was built to last. The cabin where the first of Elijah and Amey's seven children were born probably looked much the same.

It would have taken Elijah Jr., his brother Elisha, and their father two or three days to fell the trees for that cabin, cut them to the right lengths, and square and smooth them with a broadax and an adze. Another tree was found of the right size for shingles and still others to be split in half and the top sides smoothed with an adze, to make puncheons for the floor. The logs would then be laid around the site of the cabin in their proper places and the neighbors called together to raise them. Four men with axes would stand at the corners carving out each of the dovetail joints as the walls rose. When the chimney had been raised, the roof shingled, and the spaces between the logs chinked with clay, the final task was the manufacture of a few simple pieces of furniture—a table, some stools, and sometimes a bedstead. The women and girls of the neighborhood would be there with pot pies—chicken or ham with vegetables and gravy covered with a pastry crust—and perhaps some hard cider to wash it all down. From beginning to end, the process would have taken less than a week.[23] Later on, when the farm was well-established and the barns and corn cribs in place, a two-room, two-story house might have been added on to provide space for the growing family, and the original cabin relegated to the status of a kitchen.[24]

Amey's role in the family centered around the care of children and the preparation of food, clothing, and medicine. As with other borderers, a large part of her family's diet would have come from the wild game still abundant in the woods, but they would also have raised a few pigs, cattle, and chickens. In her small vegetable garden, she would have grown the crops adopted from the native peoples: the "Indian trinity" of corn, squash, and beans along with pumpkins and potatoes.[25] The herbs in her herb garden provided not only flavor but also medicines and even dyes. Her tools were iron pots and frying pans, ceramic crocks in which foods could be preserved, wooden barrels, a spinning wheel, and a loom. The kitchen also included pails for water and perhaps a carved wooden yoke that fitted over the neck and shoulders of the child who carried them.[26]

10. "This Total Want of Subordination"

After the 1774 land grants, the two Elijahs and their families disappear from the records for ten years—momentous years for Cumberland County and the country. Any guesses we can make about their experiences during those years must be based on conjecture—but conjecture informed by knowledge about their neighbors and relatives, the upheavals that were going on around them, and the accounts of a few bemused travelers. One of those travelers was J. F. D. Smyth, the Englishman whom we have already met, commenting on North Carolina forestry and the characters of Virginia gentlemen of the "second rank." Smyth, the author of *A Tour in the United States of America*,[1] claimed to have traveled widely in the American colonies and later in the new American republic, both before and after the Revolution. As he presents himself in his book, he was a young gentleman at the beginning of his travels, braver and more adventurous than William Byrd II but also callow and snobbish—a word that did not exist in his time and would have been incomprehensible to him if it had. He saw a good deal and described it vividly. His observations, like the Baptist and Episcopalian petitions in Southampton County, throw into high relief the contrast between the old, hierarchical English world he came from and the rough new one just coming into being, whose inhabitants are recognizably us.

In his account of his travels both in the cities and in the back woods, Smyth is constantly amazed by the lack of deference to rank. Traveling alone through the backcountry, he is frequently obliged to ask for shelter from the families of ordinary planters. He describes them as rude, impertinently curious, and "illiberal," a word that in that era meant not only narrow-minded but also vulgar, ill-bred, uneducated, or obliged to work with one's hands. He complains constantly about the poor quality of the food and the wretchedness of the planters' dwellings. On his way through the North Carolina backcountry, he lodges at the house of a "common plain back wood's planter, with a large family of Bel Savages, a hospitable but uncultivated mind, and rude manners." The home has only one room and one bed. The host and his wife offer the bed to Smyth, but he has the decency to refuse, " . . . as they were advanced in years, and I was young and healthy, although superior in rank and appearance to them."[2] The reader takes a good deal of satisfaction in finding him setting out across the mountains into Indian territory without food, a coat, a blanket, a gun, or anything he could use to start a fire, getting hopelessly lost, and being saved from drowning only by the intervention of a helpful slave.

Arriving at the Henderson fort in Kentucky, where all the settlers in the area have taken refuge from the Indians, he lectures the founder on having chosen the wrong place. The lack of discipline appalls him. He observes that

> . . . throughout all the backcountry, indeed I had almost said
> throughout all America, there seems to be no such thing as any
> idea of subordination, or difference of ranks in life; excepting
> from the weaker to the stronger; and from the slaves to the
> whites. In any of their forts it was all anarchy and confusion, and
> you could not discover what person commanded, for in fact no
> person did actually command entirely. This total want of subordi-
> nation renders the whole country particularly disagreeable to

strangers, such especially as have been accustomed to the polished intercourse of Europe.[3]

But eventually he does learn something, and later in his trip west he acquires an Indian hunting shirt, a blanket, provisions, and a guide—a competent young frontiersman whom he refers to as his "white savage." Of this young man he writes,

> . . . although I now call this man my servant, yet he himself never would have submitted to such an appellation, although he most readily performed every menial office, and indeed any service I could desire; yet such is the insolence, folly, and ridiculous pride of those ignorant back-woods men, that they would conceive it an indelible disgrace and infamy to be styled servants, even to his Majesty, notwithstanding they will gladly perform the lowest and most degrading services for hire.[4]

The lack of proper subordination was even more startling to a Latin American aristocrat. Don Francisco de Miranda, visiting the new country in 1783, was surprised by the surface equality on display at a celebration of the American victory—a barbecue in a public square, characterized by "promiscuous eating and drinking, the principal officers and citizens mixing freely with the coarsest elements of society, all shaking hands and drinking out of the same glass."[5]

The "polished intercourse of Europe" was certainly lacking. In both Virginia and North Carolina, travelers commented repeatedly on the brutality of the colonists' amusements. The violence involved in maintaining a slave society and in exerting control over people who had little to lose except freedom from pain bred a corresponding violence in recreation. And in a world still in the process of creation, where no man's status was entirely secure, violence and risk-taking were the primary tools for protecting one's honor. The aristocracy indulged in high-stakes gambling and horseracing in addition to the occasional duel. Common planters, according to New Englander Jedidiah Morse, "spen[t] their time in drinking, or gaming at cards or dice, in cockfighting, or horse racing" and applauded as their neighbors engaged in vicious tavern battles.[6] A jesting insult could give rise to a fight in which "kicking, scratching . . . biting . . .throttling, gouging [the eyes]," and "dismembering [the genitals]" were not only permitted but applauded by a ring of spectators.[7] The brutality extended to animals. One popular pastime was "gander-pulling," a particularly vicious game in which a gander was hung by its feet from a tree and participants galloped past it, competing to see who would be the first to pull its head off.[8]

The vigorous self-assertion of the inhabitants of the new land had positive effects as well. In William Bartram's description of the town of Cross Creek,

> . . . the creek descends precipitously, then meanders nearly a mile . . .to its confluence with the river, affording most convenient mill-seats; these prospects induced active enterprising men to avail themselves of such advantages; . . .[T]hey built mills, which drew people to the place, and these observing eligible situations for other profitable improvements, bought lots and erected tenements, where they exercised mechanic arts, as smiths, wheelwrights, carpenters, coopers, tanners, &c. And at length merchants were encouraged to adventure and settle: in short, within eight or ten years . . . arose a flourishing commercial town.[9]

Visiting Hillsborough, a Piedmont town that served as the administrative center for Orange County, Smyth commented that

> almost every man in this country has been the fabricator of his own fortune, and many of them are very opulent. Some have

obtained their riches by commerce, others by the practice of law, which in this province is peculiarly lucrative, and extremely oppressive; but most have acquired their possessions by cropping farming, and industry.[10]

This fluidity of status, this opportunity to rise by one's own efforts, reinforced the appalling lack of deference of which Smyth complained.

A fascinating footnote to Smyth's story turns up in a history of North Carolina Freemasons by the same Thomas Parramore who wrote the history of Southampton County, Virginia.[11] According to this account, one John Ferdinand Smith was a charter member of the Buffalo Lodge of Masons in Bute County in the 1760s. He appears to be the same person as the author of the *Tour in the United States of America,* since that book, published twenty years later, contains portraits of some of his fellow Masons. However, " . . . he had a dismal record of attendance and does not appear to have taken his Masonic responsibilities very seriously." Parramore describes Smyth's claims to have purchased great estates on the Roanoke River, spent many years as a physician and planter in Virginia, traveled five thousand miles west into Indian country and down the Mississippi River, and served as a captain in the British Army in the Revolution. And he points out a fact often missed by the historians and editors who have quoted or anthologized Smyth: many or even most of those stories were fabricated. The book itself may have been merely a ploy designed to support his claims for large damages from the British commissioners appointed to investigate claims of American Loyalists.

One of the witnesses summoned by the commissioners in their investigation into Smyth's petition stated that Smyth, or Smith, had come to Halifax, North Carolina, in 1763 as an indentured servant, had been bailed out of a Virginia jail where he was imprisoned for debt, and had worked at various low-level jobs in and around Halifax. Witnesses who had known him in America described him as a "disreputable and untrustworthy person who had masqueraded as a physician at Williamsburg." After hearing the testimony, the commissioners rejected most of his claims. Smyth, however, continued to pursue the matter for the next quarter of a century, in the meantime "concoct[ing] the story that he was an illegitimate child of the Duke of Monmouth, who was himself an illegitimate son of King Charles II."[12] If this account is correct, Smyth unknowingly revealed another facet of the emerging American character: the freedom afforded by the vast new country to anyone who wished to invent and reinvent himself. The snobbishness so annoying to a twenty-first-century reader was merely the self-aggrandizing fantasy of an accomplished con man.

Nevertheless, he wrote well. And whether or not he actually traveled down the Mississippi in a canoe, his descriptions of the world of the Carolina borderers seem to have been based on direct observation. What he did not describe (except to imaginatively invent his own role) was the series of conflicts that would begin to forge those borderers and their countrymen into a nation.

11. Herman Husband's Lessons in Citizenship

As Elijah Bettis and Amey Overton were clearing their farm and building their cabin on McLendon's Creek and as Amey was bearing the first of their seven children, one of the great forgotten tragedies of American history was unfolding just across the Cumberland County border. The Regulator Rebellion has been all but erased from American history texts except in North Carolina, where it has been romanticized into "the first battle of the American Revolution." Marjoleine Kars's close study of the subject, in her book *Breaking Loose Together: The Regulator Rebellion in Pre-Revolutionary North Carolina*, reveals a very different picture from the jumbled fragments that have long obscured the memory of that conflict.

North of the Cumberland County line lay the immense expanse of the Granville grant, comprising most of the northern half of North Carolina and still owned at the time by the Earl of Granville. In the Piedmont, just to the west of Cumberland, lay an area the size of Delaware owned by the speculator Henry McCulloh. By around 1750, only a few years after the almost total collapse of the indigenous population, a new group was flooding in to take its place, coming down the Great Wagon Road from the increasingly crowded farmlands of central Pennsylvania. They were predominantly Protestant dissenters: Scots and Scots-Irish Presbyterians, Pennsylvania Quakers, German Lutherans, and members of German pietist sects such as the Moravians and the Dunkers (known as the Church of the Brethren.)[1] As many as half of them may have had no religion at all.

In the area of the Granville Grant, land could theoretically be patented in the same way as in Virginia, although at a somewhat higher cost. But official corruption was endemic in the Piedmont from Anson County just west of Cumberland to Rowan and Orange Counties in the north, and the settlers were subject to extortion at every turn. Patent officials charged more than the official rate and kept the difference. Sheriffs charged high fees to make out and register deeds and then failed to do it, demanded excessive taxes and double quitrents, and gave their friends lands that had already been claimed by others. Clerks and lawyers made sure that those who came into court seeking justice had to pay double for the privilege.[2]

The distress of the backcountry settlers was increased by the high levels of debt that they incurred for necessary supplies and by the desperate shortage of the cash that they needed in order to pay their debts, taxes and fees. Since Britain banned the export of its coin and forbade colonists to mint their own, the total amount of money in circulation was probably less than what would have been needed to pay the inhabitants' taxes, let alone their debts.[3] If a debt was not paid, the debtor's goods could be seized by the sheriff and sold at auction for a fraction of their value, before the debtor had any opportunity to collect the money needed to redeem them. A 1768 petition from the inhabitants of Rowan and Orange Counties to the North Carolina Assembly pleaded that

> . . . money is very scarce hardly any to be had would we Purchase it at ten times its Value & we exceeding Poor and & lie at a great distance from Trade which renders it almost impossible to gain sustenance by our utmost Endeavours. . . . to Poor People who must have their Bed and Bedclothes yea their Wives Petticoats taken and sold to Defray, how Tremenious judges must be the Consequences, an only Horse, to raise bread or an Only Cow, to

give Milk to an helpless Family ... seized and sold and kept for a high Levy, no Part being ever Return'd.[4]

A Granville County settler was more specific about the culprits:

Are not these things, I say, taken and sold for one-tenth of their value? Not to satisfy the just debts which you have contracted, but to satisfy the cursed exorbitant demands of the Clerks, Lawyers, and Sheriffs. . . . And who buys? Why the same villains who have taken your negroes and other personal estate.[5]

At the top of the Piedmont food chain was a pair of young predators, McCulloh's son Henry Eustace McCulloh and his great friend Edmund Fanning. The conditions of the elder McCulloh's grant of 1.2 million acres required him to start paying quitrents by 1760 and obliged him to return all unsettled lands within the Granville grant by 1763. Since only a small portion of his lands had been sold by 1760, he was feeling a good deal of pressure to convert them into cash and, accordingly, sent his son out to North Carolina to do the job. Fanning, for his part, was a New Englander, a lawyer with degrees from both Yale and Harvard who arrived in the Piedmont determined to make as large a fortune in as short a time as possible.

The two young men, both strangers to the Piedmont area, started out by using their connections to acquire multiple local offices, a time-honored way for local elites to consolidate their control of their society. Fanning, who had managed to make himself commissioner for the town of Hillsborough as well as public register, assemblyman, crown prosecutor, and militia officer, became a major purchaser at the fraudulent sales described in the Granville County document and quickly began to acquire the fortune he sought.[6] McCulloh's strategy was to make allies of leading citizens in each locality and cut them in on the loot.

Many of the new inhabitants had unknowingly settled on land within the McCulloh grant and established farms and orchards. When McCulloh or one of his local agents came around, what they offered the settlers was the chance to buy their own land at its original value *plus* the value of the improvements they themselves had made. The settlers responded with threats, intimidation, and assaults on the surveyors who arrived to measure off their land. But eventually most of them settled for a price only slightly lower than that originally demanded. If they could not immediately raise the money, McCulloh would offer them a mortgage at a high rate of interest, to be paid back within three years. Their acquiescence may have been influenced by the fact that McCulloh's friend Fanning had by that time ascended to the post of associate justice on the Salisbury Superior Court, making any sort of legal redress unlikely.[7] By 1766, the Piedmont farmers' anger was erupting in increasingly frequent episodes of violence.

And here, once again, those troublesome dissenters enter our story: the Separate Baptists and the radical Quakers. Kars's greatest contribution to our understanding of the Regulator Rebellion is her detailed analysis of the relationship between the politics of the Regulators and their religious beliefs. On the basis of an exhaustive study of petitions, sermons, tracts, and other documents, she demonstrates the extent to which the course of the Regulator Rebellion was determined by the religious experience of ordinary people.

The dissenters' belief in a direct relationship between the individual soul and God, a relationship more sacred than the teachings of authority, was a profoundly subversive idea. It validated the settlers' lived experience and codified their unspoken sense of themselves as autonomous beings. Charles Woodmason, an itinerant Anglican minister whose travels took him across the Carolina backcountry in the years before the Revolution, saw the danger clearly. The religious radicals, he said, had poisoned

> the Minds of the People—Instilling Democratical and Common
> Wealth Principles into their Minds—Embittering them against
> the very Name of Bishops . . . . And laying deep their fatal
> Republican Notions and Principals.[8]

In 1755, the Separate Baptist apostle Shubal Stearns and his brother-in-law Daniel Marshall settled on Sandy Creek, a tributary of the Deep River in the central Piedmont. By 1758, he had organized several local Baptist churches into the Sandy Creek Baptist Association. He had a good deal of competition. The Piedmont was experiencing a surge of religious enthusiasm, fed by evangelical preachers of all stripes. Settlers would travel on foot for up to twenty miles to attend mass revivals where ministers of different denominations preached one after the other. After the preaching, audience members would often stay around to discuss questions of theology and politics and to receive counseling for their sins in front of an audience of others waiting their turn and commenting on the speaker's problems.[9] Exposure to a variety of conflicting doctrines, and participation in passionate arguments about those doctrines that could go on all night, encouraged people to reason for themselves and to understand and evaluate differing viewpoints, educating not only their souls but their minds as well.

Seventeen-sixty-six saw the foundation of the Sandy Creek Association, an outgrowth of the Sandy Creek Baptist Association, and the emergence of the most extraordinary figure of the Regulator Rebellion. Herman Husband, the son of an educated and wealthy Pennsylvania family, had been tormented throughout his childhood by an "inward manifestation" that he identified as Christ, constantly reproving him for not being holy enough. Beginning at the age of twelve or thirteen, he explored the doctrines of Presbyterianism, Quakerism, and the teachings of the evangelist George Whitefield. After vacillating for several years, he finally joined the Quakers.[10]

He did not remain. In 1761, then living in Orange County and a member of the Cane Creek Meeting, he became embroiled in a controversy over the right of a departing member to a "certificate of good standing" which would allow her to join another meeting in her new community. When the Quarterly Meeting ruled that she should have her certificate, Husband and several others vocally objected, then refused to apologize for their objections. All were eventually disowned, beginning with Husband, the most stubborn and outspoken.[11] Disownment was a severe punishment, a form of social death that extended to anyone, even family members, who refused to cut ties with the disowned member. When Husband later married, his wife was disowned as well along with her entire family and everyone who attended the wedding.[12] Disownments were frequent in the Piedmont, a sign that the dependence on one's individual conscience preached by the Quakers may have had consequences beyond what they expected.

Husband's religious passion was mixed with a strong impulse towards social justice. One of his surviving writings includes a "sermon" on the fifth chapter of the Old Testament book of Nehemiah, in which the writer excoriates those who prey on the poor in times of distress. Allowing people to steal the fruit of another's work is

> as contrary to Nature and Justice as the Story of the Dog in the Manger . . . . Nothing is more hurtful to the Common Wealth, than for individuals to hold unreasonable quantities of lands, and rent them out to the Poor . . . . These Sentiments of Justice are so natural, that they strike every Man in the Same Light, and it is to be hoped will do so forever."[13]

But Husband's deepest commitment, the fruit of his own lifelong religious struggle, was to the freedom of the mind. The most important duty of the clergy, he wrote, was

> to instruct men in the Principles of knowledge, and free their minds from the power of ignorance. This they cannot do without first teaching them the rights of private judgment, and the liberty they have of judging for themselves in all things that affect the conscience.[14]

The Sandy Creek Association included several of the Quakers who had been disowned along with Husband, and Husband himself almost immediately emerged as its leader and spokesman. In a series of tracts and published "sermons," Husband (who was not a minister of any religion) exhorted his fellow borderers to stand up against oppression. His writings were grounded in the natural rights philosophy of the rationalist John Locke, but shot through with religious imagery. Like many passionate moralists, he had a gift for sarcasm, which must have been particularly galling to the corrupt officials he attacked.

The anger of the settlers was not confined to Orange County but broke out sporadically in Granville, Anson, Rowan, and other counties to the west and north of Cumberland, although not in Cumberland County itself. Desperate and angry men in a culture of violence, the borderers did not hesitate to express their grievances violently. There were numerous instances when groups of men attacked and beat local officials or people whom they believed to be sympathetic to those officials. It was left to their leaders to attempt to channel this rage into organized and legal action.

The first public act of the Sandy Creek Association was to travel to the Hillsborough county court to read a manifesto that urged local citizens to form committees to investigate "unjust Oppressions." A meeting was scheduled to discuss the settlers' grievances with officials, but the officials did not show. Instead, the settlers received a message from Fanning describing the meeting as an insurrection.[15] The next few months saw a series of exchanges in which polite requests from the Association were answered by escalating threats and intimidation, first from Fanning and then from the governor, William Tryon. When the struggling farmers heard that the North Carolina Assembly had voted an appropriation of fifteen thousand pounds to build what the farmers called a "palace" for the governor—an appropriation for which they would of course be taxed—anger once again boiled over, and the members of the Sandy Creek Association once again attempted to divert their neighbors from violence.

This time they organized under the name of Regulators and persuaded the would-be rioters to subscribe to a set of Articles of Organization, which included among its provisions:

- That we will pay no more taxes until we are satisfied they are agreeable to Law, and applied to the Purposes therein mentioned.

- That we will pay no Officer any more Fees than the Law allows, unless we are obliged to do it; and then to show our Dislike, and bear an open Testimony against it.

- That we will attend out Meetings of Conference as often as we conveniently can, and as necessary, in order to consult our Representatives on the Amendment of such Laws as may be found grievous or unnecessary; and to choose more suitable Men than we have done heretofore for Burgesses and Vestrymen; and to petition the Houses of assembly, governor, Council, king and Parliament, &c for Redress in such Grievances as in the Course of the Undertaking may occur; and to inform one another, learn, know and enjoy all the Privileges and Liberties that are allowed and were settled on us by our worthy Ancestors, the Founders of our present Constitution, in Order to preserve it on its ancient Foundation . . .

- That, in the case of Difference in Judgment, we will Submit to the Judgment of a Majority of our Body.[16]

Popular protest had come a long way since Bacon's Rebellion ninety years earlier. Bacon and his followers could come up with no way of expressing their anger and resentment other than by pillaging their neighbors, burning their capital, and massacring the nearest available group of peaceful Indians. But drawing on the democratic governance structure of the Baptist churches as much as on the political philosophy of Locke, the Sandy Creek Association was teaching its neighbors how to act like citizens. Some historians see the Baptists as having educated their members in the defiance of authority.[17] A more accurate conclusion may be that they were developing a new model of legitimate authority, one more appropriate to a republic than a monarchy.[18]

In the short run, it did them no good. The popular anger continued to smolder, expressed in peaceful petitions and legal actions with an ever increasing undercurrent of violence. First Fanning and then Governor William Tryon continued to respond with ever increasing threats. Tryon issued a proclamation banning extortion. It was ignored. Extortion continued and increased while the registers and clerks raised their fees even higher. Tryon then called out the militia—but found that he could not trust the few who responded to obey his orders.

The first real violence erupted in Orange County. On April 7, 1768, a local sheriff seized a man's mare, bridle, and saddle for non-payment of a debt. As Husband later described it in his *Impartial Relation*, a crowd of sixty or seventy farmers gathered to take them back, tied up the sheriff, and carried him into Hillsborough, at the same time "firing a few guns at the roof of Colonel Fanning's house."[19] On April 21 in Anson County, a large group of farmers disrupted court proceedings, removed the judges from the bench, and held a debate among themselves about various topics including whether or not to tear down the courthouse. Shortly thereafter, five hundred Anson County men met and swore to withstand their oppressors.

Fanning wrote to Tryon to express his shock and horror:

> Clerks, Sheriffs, Registers, Attorneys and all Officers of every
> degree and station to be arraigned at the Bar of their Shallow
> Understanding and to be punished and regulated at their Will,
> and in a word, for them to become the sovereign arbiters of right
> and wrong . . . .[O]n Tuesday following I verily expect an attack
> from the whole united force of regulators or rebels at which time I
> intend . . . to *bravely repulse them or nobly die.*[20]

On May 2, " . . . ten or a dozen men, armed with Guns and
Pistols" showed up at Husband's house in Orange County to arrest
him. According to his account,

> In about two Miles, they came up to where Colonel *Faning* [sic]
> was waiting for them. He asked me, flutteringly, and with visible
> Confusion, Why I did not come to see him in so long a time.
>
> I told him, I new no call I had.
>
> He said, Well, you'll come along now.
>
> I said, I suppose I must.
>
> He said, ay, well,—and set off for Town, where *William Butler*
> and I were put into a Fort, mounted with two Swivel Guns, under
> a strong Guard.

They were threatened with hanging. Getting a bit nervous,
Husband sent for Fanning and offered to shut up and stay out of
politics if he were released.

> It took with him, and after humming a little, he repeated
> over what I must promise, which, as near as I can remember, was
> to this Effect: "You promise never to give your opinion of the
> Laws,—nor frequent assembling yourself among People—nor
> show any Jealousies [suspicions] of the Officers taking extraor-
> dinary Fees;—and if you hear any others speaking disrespectfully,

or hinting any Jealousies of that Nature, of Officers, that you will reprove and caution them; and that you will tell the People you are satisfied all the Taxes are agreeable to Law."

Butler refused to make any such promises. Nevertheless both men were released during the night, because of the authorities' fear of the large crowd that had gathered around the courthouse.[21]

There is an Old Testament resonance about this encounter. On the one side, the middle-aged farmer who had spent his entire life wrestling with his own sense of sin and with the religious passion that grew out of that sense, who had been disowned by his religious community because he could not accept that community's failure to live up to his own strict standards, who was nevertheless accepted as a leader, mentor and spokesman by his neighbors of all religions, who fought for social justice but whose deepest commitment was to the freedom of the individual conscience. On the other, the cocky would-be aristocrat, thirteen years his junior, determined to create his own fortune out of the goods and labor extorted from his less powerful neighbors. We can see even in this brief interchange the way the older man must have discomfited the younger, whose fidgety attempt at joviality was immediately followed by an attempt to reassert his own superior status. Two American futures are facing each other in this tableau. Two and a half centuries later, the conflict between them has not been resolved.

Husband was tried as an instigator of the Hillsborough riot, and acquitted. Indictments against several other Regulators were thrown out. Fanning was tried on seven counts of extortion, found guilty, and fined one penny for each offense. Husband sued the sheriff who had seized the mare for collecting an illegal tax; the sheriff was found not guilty and then sued Husband for malicious prosecution. Fanning was tried again and found not guilty. Many plaintiffs were intimidated into dropping their complaints. A few other officials were prosecuted, found guilty, and fined a penny each. When one sheriff was prosecuted for demanding extortionate fees, the judge instructed the jury that the sheriffs must be terrified because of the popular disturbances, that their salaries were really very low, and that if juries found against them no one would want the job.[22]

The courts had failed the settlers, and repeated petitions to the governor and provincial Assembly failed as well. Their next step was the ballot box. In the next election, Herman Husband and numerous other Regulator supporters won seats in the Assembly, and Fanning and many of his friends were defeated. Then, in a series of local meetings, Regulators and non-Regulators put together a remarkably sophisticated legislative platform. The list included election by secret ballot; recorded votes in Assembly; salaries rather than fees for the chief justice and clerks; a tax on property, proportional to the taxpayer's wealth, instead of a head tax that was the same for all; the establishment of a system of warehouses that would alleviate the shortage of currency by allowing farmers to pay their taxes with produce; complaints to King George about illegally large grants of land to speculators who did not settle on or farm them; a provision allowing occupants of land in Granville County to have first claim on that land whenever the land office reopened; and, in a bid for Presbyterian support, a provision establishing the right of dissenting ministers to perform marriages. Tryon, who was more concerned about the Assembly's attitude toward the looming conflict between Great Britain and her colonies, dissolved the Assembly, and none of the proposed measures were passed.[23]

Throughout the year of 1770, the confrontation continued to escalate. Fanning successfully countersued for slander two men who had previously sued him for extortion. In September, a mob of angry farmers disrupted the court at Hillsborough, dragged Fanning out from behind a bench into the courtyard, hitting him and spitting on him, and then invaded his house, threw his property out on the street, and tore the house down. Because their actions were legally only riot and therefore not punishable by death, Tryon convened the Assembly to pass the Johnston Riot Act, an *ex post facto* law making even actions committed before its passage subject to the death penalty. Husband—who had never joined the Regulators and who had constantly counseled against violence—was expelled from the Assembly and arrested on charges of being a leader of the riots and of publishing a libelous anonymous letter. He was tried for riot in New Bern, but charges were dismissed because no witnesses showed up. A grand jury refused to indict him on the libel charge.[24]

The final showdown occurred in April. Even while urging the Assembly to rectify the abuses, Tryon was planning a military expedition to crush the Regulators once and for all. He had a great deal of trouble in doing so, since members of the local militias were refusing to volunteer, and some of those who did show up declared themselves in favor of the Regulators. But at length he succeeded in raising a force of one thousand men, half the size of the one he wanted, heavy on gentry volunteers and light on farmers, and marched on Hillsborough with several cannon.[25]

On May 15, Tryon's army and a force of between two and three thousand untrained and poorly armed Regulators faced each other across Great Alamance Creek. The Regulators, who did not want to fight, sent conciliatory messages, but Tryon ignored the messages and marched against them, demanding the surrender of their leaders and their arms. When the Regulators rejected his demands, Tryon gave them an hour to surrender, then started firing. The Regulators, unprepared and without leaders or ammunition, fought back briefly and then turned and ran. Tryon pursued them through the Piedmont, burning the houses, barns, and crops of those he identified as ringleaders, cutting down their orchards, and stripping the local families of their provisions in order to feed his army.

The defeat was total. The Regulators were hunted down, captured, and whipped; a few of them were hanged. Their leaders were outlawed and had to flee for their lives to other colonies. Finally Tryon issued a proclamation granting amnesty to all who would come into his camp, surrender their arms, and take an oath of allegiance. About sixty-four hundred men complied.[26] The surrender of arms was a severe blow: in a border area where most settlers were poor, their firearms allowed them not only to protect themselves and their families, but also to procure much-needed protein. In the year following the Battle of Alamance, many Piedmont families were brought to the brink of starvation. Herman Husband escaped to Pennsylvania, where he later became involved in the Whiskey Rebellion.

The consequences of the Regulator Rebellion, however, survived its defeat. Shortly after his victory at Alamance, Tryon departed the colony to assume the governorship of New York, taking Edmund

Fanning with him as his secretary. In his place, the Crown appointed a new young Governor, Josiah Martin, who quickly discovered the actual causes of the rebellion and took effective steps to correct them. Martin's efforts to re-establish trust between the settlers and their government met with significant success. A very few years later, members of the coastal gentry who had colluded in crushing the Regulators came begging for their help in resisting British tyranny. To their dismay, the burned, beaten, and starved settlers wanted no part of another conflict. Many had already left the colony. Some fought with the Loyalists; many more refused to join up with either side.[27]

The North Carolina Declaration of Rights, adopted in December of 1776, contains several provisions designed to attract the support of former Regulators and their sympathizers for the Patriot cause:

- XVII: That the People have a Right to bear Arms for the Defence of the State. . . .

- XVIII: That the People have a right to Assemble together to consult for their common good, to instruct their Representative, and to apply to the Legislature for Redress of Grievances. . . .

- XXIV: That retrospective Laws, punishing Facts committed before the Existence of such Laws, and by them only declared criminal, are oppressive, unjust, and incompatible with Liberty, wherefor no Ex post Facto Law ought to be made. . . . [28]

Similar provisions were included in the South Carolina Declaration of Rights and the Pennsylvania Bill of Rights, both adopted in the same year, and in the Vermont and Massachusetts Declarations, adopted in 1777 and 1780 respectively. In addition, the North Carolina Constitution, adopted one day after the Declaration of Rights, contained a number of provisions dealing specifically with the complaints of the Regulators. Sections XXV-XXX all involve prohibitions against people holding a public office while at the same time having a seat in the House or General Assembly. Sections XXV and XXVI apply specifically to receivers of public money and treasurers, who are prohibited from sitting in the House or Assembly until they have settled their public accounts. Section XXXV declares "that no Person in the State shall hold more than one lucrative Office at any one Time, Provided, That no Appointment in the Militia, or to the Office of a Justice of the Peace, shall be considered as a lucrative Office."[29] In North Carolina and elsewhere, the Patriot elite had begun to grasp the necessity of paying attention to the concerns of borderers. In acting like citizens, the Regulators had staked their claim to the rights of citizens.

KEY

1. CONNOR DOWD
2. COL. PHIL ALSTON "HOUSE IN THE HORSESHOE"
3. JOHN OVERTON
4. ELIJAH BETTIS SR.
5. DR. ALEXANDER MORRISON
6. ELIJAH BETTIS JR. [DR. ELIJAH]
7. JOEL MCLENDON
8. SOLEMN GROVE ACADEMY

MONTGOMERY COUNTY

JOEL ROAD

CLAY

SAND

YADKIN ROAD

RICHMOND COUNTY

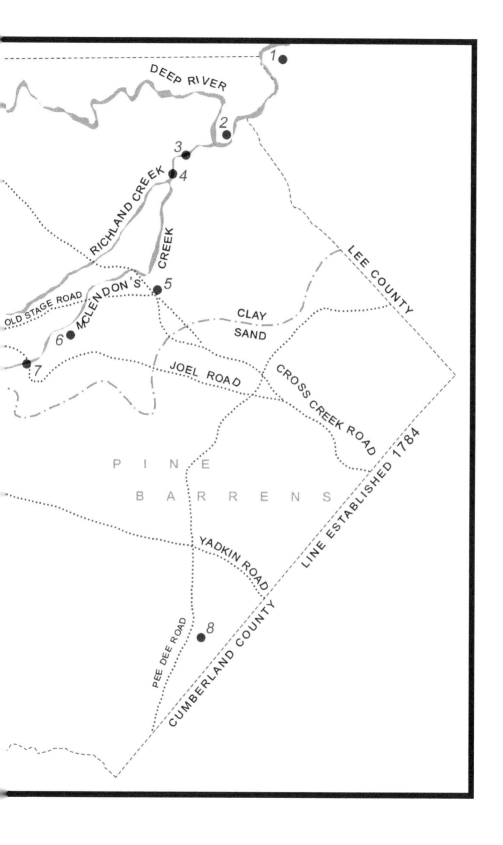

DEEP RIVER

1

2

3

4

RICHLAND CREEK

CREEK

McLENDON'S

OLD STAGE ROAD

5

6

7

LEE COUNTY

CLAY

SAND

JOEL ROAD

CROSS CREEK ROAD

LINE ESTABLISHED 1784

P I N E

B A R R E N S

YADKIN ROAD

PEE DEE ROAD

8

CUMBERLAND COUNTY

12. The Journey of the Highland Scots

In spite of the violence just to the west and north of Cumberland County, that county itself experienced no significant upheavals as a result of the Regulator Rebellion. And when we begin to examine the reasons for the undisturbed peace on the Cumberland side of the border, we find ourselves looking into a very different culture.

Ten years before the Germans and Scots-Irish began flooding into the Piedmont from the north, a very different group of settlers had begun moving up the Cape Fear River from the south, traveling in longboats and log canoes ninety miles upstream to the site of the future town of Cross Creek.[1] They were Highland Scots, members of a tightly-knit, almost feudal, clan-based society. Driven by desperate poverty and by the breakdown of their traditional social order, they came from the mountainous western edge of Scotland and the Western Islands, many of them speaking only Gaelic. They were organized and led by the aristocrats of their clans, and their arrival transformed the world of the Cape Fear Valley.

The migration began in 1739 and continued at a slow but steady pace until the 1760s, when it accelerated dramatically. Although the traditional account is that the emigrating Scots were followers of Bonnie Prince Charlie exiled from Scotland after his defeat at Culloden in 1746, most of the emigrants had not, in fact, been part of the Jacobite rebellion. The social collapse that drove them from their homeland took place more than a decade after Culloden, a result of reform measures put in place by the British government in the aftermath of the rebellion.

Traditionally, the clan chiefs of the Highlands had leased the rights to collect rents from local tenants to "tacksmen," a sort of second-level nobility who were also responsible for mustering soldiers from among the tenants as required by the lairds. In addition to providing rents and military support for the laird, a tacksman also acted as a "factor" for the cattle that constituted the primary wealth of the Highlands. It was the factor's job to buy the cattle and drive them to markets on the mainland, there to be re-sold and fattened in the greener pastures of the south. A tacksman's income depended on the amount of rent he could recover from the tenants of his "tack" and on his skill in negotiating the prices of cattle in any given year.

After Culloden, however, the British government abolished the right of clan chiefs to raise their own armies, a change that undermined the usefulness of the tacksmen by ending their military responsibilities. To compensate for that loss, lairds raised the amounts that they charged tacksmen for their leases, forcing the tacksmen to raise the rents of their already hard-pressed tenants. In an effort to maximize the profits from their estates, lairds sometimes even auctioned off leases to outsiders, weakening the kinship bonds that had supported their society.[2] New crops, modern agricultural techniques, and above all sheep were introduced—improvements that multiplied productivity several times over, reducing the risk of starvation but displacing many of the families that had formerly worked the land.

For lack of any other way to support themselves, some former tenants turned to thievery and brigandage. One tacksman, explaining his decision to emigrate, recalled that the people in my neighborhood were extremely addicted to theft and pilfering, the constant attendants of slavery and poverty . . . . For want of police, and due administration of the laws, I . . . found it impossible to defend my goods from being stolen; . . . and life was daily exposed to the resentment of murderous ruffians.

When he helped to save the cargo of a wrecked ship from plundering,

"some of the plunderers combined to destroy me and my family; and to execute their plot . . . seven desperate ruffians, armed with pistols and dirks, attacked my house in the night-time, and set it on fire in two places; and had not some of the family providentially awakened, all must have perished in the flames.[3]

The tacksmen faced financial disaster and loss of social position. The displaced tenants faced the collapse of their entire world.

Encouraged by letters from earlier emigrants extolling the amazing productivity of land in North Carolina and by eloquent puffery such as that in a 1773 pamphlet entitled "Informations Concerning the Province of North Carolina Etc." by the anonymous Scotus Americanus,[4] tacksmen began to organize emigrant groups from among their neighbors and tenants. Already experienced in commerce and negotiation, they arranged with shipowners for passage, recruited passengers, and collected the fees, keeping a portion of the fees to finance passage for themselves. In some cases, a tacksman who advertised his intention to organize such a party was besieged by poorer clanspeople begging to be included. Desperate farmers sometimes sold everything they had—livestock, furniture and farming equipment—to purchase passage below decks in appalling conditions.[5] Their destination, overwhelmingly, was North Carolina. Estimates of the number of Scottish immigrants to the Cape Fear area during this period range from ten thousand to twenty thousand, with the largest number coming from the Isle of Skye.[6]

The leaders of this immigrant community were a type of aristocrat that the American continent had never seen: warrior merchants with libraries of classical literature, whose dirt-floored Scottish homes were furnished with fine china, scientific instruments, and Hogarth prints.[7] Even the boats that carried them across the ocean had small but well-appointed libraries for the gentlefolk.[8] Despite the financial distress that had driven them to America, they brought with them not only commercial skills but also a good deal of hard money: a 1773 article in the *Edinburgh Evening Courant* estimated that the passengers in a single ship had taken six thousand pounds out of Scotland with them.[9]

They settled along the upper Cape Fear River and its tributaries, north and west of Cross Creek as far as the Deep River and McLendon's Creek,[10] the area that later became Moore County. Some became successful merchants, while others bought or patented farms and built sawmills and grist mills up and down the Cape Fear and Deep Rivers. Their poorer shipmates found a living as tenant farmers or indentured themselves as servants for a period of years to the tacksmen who had paid for their passage. By the time of the Revolution, Scottish immigrants comprised between a third and a half of the local population as well as many of the local justices of the peace and several representatives in the North Carolina Provincial Assembly.[11]

We can now begin to understand why the Regulator Rebellion never crossed the border of Cumberland County. Unlike the Piedmont farmers, the Scottish immigrants brought with them a thoroughly mercantile culture with access to credit and even to hard currency through local leaders who shared their history. When capital was not available through a single source, some groups of Scots pooled their resources to create small sawmills or other commercial enterprises. Their financial resources and entrepreneurial habits provided an effective shield against the hardships and abuses suffered in neighboring counties.[12]

More important, however, was the network of trust and cooperation among immigrants who shared not only the same language and culture but often the same names. In the atomized society of the Piedmont, newly arrived immigrants were often strangers to each other, without even kinship networks to bind them together. The only institutions capable of creating a sense of community were the churches, and even that support was lacking for the large number of settlers who belonged to no church. Men like Fanning and McCulloh had no bonds and owed no allegiance except to other ambitious outsiders like themselves. Their standards of behavior were determined by that group, and one of the most important of those standards was the acquisition and display of wealth. Their disconnection from their immediate community made it possible for them to see their neighbors not as fellow citizens, but as sheep to be shorn.

The Scottish society of Cumberland County was different. Although the Scots had left their feudal history behind them, the influence of clan leaders was still strong, and many of those leaders retained a sense of responsibility for their clanspeople. Local officials with this paternalistic orientation would have been restrained by bonds of community and kinship from the rapacity of their western colleagues, if only as a means of preserving their own position.[13]

Similarly, in Southampton County, Virginia, where, as in the Piedmont, a small elite controlled all of the lucrative local offices, grievances similar to those of the Piedmont never appear in the court records that I have reviewed. The richest members of the Southampton community were connected by multiple ties of kinship and mutual obligation to their poorer neighbors and to everyone in between. These networks helped to establish generally accepted standards of behavior and acted as brakes on the type of predatory activity that can break loose in the absence of strong community bonds. The Baptist and Quaker congregations intensified those bonds while at the same time raising community standards for morality and self-control. The only people on the outside of this protective system of relationships were free people of color, and slaves. While community censure would have deterred the justices of the peace from disregarding their responsibilities to ordinary litigants, it evidently had no effect in procuring justice for the mixed-race Allens.

The sudden arrival of the Highland Scots must have had an effect on the younger Elijah Bettis. When he first settled on McLendon's Creek in 1768, there were only a small handful of Highland names among his neighbors. Seven years later there were over two dozen.[14] And he was surrounded by tacksmen, many of them members of a single extended family. Flora MacDonald, the Jacobite heroine who had once saved the life of Bonnie Prince Charlie, settled just over the Anson County line with her husband Allan MacDonald, formerly tacksman of the largest tack on the MacDonald estates. Along with them came the families of her daughter Ann and two of her sisters. Ann's husband was Alexander McLeod, an illegitimate son of the clan chief Norman McLeod, and his cousin was Dr. Alexander Morrison.

Morrison, the son of a doctor on the McLeod estates and great-grandson of another, was born in 1717 and, before emigrating to America, was tacksman of Skinidin and factor (cattle broker) to McLeod of McLeod. Arriving in Cumberland County in 1772, with his family and three hundred of his Scottish neighbors,[15] he purchased property on both sides of Elijah, within easy walking distance of Elijah's farm.[16] On these two properties, he built a total of eighteen houses, most of them presumably intended for tenants or indentured servants. His own larger house was called Cross Hill. In his subsequent claim for losses suffered as a result of his Loyalist activities in the Revolution, he described it as "floored, framed, and lofted," which says something about the rarity of those features.[17] In addition to practicing medicine, he operated a tavern,[18] as well as a store through which he had business dealings with Elijah's brother-in-law, the enterprising Connor Dowd.

For Elijah, still in his early twenties, Morrison would have been a new species of man altogether. In spite of the differences of age and class and the brief four years during which Morrison actually lived in America, the two neighbors must have known each other. Moreover, Morrison brought with him something more important to Elijah than his wealth, his medical skill, or three hundred Gaelic-speaking immigrants. As Shubal Stearns had brought the spiritual fire of the Baptists to the Piedmont, Dr. Morrison brought with him, however briefly, the great gust of fresh air that was the Scottish Enlightenment.

The Scottish Enlightenment is the name given to an extraordinary moment in intellectual history. It was a period of two generations when men of genius in innumerable fields rubbed shoulders with each other on the streets and in the coffeehouses of Edinburgh and Glasgow, generating ideas that, in the words of one writer, "invented the modern world."[19] Among those men whose names still resonate with us are the philosopher David Hume, the economist Adam Smith, the poet Robert Burns, and James Hutton, the first modern geologist. They shared an approach to knowledge based on rationalism, empiricism, and a belief in the application of knowledge for the improvement of society. In the field of medicine, a crowd of innovative physicians occupied themselves with dismantling the moldy edifice of medieval medical theory and laying in its place the foundation for a modern medical practice based on empirical observation. Central to this new approach was an emphasis on the careful study of anatomy, which these physicians recognized as the necessary basis for an understanding of the human body.[20]

This new understanding took root in the great universities of Glasgow and Edinburgh in the early years of the eighteenth century, the time when Alexander Morrison would have acquired his medical training. Because of his wealth and his lineage, Morrison most probably attended one of those universities. There he would have been exposed to the ferment of new ideas, not only in medicine but in fields as diverse as philosophy, economics, chemistry, and even archaeology. Titles in the large library that he brought with him to North Carolina[21] indicate that he was influenced by the same intellectual excitement, the same rejection of outworn theories in favor of direct observation and experiment, that inspired his medical professors. His medical books included three on anatomy. His collection was also rich in the writings of classical authors; works of Pope, Swift, Milton, and Moliere, who at that time were thought of as "the moderns"; and books on Biblical history, "Jewish Antiquities," and "Scottish Antiquities." If the young Elijah Bettis ever came into close contact with this vigorous and sophisticated mind, that contact must have been a revelation. It may, indeed, have lit a spark that continued to burn for the next thirty years.

13. "The Most Relentless Fury"

When Flora MacDonald and her extended family arrived in Cumberland County in the early 1770s, the clouds of the Revolution were already gathering. In 1775 they burst. In April, the Second Provincial Congress assumed control of the North Carolina government, displacing the Colonial Assembly, many of whose members were also members of the congress. The Patriot committees of safety began making military preparations. British Governor Martin fled from the capital of New Bern to a warship anchored at Wilmington, at the mouth of the Cape Fear River, where he spent the rest of the war. From his floating headquarters, he called on the "friends of the Government" to unite in support of the Crown.[1] The first and most enthusiastic response came from the most recently arrived Highlanders.

People familiar with the Jacobite rebellion and the vicious reprisals that followed its defeat are often surprised by this fact. The Scottish leaders, after all, were old enough to remember that defeat and the executions, exiles, forfeiture of property, burning of farms, disarming of defeated Highlanders, and destruction of an entire way of life that came in its wake. We might have expected them to support the cause of independence because of their ancient hatred for the Hanoverian kings who continued to occupy the British throne. Among the many explanations that have been offered by historians for their failure to do so, a few stand out.

Most important, the Scottish immigrants from the Isle of Skye had not been Jacobites. Several of their leaders, including Flora's husband, Allan MacDonald, had in fact been British Army officers and had assisted in putting down the rebellion. In addition, they were not republicans. Inheritors of an almost feudal society, they were firm believers in the divinely ordained institution of monarchy. Even the Jacobites themselves never questioned that institution; they merely wanted their *own*, Scottish king to rule over them rather than an upstart German imposed on them by the British. Finally, the memory of the brutal reprisals inflicted on their defeated countrymen—and repeated only a few years earlier in the North Carolina Piedmont—probably inclined them to want to avoid a similar fate. The generous land grants provided to the immigrants by Governor Martin may also have provided a motive for loyalty.[2]

The Scottish immigrants, however, were not all of one mind. The longer they had been settled in America, the more likely they were to have been corrupted by what the Anglican itinerant Charles Woodmason called the Americans' "fatal Republican Notions and Principals."[3] Influenced by the insubordinate, self-reliant borderers who surrounded them, they were beginning to see themselves not as obedient subjects but as active citizens who deserved to have a voice in their own destiny. When the Patriot elite of Cumberland County gathered its forces for the coming war, all five of its representatives to the provincial congress and five of its militia officers were early Scottish settlers.

One of these, Alexander McAlester (or McAlister), had written to his brother a few years previously that

> . . . we did Expecte this new parliament would repeile those pernisious acts which will bring America to meare slavery. If they should be put in Execution all the Colones is unanimously agreed not to receive them on any terms. They are fully Determined

to fight to the last before they will give up ther most valuable priviledg which is ther liberty.[4]

Another, Farquhard Campbell, was described by Governor Martin as

an ignorant man who has been settled from his childhood in the County, is an old Member of the Assembly and has imbibed all the American popular principles and prejudices.[5]

The strains of divided loyalty told on some of them: Farquhard Campbell appears to have tried to please both sides, giving information to each about the other, while two of his fellow delegates switched sides at the beginning of the conflict and ended up commanding Loyalist troops.

Shortly after the outbreak of hostilities in 1775, a small group of recently arrived Highlanders, including Allan MacDonald, made their way downriver to Wilmington, where the governor's ship was anchored. They offered to raise an army of Highlanders to assist in putting down the rebellion, assuring the Governor that they would be able to provide two to three thousand men. Relying on the good relationships he had established with the former Regulators, Martin optimistically estimated that another five thousand of those men would also rally to the defense of the government.[6] On the basis of these estimates, he requested and received permission from his superiors to recruit a battalion of Highlanders and Regulators to assist in the recapture of North Carolina. Since most of these men were without arms or other military equipment, a fleet was to be sent from Ireland with seven regiments to join them at Wilmington and provide them with arms. On February 4, 1776, Brigadier General Donald MacDonald called for the Highlanders to rally to the king's standard at Cross Creek, to march to Wilmington and rendezvous with the promised fleet.

In the event, no more than thirteen hundred Highlanders actually showed up, along with about two hundred Regulators, and by the time they actually marched out of Cross Creek their number was down to about nine hundred.[7] Even with this reduced number, many of them were without arms and even without shoes. Flora MacDonald estimated that their total supply of weapons consisted of "600 bad old firelocks, and about 40 broad swords."[8] Her husband, Allan MacDonald, and their son-in-law Alexander McLeod were listed as majors, while Dr. Alexander Morrison, multi-talented like many of his fellow tacksmen, was named assistant quartermaster general with a captain's commission. In early February, Morrison was placing orders with Connor Dowd for wagonloads of provisions and "all the leather you can spare & if you can spare George to cut it out most of them can sue [sic] their own shoes."[9]

The Patriots, meanwhile, had mobilized to prevent the Highlanders from reaching Wilmington. Marching down the east side of the Cape Fear River, the Highlanders encountered the Patriot force, about a thousand strong, at Moore's Creek Bridge on February 27. The Americans, armed with cannon, had thrown up entrenchments on the south side of the creek. They had also removed the planks of the bridge, leaving only the two logs that had supported them and then greasing those logs with soap. Unfortunately for the Highlanders, the capable and experienced General MacDonald was sick on the night before the battle, and the decision on whether or not to attack was left to the younger officers. They decided to attack at dawn.[10]

In order to cross what was left of the bridge, the Highlanders had to walk single file across the two greased logs. Two captains led the way and were immediately shot, as was every man who followed them. The rest of the army broke and ran, leaving arms, wagons, horses, provisions, and everything else of value behind. Eight hundred and fifty of the Loyalist soldiers were taken prisoner,[11] including Dr. Alexander Morrison and Connor Dowd, the latter listed as a "prisoner under suspicious circumstances" for supplying the Highlanders with provisions.[12] It was the last formal military engagement in North Carolina for the next four years.

Although nineteenth-century historians could not resist the urge to romanticize the expedition, the reality was perhaps less picturesque. It is highly unlikely, for instance, that Flora MacDonald was present at the departure of the Highland regiment, urging them on with stirring speeches from atop her white horse. Her husband, Allan, and some of the other officers may have been dressed in full Highland regalia—a tartan plaid thrown over the shoulder, tartan vest, short kilt, and tartan hose [13]—but most of the common soldiers marched in their shirts and leather breeches, and some of them in bare feet. Nor is it true that Moore's Creek was the last battle ever fought with broadswords. Because of the shortage of rifles, eighty broadswords were in fact handed out in the course of the march, but the men who carried them were placed in the middle of the troops so that soldiers with guns could protect the ones without them. They never got a chance to use the swords.[14]

Most of the common soldiers were released fairly quickly after giving their word not to engage in further action against the Patriot cause. The provincial congress issued a proclamation,[15] assuring freed soldiers "that no wanton acts of cruelties, no severity shall be exercised towards the prisoners" and that their wives and families would be protected from retaliation. But official assurances were worth little when the new government was barely in control of its own territory. The homes of Loyalist soldiers were repeatedly raided and pillaged by their Patriot neighbors and the men themselves exiled to other counties or forced to hide out in the woods to avoid being beaten or murdered. The experience described by Kenneth Stewart, a Moore's Creek veteran, was typical of many. On returning home, he was forced to hide "in the woods and Swamps contiguous to his house for a space of time a little short of four years." The cries of his wife and children

> often called him from his lurking places at the most imminent
> hazard of his life, to defend them from the outrage and barbarity
> of their persecutors, who taking advantage of his situation,
> plundered them of their effects.[16]

Other imprisoned or exiled Loyalists reported that well-meaning neighbors who tried to protect their families from such pillaging were threatened into backing off.[17]

The leaders of the expedition fared worse. According to Dr. Morrison's "Memorial" in support of his claim for damages for his lost property, addressed to the British commissioners investigating the claims of American Loyalists, he was "dragged from Gaol to Gaol, & marched more than a thousand miles before he was admitted to parole in 1777." Exchanged for Patriot prisoners in 1778, he once again attempted to organize an uprising of the Highlanders, was captured again, "loaded with irons and carried a prisoner to Portsmouth, New Hampshire," then exiled to Nova Scotia before finally returning to Britain. As for his family, for five years his neighbors "swept away all the produce of his plantation, leaving only a bare subsistence for them."[18]

The treatment of Connor Dowd was only slightly more lenient. Dowd's Memorial to the same commissioners relates that

> . . . he was repeatedly imprisoned and held in contempt, but by giving large fees to Lawyers and others in Authority he narrowly escaped the Gallows . . . . After this affair [he] was always deemed obnoxious by the Enemy, plundering and quartering their Troops on him as often as they passed and repassed by his house taking and destroying whatever could be found.

Like Morrison, Dowd refused to give up the Loyalist fight. When British troops arrived in the area in 1781, hostilities resumed, and Dowd

> . . . raised Forty Horse-men who were commanded by his son in order to join Lord Cornwallis . . . which troop joined Colonels MacNeil and Fanning, and assisted at the taking of the Rebel governor Burk and his party, but unfortunately his son and thirty of the Loyalists were killed by a body of Burk's adherents who attempted to rescue him.

Dowd was forced to flee to the British army at Wilmington, "skulking in Marshes and thickets for some time."[19]

The struggle in the interior of North Carolina continued to simmer at this level for the next four years. The Loyalists were strongest in the Piedmont, where the economy was based on subsistence farming rather than slavery and commercial agriculture. The small farmers of that area were concerned with their own economic survival, which was threatened by the embargoes and boycotts imposed by the Patriot leadership.[20]

In Cumberland County, Loyalists and Patriots were probably equal in numbers, but more numerous than either was the large group of farmers who just wanted to be left alone. Unfortunately for them, they were not allowed that luxury. With its authority still weak and uncertain, it was critically important for the new Revolutionary government to persuade, coax, or coerce allegiance from the population by any means available. At the end of 1777, the North Carolina Provincial Congress passed a law requiring all male inhabitants over the age of sixteen to take an oath of allegiance to the state or else leave the state within sixty days. A large majority took the oath, but most of the Highland Scots refused.[21] The records of the Cumberland County Court of Pleas and Quarter Sessions for 1776-1778 show nearly fifty residents who were ordered to leave the state within sixty days for refusing the oath.[22]

At first the weakness of the provincial congress inclined it to treat the Loyalist population gingerly for fear of turning passive disaffection into active resistance. Some militiamen actually fought for both sides: a common way of dealing with captured Loyalists was to pardon them on condition that they take the oath of allegiance to the new government and serve for a stated length of time—three months to a year—in the Patriot militia or Continental Army.[23] As time went on, however, increasingly severe laws imposed imprisonment and confiscation of property on people who took up arms against the Americans or assisted the British in any way or even spoke out against independence.[24]

At the same time, Patriot leaders were making efforts to conciliate the disaffected backwoodsmen, among them the provisions in the North Carolina Declaration of Rights and

Constitution described above. But the ferocity of the Patriots in persecuting Loyalists and those who befriended them undermined those efforts at the local level. The Patriot militia also imposed heavy burdens on the local population, quartering their troops in farmers' houses and taking whatever provisions they found necessary. In an impassioned letter dated July 6, 1781, Patriot General Stephen Drayton described some of these abuses to Governor Thomas Burke. Denouncing the summary execution of a Loyalist named McLeod by a Patriot named Beard, he raged that

> McL. blood was not forfeit enough; they have done more, they have carryed the punishment farther. They have taken every article of Cloathing & every means of Subsistance from the Widow & the Children & have left them to the cold merciless hand of Charity rendered more so by threats to those who might relieve. My good sir could the Children partake of the Fathers Guilt? The Gentlemen in [Cross] Creek who resented the act, have their Lives threat'ned by Beard's adherents & are obliged in Consequence to keep out of the way. Another procedure, equally in my opinion, unjust, impolitical, & unlawful; is that, of an Officer bringing a Number of Men & Horses down the Country, under the pretence of being on duty, choosing capriciously, the Farmer out, & making his quarters good.[25]

Abuses of authority were rampant. One of the worst offenders on the Patriot side was Colonel Phil Alston, a neighbor of Connor Dowd and the owner of the large dwelling on the north side of the Deep River known in more recent times as the House in the Horseshoe. Alston appears to have had a particular hatred for Dowd, but he was also known to retaliate against other enemies by false accusations of Loyalism. Robert Rowan, one of his victims, described his cruelty towards neighbors who would not take the loyalty oath:

> The day of the General Muster he behaved still more like a Tyrant, tendering the oath to people under arms threatening all those with immediate imprisonment that refused it, or were not able to give security, no respect of persons . . . . One poor infirm man, seventy years of age, that many years had laid by the profits of a few potatoes, Turnips, Greens &c. was compelled to take this oath or go to jail, another poor man, from one of the back counties had his loaded wagon carrying home salt to relieve his family, brought back a dozen miles and the owner thrown into jail for saying he would not take the oath here, but in his own County . . . . I can assure your Excellency, we have not the shadow of liberty among us. The great object we are contending for, at the expence of our blood, our ruling men have at present lost sight of . . . . Our jail in the hottest of the weather was crowded with miserable objects, several ill with the flux, Bail denied them— their crime no more than some unguarded words spoke in the heat of liquor—poor wretches unworthy of the least notice.[26]

Such behavior on the part of the Patriots succeeded in turning many originally neutral inhabitants into active Loyalist sympathizers. For four years, however, the Loyalists, seeing no help in sight from the British army, generally kept their heads down and hid their sympathies.[27] Others of their neighbors spent that time trying to decide which side they were on or switching from one to the other depending on which side seemed most likely to succeed at the moment. It was not until Major Craig and 450 British Regulars reached the North Carolina border in 1780 that anarchy really broke loose.[28]

By 1781, Craig and his men had gained control of the whole upper Cape Fear Valley. Men who had supported the Patriots either surrendered to the British or fled into the swamps to hide, and most of the rest were suddenly Loyalists. No one was willing to serve in the Patriot militia or even to provide them with food. When the Patriot Captain Matthew Ramsay attempted to force the Scots of Chatham County to round up their cattle for the Patriot forces, he found that the men were all "lying out" (hiding) in the woods. When he had his own men round up the cattle, the Scots came at night and stole them back.[29] By one estimate, Loyalists under arms in neighboring Bladen County outnumbered Patriots by five to one.[30] As the military balance shifted, it was suddenly Loyalists who were attacking and beating Patriots and burning and pillaging their homes and farms.

The phrase "civil war" is woefully inadequate to describe the state of affairs in the North Carolina backcountry during that time. Violence was unceasing and from all sides—in the language of the philosopher Thomas Hobbes, a "war of all against all." Militias on both sides were the worst offenders, plundering at their own pleasure without restraint from their officers. Patriots and Loyalists, individually and in groups, terrorized the families of those on the other side. There were also men who had been driven into the swamps and had turned to brigandage in order to survive, and gangs of freelance bandits with allegiance to neither side.

Women and children were generally spared—although robbed of almost every means of survival—but not always. A petition from Rowan County, begging the authorities for the restoration of public order, relates that numbers of persons such as Women and Children have been tortured, hung up and strangled, cut down again, sometimes branded with brands ... in order to extract Confessions from them.[31]

General Nathanael Greene, perhaps the wisest of the Patriot leaders, lamented that

... the whigs and the tories pursue one another with the most relentless fury killing and destroying each other whenever they meet. Indeed, a great part of this country is already laid waste and in the utmost danger of becoming a desert. The great bodies of militia that have been in service this year employed against the enemy and in quelling the tories have almost laid waste the country and so corrupted the principles of the people that they think of nothing but plundering one another.[32]

The British General Cornwallis marched through North Carolina on his campaign to recapture the South, achieved a Pyrrhic victory at Guilford Courthouse, and marched on to defeat in Virginia, leaving the North Carolina Patriots and Loyalists to slaughter each other as they pleased.

Out of the savagery, one fascinating and almost admirable figure emerges: Colonel David Fanning, the leader of a daring band of Loyalist guerillas, whose exploits made him hated and feared by Patriot authorities in the Piedmont and the upper Cape Fear Valley. Fanning (no relation to the corrupt official Edmund Fanning of Orange County) did his share of farm-burning and summary hanging of prisoners, but as he described it in his own narrative,[33] he did it in a spirit of outraged decency and gentlemanly honor with each attack or execution a specific revenge for a particular outrage by the other side. His targets were generally the Patriot leaders in any given area. He took hundreds of prisoners but paroled most of them on their promise to refrain from future rebellious activities. Captured by Patriot forces fourteen times, he escaped nearly every time, twice when chained and once when chained and naked. When he was appointed colonel of the Loyal Militia of North Carolina in 1781, one of his lieutenants was Reuben Shields of Cumberland County, the son of Mary Overton Shields Dowd and the nephew of Amey Overton Bettis.[34] Reuben's stepbrother Owen Dowd, Connor Dowd's oldest son, also rode with Fanning. He was killed in the raid described below, when Fanning's troops captured the Patriot governor Burke and his entire council.[35]

In 1781, hearing that some Loyalist prisoners were to be hanged in Petersboro, Fanning marched his men seventeen miles overnight, surrounded the Chatham courthouse, and captured all but two of the militia officers of the county plus three Assembly delegates. Several of these prisoners subsequently wrote to Governor Burke that Fanning's troops consisted primarily of

persons who complained of the greatest cruelties, either to their persons or property. Some had been unlawfully Drafted, Others had been whipped and ill-treated, without tryal; Others had their houses burned, and all their property plundered, and Barbarous and cruel Murders had been committed in their Neighborhoods. The Officers they complain of are Maj. Neal, Capt. Robertson, of Bladen, Capt. Crump, Col. Wade and Phil Alston, the latter a day or two ago a few miles in our rear took a man on the road and put him to instant Death, which has much incensed the Highlanders in this part of the County . . . . Notwithstanding the Cruel treatment these people have received, We have been treated with the greatest Civility and with the utmost respect and politeness by our Commanding Officer, Col. Fanning, to whom we are under the greatest Obligations, and we beg leave to inform your Excellency that unless an immediate stop is put to such inhuman practices we plainly discover the whole country will be deluged in Blood.[36]

Returning to his base on the Deep River, Fanning learned that Colonel Alston was lying in wait for him. Marching all day and all night, he finally reached Alston's House in the Horseshoe, *"determined to make an example of them"* for having murdered a non-combatant named Kenneth Black, who had sheltered both Fanning and, some years earlier, Flora MacDonald. He laid siege to the house, exchanging fire for three hours until the inhabitants finally surrendered on discovering that Fanning's men were making preparations to set it on fire.[37] Four of Alston's men were killed. Fanning paroled the others on their promise to stay home and not make any more trouble. Bullet holes from the battle can still be seen in the walls of the house, since 1971 a North Carolina State Historic Site.

A few months later, after another rapid all-night march, he attacked the town of Hillsboro; his two hundred prisoners in that raid included Governor Burke, the governor's entire council, and numerous officers of the Continental Army. Even after Cornwallis surrendered at Yorktown, Fanning went on fighting while at the same time negotiating for a permanent Loyalist refuge in the Deep River area. Finally he tired of the fight, got married, danced all night, and followed his fellow Loyalists into exile.

In the midst of this maelstrom, where was young Elijah Bettis? His youngest uncle, John Bettis, served with the Continental Army, as did Aaron Tyson, who is believed to have been his brother-in-law.[38] His other brother-in-law Connor Dowd, his wife's nephew

Reuben Shields, and the aristocratic neighbor who may have been the inspiration for his later career were all Loyalists. Connor Dowd's nephew and namesake fought for the Patriots.[39] Elijah's name appears on no surviving army or militia roster for either side. He was not among those residents of Cumberland County who took the oath of allegiance to the state in 1777 nor among those ordered to leave the county for not taking it.[40] His property was not confiscated for Loyalist activity, nor did he ever receive a pension or land warrant as a Continental soldier.

We have only a few puzzling clues about his experiences during those years. One is the list of birth dates of his surviving children as passed down by their descendants. Although not all descendants agree on those dates, they appear to show an eight-year gap from about 1776 to 1784.[41] The gap roughly matches the period between 1774 and 1785, during which no Elijah Bettis can be found in any Cumberland County record with the exception of the older Elijah, listed as a taxpayer near the mouth of McClendon's Creek in 1777.[42] It hints at a story of suffering and separation, possibly involving the death of one or more babies. Equally telling is the name of the first child born to Elijah and Amey after the Revolution: Lovely Bettis, a name that breathes relief and gratitude for the restoration of peace.

The most important clue, however, comes in the form of a document that surfaced fifty years later and seven hundred miles away, in the course of the extraordinary series of lawsuits discussed in Part V. A witness who heard the document read aloud described it as the "deposition of one Folsum" accusing Elijah of "Toryisum."[43] As that witness, fifty years later, could not have known, this

"Folsum" was in fact Ebenezer Folsom, a prominent Cumberland County Patriot, colonel in the local militia, and justice of the peace who spent some time during the early years of the Revolution hunting down Loyalists.[44] Reporting to the North Carolina Provincial Assembly Council of Safety, on August 7, 1776, about the "disposition" of local Loyalists, Folsom declared it

> most Certain that they wish for nothing more earnestly than the opportunity of making a Head, and was not the strictest attention paid to all their motions, I am persuaded, numbers would fly to join the Indians.

The letter refers to an "inclosed affidavit"—possibly the same one later produced in Missouri—which I have been unable to find among the records of the provincial assembly.[45]

In the same year, Ransom Sutherland, a delegate to the provincial congress and a commissary in the fourth regiment of the North Carolina Continental Line, wrote to the same council. He requested that Folsom be sent to "lay waste to the country" around the Deep River, where the inhabitants were refusing to hand over a pair of Loyalist partisans.[46] In 1782, with the British in retreat and scores being settled in Cumberland County, Folsom was evidently still at work, since a local man was charged with threatening him with violence for reporting the man to the commanding officer of the county for "plundering."[47] Whether or not the accusation of Loyalism against Elijah was accurate, Folsom was clearly in a position to have an opinion on the subject and to have his opinions heard.

Under the circumstances, the facts behind the accusation would have been almost irrelevant: Elijah would have suffered for it in any case. In the hysteria that characterized Cumberland County during the Revolution, Toryism did not have to involve any active participation in Loyalist resistance. The records of the Cumberland County Court of Pleas and Quarter Sessions for 1776-1778, each page meticulously preserved in its plastic sleeve, reveal instances of men who were hauled into court for "speaking against this State" and "not being a friend of this State." Colin Shaw was jailed for seven days for the second offense, while John Colbreath and William Galespie, charged with "huzzahing for the king" in the first case and "speaking siditious and contemptuous words against this State" in the second, were deemed probably guilty of "Misprision of Treason" and packed off to the Superior Court in Wilmington to be tried.

Although Elijah's name does not appear in any of the records, the mere accusation could have exposed him to ferocious retaliation. Unless he and his father both left the county to fight with the Loyalists, he may have been one of those men who were forced to hide out in swamps, leaving his wife and young children at the mercy of their hostile neighbors. Even offering assistance to the families of neighbors who were imprisoned after the Battle of Moore's Creek Bridge could have had the same result.

In this scenario, another puzzling detail suddenly seems to make sense: the name of Ransom Sutherland Bettis, the first son born to Elijah and Amey after the Revolution. He was obviously named after the powerful Patriot official quoted above as requesting that Colonel Folsom lay waste to the Loyalist countryside. The original Ransom Sutherland was by no means a war hero,[48] nor is there any record of contact between him and the young family. But something that he did during those years clearly inspired a feeling of admiration or gratitude in Elijah and Amey. Did he somehow intervene to spare Elijah from the consequences of his Toryism? If so, their gratitude would have been deep and long-lasting.

14. Healing

Both for the victorious Patriots and for the remaining Loyalists, the recovery from the chaos of the Revolution was slow and hard. The economic life of the backcountry had been devastated. Where there had once been flourishing farms, by the end of the war there were only charred ruins of barns and neglected, weed-grown fields. Mills that had ground the farmers' grain for transport to market had been destroyed, mill owners and merchants bankrupted, and herds of cattle consumed by the demands of the armies and militias. Property that had been plundered by either side was impossible to reclaim.

The shattering of the framework of relationships, of trust and mutual responsibility, that had been central to the economy of Cumberland County, was as damaging to the community as any of the material losses. Those Loyalists who had not been forced to leave had seen their property plundered or confiscated and were still subject to violence and discrimination as the popular demand for revenge clashed with the efforts of the more enlightened Patriot leaders to reunite their shattered country. Reluctantly arresting a band of Patriot thugs who had been terrorizing neighbors suspected of Loyalist sympathies, Governor Alexander Martin pleaded that

> . . . however popular the decisions of our Courts may be for the present, yet they must be supported or our boasted Liberty and government will be no more, and we shall sink into a worse Tyranny than that, which we have lately escaped.[1]

An Act of Pardon and Oblivion, passed in 1783,[2] provided for amnesty for "all manner of treasons, misprision of treason, felony or misdemeanor, committed or done since the fourth day of July, seventeen hundred and seventy-six, by any person or persons whatsoever." That act, however, specifically excepted David Fanning and anyone else who had taken a British commission, had property confiscated under the Confiscation Acts, or had been guilty of murder, robbery, rape, or house burning. In 1784, another act barred from public office anyone who had aided the Loyalists in any way. But slowly, case by case, in the years following the Revolution, we can see the superior courts and the General Assembly's Committee on Petitions and Grievances intervening to right some cases of particular injustice, to restore to their positions people unfairly suspected of Loyalist sympathies, to revoke some decrees of banishment, or to restore the civil rights of people with influential friends.[3]

Dr. Morrison's son Norman, who had been exiled with his father following the Battle of Moore's Creek Bridge, made his way back into North Carolina in 1783. After "living very privately" for a while, he wrote optimistically to his father that

> . . . there's been such an alteration since I came that I am satisfied that any person that has been guilty of no cruelty to make private enemies may safely come back, as the county courts have in their power to receive any person back they please & animosities bred by difference of opinion only die away so fast that I am sure you may safely come, how soon you can.

The rest of his letter, however, seems to contradict this optimistic assessment, relating that

> . . . the plunderers from up the country carried off or destroyed all [the family's] cloathes, furniture & whatever else they could, then they came down here, & were no sooner come down than Capt. Rowen sold the land, cattle, and whatever the sheriff could find that he could get any money for.

Norman was supporting the family by giving lessons to the children of the neighborhood, and he had had to send his younger brother off to fend for himself.[4] At the same time, another friend of Morrison's was writing to him that "It is my humble opinion that a Scotchman will meet with but a slender treatment for a century to come."[5]

Connor Dowd's wife Mary[6] was experiencing similar troubles. A special act of the assembly had been passed in 1784 to allow her to sue her husband's debtors in her own name, and another act five years later allowed her to sell his property as if she were an unmarried woman in order to pay his debts.[7] But no sooner had the first act been passed than she was besieged by groundless lawsuits, seeking payment for imaginary debts. Dowd's manufacturing empire was dismantled as it had been assembled, piece by piece, month by month, between 1785 and 1800. A letter from Mary to her exiled husband, dated January 9, 1789, pleads:

> . . . your long silence, or rather, as I suppose, the miscarriage of your letters, has occasioned several of your old friends to take such advantage of the little I had left to support the children, that unless you can be here yourself, I shall be reduced to a truly deplorable condition."[8]

Dowd's son Cornelious, however, was doing very well, and quickly becoming one of the leaders in the reintegrated community. He was a delegate to the North Carolina Convention in 1788 and elected to the assembly in 1790.[9]

The 1790 federal census shows two Elijah Bettises living in the newly created Moore County, formerly the northwest corner of

Cumberland County. A comparison of their listed neighbors with the known locations of pre-Revolutionary landowners suggests that Elijah Sr. was still living on the land adjoining John Overton, near the Deep River, along with his son Elisha, two slaves, and a young family whose identity is unknown. Elijah Jr. and Amey were still (or once again) living upstream, in the area of Richland Creek. They appear to have had all seven of their children with them, in addition to an unidentified adult man and a female of unknown age. They owned three slaves, typical for a moderately prosperous family in that area. Seven years later, however, Elijah Jr.—or perhaps his eldest son Elijah III, an ambitious and energetic young man who would have been in his early twenties at the time—was keeping company with the leading citizens of Moore County. The name "Elijah Bettis" appears on a 1797 list of members of the Pansophia Lodge No. 25 of Freemasons, a select group of men that included most of the public officials and large slaveholders of the area.[10]

In the 1800 census Elijah Sr. has died, and the bachelor Elisha has inherited his farm. Three children of Elijah Jr. have left home. His two oldest daughters, Jean and Eleanor, have married and are living nearby. His oldest son, Elijah III, appears in the census as a young man between 16 and 26, living on his own with nine slaves and no other dependents; he is most likely the Elijah who in 1796 patented about 300 acres along McLendon's Creek.[11] The biggest change, however, involves Elijah Jr. himself. In 1800, instead of a mere three slaves as in 1790, he owns thirty. And in addition to becoming rich, at some point before his fiftieth birthday the obscure yeoman farmer has become a "trained medical doctor."[12]

The source of his sudden wealth is not entirely clear, but a reasonable conclusion would be that he had decided to sell some of his scattered properties, which by that time would have greatly appreciated in value, and to use the proceeds to purchase human beings. Since all Moore County deeds, starting with the establishment of the county in 1784, were destroyed in a courthouse fire in 1889, we have no way of knowing what became of any of those properties. It may be that Elijah was one of the first men to realize the enormous potential of the cotton gin, patented only six years earlier in 1794. His neighbor Benjamin Williams, the new owner of the House in the Horseshoe, was exploring the cultivation of cotton in 1801 and is referred to in Robinson's *History of Moore County, North Carolina* as "Moore County's first cotton planter."[13] But we may wonder why, if Elijah had only just managed to establish a successful cotton plantation, he would move his entire family hundreds of miles away only six or seven years later. Perhaps the accumulation of human property was simply part of a long-range plan for moving on.

Or perhaps Elijah's new wealth was a direct result of his new status as a "trained medical doctor." Trained physicians were desperately scarce in the backcountry, and their high fees reflected that scarcity. After the Battle of Moore's Creek Bridge, Flora MacDonald, alone in her plundered house and suffering from a broken arm, was "confined . . . for months, the only phishition in the collony [Dr. Morrison] being prisoner with her husband in Philadelphia Gaol."[14] When a physician was unavailable or too expensive, the demand for medical care was met by a wide variety of other practitioners. According to one estimate, there were perhaps four thousand people in America at the time of the Revolution who called themselves doctors, four hundred of them with formal training and two hundred with actual medical degrees.[15] The majority of backcountry planters acted as their own doctors with the help of popular self-help books designed to make basic medical knowledge available to the ordinary person. The great planter Landon Carter of Virginia; the backcountry Quaker housewife Rachel Stout Allen; and the mother and daughter team of Eliza Lucas Pinckney and Harriott Pinckney Horry, who managed their own plantations after their husbands' deaths, all served as healers to their households, slaves, and neighbors.[16] The term quack, applied to partially trained or self-proclaimed doctors, was not considered insulting in that era.[17]

Amid this cacophony of healers, what did it mean to be a "trained medical doctor?" University training was available only to those with the resources to travel to Philadelphia, where the first medical college on this continent was established in 1765, or abroad to London or Edinburgh. The usual method of acquiring medical training was by apprenticing oneself to another doctor, who might himself be either well or poorly trained.

All practitioners, trained, self-trained, or untrained, shared the same understanding of the human body: the venerable theory of humors, developed by Hippocrates in the fourth century BCE. They understood illness as something that arose from an imbalance in the body's four humors—blood, phlegm, yellow bile, and black bile—and could be treated by dietary regimens and by techniques aimed at depleting one or more of these humors to bring the body back into balance. Bleeding, purging, vomiting, sweating, enemas, and the application of blistering plasters were the means to this end and were applied singly or more often in combination to nearly every complaint from sore throat to cancer. Bleeding was also thought of as a general health measure and was regularly performed on healthy people. A fleam (lancet) for bloodletting, for use on livestock as well as on human patients, was part of the medical equipment of every household.

One difference between the various classes of practitioners is that domestic healers and backcountry quacks typically drew on a long list of folk medicines, collecting "receipts" or recipes from books, from neighbors, from Native Americans, and from slaves. These receipts were carefully written down in household journals or commonplace books, many of which have been preserved. Rachel Allen's recipe for curing a severe cough, for instance, included "angillico [angelica] horseradish allcompain [elecampane] Each one large handful," stewed in spring water, strained, and mixed with half a pound of fresh butter and half a pound of treacle.[18] William Lenoir of North Carolina reported that

> Colo. Koons says a woman on New River had been a long time helpless with the Rheumatism, and was advised to have fat Lightwood knobs [pieces of resinous pine typically used for kindling] split up fine & boiled in a pint of new milk till it came to half a pint and drink as much of it as her Stomac would bear & by the Experiment she got entirely well in a short time. (NB Suppose the same to be good for a horse.)[19]

Some slaves, such as James Papaw of Virginia, won their freedom by devising recipes for herbal cocktails that were thought to be particularly effective.[20] Some of the ingredients would make a modern reader blanch: animal and human dung were used in a number of recipes, including medicines for hernias and cataracts.[21]

The similarities and differences between the methods of a self-described quack and a university-trained physician can be seen in two popular self-help books, published thirty-five years apart. John Tennent's little volume, *Every Man his own Doctor, or the Poor Planter's Physician* (third edition, 1736), provides instructions for low-cost treatment with locally available herbal preparations, sparing the invalid the sometimes ruinous cost of a trained physician. Knowledge of some of the herbs named in the book, such as sassafras, sage, ground-ivy, mallow, and horseradish, was probably obtained directly or indirectly from Native Americans. Several of the herbs have since been shown to have genuine medicinal properties, particularly as antibiotics and anti-inflammatories, and are still in use in modern herbal medicine. The author comments cheerfully that a patient who uses these remedies can't complain if he dies, since at least he won't die broke. Then he jokes that he is "content to do all my Executions with the Weapons of our own Country."[22]

The majority of Tennent's "executions," however, were probably due to his preference for heroic interventions in the form of bleeding, purging, vomiting, and blistering, often performed sequentially for days or even weeks at a time. For pleurisy, he recommends that the patient be bled ten ounces on three or four successive days, with a vomit of ipecacoana on the third day, and in the meanwhile take pennyroyal water both as a drink and as a poultice; and " . . . if the Distemper should prove obstinate, you must apply a Blister to his Neck, and one to each Arm." For a quinsy (a dangerous form of throat infection), "bleed immediately ten ounces . . . in the Jugular Vein . . . apply a Blister to the neck . . . bleed again the next Day," then purge the next day and three more times on alternate days; also gargle, and wash your neck and ears every morning. Treat the bloody flux (dysentery) the same way—but don't worry, it's not catching.[23]

A welcome contrast to Tennent is William Buchan's *Domestic Medicine*, a tome of more than seven hundred pages first published in 1769 and reprinted more than thirty times over the next forty years.[24] Buchan was a Fellow of the Royal College of Physicians in Edinburgh, and his book, an admirable product of the Scottish Enlightenment, is a compendium of most of what was known about medical practice, excluding surgery, in his era. It was also one of the books brought to America by Dr. Alexander Morrison and left behind at Cross Hill when Morrison was imprisoned and exiled.[25]

Encountering Dr. Buchan after a session with the helpful Mr. Tennent feels like coming home to the modern world. In the first hundred pages, he lays out the basics of personal and public health in terms that would be familiar in 2018. Breast-fed infants are more resistant to childhood diseases. Children need vigorous exercise—girls, too! Proper ventilation is a necessity, since air pollution can be the cause of numerous diseases, particularly for workingmen who have to spend their days in confined and unventilated environments. Consumption also spreads easily in closed quarters, since the occupants are forced to breathe each other's air. Not only citrus fruits, but also cabbage, potatoes and onions— foods modern readers will recognize as high in Vitamin C—will help prevent scurvy on sea voyages. Eat more vegetables! Get more exercise! If you have a sedentary occupation, try to spend an hour a day cultivating your garden. Cleanliness is critical to health—not just personal cleanliness but also household and public cleanliness. Streets should be cleaned of filth: "Nothing is more likely to convey infection than the excrements of the diseased." Army camps must be kept scrupulously clean. Those who tend the sick or the dead must wash their hands and change their clothes after leaving the sickroom. Later on in the book Buchan also calls for a massive public education campaign to persuade people of the importance of inoculation in preventing smallpox.

In his chapter "Of Diseases," Buchan argues for an empirical approach to diagnosis, based on experience and observation as opposed to two-thousand-year-old theory.[26] At this point, however, his modernity fails. No matter how precisely he describes the symptoms of a disease, he still has no clue to its cause. Pleurisy, pneumonia, stomach inflammation, and "acute continual fevers" are all due to the same set of causes:

> ... anything that overheats the body, or produces plethora, as violent exercise, sleeping in the sun, drinking strong liquors, eating spiceries, a full diet, little exercise etc ... [as well as] whatever obstructs the perspirations, as lying on the damp ground, drinking cold liquor when the body is hot, night-watching, or the like.[27]

According to Adam Rabinowitz, Associate Professor of Classics and Archaeology at the University of Texas, Austin, this passage is an almost word-for-word translation of a passage from the Greek physician Galen, who wrote in the second century of this era. Diabetes (defined as "frequent and excessive discharge of urine") may be occasioned

> by great fatigue, as riding long journeys upon a hard-trotting horse, carrying heavy burdens, running etc. It may be brought on by hard drinking, or the use of strong stimulating diuretic medicines.[28]

With no knowledge of the germ theory of disease and little understanding of the operation of the internal organs, Buchan is forced to fall back on the old remedies of bleeding, purging, blistering, and vomiting. But he uses them with restraint, relying more on a light healthy diet, fresh air, and common substances like wine, vinegar, citrus fruits, and chamomile tea to effect his cures. His medicinal recipes include a fair number of the herbal ingredients recommended by Tennent, but unlike Tennent, he also recommends the use of more exotic substances: calomel (a mercury compound) and tartar emetic, both now known to be highly toxic, along with the miracle cures of the era, Peruvian bark (the bark of the cinchona tree, a prime source of quinine) and opium.[29] All in all, Buchan's advice certainly did less harm to the patients of his readers than did Tennent's. Apart from the stress on hygiene and proper diet, however, whether it did any more good is open to doubt.

In addition to the emphasis on hygiene and diet, a small set of questionably effective medicines, and a knowledge of the benefits of smallpox inoculation, the major advantage enjoyed by the trained physician was in the area of surgery. Although a backcountry farmer like Elijah would have had no access to formal medical education, as a "trained doctor" he would have been familiar with at least some of the previous century's research on anatomy and would have been qualified to perform many operations that the self-trained quack or lay practitioner could not. But books could go only so far. Only luck could have helped Elijah Bettis find a mentor competent to teach him the skills he needed.

Given the variety of his other concerns during the four short years he lived at Cross Hill, it is unlikely that Dr. Alexander Morrison would have had the time or the inclination to pass on much of his knowledge to a young neighbor, no matter how sharp and eager. The only known evidence of contact between the two men is a notation in Morrison's memorial to the British commissioners, to the effect that Elijah owed him one pound ten shillings for sugar, molasses, and rum.[30] Morrison may nevertheless have served as Elijah's inspiration, an inspiration that Elijah was unable to pursue for several years after Morrison's departure. It is even possible that in the course of the Revolutionary upheavals some of Morrison's books may have ended up in his neighbor's hands, perhaps as a result of a sheriff's sale at the end of the war. Whatever debt Elijah owed to Morrison, after the Revolution another physician appeared in the Cross Hill neighborhood, next door to the house where Morrison had formerly lived.[31] It may have been through that neighbor, Dr. George Glascock, that Elijah in middle age was finally able to pursue a medical career.

A first cousin of George Washington on his mother's side, Dr. Glascock would have had access to the best medical training that Virginia had to offer. He is known to have served as a surgeon in the Continental Army, tending to the wounded at the battle of Guilford Courthouse. He first appears in the Moore County records in 1784, shortly after his arrival, when he was appointed as deputy clerk of court under the former tyrannical Patriot, Colonel Phil Alston. In February of the following year, he was also appointed justice of the peace.[32] But his career in Moore County was unfortunately even shorter than that of Dr. Morrison. When Alston was elected to a seat in the North Carolina Assembly in 1786, Glascock and two others contested his election. Glascock submitted an affidavit to the Assembly, asserting that Alston was under indictment in Wilmington for the murder of a Tory prisoner,

> . . . that the said Alston did make use of sundry threats that if Henry Lightfoot aforesaid should be elected in preference to him, he would raise a riot, . . . that the said Philip Alston hath frequently declared that he believed there was no God, and that the Scriptures were set forth as a Scare-Crow to children, and that he endeavored to corrupt the conductors of the election.[33]

The Assembly ruled Alston ineligible and ordered a new election. Alston was subsequently appointed justice of the peace, but when several other citizens complained to the Senate about his actions in that capacity, the Senate found him "probably guilty" and suspended him.

On October 18, 1787, Glascock was found murdered—in circumstances that strongly implicated Alston. One of Alston's slaves was arrested and charged with the murder; Alston bailed him out, and he immediately disappeared. Alston himself was then arrested but escaped. Ultimately Alston and his whole family became such pariahs that he was forced to move to Georgia, only to be murdered in his turn in 1791, perhaps by the same slave.[34]

Three years of medical apprenticeship, from Dr. Glascock's arrival in 1784 until his death in 1787, would have been more than enough to qualify Elijah as a trained doctor, particularly if he had already managed to acquire some basic medical knowledge. The timing is also right. The time Elijah needed to devote to his medical training between 1784 and 1787 could account for the fact that he was still only a small farmer in 1790 but apparently much richer ten years later. And perhaps the sudden death of the man who may have been Moore County's only doctor resulted in a medical vacuum that he could profitably fill.

There is another, less likely, candidate for Elijah's medical mentor: the Welshman Thomas Rubottom, who first appears in Moore County in the 1790 census and whose son Ezekiel eventually married Elijah's daughter Eleanor. Rubottom is also known to have served in the Continental Army, and his descendants claim that he was also an army surgeon, although I have found no documentation for the latter claim.

Masonic lodges like the Pansophia Lodge in Moore County were attractive to doctors seeking to establish their careers, like Elijah Jr., as well as to young men with political ambitions, like his son Elijah III. American Freemasonry was just then nearing the height of its prestige and influence.[35] In the years following the Revolution, it broadened its base beyond the elite of the coastal cities to include professional men, merchants, and community leaders in inland communities, moving west with the westward expansion of the population. The fraternity offered numerous advantages to its members. The most basic were related to its original goal: to "make good men better" by teaching them the skills of self-control and genteel behavior necessary to the achievement of social harmony and by building bonds of trust and brotherhood among them.[36] All brothers were equal in a Masonic lodge. Freemasonry explicitly rejected any divisions based on religion or politics and instead mandated tolerance and respect for all opinions. Like the Separate Baptists, otherwise so different in style, beliefs, and membership, Freemasons approached the task of communi-ty-building in a complex, multi-sensory way, using touch, sound, emotion, and ritual to strengthen the impact of their lessons. A central feature of the Master Mason's ritual involved the "five points of fellowship:" "Hand to Hand, Foot to Foot, Cheek to Cheek, Knee to Knee, and Hand in Back." Group singing of Masonic songs reinforced both the Masonic ideals and the emotional bonds that supported them.[37] The emphasis was on extending the boundaries of brotherly love beyond those of the biological family but at the same time limiting membership in this broadened family to community elites and others deemed worthy.

Such expanded bonds and the trust that they engendered were of particular importance in the young republic. As the early Baptists created social capital in small communities, so the post-Revo-lutionary Freemasons created a new form of social capital that spanned the continent and bridged communities, an asset in a highly mobile society where men often found themselves among strangers. The connections forged within Masonic lodges were valuable to young men just starting their careers, to professionals like doctors and lawyers who needed connections to potential clients, and to merchants who had to rely on the credit of unknown customers and suppliers in distant towns. Masons were taught that they must "never wrong a brother," and commercial disputes among brothers were supposed to be resolved by their lodges rather than by courts.[38]

In the early years of the nation, a new set of goals came to the fore. Perhaps without realizing it, for most of the previous century the fraternity had been training its members in the skills of representative democracy. James Anderson's *Book of Constitutions,* published in 1738, laid out the organizational structure. Like that of the Baptists, it was based on semi-autonomous local lodges, which decided important matters by majority vote and instructed their representatives on what should be presented to the Grand Lodges. Article X of Anderson's "General Instructions" provided that

> the majority of every particular Lodge, when congregated, shall have the Privilege of giving instructions to their Master and Wardens, . . . because their Masters and Wardens are their Representatives, and are supposed to speak their Mind.

The rules for the Grand Lodges specified that officers must be chosen annually; that " . . . all matters are to be determined by the Grand Lodge by a Majority of Votes, each Member having one Vote, and the Grand Master having two votes;" that Grand Lodges must "receive and consider of any good Motion, or any momentous and important Affair, that shall be brought from the particular Lodges;" and that

> the Grand Master shall allow any Brother Fellowcraft, or Apprentice to speak, directing his discourse to his Worship, or make any Motion for the good of the Fraternity, which shall be immediately consider'd and finish'd, or else referred to the Consideration of the Grand Lodge at their next Communication.[39]

There was also a more subtle contribution: the idea that learning and "cultivation of the rational powers" were the necessary basis for morality.[40] In training their members to respect abstract rules of morality rather than narrow self-interest and parochial loyalties, the Masons were encouraging a new kind of cognitive growth. Like the radical Herman Husband, like the competing and disputing sects of the Carolina backcountry, Freemasons were fostering the habits of mind on which democracy is based.

Members of the Pansophia Lodge had ample opportunities to put these skills into practice. The county elite was heavily represented in the lodge. In an area where only about eleven percent of householders owned even one slave, more than fifteen percent of lodge members owned more than five. Ten of the lodge's fifty-eight members were elected to the state senate or house of representatives, and sixteen served as justices of the peace or other county officials, with five men holding both state and local offices.[41] If the Elijah Bettis who appears on the Pansophia Lodge list of 1797 is Elijah III rather than his father Elijah Jr., the younger man may have seen the fraternity as a source of contacts as well as leadership skills, since the third Elijah later demonstrated an interest in politics that his father lacked. His first cousin, the ambitious Cornelious Dowd, was a member of the lodge. If Dr. Morrison served as the role model for Elijah Jr.'s later career in medicine, Cornelious Dowd may have played the same part in the political career of Elijah III.

When the Solemn Grove Academy was established in 1804 to provide education for the young people of the county, five of the first nine trustees were Masons.[42] The emphasis on support for education followed the national trend among Masons in the years after the Revolution, reflecting a belief that universal education was central to the survival of a democratic society.[43] The University of North Carolina, the first state university on the American continent, was founded by Masons in 1793. Their portraits show them dressed in the sober clothing of the young republic, their hair worn short and natural.[44]

An examination of the membership lists of the Pansophia Lodge suggests a final goal, one specific to the devastated society of the upper Cape Fear Valley: the reconstruction of the shattered bonds of trust within their community. The large majority of the members appearing on a 1797 list bore Highland names. Because the Highlanders shared not only a tiny collection of surnames but also an equally tiny collection of given names, it is often impossible to know which Hector McNeill or Norman McLeod one is dealing with at any given moment. But there are some significant coincidences. One small group of names can be matched with those of early Scottish immigrants who signed a contract to pay a Presbyterian minister in 1759.[45] Most of these men, like other early immigrants, had supported the Revolutionary cause, and at least three other Highland names match the names of soldiers who fought in the Continental Army. Among the non-Highlanders, at least three were also either Patriot veterans or sons of veterans. Thomas Overton (no relation to Elijah's father-in-law), later General Overton, Moore county representative in the North Carolina House of Representatives and confidant of Andrew Jackson, had been a captain in the Continental Army. Thomas Matthews, the father of lodge member James Matthews and probably a close relative of lodge member John Matthews, had been a colonel in Cumberland County's Patriot militia.

The Highland names also include at least four men whose fathers or brothers had been murdered in cold blood by Patriot vigilantes, in some cases for no greater crime than befriending Loyalists.[46] At least two others, Cornelious Dowd and John

McNeill, had seen their families' property plundered and confiscated. In reestablishing the bonds of brotherhood between the families of former enemies, the members of the Pansophia Lodge were redefining themselves as Americans.

Whichever Elijah was a member of that lodge, neither the family's newly-acquired wealth nor its association with the Moore County elite was sufficient to give him the status of a gentleman. By the standards of the true gentry of the lowcountry, the Bettises were still merely rich yeoman farmers whose country manners did not allow them to associate as equals with the better sort of people.[47] Attempting to sell the House in the Horseshoe in 1803, an agent of the then owner, former Governor Benjamin Williams, described the house's location as "remote from all suitable society," evidently excluding even the richest and most educated Moore County residents from that category.[48] No Bettis held any public office in Moore County, and none took any recorded part in the building of the new Academy.

In Moore County, Elijah knew that his sons would never have the chances he believed they deserved. His oldest son, Elijah III, had the fierce determination of a boy who had known hunger, and he needed a wider field for his ambitions. When David Logan showed up with tales of the vast new lands across the Mississippi, lands where almost any ambition could be realized, the Bettises listened. Logan, who signed Elijah's will in Moore County in 1805, had been settled on the St. Francis River in southeastern Missouri since 1801. He and his brothers were putting some effort into building up their settlement; they are known to have bought land or obtained settlement permits for other immigrants on at least two occasions.[49] It was most likely

Logan who persuaded the family to move from North Carolina to that isolated corner of the Missouri frontier.

The move was a long time in the planning—perhaps as much as five years, if Elijah's heavy investment in human property was made with that end in mind. He had lived on the same land for thirty-five years; of all his Bettis relatives, only his brother Elisha had managed to stay in one place for that long. When Elijah decided to move on, he did so with great deliberation.

His will, written just before the family's departure for Missouri, recites that he has already given one or more tracts of land to each of his four oldest children. A total of twenty-six slaves were parceled out to those four and the still-unmarried Lovely, with the rest to go to Amey at Elijah's death, and after Amey's death, to Ransom and Overton.[50] Two of the children who received land or slaves remained in Moore County, one of them permanently. The others, who migrated with their parents and siblings, may have sold their tracts in order to buy more slaves.

Four of the seven Bettis children joined the migration: Eleanor Bettis Rubottom with her husband, Ezekiel, and their children; Elijah III, still unmarried at age thirty; and Ransom and Overton, still in their teens. Within a year or two, they were joined in Missouri by Sally Bettis Alston, her husband, and their infant son. Lovely Bettis Matthews followed with her husband, Edward H. Matthews, and their oldest children.[51] Jean, the oldest, stayed behind with her growing family.

With twenty wagons, several dozen slaves, and probably several other relatives or former slaves, the Bettises set out for the Cumberland Gap and the long journey west.[52] In 1810, an anonymous Moore County writer, reflecting on the changes that had taken place in the county since the convulsions of the Revolution, reported that

> ...happily for us the Scene is changed, Harmony, Cordiality, Morality, decency and Social order, appear to reign in their Sted .... The Society on Deep River is respectable the old Settlers [that would be Elijah and his relatives] have given way to men of property Decency & Character."

Gander-pulling and cockfighting had also disappeared; the writer attributed the improvement to the "present religious impressions of the people."[53] The newest wave of evangelical fervor had civilized the "barbarous" dispositions of the inhabitants.

At the time of that report, the cotton boom was gathering steam in North Carolina. As in Southampton County, Virginia, subsistence agriculture was giving way to large plantations worked by slaves, and independent small farmers were losing their place in an increasingly stratified society. The restless borderers—the ones who established the first settlements on any border, patented a little extra land, then sold out and moved further west when the area began to get crowded—had moved on.

Amey, Thinking

Somewhere in Tennessee • 1806

She's sitting by a campfire somewhere in western Tennessee, smoking a clay pipe. The firelight plays on her broad cheekbones and the wide mouth with its amused smile. The late autumn wind is cold with a hint of rain. She can hear the sleepy movements of the cattle, the slaves singing at the other end of the wagon train, her grown children talking quietly. Eleanor's little ones are asleep in their parents' laps. This journey across a continent is the greatest adventure of their lives.

Old Bear—Elijah—is playing his fiddle softly somewhere out in the darkness beyond the campfire. A big quiet man with an unexpected laugh that could always make her smile. Her marriage has been a good one. She remembers when her family would sit on the porch and sing together late into the night or listen as she told them the tales she had learned from her mother. Elijah's mama was a midwife—took care of all the families in the neighborhood. Taught Elijah the herbs and the roots long before he started studying books. But she died when Amey's oldest children were still babies. They never talk about her. Most of them don't even remember her name.

The evening before they left, Amey went out into the bare orchards to touch the trees she loved, speak to them softly, tell them good-bye: the trees she and Elijah had planted, the trees from which their children had gathered fruit, the trees her grandchildren had climbed. Cuttings from those trees are traveling with them—new orchards for a new land.

In her mid forties, already a grandmother, she suddenly found herself the richest woman in the county, with a fine big house and silk all the way from Charleston for her Sunday dress. Until then, she and her daughters had taken care of half the work of the plantation: spinning, weaving, sewing, washing, cooking, planting, weeding, milking cows, making butter and cheese and preserves and sausages—an endless round of labor. Then all of a sudden there were three times as many souls to feed and clothe and train and supervise and three times as many women and children to do the work.

She reveled in it. Her new sense of her abilities was like wine. She could organize the work and keep everything clear in her mind. She could teach the young girls how to spin and weave to her standards, oversee the dairy and the poultry yard and the vegetable garden and the hanging of the hams, and she could still find time to be in the kitchen rolling out pie crusts beside the cook. Baking was one of her greatest skills, and she wasn't about to give it up. Some of those little rich girls might let themselves be chased out of their kitchens by their own cooks, but not Amey. Her happiest memories remain back in the little log house where her children were born. Before the bad years, the years of fear and hunger.

This move to Missouri—that was her children's doing. Them and Ezekiel, who couldn't wait to be out there trading for furs with those Indians. She didn't want to move away from the place where she was born, the prosperous farm that she and Elijah had made. But they all sat down around her table and argued and cajoled until eventually she came around. This land's worn out, they said. Half the neighbors are already gone, and some of those new people look down on us like we're dirt. There ain't nothing to keep us here. She can see them, leaning forward on their elbows, faces alight with the certainty of their future. She never could refuse them anything.

Truth be told, she's mighty proud of the brood she's raised. Tall, high-spirited, adventurous, and fiercely loyal to each other. She remembers the way the older girls doted on their little brothers, the way they petted and spoiled them until each of them thought he was king of the mountain. Every one of them stood up for the others in fights. And there were a lot of fights.

Well, but who'd have thought that an old woman like her could pick up and travel all this way to build a new home out of nothing the same way she'd done thirty-five years ago? Or that she would find it an adventure too?

Part IV

The Immense Prey that Fortune Offers

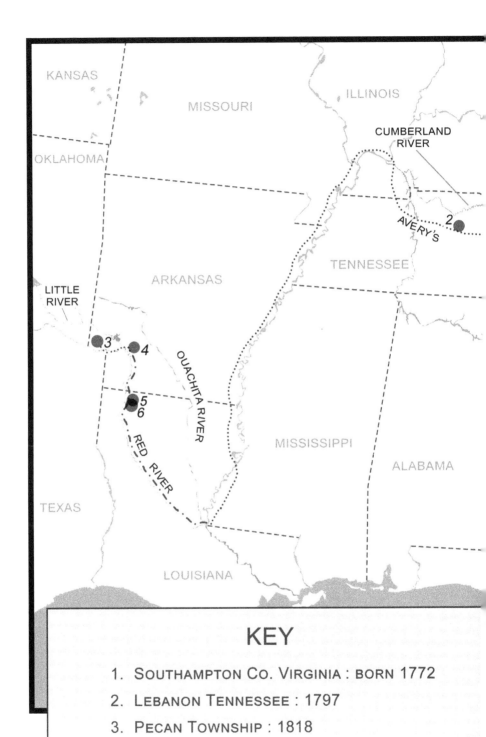

KANSAS

MISSOURI

ILLINOIS

OKLAHOMA

CUMBERLAND
RIVER

AVERY'S

2

TENNESSEE

LITTLE
RIVER

ARKANSAS

3

4

OUACHITA RIVER

5
6

RED RIVER

MISSISSIPPI

ALABAMA

TEXAS

LOUISIANA

KEY

1. SOUTHAMPTON CO. VIRGINIA : BORN 1772

2. LEBANON TENNESSEE : 1797

3. PECAN TOWNSHIP : 1818

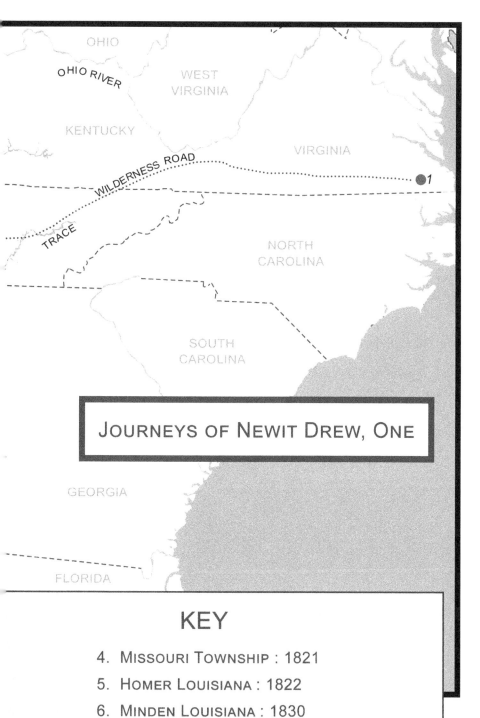

OHIO

OHIO RIVER

WEST
VIRGINIA

KENTUCKY

VIRGINIA

●1

WILDERNESS ROAD

TRACE

NORTH
CAROLINA

SOUTH
CAROLINA

JOURNEYS OF NEWIT DREW, ONE

GEORGIA

FLORIDA

KEY

4. MISSOURI TOWNSHIP : 1821

5. HOMER LOUISIANA : 1822

6. MINDEN LOUISIANA : 1830

15. Daughter of the Long Hunters

Newit Drew, age twenty-six—orphan, widower, son of an aspiring Virginia gentleman, ward of a Baptist deacon, neighbor and possibly friend of free people of color struggling to make their way in a society ever more determined to shut them out—arrived in Wilson County, Tennessee, in early 1798. In a little over a year, he had married a girl of eighteen whose early life, far harder than his own, had provided her with the strength and skills she would need to help them establish a home in the wilderness. And then another home in another wilderness, and another, and another.

Sally Maxwell Hays was the daughter of a tough Scots-Irish clan that had been moving southwest, down the narrow valleys and precipitous ridges of the Appalachian chain, for a generation before her birth. They were a different breed, the products of a culture alien to the stable and increasingly prosperous society of Southampton County, Virginia. They originated in the border lands between England and Scotland, an area warred over for centuries by English and Scottish kings but effectively controlled by neither. The savagery of those wars included the murder of whole populations and the burning and laying waste of whole districts. In the absence of stable government, smaller fiefdoms arose, ruled by petty nobles whose quarrels increased the misery of their subjects. Over time, many of these subjects took themselves and their Presbyterian faith across the Irish Sea to Ireland. By the eighteenth century poverty, oppression and social breakdown had begun to drive them further west, across the ocean to America.[1]

The violence and insecurity of their history bred a corresponding ferocity in the Scots-Irish borderers along with a fierce pride and independence. Like their ancient enemies the Highland Scots, they evolved a clan-based society in which loyalty to the clan transcended any other value. They arrived in America as extended families, connected by chains of cousinage stretching back in some cases for four generations.[2] But unlike the Highlanders they arrived in America without tacksmen, the cultivated aristocrats whose leadership in the Cape Fear Valley retained a trace of almost feudal obligation. After centuries of oppression and betrayal by their own nobility, they had no tolerance for aristocratic pretensions of any kind, whether based on birth, wealth, or education.[3]

Their culture revolved around a warlike sense of honor, along with a rejection of both external and internal control. They were given to passionate emotions, quick to take offense and slow to forgive, with a preference for settling disputes by violence. Whatever their differences in status, they treated each other as equals, causing respectable people to complain of their impudence and familiarity.[4] They settled on the mountain frontier, where the original inhabitants were still asserting their own claims, and they fought for every acre of its land. They were constantly moving on from one border to another, relying on those scattered cousins for support in their ever-expanding settlements.

Gender roles in this border society were sharply defined. Men wore loose trousers and belted hunting shirts that emphasized the breadth of their shoulders. Young women shocked the good Quakers of Philadelphia with their short skirts, tight bodices and low-cut shifts. Boys were raised to be proud and daring, girls to be hardworking and obedient. Their recreation took the form of contests of strength and skill: foot races, horse races, wrestling, and extremely precise marksmanship. In Scots-Irish families, unlike in any other immigrant culture, women routinely worked in the fields, helping to clear forests, break the ground, and sometimes even slaughter animals. They also married at a younger age than in any other American subculture.[5] Since the ability to read the Bible was as important to Presbyterians as to Quakers, almost everyone could read, but few people had more than the most elementary education.

More than one historian has seen in these Scots-Irish borderers the culture that has dominated the American South for over two hundred years. And they have found in Andrew Jackson the embodiment of that culture: belligerent, daring, hard-drinking, intolerant of authority, a lover of horses and horse-racing, jealous of his honor, and extremely possessive of his grudges.[6] He person-ified the values of his society, and the members of that society honored and followed him. The Scots-Irish were the "over-mountain men" who annihilated a British force of eleven hundred at King's Mountain, losing only twenty-eight of their own, and the Continental soldiers who stayed to endure cold and hunger at Valley Forge while the less hardy quit.[7] Scots-Irish backwoodsmen were also at the core of the Regulator Rebellion in North Carolina; although their leaders and spokesmen were Quakers and Baptists, it was a Scots-Irish ferocity that those leaders were attempting to channel and direct. At one point in that conflict, the hated Edmund Fanning tried to re-establish the old relationship of condescension and deference by offering drinks to a group of Regulators massed on the other side of a small river, if they would only send him a horse to get across. It was a Scots-Irish voice that answered, "Yer none too good to wade!"[8]

Sally's father, Thomas Maxwell, born in the Appalachians to a family of Ulster immigrants, was an inheritor of this warlike culture. By 1772, he and his brother James had settled at the head of the Clinch and Bluestone rivers, in the southwest corner of Virginia that later became Tazewell County.[9] Nearby were the Harmans, a large German tribe quite unlike their sober and industrious countrymen who had established their farms in the Carolina Piedmont.[10] Lou Poole, researcher extraordinaire of the Drew and Maxwell families, has located the Maxwell land on a ridgetop area of rocky and shallow soil and concluded that "whatever they were, the Maxwells were not farmers."[11] There was better land, still unclaimed, in the valleys all around them. Although hemp was the area's major cash crop, Thomas's name is absent from the lists of settlers whose hemp crops were certified by the local authorities. His livelihood, like that of the Harmans, was based on free-range cattle herding, small family plots, and above all hunting.

A Jacob Harman is known to have been among the Long Hunters, who hunted the teeming game on the Cumberland Plateau in the late 1760s and early 1770s. The famous German frontiersman Kasper Mansker and Uriah Stone, both among the first settlers of the Nashville area, were others.[12] Tazewell County court records show that Mansker and other Long Hunters, including Uriah Stone and four of the Harman brothers, were closely associated with both Thomas Maxwell and his brother James.[13] The Mansker family remained associated with Thomas's descendants for the next two generations.

The Long Hunts, which lasted for months and sometimes years, were journeys of exploration as well as profit. Long Hunters lived entirely by their own resources. They generally set out for the wilderness with two horses, a rifle, a saucepan in which to melt lead for bullets, a tomahawk, knives, traps, and the tools needed to fix these implements. In constant danger from Indians who resented their intrusion into those hunting grounds, they often slept with their guns loaded and primed, and their moccasins tied around their knees so as to be available at a moment's notice.[14] Their kills were enormous: on some hunts, hundreds and even thousands of skins were sent down the Cumberland River on flatboats and canoes for sale in the Spanish town of Natchez.[15] But their time was brief. In 1767 the hunters found the Cumberland Valley teeming with game, with herds of buffalo so thick it was difficult to ride a horse through them. Nine years later the game was almost entirely gone.[16]

Before that happened, Thomas was back in the mountains serving as a militia scout during the period of Indian conflict known as Lord Dunmore's War. The frontier was a place of peril, where settlers crowded for safety into a series of blockhouses and fortified "stations." On one occasion, Thomas was almost court-martialed, when Captain Daniel Smith complained that he had sent Thomas and Thomas's friend Israel Harman out as scouts on the Sandy River, and the two had abandoned their post in order to get the Harman family to safety.[17] In the opinion of many genealogists, Thomas's future wife Rebecca was a member of that family.[18] During the Revolutionary War, a Thomas and James Maxwell are recorded as having fought with the Patriots at the battle of King's Mountain, although it is not clear that these men are the same people as the Tazewell brothers.

In 1782 Thomas and Rebecca were the parents of two small daughters: Sally, age one, and her older sister Mary. It was in that year that Indians attacked the home of Thomas Ingles in the little valley of Burke's Garden, taking prisoner his wife, three children, and two slaves. Hearing the cries of the captives, Ingles went in search of help, and found Thomas Maxwell drilling a company of militia in the next valley. Maxwell and his twenty volunteers pursued the Indians for five days, finally catching them asleep before daylight. The party split in two in order to attack from both directions before dawn, but Maxwell failed to make it to his place on time, and when Ingles decided to attack, the Indians were already awake. On hearing the first shot they began to tomahawk the prisoners, killing Ingles's small son and daughter and badly wounding his wife. His wife and infant daughter were rescued, but as the Indians fled, they ran past Maxwell and his party and fired on them, killing Maxwell. Only a few weeks later, the two young daughters of Thomas's brother James were also killed.[19]

By 1786, the widowed Rebecca had married John Hays, another restless Scots-Irish neighbor. When Sally was about eight years old, John moved his family still further west, to the Cumberland plateau, by then empty of game and ready for the plow. His brother Robert had preceded him, and by 1788 was married to Jane Donelson, whose father was the leader of the first party of settlers to reach the site of the future Nashville. Two young lawyers, friends and fellow students, arrived in the same year as Robert: John McNairy, who had recently been appointed as Davidson County's first judge, and Andrew Jackson, who by 1791 was married to Jane Donelson's sister Rachel.

The first permanent settler, however, was the old Long Hunter Kasper Mansker. Mansker's fortified station—half a dozen small cabins and sheds built into a stockade of sharpened poles and guarded by two two-story blockhouses—sheltered many of the earliest arrivals, including the Donelson family and most probably the Hays family as well.[20] Other stations up and down the river eventually protected as many as five thousand people.[21]

Indian attacks were frequent and deadly. Until Sally was twelve or thirteen, the Cumberland plateau experienced weekly raids, and during some periods a man, woman, or child was killed roughly every ten days.[22] No man left the safety of his cabin without his rifle.[23] Every able-bodied man was expected to serve in the militia and to be ready at a moment's notice to defend his settlement.

Sally's older sister Mary died in childhood, and as time went on, Sally would have become responsible for the care of her four

replica of Kasper Mansker's station, Moss-Wright Park, Goodlettsville, Tennessee

half-siblings. Under the protective gaze of armed adults, she would have weeded the family's garden, picked berries, fetched water, or fed chickens in addition to helping her mother with household chores. As the eldest daughter, she would also have been the designated spinster, responsible for spinning the thread that was woven into cloth for the family's clothes. In 1794, the Indian danger decreased dramatically with the final defeat of the Chickamauga Cherokees, but sporadic attacks continued for another twenty years. The fear that had haunted the settlers dissipated little by little, but hatred of Indians lived long in many memories.

Like most of his pioneering neighbors, John Hays was interested in land. Land speculation—buying, mortgaging, and reselling wherever one could realize the greatest profit—was the best way to get rich on this or any other American frontier. Land ownership was in chaos, a result of primitive and often ignored systems of record-keeping. Each man's claim was likely to conflict with that of someone else, and temporary success was often followed by financial disaster.[24] But in spite of that chaos John did well, at least at first. In 1793, he received a grant of 274 acres on Little Cedar Lick Creek, about 25 miles east of the raw little village of Nashville, near the future border between Davidson and Wilson Counties.[25] In 1790, the Davidson County Court ordered him, his brother Robert Hays, and Andrew Jackson to keep a ferry across the Cumberland River at the mouth of Dry Creek, and over the next ten years, he acquired 1280 acres near the Cumberland River and Cedar Lick Creek.[26]

By the time Newit Drew arrived in Wilson County in 1797, Sally was sixteen years old, the daughter of a prosperous and respected family, connected by her uncle's marriage to the leading citizens of the area. Despite the Scots-Irish distrust of pretension, she may have been attracted to the good education and cultivated manners that Newit had acquired from his gentlemanly father. She may have admired the sobriety and the deep religious faith inspired by his Baptist guardian. Whatever she saw in him, Newit was a very different man from her stepfather John Hays.

16. "To Walk Circumspectly in The World"

In 1798, the area around Big Cedar Lick Creek was still mostly wilderness. A writer who arrived in Wilson County as a child ten or twelve years later reported that there were

> no improvements, the sound of the axmen had never been heard.
> Nature stood in all her wildness in profusion. By constant labor
> we erected some log houses, rude but comfortable, and . . . began
> felling the forest trees, clearing the land of brush . . . which
> afforded constant and ergent employments for all of every age.

At seven or eight years old, the writer was put to work "piling and burning the brush of the trees cut down by the men. Often all would burn brush at night until the Oclock." The women and girls of the family "found constant employment in their department: carding and spinning, weaving cloth for clothing for the family." They raised flax, which was made into clothing, towels, and dish cloths, and sheep whose wool provided warm coats and blankets. The writer described his parents as "industrious close laboring persons . . . independent and above want," who "taught us by precept and example the good and right way."[1]

The houses of these borderers, like that of Joel McLendon in Moore County, North Carolina, were built of squared-off beams, split from the heartwood of trees five feet or more in diameter and held together at the corners with elaborate dovetail joints. Unlike the houses of ordinary Virginians, they consisted of only a single room, but they were solidly built, typically with a puncheon (split log) floor and a proper foundation, and some of them are still standing today.[2] There was usually a separate kitchen as well as a collection of smaller outbuildings. A larger "dogtrot" house would consist of two cabins side by side, with a plank corridor between them covered by a roof. If the inhabitants of those houses owned slaves, like the early Virginia borderers they saw no shame in working alongside them in the fields.[3]

But while those industrious laboring persons were clearing the forests, wealth and fashion had already leapfrogged the mountains and rowed themselves up the rivers. Inequality of wealth was unusually high on the Tennessee border, with some large landholders owning thousands of acres and more than a hundred slaves.[4] In Moss-Wright Park near Nashville, next to a replica of Kasper Mansker's original station, stands a two-story brick house built only ten years later with a large parlor and dining room. By 1800, silk rugs and mahogany furniture were being sent by river from New Orleans to Nashville merchants, and ladies' tailors were advertising silk ball gowns and fashionable beaver hats. Hunting shirts and leggings had disappeared. Even moderately prosperous farmers wore linen shirts, knee breeches, stockings, and sometimes red silk vests, and their wives might own calico petticoats, lace, ribbons, embroidered aprons, and silk parasols.[5] Judge John McNairy, who had arrived with Andrew Jackson in 1788, was giving grand balls, and members of the Hays clan were mentioned among the town's richest citizens.[6]

Newit Drew was not a speculator, and he did not get rich. For most of his time in Tennessee he lived on 200 acres bordering the land of his father-in-law,[7] and there is no indication that he ever acquired more than another 120. He may have raised cotton, then a major crop in Tennessee,[8] but his ambitions were elsewhere. In April of 1801, three years after he arrived in Wilson County, he became a founding member and one of the first three deacons of the Big Cedar Lick Baptist Church, the first Baptist church in Wilson County.[9] When the charismatic preacher Moore Stevenson was called to lead the church a year later, Drew named his second son Thomas Stevenson Drew in his honor.

The leading spirit in the foundation of the Big Cedar Lick Church was Elder James Brinson, a pioneering Baptist who had been whipped and imprisoned for his preaching in eighteenth century North Carolina.[10] The parishioners were a decidedly mixed lot, drawn from a scattering of counties in the Piedmont and mountains to the east and mostly from a relatively modest social stratum. Isham Davis owned a grist mill, and several other members were storekeepers, but with the exception of John Dew, an important member of the local community unrelated to the Drew family, no member of the church seems to have held any public office, and no church member is mentioned anywhere among the county's gentry.[11] As was usual among early Baptist churches, about ten percent of members were slaves; their names are mixed in randomly on the membership list as in the early Black Creek Church in Southampton County. Others bore the names of Indian traders of a previous generation, a group that included many members of mixed-race or tri-racial ancestry.[12] Kanady and Fanah Bay may have been freed slaves of Moore Stevenson, whose 1818 will directs his executors to give Kanady "all legal rights due to him" along with the fifty acres on which he was then living.

At least seven names, although not appearing as "other free" in any surviving Tennessee census, can be identified with greater or lesser certainty with people earlier listed as "mulatto" or "free negro" in Virginia or North Carolina. Of particular interest among this group are Moses and Elizabeth Brown, who appear to be members of a group of prosperous interrelated mixed-race families including Browns, Stewarts, and Drews, originating in the Virginia border counties of Mecklenburg and Dinwiddie. Elizabeth was probably the daughter of Dr. Thomas Stewart of Dinwiddie County, described by his granddaughter as "a black man but a great doctor," who at the time of his death owned at least twenty slaves. Born around 1780, this Elizabeth Stewart married an "other free" Moses Brown in Southampton County, where the family was living in 1810.[13] In Wilson County in 1812, a mixed-race Rebecca Brown married a mixed-race James Drew, and subsequent records indicate that a "mulatto" Moses B. Drew was born a year later and married a Stewart. Census records show 384 free people of color in Wilson County in 1810, more than twice the number recorded in any other Tennessee county, but by 1820 most of them had moved on.

As Baptist churches spread across the continent with the spreading population, they formed the nuclei of communities and often the earliest community institutions. Members of Baptist congregations migrating to the west would take with them letters of dismissal from their home churches attesting to the sincerity of their conversions and their good standing in the church, and those letters would gain them membership in new churches in the communities into which they moved.[14] These churches, in turn, provided their members with new opportunities to build consensus and hammer out differences—additional training in the habits of democracy.[15] As each frontier Baptist church was established, its first members collaborated in drawing up a constitution, defining the specific doctrines to which the church subscribed; a church covenant, describing the rules of behavior expected from all members; and Rules of Decorum specifying the manner in which its business would be conducted.

The Rules of Decorum for the Big Cedar Lick Church contained some typical provisions:

> 7. Only one person shall speak at a time who shall Rise from his Seat and address the Moderator under the appellation of Brother Moderator.

> 8. No person may Speak more than Twice upon the Same Case or question without leave of the Church . . . .

> 10. There shall be no light or canting Expression used.

The church's founding covenant, however, went further than most in laying out a distinctive set of values. Among other commitments, its members engaged themselves,

> by the aid of the Holy Spirit . . .

> + To walk circumspectly in the world; to be just in our dealings, faithful in our engagements, and exemplary in our deportment;

> + To avoid all tattling, backbiting, and excessive anger;

> + To abstain from the sale and use of intoxicating drinks as a beverage, and to be zealous in our efforts to advance the kingdom of our Saviour;

> We further engage to watch over one another in brotherly love;

> + To remember each other in prayer; to aid each other in sickness and distress; to cultivate Christian sympathy in feeling and courtesy in speech;

- To be slow to take offense, but always ready for reconciliation, and mindful of the rules of our Saviour to secure it without delay.[16]

This statement of commitments amounts to a direct challenge to the culture of pugnaciously defended honor, of horse racing, hard drinking, quick anger, and stubborn grudges that characterized the Scots-Irish gentry of Middle Tennessee. Its inclusion in the church covenant gave it a religious significance and meant that church members could be disciplined for ignoring it. A generation after early Baptists so terrified the Virginia elite, the Baptist churches of the Tennessee border were still providing their members with a clear alternative, a community of conciliation, order, and mutual support, a refuge from the anarchic individualism of the surrounding society.

Of course the church's members did not always live up to that vision. One member, quitting in 1811 to join the Methodists, stated that his decision was based in part on

prayerless families . . . neglect of keeping the Sabbath, also large drams and a great many of them, family broils, and sometimes a Ewe lamb chased too far from the fold on forbidden ground.[17]

Nevertheless, the covenant marked a deliberate decision to reject the struggle for preeminence that shaped the church's frontier community and to emphasize virtues unlikely to lead in that direction.

An interesting detail illuminates this divide. In 1808, Judge McNairy donated land to Newit Drew to be used for the construction of a new church building on the west side of Hickory Ridge, a small rise near the intersection of twenty-first-century Route 106 and Hickory Ridge Road, a few miles west of the town of Lebanon.[18] Although McNairy had been a close friend of Andrew Jackson when the two of them arrived in Nashville, the friendship had already soured by the time Newit got to Wilson County. In 1797, Jackson got into a verbal brawl with Governor John Sevier, who was then staying at McNairy's home. By 1803, their animosity, fueled by competing political ambitions, had escalated as far as a challenge to a duel. Meeting by accident on the road one day, Jackson and Sevier drew pistols and came within an inch of shooting each other before their companions intervened.

Two years later, a different quarrel, this time over a horse race, resulted in a duel in which Jackson killed his opponent, a young lawyer named Dickinson. The incident brought general condemnation down on Jackson's head, and members of the McNairy family were among those who signed a public letter of condolence to the widow. Then, in 1807, McNairy filed a lawsuit against Jackson, insisting on payment of the mortgage on a piece of land that Jackson had bought and given to a relative. Perhaps the professed meekness and circumspection of the Big Cedar Lick Church struck McNairy as a favorable contrast to the values of his ex-friend.

The list of Big Cedar Lick Church members, covering a period between 1801 and about 1816, offers a hint of the church's complex gravitational pull on the Hays family. If, as seems likely, names of members are listed in the order in which they joined the church, the list indicates that Sally Drew and her mother Rebecca Hays were both among the founding members but that John Hays never joined. Further down the list appear the names of Sally's younger sister Rachel Hays Davis and her husband, Isham F. Davis, son of a church member of the same name. Still later we find the name of

Sally's youngest brother, Thomas Thompson Hays. Neither Sally's sister Ann Hays Alford nor her brother Harmon Atkins Hays appears on the list.

These names on the church list find a reverse mirror in a list of "Intruders on Cherokee Lands," drawn from the papers of the Cherokee agent Return Jonathan Meigs.[19] Around 1808 or 1809, eighteen years after he had first arrived on the Cumberland River, John Hays sold much of his Wilson County property. He then joined a large group of settlers moving to Alabama, taking with him his wife Rebecca (who, as a dependent, does not appear on the list), his sons Harmon and Thomas, his daughter Ann, and Ann's husband, Julius Alford. They settled on land just south of the Tennessee River, which the Cherokee chief Doublehead had acquired and was leasing to white settlers. The leases were illegal under both United States and Cherokee law, and in 1809, Meigs was dispatched to remove the intruders.

When John died in 1811, he and the rest of his family were back in Wilson County. His son Harmon enlisted under Andrew Jackson in the War of 1812, named his oldest son John Coffee Hays after Jackson's general John Coffee, and according to family lore was given the honor of accompanying Rachel Jackson to New Orleans to celebrate the end of the war with her husband. The only family member whose name appears on both lists is the youngest Hays son, Thomas.

What did the Baptists have to offer this family that they could not have found in their Scots-Irish Presbyterian church? Baptists adhered to the same Calvinist theology as Presbyterians and put an equal value on the direct relationship between God and the individual soul. They shared with the Scots-Irish Presbyterians a fiercely egalitarian world view and a rejection of any claims to authority based on birth or education. But Baptists took the individualism of the frontier one step further, and at the same time counterbalanced it with a passionate assertion of community. The governance of each Baptist church was solely by vote of its members, not by a group of elected elders subject to the authority of a higher assembly of presbyters. Baptist churches, as we have seen, also placed a heavy emphasis on harmony and conciliation, working with the parties to any dispute to try to bring them back into fellowship before making a judgment about rights and wrongs. To a greater extent than Presbyterians, Baptists aimed to create a spiritual family, bound together by the love of brothers and sisters and cemented by emotional outpourings of faith.

If some sections of the Big Cedar Lick Covenant declared the church's opposition to the dominant values of its society, one striking provision in its Constitution seems to run counter to the evolving values of the Baptist Church as a whole.[20] The first eighteen statements of belief cover standard Calvinist doctrine, but the nineteenth stands out:

> 19. We believe that full Liberty ought to be allowed for every male member to Improve his Gift according to the Gospel and that the Church should Encourage and Recommend such as are qualified for the Gospel Ministry.

"Every *male* member." Not "every *free* male member" or "every *white* male member." In Big Cedar Lick, as in most Baptist churches, the idea of leadership roles for women had long been abandoned,[21] but in conformity with this statement of belief, we find a slave,

"Brother George, Negro," among the four men licensed to "exercise their gifts."[22] "Exercising one's gifts" was a lesser function than preaching but still one that allowed for a voice and a respected role. Furthermore, neither the Big Cedar Lick Constitution nor its Rules of Decorum placed any limits on the categories of members entitled to a vote. These decisions stand out in contrast to the recommendations of the Roanoke and Dover Baptist associations of Virginia, at about the same date, that black church members should not be allowed a vote in matters affecting whites.[23]

Article 19 was not unique in Middle Tennessee. Elder James Whitsitt, one of Moore Stevenson's spiritual mentors, was the pastor of four Baptist churches in the Nashville area. Records of one of those churches, the Mill Creek Baptist Church, offer a more detailed version of this article, which clarifies its intent and effect. In 1806 that church " . . . resolved that the Black Brethren at the time of the Church's Society Meeting have, and enjoy the same liberty of exercising public gifts as white members do have or do enjoy." They could "sing and pray with and exort[sic] . . . fellow servants," exhort "within the bounds of the Church," and take responsibility for oversight of other black members.[24]

The liberty set out in these covenants and resolves was not absolute. The Mill Creek Church confined its black members to exercising their gifts in separate meetings with people of their own race but did not attempt to license or control their activities within those meetings. At the Big Cedar Lick Church, there was no recorded limitation on the times or places where Brother George could exercise his gifts, but, like white men who were similarly licensed, he could do so only with permission of the church. Nevertheless, the two churches were making a deliberate commitment to honor the participation of their black members. Their records reveal an ongoing struggle on the part of frontier Baptists to reconcile their egalitarian creed with the realities of a slave society.

Even on the frontier, however, black and white Baptists were drawing ever farther apart as the whites increasingly rejected both the emotional expressiveness of black worship and the idea that black members ought to be allowed an equal voice with whites. By 1831, black members, free or slave, no longer had a vote in most white-dominated churches.[25] At around the same time, the new minister of the First Baptist Church of Nashville explained why he had to preach differently to blacks and whites: "[Black members] are generally dull of apprehension; they are, for the most part, strongly inclined to fanaticism; and as church members they are litigious, and difficult to govern."[26]

The Big Cedar Lick Church was fighting a rear-guard action against remorseless history. Little by little, black Baptists were withdrawing into separate congregations where they could worship as they pleased. When the church covenant was restated in 1821 by a daughter church at Little Cedar Lick, Article 19 had vanished.[27]

The doors were closing in other ways as well. In 1834, Tennessee, which had been one of only three southern states to continue to extend the suffrage to all free males after the beginning of the nineteenth century, changed its constitution to disenfranchise free people of color.[28] After 1831, emancipated slaves were required to leave the state. Over a hundred years after Virginia solidified its own racial caste system, the relatively open society of the Tennessee border was following the same path.

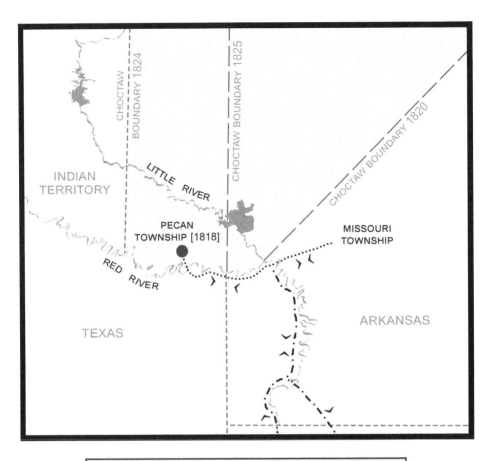

CHOCTAW BOUNDARY 1824

CHOCTAW BOUNDARY 1825

CHOCTAW BOUNDARY 1820

INDIAN
TERRITORY

LITTLE   RIVER

PECAN
TOWNSHIP [1818]

MISSOURI
TOWNSHIP

RED   RIVER

ARKANSAS

TEXAS

KEY

·························· ROUTE

—··—··—··—··— PROBABLE ROUTE

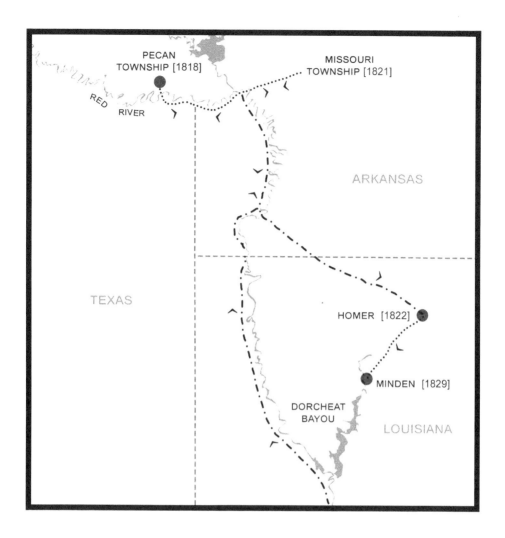

PECAN
TOWNSHIP [1818]

MISSOURI
TOWNSHIP [1821]

RED
RIVER

ARKANSAS

TEXAS

HOMER [1822]

MINDEN [1829]

DORCHEAT
BAYOU

LOUISIANA

JOURNEYS OF NEWIT DREW, TWO

17. Bear Lard, Parched Acorns, and Hog Potatoes

The first high school in Wilson County was founded in 1810 on Hickory Ridge near the Nashville Road in the immediate vicinity of the Big Cedar Lick Church.[1] Newit's oldest son, James Cloyd Drew, was ten, and Thomas Stevenson Drew was eight. Newit, who knew the value of words and ideas, made sure that his sons received a good education, and it seems almost certain that his two oldest would have attended this school.

By 1816, however, membership in the Big Cedar Lick Church was beginning to decline as some members split off to constitute new churches and others pulled up stakes and moved on. In 1816, the church's business conference resolved "that each and every brother here present, is commanded to cite each and every member of our body to attend their church meetings, otherwise they may expect to be dealt with according to our covenant." The decline in attendance may also have had something to do with doctrinal disputes. Developing conflicts about the issue of missionary work and about the Calvinist doctrine of predestination ultimately led to a series of schisms within the Concord Baptist Association, of which the Big Cedar Lick Church was a member.[2] A puzzling entry in the church minutes for 1813 seems to refer to such a controversy, noting that a member of the Concord Baptist Association had charged that the Cumberland Baptist Union "was built upon falsehood deceit and schism."[3]

1816: the Year Without a Summer. The gigantic explosion of Mount Tambora in Indonesia in 1815, following on a series of other large volcanic events, had resulted in a globe-spanning haze of ash that veiled the sunlight over much of the northern hemisphere. In New York, New England, and as far south as the mountains of eastern Tennessee, there was snow, ice, or killing frost in every month of the year, causing widespread famine and sending desperate emigrants south and west. Although the frosts did not extend as far as the Cumberland River, loss of sunlight most likely reduced crop yields there as well. As a result of Jackson's victory at the battle of New Orleans and the successful end of the War of 1812, the southern Mississippi Valley seemed increasingly attractive to prospective migrants. Between 1815 and the end of 1816, Newit Drew sold his 320 acres for twice what he had paid for them,[4] loaded his family—then consisting of Sally, seven children, and perhaps three or four slaves—onto one or more flatboats, and headed south, following the Cumberland, Ohio, and Mississippi rivers. He had been in Wilson County for about twenty years.

Flatboats—giant rafts sometimes as much as a hundred feet long carrying living quarters, household goods, furniture, tools, canoes, and livestock—were a major means of transportation for settlers heading south and west. Journeys down the rivers were leisurely. Along the way, travelers would stop to hunt and fish or gather wild greens and berries. Livestock was carried downstream on the boat or driven along the banks as the family and their possessions floated down.[5] John James Audubon, who traveled widely in the Mississippi Valley in the first half of the nineteenth century, left us a word picture of one of these flatboats:

> The roof or deck of the boat was not unlike a farm-yard, being covered with hay, ploughs, carts, wagons, and various agricultural

implements, together with numerous others among which the spinning-wheels of the matrons were conspicuous. Even the sides of the floating mass were loaded with the wheels of the different vehicles, which themselves lay on the roof.[6]

The Reverend Timothy Flint, who moved his family to several places in the Mississippi Valley between 1815 and 1825, was less charitable, describing the boats as "very nearly resembling a new England pigsty." The great rivers were crowded with boats of all sorts—long elegant keelboats manned by crews of a dozen or more boatmen, pirogues hollowed out of a single giant tree and carrying as much as four tons, small dugouts and canoes, and a variety of eccentric and idiosyncratic craft, creations of imaginative boat builders unacquainted with river travel.[7]

The second decade of the nineteenth century is close enough to our own time for a few scraps of oral history to have been handed down and recorded by the Drew and Bettis families. Some of these narratives contain surprisingly accurate nuggets of fact; others consist of bits of fact partially obscured by a jumble of errors; and a few display family legends embroidered to the point of fantasy. Among the second group is an unpublished narrative entitled "The Drew Family Moves to Louisiana," recorded in 1943 by Doris Whitaker Tynes, edited in 1992 and 1993, and containing at least as much legend as fact. In spite of some embroidery in other sections, Tynes's vivid description of the family's journey matches narratives of similar journeys by other authors.

> … (R)opes were attached to [the rafts] and men ran along the river bank holding them, to keep from letting these precious supplies get away from them …. It took some time to make the journey. Lard was made from bears killed in the wintertime and

it was stored in wooden barrels which they made themselves. Occasionally they had wild hog potatoes for food. This is a root which grows wild and resembles the sweet potato. "Coffee" was made from parched acorns, ground up using a mortar and pestle which is today in the possession of Ulracca Thankful Evans of West Monroe.[8]

It was here that the Drew family stepped out of the world of knee breeches, silk petticoats, and red silk waistcoats. The next six years of their lives were hard ones. Louisiana descendants of the Drews insist that James and Thomas, Newit's two oldest sons, left Tennessee at the ages of sixteen and fourteen, headed down the Mississippi in a canoe to scout out a place for a new settlement, then came back upriver and recommended that the family move to Louisiana.[9] But if the first stop on the family's journey was somewhere in Louisiana, there was something about the area that displeased them, and they did not remain there long.

In 1819, Newit Drew and Joab Scallorn, whose son later married one of Newit's daughters, appear as grand jurors in Pecan Township, a remote area between the Red and Little rivers on the western edge of Hempstead County, Arkansas. The Drew family may have moved there in order to join a tightly knit group of families that had recently migrated from Williamson County, Tennessee, since several other men from these families eventually married Drew daughters.[10] However they got there, the journey must have been grueling. If, like many early Arkansas pioneers, they went up the Red River from the Mississippi in a keelboat, the trip would have involved several months of backbreaking labor. They would have had to push the boat upriver for long stretches through waist-deep water or haul it up by means of overhanging trees, hand over hand or with ropes called cordelles, through the impenetrable mass of floating logs known as the Red River Raft.[11] If, on the other hand, they went up the slightly more navigable Ouachita, then overland to the Red River, they would have had to make the last part of the journey by way of Trammel's Trace, not even a trail but rather a path marked by blazes on trees and named for the family of horse thieves who had first blazed it.[12]

The first white inhabitants of the Red River Valley were hunter-farmers who settled in the higher, drier areas on the edge of the valley where the land was less fertile but game abounded. The travelers who described these migrants concurred that they were of " . . . the worst moral character imaginable, being many of them renegadoes from justice, and such as have forfeited the esteem of civilized society."[13] They were hunters and Indian traders, skilled in the arts of wilderness survival, dressed in hunting shirts, leather leggings, and moccasins and at that time still exposed to the dangers of raids by the warlike Osage who inhabited the area to the west. The bear lard and parched acorn coffee described by Tynes were staple features of their diet.[14] After 1812, however, a new group of yeoman farmers began moving in, hoping to settle on the deep, rich soil of Long Prairie. By 1821 there were twenty-two hundred inhabitants growing cotton and sending it down the Red River by keelboat to market.[15]

The Drew family was part of the second group, arriving around 1818 in the middle of the transition. The task that faced them was arduous, and many of their neighbors failed at it. One such neighbor was John Murrell, whose family had previously lived near the Drews in Tennessee. The lowland areas were brutal to clear and hopelessly disease-ridden, with malaria, typhoid, and cholera constant dangers. Wealthier planters had slaves to do the hard work of clearing the land, while the white families established their homes in the drier uplands. For Murrell, who owned no slaves and had no grown sons, it was impossible. Within a year, both his horses and one of his children had died, and the family had given up their land and moved to the drier climate of northern Louisiana.[16]

Newit and Sally, too, lost a child in those years—Margaret, age two. But whether Newit, whose household then contained only one grown son and perhaps two adult slaves, could have succeeded where Murrell failed was soon beside the point. In 1820, his old neighbor Andrew Jackson—by then General Jackson and a national hero—negotiated a treaty with the Choctaw Indians, who were being forced out of Mississippi, granting them land between the Arkansas and Red rivers. The grant included all of the land previously identified as Pecan Township. Of course, the treaty did not last: five years later the boundary was moved west to the current Arkansas state line, and the Choctaws were coerced into giving up the land they had recently gained. But in the meantime hundreds of white settlers, including the Drews, had been forced to move east to establish new settlements. In 1821 Newit Drew and Joab Scallorn were appointed as "Judges of the Election within and for the Township of Missouri," on the other side of the large territory that was then Hempstead County, forty miles east of their former land.[17]

By the end of 1822, the Drew family, which by then included two sons-in-law, had followed the Murrell family to Claiborne Parish, Louisiana. With each of their moves, they had to clear new fields and build new cabins, only to leave them again after less than two years. Before the marriages of their daughters, no members of either Newit's or Sally's extended families had accompanied them on these journeys. But they had a more important family in their church.

Elders James Brinson and John Impson, two of the founders of the Big Cedar Lick Church, along with two daughters of Elder Brinson and their husbands, had left Tennessee within two or three years of Newit's departure. John Murrell and Isaac Alden, members of other Middle Tennessee churches connected to the preacher Moore Stevenson, migrated at around the same time.[18] By 1823, they were all in Claiborne Parish and founding new churches. Newit and Sally were founding members of the Black Lake Church, which met in Murrell's large house with Newit and Elder Brinson leading the monthly services.[19] A little later, Murrell initiated the first school, also in his own house.

A *History of Claiborne Parish*, written in 1886 by two early settlers, D.W. Harris and B. M. Hulse, relates that at the time of the first settlement,

> . . . we could almost daily see Indians, for there were many of them in the country. They lived in small villages, and moved from place to place as their hunting expeditions required. But these Indians were inoffensive, committing no depredations on stock or other property . . . . The country then was almost entirely covered with a dense thicket of brush, briars and vines. Cane was abundant on all the streams and abutting hill points.

Two successive fires, most likely intentionally set by either whites or Indians, cleaned out the brush,

> leaving it an open and beautiful country. You could see a cow or a deer as far as the eye could reach, through the intervening living

timber. New grasses sprang up, the wild pea vine and switch cane, and a better range for farmers' cattle, hogs, deer and turkey was never seen . . . . A turkey for dinner required only a few minutes hunt, venison steak was to be had at any hour, and bear in the proper season was readily converted into the best of bacon. Wolves, too, abounded. It was common to see them, of moonlight nights, traveling around the house or cow pen.[20]

There were no roads, only trails, and until 1825, no store-bought goods. As in the mountains where Sally was born, clothing consisted of buckskin pants, moccasins, and home-spun and home-woven cloth. It was very far indeed from Newit's childhood and from the comfortable life of the Southampton County planter with his riding chair and his thirteen slaves. Newit had learned some things about wilderness survival from Sally and her family.

The first public road through the area was established in 1829 from Russellville, near the town of Homer, to what was then called Minden lower landing, the head of navigation on the Dorcheat Bayou. By this time steamboats were everywhere, even on the smaller bayous, and the new ease of transportation raised hopes for the rapid expansion of the local economy. At around the same time, four of the churches established by Elder Brinson were torn apart by a scandal involving allegations of marital misbehavior by a popular minister, a rift that was then aggravated by another doctrinal dispute. The majorities of the four churches voted to expel the minister. His supporters, including the family of John Murrell, split off and re-established themselves as "the Christian Church (Disciples of Christ) at Union Grove."[21]

The Disciples of Christ, a loosely organized faith that had recently separated from its Baptist and Presbyterian parents, rejected all of the doctrinal disputes then roiling frontier Baptist churches, along with any dogma or ritual not specifically derived from the New Testament. It championed the right of each believer to interpret the Scriptures for himself or herself. Its creation and rapid growth were part of the seemingly endless process of fission and refashioning that characterized the American religious landscape in the nineteenth century, a product of Americans' stubborn insistence on thinking for themselves. It is unclear whether it was the church dispute or the arrival of the new steamboats that was more responsible for the Drews' next move, to the Minden lower landing, where Newit Drew founded the town of Overton. The *History of Claiborne Parish* suggests a motive: "Being the head of navigation it was thought [the town] would become a big inland city."[22]

Around the time of that move, Newit, then fifty-eight years old, finally decided to leave the religious controversies to the preachers and settle down to making money. He and his sons and slaves built a grist mill, like his father's, and then a saw mill. According to census records, the Baptist families who had moved with him from Wilson County doggedly refused to acquire any slaves; but Newit's human possessions increased from seven in 1830 to thirteen in 1840.[23] "Much might be said," says the *History*, with maddening reticence, "of this good old go-ahead pioneer. Himself and wife were true old Tennessee Baptists .... Some of his daughters married well, others, contrary to the old man's wishes, not so well."[24]

"It would be difficult," said de Tocqueville,

> to depict the avidity with which the American throws himself
> on the immense prey that fortune offers him .... Before him lies
> an almost boundless continent, and one would say that, already

afraid of losing his place in it, he hastens for fear of arriving too late . . . . It is not rare, when passing through the new states of the West, to encounter abandoned dwellings in the middle of the woods; often one discovers the debris of a hut in the deepest solitude, and one is astonished to come across partial clearings which attest at once to human power and human inconstancy.[25]

But avidity, for families like the Drews, was not the only reason for repeated moves. Some yeoman farmers failed and gave up; some were cheated out of their land; and some, like the Drews, were forced off it. In the Drews' case, the pull of their church community and the subsequent dissolution of that community appear to have been as important as the call of new and better opportunities. If we look for a theme in Newit's life, an explanation for his endlessly repeated moves, we should consider the tension between the demands of his faith and his continuing need to build something of his own, a church, a town, or a grist mill, to start something from scratch and leave it as a legacy behind him. It may also be true that, restless, driven, and perennially dissatisfied, he was simply a difficult man to get along with.

Newit and Sally named their children with an almost Quaker conscientiousness, alternating names of his family members and hers in a way that points to a Quaker-like sense of equality between the spouses: James Cloyd Drew for Newit's older brother and for his father's wards Newit and Joshua Claud/Cloyd; Thomas Stevenson Drew for Sally's father and the family's pastor; Susannah Adeline Drew for Newit's deceased sister; Jane Hays Drew for Sally's aunt; Mary Parker Drew for Newit's mother; Rachel Ann Drew for Sally's two sisters; Caroline Sally Drew; Margaret Drew for another of Newit's sisters; Richard Maxwell Drew for Sally's father; Harmon

Atkins Drew for Sally's brother. No child was named for either Newit's father or Sally's stepfather; Newit and Sally had chosen another path. Nine out of their ten children survived to adulthood. Three became lawyers and then judges, one of them, Richard Maxwell Drew, at the age of twenty-three. Unlike many borderers, Newit did not bother acquiring enough land for his sons to establish their own plantations. Their education was their patrimony.

Yet in this deeply family-centered world, Newit had some trouble holding on to his children. By the time the Drews returned to Louisiana their two oldest sons, James and Thomas, had already left home.

James, the oldest, seems to have inherited the restless independence of his Scots-Irish ancestors. By the time his parents and siblings moved on to Pecan Point, he had settled on the Ouachita River near the former Spanish trading post that was soon to become Monroe, Louisiana. There he set out to make his fortune in the booming cotton economy. He trained as a surveyor, started acquiring land, and by the time of the Civil War was one of the richest planters in the area, with four large plantations, four hundred slaves, and a taste for the kind of gambling that would have appalled his Baptist father. In one entry in his journal, he speaks of betting one of his plantations on a horse.[26]

Susannah Adeline Drew, at fifteen, and Jane Hays Drew, at sixteen, had already embarked on a long series of marriages, three for each of them, creating a tangle of stepfamilies and family squabbles that is almost impossible to unravel. Jane may have been intentionally disinherited by her second husband, and later on, her sister's third husband seems to have tried to remove her from guardianship of her own children.[27] A couple of Susannah's and Jane's siblings appear to have been married as Presbyterians rather than as Baptists. Perhaps the zealous faith of their parents was a bit too controlling for the next generation of Drews. Or perhaps the children were simply seduced by the newer American faith—the belief in getting rich as quickly as possible.

It is against the background of this restless, driven, occasionally tumultuous family and this constantly shifting community that the figure of the young Thomas Drew begins to emerge. Given what we know of his later personality, we can imagine him as the conciliator among his strong-willed family members. Perhaps he simply got tired of his domineering father and rambunctious sisters. At any rate, when the rest of the Drew clan moved south from Arkansas to northern Louisiana, Thomas stayed behind.

Sally in the Cookhouse

Hempstead County, Arkansas • an autumn morning, 1822

Sally is standing in the cookhouse, preparing beans and cornbread for her family's midday meal. She is thirty-nine years old, small, tough and wiry. Her long hair, still red-blond, is pulled back tightly from her face.

Outside, the sunlit yard is full of little girls, Lydia's and Sally's, four in all. Lydia, the servant woman, bends over the washtub. The children are weeding the vegetable garden, helping Lydia with the laundry, sweeping the dirt yard with a dogwood-branch broom. In the dogtrot house across the yard, the spinning wheel hums as thirteen-year-old Mary paces back and forth beside it. The loom has already been dismantled for the journey.

What would she ever do without Lydia? It's been awfully lonesome out here since she left her brothers and her sisters and her church back in Tennessee. It's been a blessing to have another woman to talk to, another mother to share her worries about her daughters, to comfort her in the bad time after little Margaret's death. Lydia's not just a servant. She's a dear friend.

It's November again, the fifth November since they left Tennessee. The cotton crop is in, and they're getting ready for another move. Elder Brinson is preaching the Word down in Louisiana, and they need to join him. Some of their old Tennessee neighbors are already there. What a joy it will be to see them all again! She needs to hear the preaching, to stand shoulder to shoulder with her family in Christ, all raising their voices to praise him, to lose herself in the glory of his salvation.

Praise the Lord, He gave her strength. She could do the work of a man when it was needed. Been working ever since she can remember, ever since she was old enough to walk. Fed the cows, cleaned the house, looked after her little brothers and sisters. It was lonesome sometimes after sister Mary died, but she didn't have time to mind.

Her husband, now, he was a rich man's son. Waited on by servants hand and foot when he was little. Never had to learn to work until his Ma died. And then when the Lord called him out into the wilderness, there he was working the fields side by side with the Negroes. Worked as hard as any of them, too. Still does.

Oh, but he's a learned man. Talks like a whole book full of sermons. He is her true partner in faith, diligent in all his works, a stern but just father. People look up to him, people listen. Elder Stevenson relied on him like nobody else. Sometimes, though, they didn't listen like they should. That was one reason for the move from Tennessee—disunity among the brethren.

That journey down the Mississippi, that was a good time. For once in her life, the freedom of just sitting back on the flatboat, watching the banks slide by with their high bluffs, their willows and their great sycamores, their flocks of swans and cranes, letting the river take her where it would. This one will be overland again, wagons and animals laboring down the muddy paths. And when they get down to Louisiana, new fields to clear, new house to build, new cookhouse, smokehouse, barn. But Elder Brinson and the others will be there to help. Maybe that means they'll stay awhile.

The Lord has given them seven healthy children, every one of them smart as a whip. The older ones could read the Bible like their own names by the time they were ten. She taught them all, although Tom helps out now with his little sisters. Every evening after dinner the family and servants sit down together. Her husband reads from the Bible, and then the children take turns.

A bit too much of the devil in them, though. James, her firstborn, the one she loves best—he inherited his father's talent for hard work and his temper, too. Their quarrels were terrible. It made a hole in her heart when he had to go, but she knew it was for the best. Wants to be a rich man like his grandfather. But the Book says, thou canst not serve God and Mammon. How will he keep his eyes on the Lord? Praise the Lord, those two oldest girls found themselves husbands already. A couple of extra hands are always useful.

Tom, he's different—meek as a lamb, always ready to jump in and try to reconcile a quarrel. Blessed are the peacemakers, but when you need him, he's never around. He'll be out back of the barn with one of those old dusty books his Pa brought with him from Virginia. When you look for him to do the plowing or chop the wood or bring the stock in, he's nowhere to be found. Both of them restless, dissatisfied, always looking over the next horizon. Just like their Pa.

Part V
The Town Builders

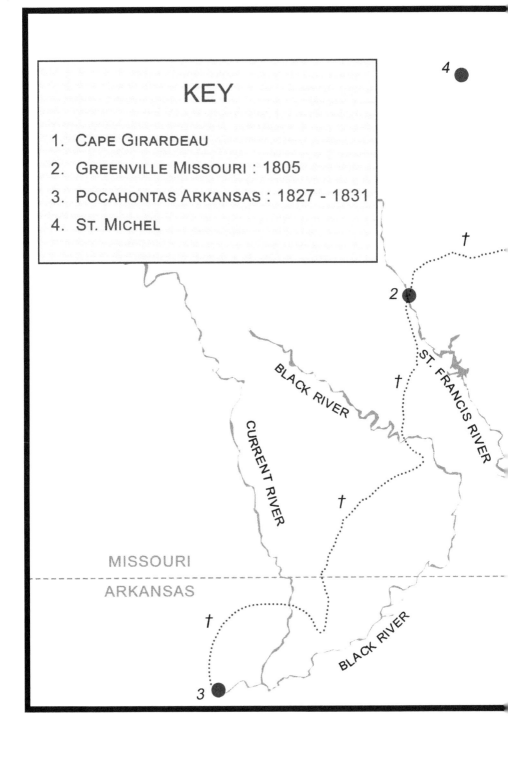

KEY

1. CAPE GIRARDEAU
2. GREENVILLE MISSOURI : 1805
3. POCAHONTAS ARKANSAS : 1827 - 1831
4. ST. MICHEL

BLACK RIVER

CURRENT RIVER

ST. FRANCIS RIVER

MISSOURI

ARKANSAS

BLACK RIVER

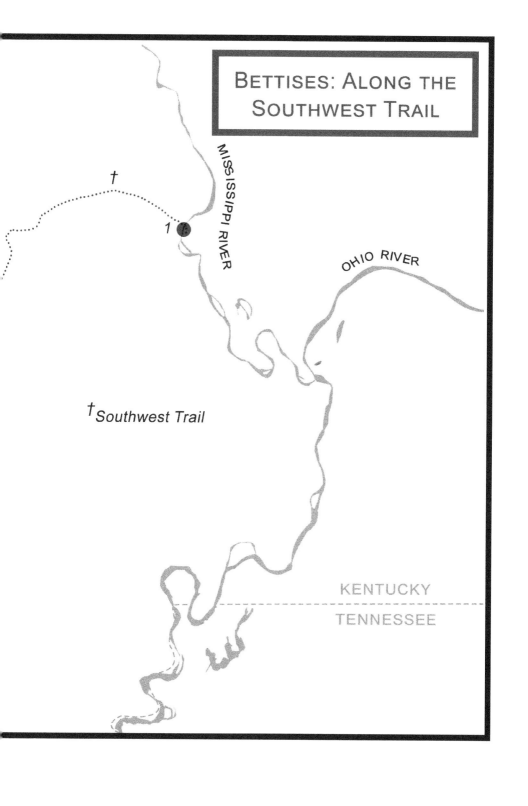

18. In the Rough Hills

If the story of Newit and Sally Drew is a story of wandering, the story of the Bettis family is a story of building. In the lives of Dr. Elijah Bettis's children and grandchildren, we can see the changes wrought by the opening of the trans-Mississippi West and by the migrations of the hundreds of thousands of settlers who rushed to fill it. We can also see the effects of their contacts with the multiple cultures they encountered. The Bettis men of the next two generations were merchants and entrepreneurs whose exposure to different cultures helped foster the flexibility of mind they needed in order to profit from each new opportunity. No longer confined behind the Appalachian mountain chain or treated as unsuitable by their wealthier and more cultivated neighbors, such borderers discovered in themselves the energy and initiative that came to be seen as uniquely American. The Louisiana Purchase in 1803 was another hinge, a bend and a broadening of the path that ultimately led to us.

Heading out from North Carolina with twenty wagons and perhaps three dozen slaves, the Bettis caravan probably crossed the Mississippi at Cape Girardeau and followed the Southwest Trail to the place where it forded the St. Francis River in the southeast corner of the future state of Missouri. The Southwest Trail, later known as the Red River Road and later still as the Military Road, was the main route from St. Louis to Arkansas and Texas, the route that would be followed by tens of thousands of emigrants in the years to come.

Unless they were accompanied by overseers and relatives, the white adults in this party—four men, two women, and a teenage boy—were outnumbered five to one by their slaves. If any of those slaves had decided to run away in the middle of their seven-hundred-mile journey, their owners would have had no time to stop, post advertisements, and wait for the slave patrols to catch them. But there is no record that any slaves did attempt to run. Among the narratives of elderly ex-slaves collected in the 1930s by the Federal Writers' Project, there are many accounts of similar migrations.[1] One of those narrators remembered walking to Texas behind his owner along with five hundred other slaves, singing as they walked. "It was hard," he recalled, "but we enjoys the trip."[2]

What kept these parties together?

The slaveholding South was a crazy quilt of cruelty, generosity, indifference, sadism, kindness, hatred, affection, and despair. On one plantation, slaves might be well-fed and adequately clothed and housed, whippings rare or nonexistent, families kept together, and slaves given time off to "frolic" together or tend their own vegetable patches. People in their nineties who had grown up on such plantations—particularly if they or their parents had been house slaves—remembered their childhoods as happy, described their reluctance to leave the plantation even after they were freed, and told the interviewers of their love for their masters and mistresses.[3] On the next plantation, enslaved people might be whipped to death, families torn apart, and field hands forced to work eighteen-hour days on rations barely sufficient to keep them alive. But even in those hellish places, the human preference for the secure known over the dangerous unknown and the spectacle of the brutal punishments meted out to recaptured runaways kept most of the enslaved in place. If the master and his family decided to move west, the slaves went with them. It was the way of the world, and they were powerless to change it.

The Bettis clan settled on the St. Francis River five or six miles upstream from the place where the Southwest Trail crossed the river.[4] In many ways, it looked like an unpromising spot. It was located in the "rough hills" of the Ozark Plateau, a vast expanse of rocky ridges and precipitous slopes stretching westward from the rich alluvial soil of the Mississippi bottomland and the fertile plain above the river. The St. Francis River itself was not navigable, and its banks were broken by granite knobs that made travel up and down it difficult even on foot. The knobs created shut-ins, isolated patches of rich bottomland suitable for small farming settlements but cut off from neighboring farms by the difficulty of travel.[5]

The hillsides and ridges, however, were covered with widely spaced oak and hickory trees with plentiful grass underneath. In low places around marshes and riverbanks grew great thickets of American cane, *arundinaria gigantea*, a favorite food for cattle and other stock. Such canebrakes, another piece of the vanished American landscape, once covered thousands of square miles in the South and Midwest, sometimes reaching heights of twenty or thirty feet and so densely packed that the only way to get through them was to turn around and force one's way in backwards.[6] Along with the open woods, they created an environment well-suited to the type of open-range cattle and hog farming practiced in southside Virginia, in the Carolina Piedmont, and throughout the southern frontier. Before the arrival of Europeans, annual fires, both natural and man-made, kept the woods free of underbrush.[7] When the first farms were established, fields and stock pens were located in the valley bottoms. Cattle were pastured in the woods along the ridges during the warm weather and brought down in winter to graze on the cane by the river. The Bettises, whose grandfather, great grandfather, uncles, and great-uncles had been chasing the border for a century, found the location congenial.

In order to stay on that land, one had to be stubborn. In earlier days, the Spanish authorities had given out land for the asking, and after 1795, they had encouraged immigration by Americans. To secure a "concession" under the Spanish system, one first had to ask the district commissioner for a settlement permit. Permits were issued subject to a formula based on the size of the family, up to a maximum of eight hundred "arpents" or a little over one square mile. The commissioner would then forward the permit to the lieutenant governor, who would order a survey and pass the documents on to the governor general in New Orleans, whose approval was the final requirement for an official concession.[8] The requirement of a survey, however, was often ignored. Surveys were expensive and surveyors hard to find, especially after the Osage Indians burned one of them to death.[9] Many settlers claimed their lands with nothing but a bare settlement permit.

In 1800, the Spanish re-ceded the land to the French, who left the existing Spanish authorities in their places, effectively responsible to no one. By then, it was common knowledge that the Americans would most likely acquire the whole of the Louisiana Territory. Outgoing French Lieutenant Governor Delassus started handing out concessions like so much candy—with particular attention to his friends and those who offered bribes. Savvy prospective settlers, who knew that once the Americans took over they would start charging for the land, rushed to acquire free concessions before the date of the transfer.[10] It was in this period that the Logan brothers acquired their concessions on the St. Francis River. Other settlers didn't bother with permits or concessions. In defiance of all laws and restrictions imposed by distant governments, they simply came and squatted, hoping eventually to acquire their lands by right of settlement.

In 1805, two years after the transfer of the territory to American authority, all concessions acquired during the three years of French ownership were declared invalid unless the grantee had made an actual settlement before December 20, 1803 with proper permission from the Spanish authorities. A board of commissioners was set up to judge the validity of existing land claims. But then, year by year, the law invalidating the concessions was relaxed. In 1806, for instance, Congress decided that people who had been inhabiting and cultivating land before October 1, 1800, should be deemed to be doing so with proper permission, whether or not they had documents.[11]

The board of commissioners finished its work in November of 1811. It rejected the majority of claims that had been presented to it, including every claim on the St. Francis River. That same year, however, Congress relaxed the requirements again. A new law allowed owners of rejected claims to appeal them to the recorder of land titles based on settlement and cultivation, even without permission. This time, two-thirds of the claims were approved, including all of those on the St. Francis. In 1814, all pre-1803 claims were validated as long as they referred to a specific ascertainable place, even if they were *not* inhabited or cultivated in 1803. The stubborn and patient, who had stuck it out during the prolonged and sometimes violent period of uncertainty, obtained title to their land at last.[12]

Isaac Kelly was not one of the patient. Part of the first wave of white settlement, a member of a family whose mode of living combined hunting, trapping, small-scale farming, and Indian trading, he had obtained a concession of 300 arpents, or about 338 acres, in 1801 as a reward for participation in a brief militia expedition. He exercised that concession by settling on the St. Francis with his younger brother at the ford where the Southwest Trail crossed the river. Two or three years later, they were joined by the rest of their family.[13] As in southwest Arkansas a few years later, travelers who described such hunter-trader families painted a picture of poverty and squalor: ten or a dozen people living in a single log cabin with dirt floors, minimal furniture, and a diet consisting only of fried pork and corn bread.[14]

When the territory was transferred to American jurisdiction, Isaac filed a claim for his land, which was turned down like all the others on the St. Francis in 1811. By this time, however, Isaac had already moved south to the Current River in northeast Arkansas, where he traded with Cherokees recently arrived from the East.[15] After his departure, Elijah Bettis III, oldest son of the patriarch Dr. Elijah, took up residence on his land. When Isaac's claim was finally approved in 1816, he sold that land to Elijah III in two separate parcels.[16] The land included a large stretch of fertile floodplain that became a state recreation area more than a century later, when the river was dammed to create Lake Wappapello. The four-lane highway that tracks the old Southwest Trail crosses the lake near the site of the original ford.

Many things changed in 1811 and 1812. The most devastating event was the series of violent earthquakes known collectively as the New Madrid Earthquake, at magnitude 8.4 the strongest earthquake to have occurred in the continental United States in the past two hundred years. The heaving and shaking of the ground was so violent that the Mississippi River briefly ran backwards and permanently changed its course in some places while church bells rang in Charleston and masonry cracked in Washington, DC.[17]

In the course of those years, Dr. Elijah Bettis died. His estate inventory, obviously incomplete, identifies him as the owner of twenty-five slaves and, surprisingly, only four books.[18] His son Ransom married Isaac Kelly's daughter Mary Kelly,[19] and their only child, a daughter named Cinderella, was born. The date of Cinderella's birth is usually given as 1810, which would make her seventeen at the time of her marriage; Rose Fulton Cramer, the author of *Wayne County, Missouri*, gives the date of Cinderella's parents' marriage as 1811.[20] And the three Bettis brothers—like Connor Dowd, the Loyalist uncle whom none of them could remember—set out to make a profit out of their new location.

As it turned out, there was a good deal of profit to be made at a ford on the main route from St. Louis to Texas. The Bettises' extensive slaveholdings gave them the means to take advantage of that opportunity. By 1816, when the Cape Girardeau Court of Quarter Sessions ordered the first real roads laid out, the place where they converged was known as Bettis Ferry.[21] Two years later, Bettis Ferry had become Greenville, the county seat of the newly established Wayne County. Overton Bettis, James Logan, and Overton's brother-in-law Ezekiel Rubottom were among the five commissioners appointed to choose the county seat and secure land for public buildings, presumably by purchasing it from the Bettises. The legislation that established the county provided for court to be held at the home of Ransom Bettis until a proper courthouse should be built. [22]

At the time the county was established, the town of Greenville consisted of ten to fifteen log houses, a grist mill, and from sixty to seventy-five inhabitants, the majority of them Bettises and their slaves.[23] Wayne County itself had just over a thousand inhabitants, but like the rest of the Missouri Territory it was growing rapidly. By 1820, there were 1443 inhabitants and eight years later, 3009.[24] The farms surrounding Greenville were prosperous and well managed. Cattle, the mainstay of the local economy, were driven to markets as far away as Kaskaskia, Illinois, ninety miles to the north, and St. Louis, over a hundred and twenty.[25] Ransom Bettis held the license for the ferry (issued by Overton as Sheriff), but Elijah III is said to have run it besides building a grist mill—one sign of an enterprising person on any border—and practicing medicine on the side. At some point, the brothers also added a store.[26]

Like nearly all other houses in the newly settled areas of the South and West, theirs were built of logs, but the comfort level of those houses was steadily increasing. Manufactured goods were becoming increasingly common, and small luxuries were available even for a child. As of the 1940s, the sole remaining artifact connected to Cinderella by family tradition was a child's "chastely garlanded" china teacup.[27] In the 1820 territorial census, members of the extended Bettis clan were recorded as owning more than a third of the county's 204 slaves. Assuming a relatively equal distribution, that would average out to about twelve slaves per family.[28]

The Bettis brothers and their in-laws also dominated the area politically. Elijah III, the oldest, was the most prominent, serving as Wayne County representative to the Missouri Constitutional Convention in 1820, and after Missouri became a state in 1821, serving three terms as a representative in the Missouri General Assembly and two in the Missouri Senate.[29] Ransom was a county court judge in 1822.[30] Overton was the first sheriff and collector of Wayne County,[31] while Ezekiel Rubottom, the husband of their deceased sister Eleanor, was a justice of the peace in five separate years between 1819 and 1834, a representative in the General Assembly in 1820, and a county court judge for three separate terms.[32] As far as we can tell, none of them had any legal training, but the lack of such training was pretty normal for that era.

Two of their sisters, Sally Bettis Alston and Lovely Bettis Matthews, settled with their families on Otter Creek, at least ten miles away to the south. Ezekiel Rubottom and his second wife settled a few miles to the north, near Lake Creek.[33] Since there were no Spanish grants in the area except Isaac Kelly's and federal lands had not yet gone on sale, they must have simply squatted like most other early settlers and waited for the chance to establish a legal claim.

In this isolated place, where the Bettises knew every white resident and were related to a large number of them and where they had to rely on a small group of family members, neighbors, and enslaved people in order to survive, relationships developed a particular intensity. The enduring relationships among the cousins in the next generation are testimony to the strength of those bonds. For the child Cinderella, the isolation must have been particularly powerful. Her childhood was much easier than that of her mother, who would have had to work to keep her family fed and clothed from the time she was small. Cinderella still had work to do, learning the skills of gardening, food preparation, and household management as she grew, but she would also have had time for lessons and for play. The oldest legitimate children of her uncles Elijah III and Overton, the only white cousins in their little settlement, were at least six years younger than she was.[34] She had Alston, Matthews, and Rubottom cousins of about her own age, but they lived near enough only for Sunday visits, not for daily contact. Although there were some non-Bettis residents in Greenville, it is possible that for much of her childhood Cinderella was the only white child of her age there.

This does not mean that she did not have playmates nor that some of those playmates were not her cousins. Elijah III apparently waited until he was in his forties to settle down and start having legitimate children, but he had been busy enough before then. The story passed down by his mixed-race descendants is that he had seven enslaved daughters by seven different enslaved women and that all of them considered themselves sisters and remained close after they were freed. A letter from one descendant describes them as all " . . . of olive complexion, high noses and dark straight hair."[35] Some of their names were passed down as well: Jane, Elizabeth,

Martha, Celia.[36] The letter writer, Bettie Hurd, also passed on a generous helping of family fantasy, including a description of the elder Dr. Elijah as a refugee nobleman who had escaped from the French Revolution.

Her letter, however, is only partly fantasy. At the 150th anniversary celebration for the town of Pocahontas, Arkansas, in the middle of the Pocahontas history pageant, I was startled to hear those same names read from the stage, as part of a deed by which Elijah III freed seven slave women while keeping their children in slavery.[37] In the deed they were called by children's names, although most of them were grown women with children of their own: Jenny, Charity, Haly, Litty, Polly, Patsie, and Celia. Patsie, a tall girl[38] later known by her adult name of Martha, was four or five years older than Cinderella, while two of her sisters were roughly Cinderella's age. Most or all of them were probably born between 1795 and 1811.[39] An 1830 census listing, discussed below, suggests that Elijah's oldest legitimate white child was born around 1815.

That slaveholding men often fathered children by enslaved women was something everyone knew but no one could say aloud. Since Elijah III eventually freed his daughters, there must have been some acknowledgment and some form of paternal benevolence, however limited. Martha/Patsie herself is said to have boasted to her grandchildren that her mother was Elijah's favorite.[40] As Cinderella grew up, she would have absorbed this knowledge in some part of her mind, perhaps without knowing that she knew it.

On those plantations where childhood was possible, where slave children were not made to work from the time they were able to walk, it was normal for white and black children to play together.

Harriet Bailey Bullock, born on her father's Arkansas plantation a generation later, remembered stealing watermelons with her black playmates, chasing small animals, and staging a pretend church service in which one child stood on a board to preach to the others.[41] An elderly ex-slave named George Rogers, one of hundreds who were interviewed in the 1930s through the Federal Writers' Project, recalled playing marbles, prisoner's base, blindfold, and tag with the white children on the plantation and said that his master "whipped us all together when we stole watermelons and apples." Young boys, white and black, fished and hunted small game together.[42]

Even in childhood, however, the racial hierarchy was evident. Delicia Patterson, another ex-slave, remembered a time when she was weeding the garden with her master's daughter and pulled up the wrong plant. The white child slapped her. Delicia picked up a hoe "and run her all the way to the Big House, and of course I got whipped for that." The white child had learned that it was acceptable to slap a slave; the black one had not yet learned that she was expected to take it.[43] A few years later, the caste system would have fully reasserted itself, and the former playmates assumed their adult roles of owner and owned.

As time went on, there were also some illegitimate white children in the Bettis settlement. Overton was said, by an unofficial Greenville historian named Hal Bennett, to have had several children by his housekeeper, Mrs. Timmons, the wife or widow of his neighbor Moses Timmons.[44] There are people living in Pocahontas as I write this who claim descent from Ransom but not from Cinderella, in spite of Cinderella's rather belligerent assertion on her father's tombstone that the monument was "erected by his only child."[45] But in her early years, Cinderella must have been queen of her little kingdom, the child whom everyone spoiled and to whom all other children deferred—except, just possibly, Patsie. It was not the best training for the troubles she would face as an adult.

As their master's daughters, Patsie and her sisters were probably raised as house slaves, a condition superior to that of the darker-skinned field hands. In many households, light-skinned children of the master were mocked and ostracized by other enslaved children and even by enslaved adults,[46] but here there were so many of them that they could have formed a little tribe of their own, a protective group that strengthened the bonds of their sisterhood. Although they were most likely spared the lash that was a feature of everyday life on most plantations, they may still have been subject to slaps, whippings, or beatings by their mistress for flaws in their housekeeping, because Elijah's wife was jealous of the attention he paid to them, or for no reason at all.[47] The kindness or brutality of a plantation mistress—and there were more than a few who were brutal—could make the difference between a hell on earth and a life remembered with fondness seven decades later.

Black or white, few women on a frontier farm were exempt from hard work. As the sisters grew, their responsibilities may have included caring for their younger white half-siblings, emptying the chamber pots of the white family, standing behind the white adults at dinner to shoo away the flies as they ate, cleaning the house, boiling lye to make soap, milking cows, feeding hogs, working in the garden, preserving food, and above all, spinning, weaving, and sewing clothes for both white and black members of the household. In households like the Bettises' "good" clothes for the white family members were made of silk or calico shipped from New Orleans, but slaves' clothing and everyday clothing for whites was generally made at home, often in a loom house where women worked together at spinning and weaving.[48]

A surprisingly detailed glimpse of Elijah's enslaved daughters as young women, as well as of the rest of their black and white family, is provided by the 1830 federal census listing for Elijah Bettis III, taken two or three years before the family's move to Arkansas. Elijah appears as a middle-aged widower (over sixty, although his actual age as calculated from earlier censuses was about fifty-six) with five children between the ages of five and fifteen and thirty-six slaves. His slaveholdings have at least doubled from their number ten years earlier. The most interesting aspect of the listing, however, is the composition of his enslaved household. More than four-fifths of them are women under thirty-five—Patsie, her sisters, and a few others—and young children. The young men who might have been their brothers or the fathers of their children are almost entirely missing, as are the middle-aged women who might have been their mothers.

The absence of middle-aged women may have reflected the common practice of selling the white owner's enslaved concubine or concubines away at the time of his marriage. The shortage of enslaved men, which would seem to leave the elderly Elijah without an adequate labor force, may have been a result of their having been rented out to other planters, a common arrangement in that era. Or they may have been sent to Arkansas to clear fields and build houses and cabins for a new plantation. A slaveholder planning a move would often send slaves ahead with an overseer to clear the land, plant the first year's crop, and make sure that the white family could live in comfort when they arrived.[49]

The lack of male slaves, however, may also have been the result of the highly profitable trade through which tens of thousands of young black men, even those who were the sons of their owners, were sold down the river to the cane and cotton plantations of the deep South. Before the arrival of steamboats, they would have made the journey on foot, chained together under conditions that would have been considered too cruel for animals. With the advent of steamboats, the journey may have been even worse: on many boats, men and women were not only chained together, but each one was chained separately to the railing of the lower deck and left there in their own filth for the entire voyage.[50] The strange and terrible form of paternal affection that involved keeping one's child while selling her brothers and tearing her away from her mother was only one of the unfathomable complications of slavery.

If we look a bit closer, however, we see something else as well. The orderly running of a plantation or a large farm depended to a high degree on the plantation mistress, usually the master's wife but sometimes a grown daughter or unmarried sister. The mistress was responsible for all facets of household management, including the maintenance of household accounts. She supervised the procuring, processing, and distribution of food supplies, the production of clothing for white and black members of the household, the maintenance of vegetable and herb gardens, and the cleaning and ordering of the house. While most of the routine work of caring for the white children was performed by slaves, the mistress was responsible for the children's academic and social education.[51] But in this 1830 census listing, there is no mistress. Unless the sole black man over thirty-five is acting as an overseer—unlikely, but possible—Patsie and her sisters are running the household and raising their white half-siblings on their own without much discernible supervision, and may have been doing it for as much as five years. Elijah must have provided a tutor for his legitimate children, since his illegitimate ones, being illiterate, could not have fulfilled that function, but in all other respects his enslaved daughters seem to have been in charge. As far as can be determined from the records and from oral tradition, he never married again.

19. The Multicultural Border

As isolated as the Bettises' St. Francis settlement was, it nevertheless straddled the borders between several cultures, two of which had been living together on terms of harmony and mutual benefit for nearly a century. By 1806, the area around the French town of Ste. Genevieve was home to a growing crowd of Indian peoples, some of them long-time inhabitants and others only recently arrived. To the west lived the powerful Osage, who controlled the fur trade, and who had managed to maintain their regional dominance for generations by skillfully playing off competing European empires against one another. Numerous smaller tribes maintained a presence in the same area. More recent arrivals were Shawnees, Delawares, Cherokees, Choctaws, and Chickasaws who had been migrating westward for several decades in response to the pressure of European settlement in the east.

The Shawnee and Delaware, who had been living in proximity to white settlers for some time, had established permanent villages virtually indistinguishable from those of whites.[1] Like the whites, they farmed their fields and let their stock range free in the woods. All recently arrived tribes feared and resented the Osage, who reacted to the pressure on their hunting grounds by raiding the villages of newcomers, both white and Indian, and stealing horses and whatever else they could find.

On the two-thousand-mile ribbon of territory that historian Jay Gitlin calls the Creole Corridor, stretching down the Mississippi River from the Great Lakes to New Orleans, earlier European settlers had taken collaboration a good deal further. Theirs was a society based on trade, and trade imposed its own imperatives. Like other Indian traders, the French fur traders knew from the beginning that the only way to establish a solid trading relationship with another culture was to join it. From the early eighteenth century onwards, French and Indians lived in neighboring villages, learned each other's languages and customs, and intermarried.[2] Indian wives were an essential part of the trading culture. The food they grew nourished their families, their relationships with their villages facilitated trade, and their work cleaning and preparing skins made it possible to transport and sell the tanned hides.[3]

In the fur-trading town of St. Louis, the rich and cosmopolitan Chouteau family sent its sons to live in Osage villages and marry Osage wives.[4] In the agricultural village of Ste. Genevieve eighty miles north of Greenville, the children of Indian mothers, known as "métis," were often raised in their fathers' French families, married respectable French citizens and were accepted as French themselves.[5] Indians traded, visited, and strolled through the streets of Ste. Genevieve, and their children played in the streets with the white and black children of their neighbors.

The openness of the French "habitants" to a relationship of equality with their Indian neighbors reflected their long experience in the intercultural "middle ground" plus a habit of mind generally more relaxed and tolerant than that of the Anglo-American settlers. Like the Americans, the French owned slaves, but compared to the Americans, their acceptance of slavery was noticeably lacking in racial contempt. Their records contain several instances of black women who were freed and who subsequently married white husbands. One freed slave, Elizabeth D'Archurut, successfully sued the estate of her former owner, the father of her ten children, claiming that she and her children were entitled to a share of his estate.[6] The French Code Noir, slightly more humane than the slave laws of most southern states, allowed whipping and mutilation of slaves but not the separation of children from their parents, limited work to daylight hours, mandated proper clothing, food and shelter, and forbade sexual coercion of enslaved women. In St. Louis and Ste. Genevieve, slaves had Sundays to themselves and could hire out their own time and keep their wages, even though that practice was in violation of the Code.[7]

French women also enjoyed greater influence and a more active role in society than their American counterparts. Most contemporary observers attributed this influence to the women's control of their own property.[8] Under French law, unlike Anglo-American common law, sons and daughters inherited equal shares of a parent's estate, and when a woman married, her property did not become the property of her husband but rather part of the family "communauté." On the death of either spouse, half of that communauté went to the survivor as opposed to the one-third that was the widow's share under Anglo-American common law. Marriage contracts also provided for a dower, contributed by the husband for the support of his wife if he should predecease her.

Another source of women's influence in French community life was their responsibility for family affairs during their husbands' prolonged absences. Hunting, fur trading, mining, and river-based commerce took men away for long periods, during which their wives had to manage the family farms and businesses, collect debts, and pay the bills. Names of white and free black women appear as plaintiffs in numerous court cases, even though the women themselves were generally illiterate.[9]

One of the most striking differences between the culture of the French towns and that of the English-speaking borderers who were soon to overwhelm them was the French emphasis on communal harmony. The typical French village in the Mississippi Valley consisted of three parts: a cluster of closely spaced houses; a large field, divided into long strips owned by individual families but enclosed by a communally maintained fence; and a common area of woodland where everyone's livestock was pastured. Both French and American commentators described the geniality and family-like feeling of French village society. The church rather than the courthouse was the center of the community, and the house of the village or town commandant served as both court and social center. Lawsuits were regarded as an evil to be discouraged at all costs, and conflicts were normally resolved through informal arbitration by a local authority. Dancing was a universal passion. Children danced at their own balls, where manners and proper decorum were taught along with the dances. Astonishingly, the colonial records of Ste. Genevieve contain no instance of French-on-French violence.[10]

Some features of American border society were strikingly lacking in the French towns. Self-sufficiency, for instance, was not a value. The inventories of French estates contain no spinning wheels or looms; French colonial policy decreed that colonists should produce and export only raw materials and should import all their manufactured goods from the mother country.[11] There were also no water-powered grist mills. In spite of several attempts, no

French entrepreneur in the upper Mississippi Valley succeeded in getting one to work properly until the beginning of the nineteenth century. Before that, grain was ground in the most ancient way, by a horse-driven mill.[12]

Everything changed with the Louisiana Purchase—slowly at first, and then with the force of an avalanche. When the Bettises arrived on the St. Francis, traditional patterns of intercultural trade and cooperation were still the norm. But by 1818, the American victory in the War of 1812 had made the newly acquired territory safer and more inviting, the board of commissioners had finally finished sorting out the Spanish land claims, and federal land had finally gone on sale. The thousands of new settlers descending on the trans-Mississippi frontier brought with them new technology, new skills, new agricultural methods, and new entrepreneurial energy. By the time Missouri achieved statehood in 1821, they were establishing taverns, ferries, stores, tanyards, and ropewalks. They had founded newspapers—two of them in Jackson, the nearest sizable town to Greenville. They founded schools, spurring the conservative and mostly illiterate French habitants to start educating their own children.[13]

They also brought with them a culture of violence, lawlessness, and racial contempt. Even before the transfer, a horrified French priest had described the society on the American side of the river: "Wantonness and drunkenness pass here as elegance and amusements quite in style. Breaking of limbs, murder by means of a dagger, sabre or sword are common, and pistols and guns are but toys in these regions."[14] After the transfer, violence, fraud, robbery, and mayhem spread up and down the river and out onto the plains and the rough hills. Pirates hid out on islands waiting to rob travelers while organized gangs of robbers terrorized towns.[15]

In the longer-settled areas of the South, dueling had evolved into a formal ritual that rarely involved the death of a combatant. As one traveled farther west, however, such combats became less controlled and far more deadly. The duel in which Andrew Jackson killed Dickinson was not his only combat: he and Governor Sevier once almost killed each other in a chance meeting on the road, and later on, Jackson and several armed friends were involved in a brawl with the future Missouri Senator Thomas Hart Benton that nearly cost Jackson his life. Still later, in Missouri, two political rivals got into a quarrel that began with aspersions on each other's character. When they met in a public square, they both started shooting, and one ran into a nearby tavern with the other in pursuit. The gunfight continued in the tavern with the pursuer eventually dying of his wounds. The survivor was not prosecuted. Whether or not a malefactor was prosecuted for such an offense apparently depended on his social standing and political connections, or perhaps on whether the authorities were too scared of him to indict.[16]

The arriving Americans thought the French were lazy, conservative, unambitious, and much too fond of dancing.[17] The French thought the Americans were rude, thieving, litigious barbarians.[18] The Reverend Timothy Flint, who spent several years in this area, thought that the Americans profited by the comparison. "They are destitute of the forms and observances of society and religion," he remarked,

> but they are sincere and kind without professions, and have a
> coarse, but substantial morality, which is often rendered more

striking by the immediate contrast of the graceful bows, civility, and professions of their French Catholic neighbors, who have the observances of society and the forms of worship, with often but a scanty modicum of the blunt truth and uprightness of their unpolished neighbors.[19]

Along the St. Francis River, relations between white settlers and relocated Indian tribes remained good. But elsewhere in the state, newly arriving Americans, many of them from Tennessee and Kentucky and with recent memories of deadly conflicts, brought with them a ferocious hatred of all Indians. The hatred was exaggerated by the growing scarcity of unclaimed land and by the new settlers' insistence on ignoring restrictions and on settling wherever they wanted, whether or not the land had been granted to Indians. Popular voices began to call for "slaying every Indian from here to the Rocky Mountains." Senator Thomas Hart Benton described the existence of Indian communities within the state as "a palpable evil."[20] When William Clark, who as territorial governor had attempted to ensure fair treatment for the Indians, was overwhelmingly defeated in the first post-statehood election, the end of the multicultural border was in sight.

20. Six Indictments, Four Lawsuits, and Perhaps a Murder

The Bettises and their relatives were among the early arrivals, and their isolated location allowed the collaborative patterns of intercultural life to continue longer than in other areas of Missouri. Supporting these patterns were commercial interests much like those of the peoples who were there when they arrived. Perhaps a day's ride to the north of Greenville, on the upper St. Francis, were two Shawnee villages, while a Delaware and three more Shawnee villages lay near Cape Girardeau to the east.[1] To the south and west, on the White and Current rivers, lived a large group of Cherokees.[2] The Bettis clan and other St. Francis residents maintained peaceful and mutually beneficial relationships with all of them except for the still unpacified Osage. Ezekiel Rubottom, a blacksmith and gunsmith, is said to have been a favorite with the Delaware because he kept their guns in good working order.[3] Isaac Kelly and his family, resettled on the Current River, traded with the Cherokees.

The commercial activities of the Bettis clan also brought them into contact with the tolerant, diverse, and thoroughly mercantile French (but increasingly French-American) community to the north. One clue to this contact is what local historian Hal Bennett called the "French" style of an old log house still standing in the 1940s. Bennett described this house as "the old Bettis house," and commented that " . . . the method of construction . . . certainly looks French. This was the style in old St. Louis as well as Cape Girardeau and Ste. Genevieve."[4] The houses of those old French towns were strikingly different from the boxy houses of the newly arrived

Americans. They were built of vertical rather than horizontal logs, with a steeply pitched central roof that spread out at the level of the first floor ceiling into two gently sloping symmetrical sides, giving the roof the look of a witch's hat or a large bird in the process of alighting. Under one or both of these side roofs, a wide porch ran the full length of the house, sometimes turning a corner to run the full length of the adjacent side.[5] If a house of this distinctive pattern was built in Greenville during the years the Bettises lived there, it would almost certainly have been built by a Frenchman.

Perhaps Joseph Labbé built it. The Labbé family appears to have had an ongoing relationship with the Bettises. They lived in the village of St. Michel about thirty-six miles north of Greenville on the former Southwest Trail, which by then had come to be known as the Red River Road. By 1822, that road was already a major north-south route, and Joseph Labbé and Ransom Bettis were doing business with each other. An affidavit from a long-running lawsuit, lasting until 1827 and costing the parties far more than the amount at issue, indicates that Ransom sold several lots of "cider royl" to a third party, who then sold three of them back to Ransom in a complicated transaction involving a note from a fourth party and a partial payment by Labbé. When the deal went bad and one of the other parties filed suit, Ransom (whose name switches between Ransom and Ranson in the course of his deposition) acted as a witness for Labbé.[6]

By 1831, the three Bettis brothers had left Missouri and moved south to Lawrence County Arkansas—and so had Joseph Labbé, his wife, Roddé, and two sons, Alfred and Ambrose. After only a few years, however, the Labbé family began moving back to Missouri, one member at a time. In 1839 in Ste. Genevieve, Ambrose Labbé married an Ann Betts, whose parentage is unknown. A year later the entire family had moved again, to the free state of Illinois.[7]

Labbé's wife, Rhoda or Roddé Christie, began life as a mulatto slave in Virginia. She was sold two or three times, transported to Missouri, and purchased in 1800 by a Frenchman named Pierre Viriat, part owner of Mine La Motte in the center of the lead mining district west of Ste. Genevieve. A year later, Viriat freed her, and two days after that he married her. The list of witnesses at their wedding includes the names of several of the leading families of Ste. Genevieve and St. Louis, some of whom had traveled thirty or forty miles to be there.

In violation of the provisions of the Code Noir prohibiting the separation of enslaved children from their parents, Roddé's two children had remained in slavery with her former owner. Viriat only bought and freed them towards the end of his life, perhaps to ensure that Roddé would stay with him. Shortly before Viriat's death in 1806, Joseph Labbé, who was soon to become his executor, devised an elaborate protective scheme that ensured that the children would not be reenslaved. By 1809, Joseph was married to Roddé.[8]

But when the Labbé family returned from Arkansas to Missouri thirty years later, the world had changed. Beginning in 1836, free people of color like Roddé and her children had to show proof of their freedom and pay to post a bond in order to remain in the state. Like many other free mixed-race families, they had to move on.

The names of Bettis girls born in Missouri between 1805 and 1830 suggest an effort to assert the family's social status within this fluid and constantly changing world. Dr. Elijah's daughters, Sally

Bettis Alston and Lovely Bettis Matthews, named most of their sons after their brothers Ransom, Overton, and Elijah III—an indication both of family closeness and of just who counted on the St. Francis River. But their brothers did not return the compliment. Instead they gave their daughters fanciful literary names—Cinderella, Narcissa, and Charnelcy.

The family's ascendancy, however, was short-lived. Along with their entrepreneurial energy and their generous supply of enslaved labor, the Bettises brought with them the American habits of violence, self-assertion, and litigiousness that so horrified the civilized French. The black sheep of the family was apparently Lovely's husband, Edward H. Matthews. Or at least Edward, at one point, had a really bad three years. Between 1814 and 1816 he was indicted no fewer than five times: twice for assault and battery, once on his wife's nephew Pleasant Rubottom and once on David Logan's brother Alison/Ellison Logan; once for brawling in the street with a neighbor "to the great terror and fright and disturbance of the good people of the Territory;" and twice for obstructing a constable. Lovely herself played some role in the ongoing hostilities: among the yellowed files is another containing an indictment against Isaiah Swann for assault and battery on "Loveda" Matthews.[9]

All post-statehood judicial records of Wayne County were destroyed in a courthouse fire in 1854. And many of the surviving territorial records in the Cape Girardeau County Archives had not yet been collated or indexed as of 2013, but were still gathering dust in boxes on the archive shelves. So we cannot tell whether the absence of any indexed records of the dispositions of these cases indicates that Edward was convicted or acquitted or whether the charges were simply dismissed. Nor can we tell whether he settled down after 1816 or whether the records of his subsequent misdeeds have been lost. But his reputation for violence seems to have spawned a favorite myth among the later residents of the county. "The fatal quarrel between the sons-in-law of Doctor Elijah Bettis is well known," says Rose Fulton Cramer without providing a date or documentation for this knowledge. Elsewhere she cites "several histories" for the story that Lovely Bettis's husband "Elijah Matthews" killed Sally Bettis's husband "William Alston" with a handspike but was acquitted at trial on the grounds of self-defense.[10]

There are several problems with this story. According to Janet Puckett, a descendant of Edward and Lovely, Elijah Matthews was their eldest son, born about 1806 and probably still a child when Alston died.[11] The alleged trial does not appear anywhere in the surviving territorial or post-statehood records of Missouri, or at least in those that have so far been indexed. And there is strong evidence that Mr. Alston's first name was not William. Whatever his name, he appears in no record of the area either pre- or post-statehood—not as a landowner, not as a town official like every one of his in-laws except Matthews, and not as a plaintiff, defendant, or victim in any available court case. The pre-statehood Missouri censuses have not survived, but in the leading family of a community this small, this absence is nevertheless striking. It is possible that the alleged homicide and trial took place after the establishment of the county in 1819 and that the records were among those lost in the fire. But it seems more likely that Alston died early on, before the county was established.

This conjecture is supported by the statement of a descendant of Ezekiel Rubottom to the effect that the quarrel occurred "a short time" after the two families had moved to Otter Creek.[12] In 1825, Edward Matthews was still around and apparently on good terms with his in-laws, since, as we shall see, Ransom was present at a pre-election gathering at his house. Perhaps there was a quarrel followed by an accident for which Matthews was blamed or a homicide that for some reason was never prosecuted, but the story of the famous murder appears less and less likely the more closely it is examined. But who was the victim, anyway?

Sally Bettis was about thirty years old when she married him in 1805 or 1806. She had four known sons in the next ten years, and like her sister Lovely, she named the first three after her brothers: Elijah Bettis Alston, Overton Bettis Alston, and Ransom Drew Alston. The fourth one was James S. (Smith?) Alston. All four appear as householders in the little town of Spadra, Arkansas, between 1834 and 1839, suggesting that the youngest was born no later than about 1815.[13] Ransom Drew Alston had a son named Drew. There were no Drew families in Wayne County, Missouri; Moore County, North Carolina; nor any of the counties adjacent to Moore; and no Drews plausibly associated with any member of this line of Bettises before about 1826. A Drew Bettis, born between 1810 and 1820, parents unknown, can be found in Crittenden County, Arkansas, in 1840, but he does not appear in any genealogy of the Elijah line and is probably the descendant of a distant or unrelated branch of the family.[14]

There is only one convincing explanation for the appearance of the name Drew in this Bettis family. At the time of the siege of his House in the Horseshoe by David Fanning's Loyalist guerillas, Colonel Phil Alston, the "tyrannical" Patriot leader, Moore County official, and possible instigator of the murder of Dr. George Glascock, was married to Temperance Drew Smith, the daughter of Drew Smith, a distant cousin of Newit. Temperance won fame during the siege by coming out of her house with a flag of truce, facing her husband's enemies, and persuading them not to burn the house down with the family inside.[15] According to a later history of the Drew Smith family, "Temperance Smith and Philip Alston had sons James, John, Philip, and Drew."[16] The wives and children of the first three are known in detail. James, the oldest, took an active role in the sale of Connor Dowd's property after the Revolution. Of Drew Alston, however, almost nothing is known: no wife, no children, no place of death. Only one fact can be gleaned from the records on ancestry.com: the year of his death, 1813.

It is at least plausible that Sally was married to the son of Phil Alston, the ferocious enemy of her uncle Connor Dowd and the man whose house her cousin Reuben Shields had helped to besiege. Supporting this hypothesis is the notation in the 1850 federal census that her oldest son, Elijah Alston, was born in 1805 in Georgia, where Phil Alston's family remained after his death. The given name James, which like Drew appears nowhere else in the family, may have been given to her youngest son in honor of Drew Alston's oldest brother.

The reformation of Edward Matthews, if that's what it was, did not bring peace to Wayne County. Within a year or two of the establishment of the county, tension had begun to develop between the sons of two of the original settlers, David Logan and Dr. Elijah

Bettis. The gathering animosity came to the surface in the course of an election campaign in 1825 in which Elijah III was a candidate. The resulting dispute nearly broke the county apart and illuminates for us not only the combative spirit of this border community but also the dramatic change in the public perception of Freemasonry in the course of the 1820s. Nearly two hundred years later, the staff of the Cape Girardeau County Archives disinterred the records for me, a stack of crumbling documents in manila file folders stored in a cardboard box on the archive shelves among the one-third of the archive records that have so far been indexed—and they let me handle them without gloves.

As related by Isaac Kelly and numerous others in depositions given in two of the four lawsuits arising from the incident, a group of men including Elijah III's brother Ransom Bettis and David Logan's son James were gathered at the house of Edward Matthews on March 10, 1825, shortly before the election. Logan, who opposed Elijah's candidacy, offered to read an affidavit by "one Folsum"—apparently the Patriot colonel mentioned earlier in this narrative, who spent his time during the Revolution hunting down Loyalists—containing an accusation of "Toryisum" against the elder Elijah. Ransom challenged him to read it aloud, and he did so and then went on to say that he would read them something else.

While hardly anyone could remember the content of the first document, the second one caught their attention, because Logan was reading from a book or sheaf of paper that he held in his hand which he said was a copy of the Masonic *Book of Constitutions* belonging to Elijah Bettis III. He said that he had obtained the book from his aunt several years earlier when they were gathering together the scattered possessions of his aunt's family left behind by Osage Indians who had raided their house. He also said that he had kept the book concealed in hollow logs and hollow trees for six or seven years, knowing that it was Elijah's.[17] Several other members of the Logan family were in on the secret. One witness testified in his deposition that he had remarked to John Logan, the justice of the peace in whose house many of the depositions were taken, that "... if Doctor Bettis [Elijah III, who also practiced medicine] could get holt of the book he might put some of us to trouble. Mr. John Logan stated that [illegible] he don't get holt of it I have it under lock and key."[18]

There is no evidence that Logan's public readings did any damage to Elijah's political career. He was elected to a third term as state representative for the term beginning in 1826 and then to the state Senate in 1828. There were numerous Masons in the French towns to the north,[19] and Elijah's brother-in-law Ezekiel Rubottom, who is also said to have been a Mason, had an even longer and more distinguished political history than Elijah. Nevertheless, Logan's public contempt for Elijah and his family, his boasts about his theft and concealment of the book, and his revelation of Masonic secrets supposed to be guarded from the general public infuriated Elijah. If he and Logan had aspired to the status of gentlemen, the insult might have resulted in a duel. As it was, Elijah merely insisted that a grand jury be empaneled to indict Logan for the theft of the book. The grand jurors—at least three of whom had actually been among the witnesses to the incident!—returned the indictment. Evidently no trial took place, for in subsequent documents Logan referred only to "my indictment" and not to "my trial" or "my conviction."[20]

Logan, however, was not about to let Elijah get the better of him. It was not merely the reputations of the two men that were at stake but the deeper question of which family would exercise power in the community. Logan's next move was a suit against Elijah for "Trespass on the Case" (slander), based on a statement by Elijah to the effect that Logan was a "dam'd thief." The suit, which was eventually transferred to Cape Girardeau County in spite of Elijah's objections that Logan exercised "an undue influence over the minds of the inhabitants of said county," took two years and involved a total of nineteen witnesses. Astonishingly, although everyone involved, including Logan himself, agreed that Logan had taken the book and concealed it for several years while knowing it belonged to Bettis, Logan managed to win the case and to recover six hundred dollars in damages.

While the first case was still in progress, Logan filed another. It appears that Elijah had incautiously allowed himself to become indebted to his enemy in the amount of $1,200—the price of two or three prime slaves—and Logan sued him for that too, and won. Elijah countersued for "trespass and false imprisonment," in a case that took twelve days and involved thirteen witnesses, many of them the same people as in the previous case. He won the case but was awarded only his costs, a total of $196.37¼. At the end of the original suit, Logan paid him those costs with a scrawled note designed to remind him that Logan had, after all, come out on top. In all other documents in these cases that bear Logan's signature, that signature appears in a scrawl similar to the handwriting in the note. On this note, however, the signature is formal, upright and

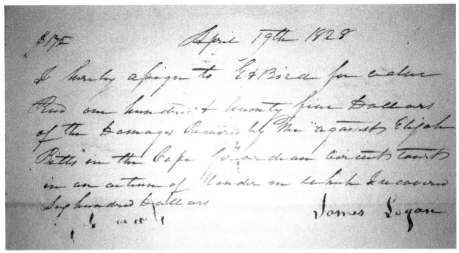

Assignment by James Logan to Elijah Bettis of $175 out of the $600 damages recovered by Logan from Elijah. The difference between the assigned amount and the judgment of 196.37^{1/4}$ in Elijah's favor most likely reflects the sheriff's fees involved.

stylized, in elegant italic script with broad artistic downstrokes. If ever a signature could be said to express sardonic contempt, this is the one.

Logan was not yet finished with Elijah. After the judgment in the suit for debt, but while the first suit was still in progress, he filed another, this time for "Trespass and Malicious Prosecution." The claim here was that Elijah, in obtaining the original indictment, had acted out of malice and somehow tampered with the grand jury. Twenty witnesses were deposed in this third suit. All of the members of the grand jury were subpoenaed and asked to state the exact reason for their vote on the indictment, what evidence had been presented, and by whom. Other witnesses were asked about a statement allegedly made by Elijah to the effect that, if he had a jury like those they had had in North Carolina, he would have made

Logan "hug the widow Sharan"— the nickname for a tree on which a horse thief had once been whipped.

In 1828, after Elijah had already been elected to the state Senate, the first suit was finally decided in Logan's favor, and the third was settled, on what terms we do not know. A significant percentage of the white men in the county had been required to testify on one side or the other. Logan had not only defeated but humiliated Elijah on all counts. The balance of power in Wayne County had shifted decisively. "The lawsuit was said to have had a bad effect on the county," says Rose Fulton Cramer with spectacular understatement.[21]

The verdicts in these cases leave one question unanswered. Why would Logan's public reading of the *Constitutions* have been expected to injure Elijah, as Logan obviously meant to do? Ever since the Revolution, Americans had largely accepted the Masons' own self-image as a corps of enlightened leaders committed to the advancement of education, religion, and democracy, training their members in courtesy and self-control for the benefit of all. One would have thought that an association with Freemasonry was something to be published rather than concealed. But the public consensus was already shifting in ways that were invisible to members of the fraternity and to many later historians as well.

American Freemasonry in 1825 was at the peak of its power and prestige. Religiously-based hostility, which had been widespread a generation earlier among Christian sects jealous of their own hold on ultimate truth, was diminishing as more and more respectable clergymen joined the Freemasons.[22] Everywhere in the nation, in communities large and small, a significant proportion—sometimes even the majority—of officeholders and community leaders were

Masons.[23] Ambitious men like Elijah Bettis III found in the fraternity connections that helped to propel them into positions of power. Grand new Masonic halls were erected, their sumptuous furnishings proclaiming both the dignity of the fraternity and its increasing claims to quasi-religious significance. A multitude of new degrees was also established, centered on highly emotional rituals that served to identify the organization with Christianity itself.[24]

Intoxicated with its own success, the fraternity was overreaching. Although it claimed to be promoting the welfare of society as a whole, its increasing size and diversity meant that more and more of its charitable efforts were directed specifically to fellow Masons. Most dangerous, from the point of view of its public image, was the requirement that brothers give preference to fellow Masons in business transactions, as well as in hiring, over "any other person in the same circumstances."[25] The growing sense that Freemasonry was perhaps too powerful, that it conferred an unfair advantage upon its members in a competitive and individualistic economy, created a combustible layer of suspicion and resentment that wanted only a spark to set it aflame.

The spark that ignited this tinder was the kidnapping and presumed murder of William Morgan, a renegade Mason from Batavia, New York, who had been threatening to publish a book revealing the secrets of Masonry. On September 10, 1826, local brothers procured the arrest of Morgan on an imaginary charge. He was bailed out the next day by a man who then forced him into a carriage and carried him off as Morgan shouted "Murder! Murder!" He was never seen again.

As always in such cases, the cover-up by powerful local Masons was more damaging than the crime itself. Investigations were blocked, juries were packed with Masons, potential witnesses were intimidated into keeping silent; the fraternity, in short, did everything it could to justify the hostility that had already begun to smolder.[26] Within a year, the case had flamed up into a wildfire of antimasonic hysteria that all but destroyed the organization in the northern states. The fire gave birth to the first national single-issue party, the Antimasonic party, which lasted for six or seven years before finally sputtering out. It took the fraternity until the 1840s to recover, and it never regained its former influence.[27]

Even Steven Bullock, the most thorough and objective of all writers on the subject, tends to attribute the Antimasonic catastrophe solely to the Morgan kidnap/murder. But like any other flareup of popular hatred, this one needed the right conditions for ignition. James Logan's purloining and concealing of Elijah Bettis's Masonic book sometime before 1820 and his use of that book in an attempt to discredit Elijah in 1825 give us a clue about the resentment against the fraternity that was already simmering, a resentment of which its members were largely unaware. And the astonishing verdict in Logan's favor in the slander case in 1828, in spite of the fact that Logan had publicly admitted to the theft of the book, can perhaps be understood in the light of the crime and coverup that had discredited all Masons two years earlier. Some of the next generation of Bettises, however, remained committed to Masonry, showing up later on in California as high-level members.

21. Departures

By the time the lawsuits ended, Missouri had changed in many ways. The most dramatic of these changes was the arrival of the steamboats, beginning in 1817. Before steam, the journey upriver from New Orleans to St. Louis had required weeks or even months of backbreaking labor. Steamboats cut this time to nine days there and back.[1] Timothy Flint, who lived through the transition, describes the exhilaration of the new mode of transportation:

> It is now refreshing, and imparts a feeling of energy and power to the beholder, to see the large and beautiful steamboats scudding up the eddies, as though on the wing; and when they have run out the eddy, strike the current. The foam bursts in a sheet quite over the deck. She quivers for a moment with the concussion, and then, as though she had collected all her energy, and vanquished her enemy, she resumes her stately march and mounts against the current, five or six miles an hour.[2]

The new ease of travel was a stimulus to commerce, providing the farmers and merchants of half a continent with new markets for new and more varied goods and increasing the flow of settlers to lands across the river.

That influx had less positive results for some of the inhabitants. By 1815, game was already disappearing from the Shawnee and Delaware lands, and pressure from white settlers was becoming too powerful to be resisted either by Indians or by American authorities. When the Shawnee and Delaware formally ceded their lands in 1825 and 1829, they had already left the state, and reluctantly relocated to less productive lands across the Missouri-Kansas border. The Osage, plagued by internal divisions, no longer in a position to control the fur trade, and under siege from all sides by migrating eastern tribes, ceded the last of their Missouri land in 1825. By 1829, the state of Missouri was officially empty of Indians.[3] So complete was the break with the past that some French and American fathers actually severed ties with their métis children.[4]

As the Indians were vanishing from Missouri, the familiar pattern of American race relations was reasserting itself. As on previous frontiers, once the borderers felt secure in their possession of the land and had begun to establish a stable and stratified society, they tightened the restrictions on slaves and free people of color. Slaves lost the right to do business for themselves or even to use ferries without the permission of their owners. Free people of color were forbidden to carry firearms without a special permit, and they also lost the right to testify in court against whites, a restriction that, as in eighteenth-century Virginia, effectively denied them the protection of the laws.[5] In 1825, the Missouri General Assembly passed a law forbidding any free person of color to enter or settle in the state under penalty of ten lashes and a jail term. Since the law included exceptions for people who were emancipated while in the state as well as for those who could prove that they were citizens of any state,[6] it is difficult to determine who was actually affected; but the spirit behind the law was clear.

In 1827, twenty years after their arrival in Missouri and a year after the filing of the first lawsuit, Ransom Bettis initiated the family's next move, on down the Red River Road to northeast Arkansas, just downstream from the confluence of the Black and Current rivers. There, on the high ground overlooking the Black River, he established a trading post, giving his new settlement the name of Bettis Bluff. Within a few years, his brothers Elijah and Overton had followed. Sally Bettis Alston and her four sons also moved south and then west up the Arkansas River to Johnson County, where there were numerous recently arrived Cherokees and where relations between white and Cherokee immigrants were still collaborative and sociable.[7] Edward and Lovely Bettis Matthews, still in Wayne County in 1830 with thirty slaves, moved in the opposite direction, north to the lead-mining country around Potosi.[8] Only Ezekiel Rubottom remained in Wayne County, reaching old age as a Baptist minister and respected community leader.[9]

The twenty-year rhythm that we have seen in the migrations of the Drew and Bettis families is not hard to understand. One factor was the agricultural regime that they shared with other borderers. On arriving in the new world with its sparse population and its apparently endless supply of land, English-speaking settlers abandoned such European practices as manuring and crop rotation, preferring to let their stock roam free and to exploit the cultivated land until they wore it out. Even if you moved your fields every few years, the cultivation of corn, tobacco, or cotton would eventually impoverish the soil, and wild game, a major part of most families' diets, would eventually be hunted out. In spite of the worn-out soil, however, there would be new settlers moving in behind you, hungry for cleared and settled land. And in twenty years, with any luck, you would have a couple of teenage sons to help you clear a new farm in more fertile territory.

In fact, there is a surplus of explanations for the latest move of the Bettis clan. Elijah's defeat and humiliation in the Logan lawsuits and his resulting loss of prestige in the Wayne County community may have been one of the strongest. The arrival of a group of rich slaveholding families from Virginia on the upper St. Francis, creating a neighborhood known as the Virginia Settlement, may have helped to deprive the Bettises of the pre-eminent position they had worked to achieve. The most powerful inducement, however, was the same as the one that sent Newit Drew to the Dorcheat Bayou: the new possibilities of steamboat travel. With water travel both upriver and downriver so easy, a location on a non-navigable river was becoming less attractive to aspiring entrepreneurs. The new settlement in Arkansas was on a navigable river. The Red River Road (soon to be known as the Military Road) ran past it just a few miles to the west. The Kelly family was already there as well as the former postmaster, Thomas O. Marr, then or later married to Elijah's daughter Amy Bettis, along with the niece and nephew of the old frontiersman Kasper Mansker.[10] The names of the Marr and Mansker families are preserved in the names of creeks running into the Black River near twenty-first-century Pocahontas.

A year or two before the move, a newcomer had arrived in Greenville, coming up the Red River Road from the Red River itself, in the farthest corner of Arkansas. In his mid twenties, short in stature with a gentle manner and a bookish disposition, he had already tried his hand at several occupations, including schoolteacher, clerk of the Clark County court, major in the First Regiment of Arkansas Militia,[11] and, most recently, mailman. It was probably the last of these that brought him to Greenville, since the principal mail route ran through the town along that same road. With the ambitious, entrepreneurial Bettises, with their lawsuits, their businesses, their flocks of natural children, their intense family bonds, and their rumors of fratricide, he found himself oddly at home—and most of all with the imperious, dark-eyed daughter Cinderella. Thomas Stevenson Drew was about to join the clan.

The migration to the West had changed both families. It gave scope to energies and ambitions that had no outlet in the communities from which they came. It offered them experience in creating institutions, in building and leading communities, in developing commercial enterprises, in navigating complex relation-ships between various cultures. In tightly-bound local churches and in Masonic lodges connected to continent-spanning networks, they had acquired skills needed for democratic self-government. The independence of the French women of Ste. Genevieve and the strength and self-confidence of Roddé Labbé, the former slave whose marriage to a white mine owner had been attended by the elite of the French towns, may also have served as an inspiration for more than one young Bettis woman.

Timothy Flint noticed another change among the migrating borderers. The diversity of the West, he thought, served as a spur to intellectual development and openness to new ideas. "The collisions of minds," he writes,

> that bring together different opinions, that have been swayed by
> different prejudices, and have been compelled by comparing them
> with other prejudices, which have become obvious to them when
> seen in another, to lay them aside; the result of different modes of
> education and thinking compared together—all these things tend
> to form a society, when it becomes new molded and constituted
> in such a state of things, more free from prejudices, and in some
> respects more pleasant, than in those older countries, where the

population, manners, opinions and prejudices are more generally of one class.[12]

But more than all these, their journeys had imbued the Drews and Bettises with the belief that there would always be something better, just over the next horizon. For better or worse, their migrations had taught them the habit of hope.

Part VI
The Accidental Governor

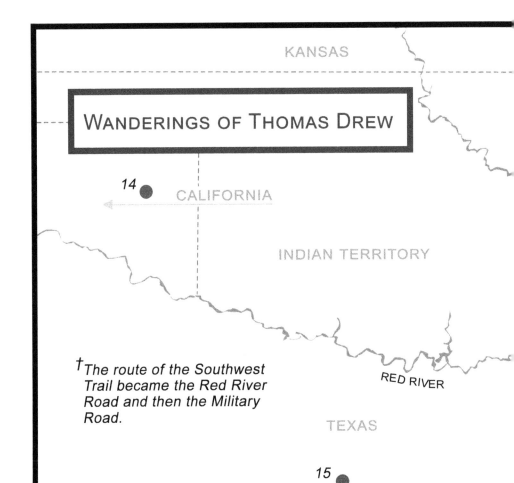

WANDERINGS OF THOMAS DREW

KANSAS

CALIFORNIA

14 ●

INDIAN TERRITORY

†The route of the Southwest
Trail became the Red River
Road and then the Military
Road.

RED RIVER

TEXAS

15 ●

KEY

1. PECAN TOWNSHIP : 1818
2. MISSOURI TOWNSHIP : 1821
3. MONROE LOUISIANA : 1823
4. CADDO TOWNSHIP, CLARK COUNTY : 1824
5. GREENVILLE MISSOURI : 1827
6. POCAHONTAS ARKANSAS : 1828
7. LITTLE ROCK/POCAHONTAS : 1836 - 1848
8. DESHA COUNTY : 1850

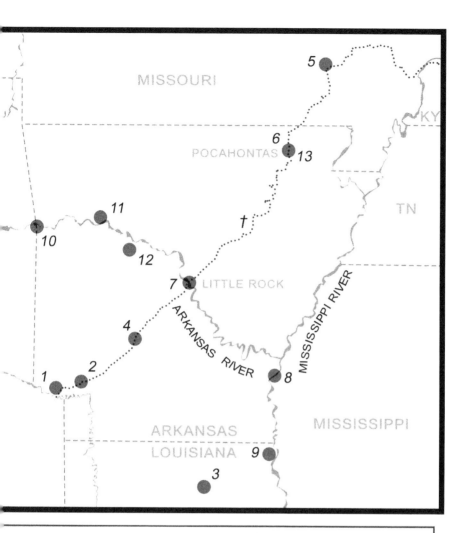

KEY

9. LAKE PROVIDENCE LOUISIANA : 1852
10. FORT SMITH : 1853 - 1861
11. CLARKSVILLE : 1862
12. DARDANELLE : 1863
13. POCAHONTAS : 1866
14. SAN BERNARDINO CALIFORNIA : 1875
15. LIPAN TEXAS : 1877

22. Cherokee Bay

De Tocqueville hitched a ride with a frontier mailman in 1831 and left us with an unforgettable image:

> We advanced briskly night and day by scarcely cleared paths in the middle of immense forests of green trees; when the darkness became impenetrable, my guide lit branches of larch and we continued our route by their light. Here and there one encountered a cottage in the middle of the woods; it was the post office. The courier threw an enormous packet of letters at the door of the isolated dwelling and we continued our course at a gallop, leaving to each inhabitant in the neighborhood the care of coming to seek his part of the treasure.[1]

He might have been describing one part of Thomas Drew's early life.

The mail route, however, was only one part of Drew's activities during the 1820s. His education served him well; traces of it can be seen in his elegant handwriting, his usually clear and cogent prose, and his unusually good spelling. We know from one of his later letters that in the winter of 1823 he was teaching school in Monroe, Louisiana, where his brother James had settled.[2] Some rather dubious versions of his life story have him traveling through Arkansas as a peddler during the summer; other historians dismiss that idea as absurd.[3] From 1824 to 1827 he served as clerk of court for Clark County, Arkansas, and justice of the peace in Caddo Township, positions in which he could have acquired the legal training that formed the basis for several of his future careers.[4] He was a major and then general in the First Regiment of Arkansas Militia,[5] was appointed postmaster of Clark County in 1825, and at the same time contracted for several postal routes. When a federal law barred postmasters from taking on both positions, he opted for the postal routes, which allowed him to earn more money.[6] A faint whiff of his future troubles can already be detected in a court notice published three times in the *Arkansas Gazette* in April of 1828: in the case of John Clover vs. Thomas S. Drew, since Thomas S. Drew was no longer an inhabitant of Clark County, an order was to issue for the attachment of his remaining Clark County estate "in the penal sum of one hundred dollars."[7]

With his marriage to Cinderella Bettis on February 3, 1827,[8] much of this earlier history became irrelevant. His father-in-law, by then spelling his name "Ranson,"[9] set him up as a landowner in the area known as Cherokee Bay on the east side of the Current River, with eight hundred acres and twelve slaves.[10] With his newly-acquired land and slaves, he was transformed overnight from a penniless mailman to one of the richest ten percent of Arkansas settlers.[11] Separated by choice from his own family, he threw himself into the arms of the Bettis clan. For the rest of his life, many of his closest associates were Cinderella's cousins.

Thomas and Cinderella were my great-great-grandparents, and Thomas is the only character in this history who left enough traces for us to form a picture of him as a person. One of the discoveries that set this book in motion was a small green folder in a back corner of my attic. It contained handwritten scraps of his correspondence and a couple of puzzling drafts of official documents, the only bits of his writing that had managed to survive the passage of four generations. They reveal a complex personality, a mild and conciliatory man struggling for wealth and status in a chaotic era and finding them more than once only to lose them again. His experiences, entirely individual, help to illuminate the dreams, disorders, and cataclysms of the times and places in which he lived.

Cherokee Bay was located in the area that later became Randolph County, on the border between two major regions of the Arkansas Territory. To the east of the Current River stretched the rich, level lands of the Mississippi delta. Immediately to the west rose the gentle foothills of the Ozarks. The area is far north of the thirty-fourth parallel, usually considered the northern limit for profitable cotton production, and although cotton was grown there for most of the nineteenth century, it produced no great fortunes. The town of Bettis Bluff was not located on the new Military Road, formerly the Red River Road or Southwest Trail, which crossed the Elevenpoint River a few miles to the west at Pitman's Ferry. But if your ambition was to operate a trading post, a location at the confluence of two navigable rivers may have been a better bet than one on a road whose design requirements were that twelve-inch-diameter trees in the roadbed be cut to a height no greater than eight inches.[12]

Ranson's trading post served the hunters and trappers of the Ozark highlands to the west as well as the increasingly numerous farmers on the Black and Current rivers to the north. Deerskins, furs, and beeswax along with some agricultural products came down to the post on packhorses. Up the river, at first by keelboat but very soon by steam, came flour, salt, whiskey, coffee, and calico.[13] The first steamboat arrived on the Black River in 1829, and a few years later, they were running up the Current River as far as the Drew Farm.[14] By 1836, Ranson was also managing the ferry across the Black

River, paying an annual license fee of two dollars. Mr. Pitman, on the Elevenpoint, was paying five dollars.[15]

In the fertile lands to the east of the Current River, the Drews and their slaves set up their farm. Their house would still have been built of logs, but it was probably either a two-story house or a dogtrot house consisting of two adjacent cabins with a roofed corridor, open at both ends, running between them. In either case the house would have had at least two and perhaps as many as four rooms plus a separate kitchen and other outbuildings, including a smokehouse, a barn, and smaller cabins for the slaves.[16]

For the young wife, Cinderella, the first years must have been difficult in the extreme. Her mother, Mary Kelly, the daughter of an Indian trader, was certainly no stranger to work. Married into a richer family, she would still have been actively involved in the running of her household and would have been careful to pass her housekeeping skills on to her daughter. One skill, however, was never easy for a seventeen-year-old bride to master: the effective exercise of authority in the management of slaves. Giving orders to the nurse who raised you, the cook who had chased you out of the kitchen, or the men or women of your own age with whom you had played prisoner's base as a child demanded a degree of self-confidence and maturity rare in any young woman. Enslaved people in such a situation knew what they could get away with and occasionally responded with sauciness, deliberate incompetence, or outright defiance. In the first years of Cinderella's marriage, her efforts to establish her authority could easily have involved shouts, slaps, or the use of the small whip that wives in slaveholding families often carried with them.[17]

By the time she was twenty-one, she had given birth to three children and lost two of them within a day of each other, one at birth and the other, little Samuel, at the age of two.[18] Their nearly simultaneous deaths suggest a contagious illness from which Cinderella herself may have been lucky to recover. Lawrence Dalton's *History of Randolph County* provides a clue, citing local memories of a devastating cholera or typhoid epidemic said to have wiped out the town of Davidsonville, where Cinderella's relatives Charles and Isaac Kelly were then living.[19] Within months of this catastrophe, Cinderella must also have learned of the birth of a new baby, born in Missouri into her Uncle Elijah's slave family, the son of her twenty-five-year-old cousin Patsie. The child's name was Drew.

It would be eight years before Cinderella and Thomas had another child. Their surviving son, Ranson, perhaps a twin of the baby who died, remained for much of his childhood his mother's only consolation. We have few clues to help us imagine her life during this period. Did she move back with her parents, a short distance away in Bettis Bluff? Did she remain in angry misery on the Cherokee Bay farm until her anger finally faded and, bit by bit, she matured into her adult role? Or did the illness that killed her children leave her with such severe health problems that she was unable to resume normal life for a number of years?

We know even less about the relationship between Thomas and Patsie. It is almost certain that Elijah's enslaved concubines had no choice about whether to accept his advances: they may have resigned themselves to the inevitable or tried to gain what advantage they could out of their situation, but in our modern understanding of the term, those relationships were rape. But Thomas was not Patsie's owner, and his wife's rich uncle might have objected to an attempt to force one of the daughters on whom he had been relying for so long. And it would have been odd indeed for Patsie to have named her son after a man who had coerced her into sex. All the signs point to a consensual relationship, perhaps even an affectionate one. In giving her son that name, she was both boasting of her connection with Thomas and laying a claim on him for future support and protection—not to mention sticking a finger in the eye of her spoiled young cousin. Drew Bettis's descendants have passed down the story that Drew himself "spoke highly of both Thomas and Cinderella and said that Cinderella always treated him well."[20] If that story has a basis in fact, it indicates that at a minimum Thomas acknowledged his son and suggests the possibility of an extended connection between Thomas and Patsie, to which Cinderella, like many other southern wives, somehow managed to reconcile herself.

It is somewhat easier to imagine the experience of young Ranson during those years. He was an only child; his parents appear to have been to some degree estranged; his father was away a good deal; and in his tiny town, at the periphery of his vision, there was a light-skinned slave child exactly his age who looked a good deal like him, to whom his father paid an unusual amount of attention, and who he may already have suspected was his brother. Are we surprised to learn that he left home at nineteen and never came back?

23. "Around You Everything Moves"

The name of Cherokee Bay acknowledges the very recent presence of the several thousand Cherokees who had migrated from their eastern homeland in 1817 under pressure from white settlers and the United States government. Perhaps five thousand of them had settled in the area just to the west, between the White and Arkansas rivers.[1] For many of the full-blood Cherokees, the move was seen as a way to preserve their culture and traditions from the influence of the whites, allowing them to continue to hunt in a land where game was still plentiful and to make war on the resident Osage when war with whites had become a losing proposition. For the mixed-blood elite, on the other hand, the new territory offered the chance to establish large plantations modeled after those of the whites. The richest mixed-bloods raised cattle, fenced their fields, and acquired scores of slaves. Their wives wore English fashions and ate from English tableware. Both full-bloods and mixed-bloods preserved their own religious customs, the most important of which was the annual Green Corn Dance.[2]

S. C. Turnbo, who visited the White River area at a later date, collected stories of life in early Arkansas. They tell of white men joining the Indians on hunts, of visits by settlers to Cherokee camps to drink and gamble, and of visits by Cherokees to white settlements for similar reasons. "They were a lively crowd," recalled one informant. "White settlers visited them from far and near." When whites were present at a Green Corn Dance, they would be invited to participate, and the Indians would laugh at their awkwardness. If they smoked tobacco with the Indians, the Indians would consider them friends.[3] But those relationships changed quickly when white farmers like the Bettises started pouring in to replace early hunters and traders like the Kellys. Between 1820 and 1830 the white population of Arkansas more than doubled, from fourteen thousand to thirty thousand. Settled in Arkansas for barely a decade, the Cherokees, along with other tribes both native and resettled, were forced to move again.

Having prided themselves on their friendly relationships with white society and on the help they had given to Andrew Jackson during the Creek War, the Cherokees protested vigorously against the removal. In April of 1828, a Cherokee named Nu-Tah-E-Tuil, or No-Killer, wrote to the *Arkansas Gazette*, arguing correctly, but to no avail, that his nation was at least as "civilized" as the whites among whom they lived. The farms and gardens of the Cherokees were better tended and more productive than those of the whites, their houses better constructed, and their children more literate. "Our people have built," he wrote

> mostly at their own expense, the only Meeting house in the Territory; and though the number of truly religious people is small, and though many immoral practices prevail, yet I believe we might compare with your very best settlements in these respects. … I believe a larger portion of our youth can read and write than those in your own settlements.[4]

It was all in vain. When a delegation of Cherokees went to Washington in the same year, they were met with contempt and hate-filled rhetoric and described by the House Committee on Indian Affairs as "a miserable and degraded race."[5] The final expulsion was accompanied by more verbal abuse, as if the victorious whites felt the need to shout loud enough to drown out the voices of their own conscience.

The expulsion of the last Indians from Arkansas and Missouri was only one aspect of the social and economic transformation that began in the first half of the nineteenth century with the dawn of the industrial revolution. In many areas of the country, living standards were rising rapidly. The revolution in textile production meant that moderately well-to-do families could acquire such luxuries as curtains and rugs, and by the 1830s even upholstered furniture.[6] The availability of ready-made cloth meant that women, even in the country, could have larger wardrobes, and magazines promptly appeared to tell them what fashionable ladies of the cities were wearing.[7] Even the poorest white families could have chairs, knives, and forks. In towns and cities of the North, domestic comfort took a giant step forward with the introduction of iron cookstoves, which eliminated much of the labor of cooking in an open fireplace, while the parlor stoves that began to appear a few years later provided an even heat that made an entire room habitable in the winter months.[8]

Arkansas, poor and remote with a small and widely scattered population, experienced little of this material improvement. Up to the time of the Civil War, nearly all of its inhabitants were still living in log houses, the most elegant of which might have plank floors and inside walls finished with smoothly planed boards.[9] As late as the 1840s, in the Ozark highlands fifty miles west of Pocahontas, settlers were still subsisting on wild game and wild honey. Animal pelts, barrels of honey, and cakes of beeswax were the currency in which taxes were paid.[10]

In spite of this isolation, Arkansas was powerfully affected by the revolutions in transportation and communication that came with the arrival of steamboats and with improvements in the printing process. Steamboat travel not only increased the availability of manufactured goods, it increased the flow of knowledge and ideas. Combined with the abundance of newly inexpensive newspapers, it provided readers with access to up-to-date information about politics and events in all corners of the country. Most newspapers were openly partisan, and practices that today would be classified as libel or plagiarism were part of the normal course of business. Literate citizens, even in remote areas, were exposed to new ideas and information, and to the clash of opinions on a broad variety of local and national topics, and they consumed them all voraciously.[11]

There has never been such an age of newspaper readers. Intoxicated with the idea that they, the sovereign people, were in charge of their own government, shop clerks would put down their newspapers to give you change and draymen would read them two at a time on their way to deliver bread.[12] The noisy and ubiquitous papers connected people in distant communities with others who shared their interests and ideas. Accessible not merely to the moneyed elite, but to ordinary yeoman farmers, merchants, and lawyers, they made possible discussions about a wide range of national issues. They supported the development of broad-based political parties, allowing people of differing regional and economic backgrounds to begin to understand themselves as citizens of a national community rather than one based on face-to-face interactions within a church congregation or isolated small town. Slowly but inexorably, the chaotic society of the border was evolving towards a society of American citizens.

De Tocqueville rightly understood the wide availability of newspapers as essential to a democratic society.[13] Other foreign observers, however, were less enthusiastic. In 1827, the year of Thomas and Cinderella's marriage, the English novelist Frances Trollope came up the Mississippi River by steamboat. A few years later the English geologist George W. Featherstonehaugh (pronounced "Fanshaw") crossed Arkansas in the opposite direction over the Military Road. While de Tocqueville, the young French aristocrat, was fascinated and impressed with the workings of American democracy, the two English travelers were appalled by nearly all of it.

Mrs. Trollope's stated goal, in reporting on the new country in *Domestic Manners of the Americans*, was to convince her fellow countrymen of "how greatly the advantage is on the side of those who are governed by the few, instead of the many."[14] Featherstonehaugh was a bit more optimistic: he hoped that Americans might someday come to their senses and abandon the foolish ideal of universal (white male) suffrage in favor of government by the wise and disinterested. Featherstonehaugh was offended by the fact that *"cheap"* newspapers could distract and corrupt the minds of the working class, who couldn't have afforded them in England and would have had to read the Bible instead.[15] Trollope was considerably more offended by the third-rate poetry and literary criticism often published along with the news.[16]

All three foreigners looked around them at a rude, vigorous, graceless, and sometimes frighteningly violent society. "Around you everything moves," said de Tocqueville.

> The universal movement reigning in the United States, the frequent turns of fortune, the unforeseen displacement of public and private wealth—all unite to keep the soul in a sort of feverish agitation that admirably disposes it to every effort and maintains it so to speak above the common level of humanity.[17]

Patriotism was intense, political opinion fervent, and equality a sacred doctrine to be proclaimed on any and all occasions. Along with these beliefs came insatiable greed, disgusting table manners, and the constant spitting of tobacco on the floor, the rugs, and the dresses of any women unlucky enough to be standing near. And the appalling familiarity! On one occasion, while Trollope was living outside of Cincinnati, she went in search of two of her children who were late coming home from a walk in the woods. When she stopped at a store to ask if anyone had seen them, a woman dressed like a "Covent Garden market woman" came out and decided to accompany her in her search. "She passed her arm within mine," reported the writer with amused dismay,

> and . . . dragged me on, talking and questioning me without ceasing . . . .[M]y children, including my sons, she always addressed by their Christian names, excepting when she substituted the word "honey."[18]

All three travelers also remarked on the "want of gaiety" of Americans, who refused to let any public amusement or any influence of art or culture distract them from their total preoccupation with making money. Money, said Featherstonehaugh, was "the grand exclusive object of their existence," "the all-prevailing passion," and the sole measure of standing or distinction in American society.[19] And everyone ate everything, even pudding, from the points of their knives.[20]

There were few subjects on which Trollope and de Tocqueville saw eye to eye, but on one topic they agreed: the rigid restrictions on the social and economic roles of American women. de Tocqueville noted that public opinion "carefully confines woman within the small circle of interests and domestic duties, and forbids her to leave it."[21] Trollope deplored the "sevenfold shield of habitual insignificance" that denied women any role or voice in public affairs. Throughout her travels in the western states, on steamboats, in hotel dining rooms, in private gatherings, and at public balls, she noted the enforced segregation of the sexes, by which women were literally denied seats at the tables and entrance to the more comfortable public spaces. At Cincinnati's elegant Washington's Birthday ball, the men ate their dinners off a table in a large, well-furnished room while their wives and daughters had plates brought out to them in the ballroom and balanced them on their laps. When Trollope asked about the reason for this practice, she was told that "the men liked it better."

Not unreasonably, she blamed the segregation of the sexes for what she called the "total and universal want of manners" and "the total want of all the usual courtesies of the table." Rather than a social occasion, Trollope said, a meal at a hotel or on a steamboat more nearly resembled a collection of swine at a feeding trough, where male diners rushed to the table to devour their food in the shortest possible time, and then rushed out again, without having exchanged a word. In fact, she would have " . . . infinitely preferred sharing the apartment of a party of well-conditioned pigs to . . . being confined in [a steamboat's] cabin."[22]

There was, however, one sphere of life in which women were allowed a voice, a public emotional outlet, and sometimes even a leadership role, a sphere that only Trollope bothered to discuss. De Tocqueville, the French rationalist, paid it only minimal attention. Featherstonehaugh ignored it entirely. Trollope, who in spite of her disdain remains one of our best observers of everyday life in that era, investigated it thoroughly and with what seems like a rather pleasurable thrill of horror. The "second Great Awakening" was underway, and Methodist, Baptist, Congregationalist, and Presbyterian preachers were fanning out across the western states to bring religion to the multitudes of the unchurched. At prayer meetings in private homes, at revivals in large churches, and at multi-day camp meetings attended by thousands, Trollope observed the same "frightful" paroxysms of faith. At a camp meeting attended by two thousand people, the young women who had come forward ended up "lying on the ground in an indescribable confusion of heads and legs," while " . . . hysterical sobbings, convulsive groans, shrieks and screams the most appalling, burst forth on all sides." When the shrieking subsided the penitents began to confess their sins, at first in murmurs and then loudly, publicly, and repetitively, sometimes for hours on end.[23] Both Methodist and Baptist preachers were holding camp meetings and revivals in the area of Greenville, Missouri, during the years the Bettises lived there,[24] but there is no record of any Bettis relative except Ezekiel Rubottom being associated with any church.

In her horrified fascination with the behavior of worshippers, Trollope seriously undervalued the preachers. Although clergymen of most major Protestant denominations participated in the evangelical movement, the Methodists were in the lead, and their success was based upon a combination of heroic dedication and what historian D. W. Howe describes as a brilliant and uniquely American marketing strategy. The first component of this strategy was door-to-door outreach. They sent out circuit riders, men of great faith but typically of limited education, to all corners of the frontier. Alone, dressed in black, these itinerant evangelists scattered through the hills and swamps of the backcountry, relying for food and shelter on whatever hospitable inhabitants they chanced to meet. Each one carried with him a Bible, a hymn book, and a copy of the *Methodist Discipline*, a set of rules for godly living that were often more important to his hearers than the doctrine itself. Wherever he found shelter, he would pray with the family and instruct them in Methodist rules and doctrine. In a counterpoint to the emotional release of the revivals, the *Discipline* provided religious support for the principles of temperance, cleanliness, hard work, and sexual restraint.[25]

Methodist theology itself was their second advantage. The Methodists rejected the Calvinist doctrine of predestination. Itinerant evangelists described salvation as a choice to accept God's grace, made freely by an autonomous individual rather than by the arbitrary intervention of God. Their doctrine on this issue must have lightened the spiritual burden of many worshippers who had never known the ecstatic experience of being chosen and who feared that the absence of that experience meant they were damned.

A third contributor to the Methodists' success was the establishment of classes, groups of about thirty laypeople who met together on a regular basis to study and discuss Methodist doctrine. Short on traveling clergy, the Methodists entrusted the management of these classes to respected lay leaders who not only led worship but also managed the groups' finances and monitored the behavior of their members. Female worshippers, hungry for a role in the world outside of their own kitchens, played an important part in organizing and supporting prayer meetings and revivals and sometimes even in leading classes.[26] These techniques were so effective that by 1850 the Methodists were the largest religious denomination in the country.[27]

Once again we see an evangelical religious organization, attuned to the needs of a self-reliant and fiercely independent population, creating islands of community and social order, nuclei of social capital that bit by bit enabled the isolated borderers to organize themselves into a functioning democracy. In interrogating clergymen of various denominations about the prominence of religion in American life, de Tocqueville found a universal agreement that religion was "necessary to the maintenance of republican institutions." And one and all

> ... attributed the peaceful dominion that religion exercises in their country principally to the complete separation of church and state. I do not fear to affirm that during my stay in America I did not encounter a single man, priest or layman, who did not come to accord on this point.[28]

As early as 1845, however, Methodists were already splitting apart over the issue of slavery, with southern members increasingly abandoning their denomination's longtime opposition to the practice. In June of 1845, a Batesville correspondent published an anonymous letter in the *Arkansas Gazette* expressing concern that the division between the pro-slavery and anti-slavery Methodists would weaken the bonds of the Union. Another writer dismissed that possibility, accused the first writer of abolitionist tendencies, and invited all Methodists of similar views to leave the state. At the end of that year, the delegates to the Methodists' Arkansas Annual Conference unanimously announced that slavery was not a moral evil.[29]

24. "An Agglomeration of Adventurers and Speculators"

Nothing we know of Thomas Drew suggests that he had much aptitude for the life of a farmer, even a rich one with plenty of slaves. Although he was successful enough by 1832 to have acquired twenty slaves, he was already turning his eyes elsewhere. In that year he was elected a judge of Arkansas's Lawrence County, an office he held until Randolph County split off from Lawrence in 1835.[1] Like physicians, lawyers and judges in that era received their training through apprenticeship, sometimes of remarkably brief duration. One of Thomas's brothers, Richard Maxwell Drew, was practicing law in Louisiana at the age of seventeen and serving as a judge by the age of twenty-three.[2]

Nor does Thomas's life show any evidence of the Baptist piety of his parents. Until the very end of his life, there is no evidence that he ever belonged to a church. But one thing he did carry with him from the Big Cedar Lick Church of his childhood: the covenant by which church members bound themselves to "be slow to take offense, but always ready for reconciliation, and mindful of the rules of our Saviour to secure it without delay." By 1834, the United Baptist Church of Christ had been established in Cherokee Bay.[3] Although there is no record that he was a member of this church, there is an amusing resonance in the church's name, which suggests an attempt to reconcile the warring factions whose disputes had troubled his father's family. Such an attempt would have been characteristic of Thomas, who spent his life trying to reconcile conflicting opinions and to bridge gaps between opposing groups.

Reconciliation was in short supply in northeast Arkansas. Lawrence Dalton's *History of Randolph County, Arkansas*, notes that the records of the Randolph County Circuit Court for 1837 and 1838 contain a number of names of the area's leading citizens, charged with such offenses as "assault and battery" and "creating an affray." Dalton observes that the men of the time "often scorned conventional things and were not much for formality." There were few ways for a mild-mannered consensus-builder to attain prominence, but Thomas and Ranson found one.

When Randolph County split off from Lawrence, there was a question as to which of the local towns would become the county seat. Ranson Bettis, who already had some experience in turning a small settlement into a county seat, decided to do the same for Bettis Bluff. The town of Columbia was also a contender. The decision was left up to a vote of the residents, who could vote anywhere in the county.

The story universally accepted in present-day Pocahontas is that on the day of the election, Ranson Bettis and Thomas Drew laid out a huge barbecue and invited all the men in the county. Food was plentiful and liquor more so, and at the end of the feast, the guests, "much invigorated," voted for the town they preferred. Bettis Bluff, not surprisingly, was the winner.[4] The town was renamed Pocahontas, allegedly because the county seat of Lawrence County was Powhatan, and Randolph, being a daughter county, needed Powhatan's daughter's name for its county seat. Two years later, on July 27, 1837, Drew followed up on this victory with a donation of more than fifteen city blocks' worth of land in the center of Pocahontas for the purpose of constructing a courthouse and other public buildings.[5] He also executed a bond in the amount of three thousand dollars for construction of the courthouse, provided that it was located in Pocahontas. T. O. Marr, the former Greenville postmaster and the husband of Amy Bettis, daughter of Elijah III, was paid twenty-four hundred dollars to build it.[6] The donation may well have marked the zenith of Thomas's fortunes.

His first foray into state politics occurred in 1836, when he was elected as a delegate to the constitutional convention for the soon-to-be state of Arkansas. The convention delegates were deeply divided on the subject of representation in the state senate. The rich slaveholding and cotton-growing areas of the south and east contended for a system of representation similar to that established in the United States Constitution, based on the number of white male inhabitants plus three-fifths of the number of slaves. The poorer but more populous counties of the north and west, where there were few slaves and where the economy was based primarily on hunting and free-range cattle farming, demanded representation based on free white males only.[7] As a result of a compromise worked out before the convention, delegates were elected by geographical districts rather than by either measure of population, with each of the two major regions having exactly the same number of delegates as the other. The majority report on the question of senate represen-tation, however, favored the demands of the south and east.

The final draft of the constitution established a compromise system of representation based on an amendment to the northern minority report. The amendment was offered by Thomas Drew, to resolve a tie vote that had prevented the adoption of his previous motion to substitute the minority report for that of the majority. It was supported by a select committee of three members, one of them Drew.[8] The "north and west" and the "south and east" were each allotted eight senatorial districts, but a new district was also created in the center of the state, including Little Rock and Pulaski County—a rich area with a large number of slaves and closely connected to the commercial interests of the south and east. Initially, this scheme gave the landowners of the south and east a greater weight per voter than those of the north and west, but as the state population grew and new districts were added, representation in all districts was to be based solely on the number of free white males—a victory for the north and west.[9] A moderately rich slaveholder in a poor district located precisely on the border between the two great regions, Drew was perfectly positioned to propose such a solution. His amendment is the first recorded example of the search for consensus that would characterize his later life.

In 1837, another event occurred that may have been significant for Thomas and Cinderella. Before Elijah Bettis III died in 1836, he executed a deed—the same deed that was read from the stage at the Pocahontas Sesquicentennial—freeing all seven of his enslaved daughters but specifying that their children were to "remain in slavery and bondage."[10] The deed, by its terms, took effect one year after his death. As we have seen before, effecting this legal transaction by way of a deed, rather than a will, served to prevent Elijah's heirs from challenging it.

Six of his emancipated daughters immediately disappear from the records. Charity remained in Pocahontas and by 1852 had saved enough money to buy a house.[11] Patsie resurfaces in 1849 as Martha

Cooper, buying land in the busy river town of Jacksonport. 1838, the year after the emancipation of Patsie and her sisters, saw the birth of Mollie Drew, the first child born to Thomas and Cinderella since the birth of their son Ranson in 1830. Whether or not there was a connection between her conception and Patsie's emancipation is anyone's guess.

In the early days of the new state, Drew became increasingly active in Democratic party politics. He did not attempt to run for office but instead stayed in the background, making allies rather than enemies.[12] It was a wise decision. Arkansas politics was a pool of sharks, corrupt and frequently violent. The majority Democratic party was dominated by an intermarried group of powerful men known collectively as "the Dynasty" or "the Family," whose members included Governor James Sevier Conway, his cousin Senator Ambrose Sevier, and Sevier's brother-in-law, the future Senator Robert Ward Johnson, as well as the wealthy land speculator Chester Ashley. Members of the Family controlled patronage appointments and typically picked the Democratic candidates for elected offices as well.[13] They were supported by William Woodruff, the publisher of the state's major newspaper, the *Arkansas Gazette*.

The Family flourished within a society more violent than any the Drews or Bettises had yet encountered. Both Featherstonehaugh, the English geologist, and Timothy Flint, the New England clergyman, remarked on the ungovernable young men who populated the streets of the capital, deracinated and feral, lacking any of the restraining influences of family or community, in that wild corner of the frontier the wildest of their breed. According to Featherstonehaugh,

... a common practice with these fellows was to fire at each other
with a rifle across the street, and then dodge behind a door: every
day groups were to be seen gathered around these wordy bullies,
who were holding knives in their hands, and daring each other to
strike, but cherishing the secret hope that the spectators would
interfere .... One of the most respectable inhabitants told me,
that he did not suppose there were *twelve* inhabitants of the place
who ever went into the streets without ... being armed with
pistols or large hunting knives about a foot long and an inch and a
half broad.[14]

Flint understood the violence as the product of young
adventurers who "ha[d] not yet had their place or their standing
assigned to them in public opinion" and who could only gain respect
through reckless courage in matters of honor.[15]

Nor was deadly conflict confined to the young and rootless. The
Southern concept of honor, reflected in ostentatious daring and
eagerness to resent a slight, found even more dramatic expression
on the Arkansas frontier than in Tennessee or Missouri. Leading
citizens of Arkansas—politicians, judges, and journalists—regularly
injured and occasionally killed each other over personal insults and
political disagreements. In 1824, one judge killed another in a duel;
the survivor later killed a political rival with a spear drawn from his
sword-cane. In 1828, an opponent of the Family entered the office
of the *Arkansas Gazette* and fired at Chester Ashley; shots were
exchanged and the attacker was mortally wounded. In 1831, a duel
over a newspaper article resulted in the death of the challenger.
The editor of the *Arkansas Banner*, Solon Borland, got into a street
fight with a rival journalist in 1842, then challenged his opponent
to a duel in which, fortunately, no one was killed. His fellow

newspaperman William Woodruff described Borland approvingly as "a ready, expert fightist, and equally ready with the pistol or the knife," a skill that made him "quite an acquisition to the democratic cause."[16] By 1851, Borland was a US senator and still brawling, on the streets of Little Rock, the streets of Washington, DC, and the floor of the US Senate. As a US congressman, Robert W. Johnson did the same on the floor of the House. The preoccupation of these men with the defense of their "honor" was actually written into the Arkansas Constitution, whose opening Declaration of Rights listed, among the inalienable rights of free men, the right of "acquiring possessing and protecting property and reputation."[17]

Their sense of the rightness of their world view may have been derived, in part, from the books they were reading. Albert Pike, a lawyer, journalist, Confederate general, and later a major figure in American Masonry, kept a circulating library in his office at the *Arkansas Advocate*. We know the titles of some of his books because borrowers often failed to bring them back, and he had to place ads (and poems) in his paper begging for their return. *The Countess Ida; Fair Rosamond; The Partisan; The Black Riders of Congaree; Tylney Hall; The Slave King*. Books for sale in the offices of the rival *Arkansas Gazette* included *Minstrel Love; Geraldine, Or, Models of Faith and Practice; Mandeville, a Tale of the 17th Century*; and the *Poetical Works* of Byron.[18] In a famous passage in *Life on the Mississippi*,[19] Mark Twain argued that the gauzy medieval romanticism of these books had fatally corrupted the minds of generations of Americans, particularly in the South, with their "sham grandeurs, sham gauds, and sham chivalries of a brainless and worthless long-vanished society."

It was all the fault of Sir Walter Scott. In Twain's view, what Scott and the writers who followed him did was to create an intoxicating medieval fantasy, allowing Southern men to gloss over the horrors of slavery with myths of chivalry, honor, and heroism and to imagine their own thuggish behavior as deeds of daring in the service of noble ideals. "Sir Walter," he wrote," had so large a hand in making Southern character, as it existed before the [Civil] war, that he is in great measure responsible for the war."

Despite these ideals of honor and chivalry, the violence of Little Rock society was intensified by pervasive corruption in a culture where political office was seen more as a means to private gain than a calling to public service. As rapacious as the early Virginia Cavaliers but with fewer pretensions to gentility, Family members and other powerful politicians were involved in some of the most outrageous land frauds of the era.[20] "As one descends toward the south," wrote de Tocqueville,

> into states where the social bond is less old and less strong, where instruction is less widespread, and where the principles of religion, morality, and freedom are combined in a less fortunate manner, one perceives that talents and virtues become ever rarer among those who govern. When one finally penetrates into the new states of the Southwest, where the social body, formed yesterday, still presents nothing but an agglomeration of adventurers and speculators, one is confounded to see into whose hands public power is placed."[21]

The nascent society of mid-nineteenth century Arkansas differed in many ways from that of the North Carolina Piedmont three generations earlier, and the corrupt officials of the two eras differed in the same degree. The Piedmont officials still operated out of an aristocratic, European frame of reference in which powdered wigs set them apart from the rude backcountry settlers, and their status as "gentlemen" allowed them to plunder their neighbors openly by means as simple as direct extortion. But the broadening of the franchise in the new states of the trans-Mississippi West, along with the elevation of equality to a sacred principle, had changed all that. Mid-century Arkansas was enjoying the heyday of Jacksonian democracy, in which every white man's voice was—at least in theory—the equal of every other. Political conflict was fierce and personal, but it was carried on—for the time being—by means of newspaper articles, party conclaves, and street fights rather than by mobs and armies. And the rise of mercantile capitalism had provided the powerful with more sophisticated means of self-enrichment, allowing them to plunder, not their neighbors directly, but their state and their own future.

The most dramatic incident in the catalogue of violence and corruption occurred in 1837 on the floor of the Arkansas House of Representatives in the course of a debate about the Real Estate Bank of Arkansas. The newly drafted constitution provided for the establishment of two banks, the State Bank of Arkansas and the Real Estate Bank, both of them exercises in imaginative financing. State revenues had originally been based on a tax of one-quarter of a percent of the assessed value of property, but when a surplus of revenue was projected from that tax, the lawmakers voted to cut the rate in half. They then faced a deficit, which they proposed to make up with the profits from the publicly-owned State Bank, hoping that eventually those profits would be so great that no property tax would be necessary at all. All state funds were to be deposited in the various branches of the State Bank, with additional capital to be raised through the sale of notes and bonds backed by the state. The bank was empowered to issue notes in denominations as small as five dollars, and the directors of its various branches were paid in those notes.[22] Until the day the State Bank started making enough profit to cover the state deficit, that deficit was to be financed by surplus federal funds that had been turned over to the state at the inception of statehood.[23] In March of 1838, Thomas Drew was appointed as one of the directors of the Batesville branch.[24]

The Real Estate Bank, on the other hand, was established as a semi-private corporation—private in the fact that its stockholders controlled its operations and received all of its profits, public in the fact that the state assumed all of its risks. The initial capital of both banks was composed of bonds issued by the state and then transferred to the banks; the Real Estate Bank was also authorized to raise two million dollars of additional capital through the sale of bonds and stock. The debt represented by the additional bonds was to be guaranteed by the state.[25] If the bank failed, the state, as the issuer of the bonds, would be responsible for the lion's share of its debts. Each of the four branches of the Real Estate Bank had nine directors, seven of whom were appointed by stockholders and only two by the government, leaving the state with financial responsibility for risks over which it had no control.[26]

It was here that the imaginative part came in. Stock in the Real Estate Bank could be purchased with agricultural land or town lots, both of which could be mortgaged, or even with crops. Stockholders could then use one-half of the value of their stock as collateral for loans or mortgages with which to buy additional land.

Although land offered for the purchase of shares was supposed to be assessed at fair market value and at least partially improved or in cultivation, the so-called independent appraisers were in the pay of the landowners. Not surprisingly, the land used to purchase shares was often grossly overvalued and sometimes not in cultivation or even suitable for cultivation. By obtaining loans on the basis of overvalued assets and using those loans to purchase additional assets that could be used, at similar inflated valuations, as collateral for new loans, the shareholders, who controlled the bank, could multiply their initial investments many times over at the expense of the state. When shares in the bank were offered for sale, they were ultimately distributed to only 184 people: powerful Arkansas politicians, their relatives, and a selection of their landowning friends.

The Real Estate Bank, in other words, was conceived and operated as a mechanism for the wealthy planters of Arkansas's cotton-growing south and east to plunder the state—and the state's most powerful politicians, including Ambrose Sevier, were among the plunderers.[27] The privatization of profit and socialization of risk, accompanied by the fantasy that money could be created out of thin air by repeated asset transfers and the near impossibility of explaining this scheme in any way that makes sense, is not unknown in our own time.

The birth of the Real Estate Bank was marked by a highly public murder. The bank president, John Wilson, was also the speaker of the state house of representatives, and had acquired a reputation for corruption in connection with bounties offered for wolf scalps. Major J. J. Anthony, a Randolph county legislator and a fierce opponent of the bank, had repeatedly accused its officers of corruption, mismanagement, and disregard of the interests of the state. He made no secret of his desire to put the whole operation out of business. When a bill was introduced providing that certificates for wolf-scalp bounties should circulate as legal currency, Anthony proposed an amendment to the effect that the certificates should be signed by a "great dignitary" such as the president of the Real Estate Bank—an amendment designed specifically to insult Wilson.[28] At that point, Wilson abandoned the speaker's podium, drew out his Bowie knife, and advanced on Anthony. A knife fight ensued, and Anthony was killed.

Three days later, Wilson was arrested, then let out on bail. At his trial, which took place several months later in another county, his friends testified that the murdered legislator had violated parliamentary procedure by insulting him and was just as aggressive as Wilson in the conduct of the fight. Other testimony revealed that on the day of the fight, Wilson was carrying a loaded pistol for the purpose of seeking "satisfaction" from another legislator who he believed had also insulted him. The jury quickly returned a verdict of "excusable homicide," whereupon Wilson took them all out for drinks to the accompaniment of tumultuous cheers from the assembled mob.[29] Despite his acquittal, he was expelled from the legislature. He was then reelected at the first opportunity.

This, then, was the pool of sharks in which Thomas Drew aspired to swim. His education and early life had provided him with many of the skills that he needed to survive in such a culture. He was sadly lacking in others.

The Batesville branch of the State Bank opened in January of 1838, and, like its sister branches, immediately embarked on a reckless lending spree. A large portion of its loans were made to its own directors, most likely including Drew.[30] At the same time, Drew and his father-in-law started patenting more land in and around Pocahontas—337 additional acres for Ranson and 440 for Thomas.[31] In the Randolph County tax list for 1839, Thomas appears as the third largest landowner in the county, with a state tax of $14.36 and a county tax of $29.47, ten times higher than those of most of his neighbors. Only Mr. Pitman, the owner of the Elevenpoint River ferry, and T. O. Marr were taxed on more land.

Tax lists for the next three years show a bewildering series of changes in land ownership, with Drew's possessions dropping from 1,278 acres in 1839 to 383 in 1840, then rising again to 1,140 in 1841, while Marr's totals move in the opposite directions. Still more bewildering is the fact that there are no land sales in the deed records that would account for these changes in ownership. Ranson's acreage fluctuated in a similar manner, while his brother Overton and his nephew Elijah IV were players in the same game, though on a smaller scale.

Ranson and Thomas quickly subdivided their town land and sold it off in small parcels of one or two lots. One of Ranson's purchasers made a killing on those lots, reselling one of them within a day for three times what he had paid for it and two others nine months later for six times their cost.[32] That purchaser bore the interesting name of John Glascocke, who with his brother George appears very briefly in the Randolph County records. The murdered Dr. George Glascock of Moore County North Carolina, who may have been mentor to Ranson's father, had sons named John and George, but I have been unable to trace any connection between them and the Randolph County pair. The large majority of Ranson's and Thomas's new land, however, was located not in the town itself but in the flat delta country to the southeast of the town, possibly swamp land and most likely not yet cleared for planting.[33]

For a long time I believed that the collapse of Thomas's fortunes must have had something to do with a reckless investment in shares of the Real Estate Bank, perhaps in an attempt to emulate the powerful politicians who were doing the same thing. But the deed records reveal no mortgages in Thomas's name and no transfers of any of Thomas's land to either bank. The actual explanation is probably simpler: hope of establishing a profitable cotton plantation and lack of skill or effort, or both, in carrying out that project. Ranson quickly sold most of his delta land, but Thomas held onto his for another six or seven years until his accumulated debts finally forced him to sell.

In the meantime, the banks were collapsing. By 1840, the Real Estate Bank needed to borrow money to pay interest on the money it had already borrowed. In an extraordinary display of banking ineptitude, the commissioners who were sent east to sell more bonds agreed to take only half of the price for those bonds in cash and the rest on credit, then physically handed over the bonds to the purchaser, North American Trust and Banking Company, which resold them to a London bank. The London purchaser demanded payment from Arkansas for the full value of the bonds, even though North American had already defaulted on the second half of the agreed-upon price. Arkansas stonewalled. The legislature proposed to examine the bank's affairs, but the judiciary committee ruled that it had no power to do so.[34] The bank finally closed in 1841, having survived for less than three years. The directors appointed themselves as receivers, kept the remaining money, and refused to turn over the books.[35]

The State Bank lasted only a little longer. When Arkansas Senators Sevier and Fulton were directed to sell two hundred thousand-dollar bonds in Washington, they only managed to sell thirty, and those went to Vice President Richard Mentor Johnson, the uncle of Sevier's wife, in exchange for a mortgage which the senators neglected to record and which was therefore invalid.

The nationwide depression that followed President Jackson's abolition of the Second Bank of the United States was spreading to Arkansas, and by 1840, the notes of the State Bank were being discounted by between twenty percent and fifty-five percent in New Orleans. A legislative committee investigated the situation and directed the bank to reduce the salaries of its employees along with the amount of the loans it had been making to its directors. At the same time, the debtors of both banks were increasingly unable or unwilling to repay their loans. To top it all off, the federal surplus funds had finally run out, and the state government was raiding the bank's assets to cover its own deficits. By 1842, however, the bulk of those assets consisted of near-worthless notes of the Real Estate Bank.[36]

The legislature then stripped the State Bank of the power to make further loans and began appointing receivers for its various branches. Drew was named as receiver of the Batesville branch, which was still trying unsuccessfully to recover against its debtors in 1845, as the debtors muttered about burning its books.[37] The collapse of the two banks was disastrous for the state, which was left with millions of dollars' worth of obligations that it could not repay and never did, in addition to an ongoing budget deficit equal to half of all state expenditures.[38]

In 1842, Ranson Bettis died. His impressive tombstone resides in the museum of the Randolph County Historical Society, bearing Cinderella's declaration that it was erected "by his only child." His estate inventory provides a picture of the life of a successful western entrepreneur in the mid nineteenth century: stables, gardens, an orchard, several town lots, a store, a mill, a warehouse, a barouche (an open carriage seating four) worth seventy-five dollars, and sixteen slaves along with fine furniture including three writing desks, three looking glasses, a brass clock, two brass candlesticks, a dining table, a set of Windsor chairs, a "sundries cupboard," a tea service, and a silver watch. Rugs and upholstered furniture do not appear in the inventory, having apparently not yet made it to the small towns of northern Arkansas. The seven books listed as part of the estate sale demonstrate the family's continuing aspirations to respectability: *Statutes of Arkansas*, Robinson's *England*, Murray's *Grammar*, *Western Navigation*, *Life of Franklin*, *Polite Learning*, and *Arithmetic*.

Ranson did not die poor. Whatever the cause of Thomas's financial disaster, Ranson was evidently spared. So was T. O. Marr, who by 1850 had acquired everything: Drew's land, Ranson's land, Overton's land, and the land of Elijah IV in addition to the license for the Black River ferry.[39]

As the banks disintegrated along with his own finances, Drew's political star unexpectedly rose. Somewhere along the line, he had caught the attention of the Family without at the same time antagonizing the more independent elements of the Democratic Party. In July of 1844, at a Democratic Party caucus in Little Rock, he was nominated for governor. The party had already held not one but two conventions, but the successive candidates nominated at these conventions had both backed out. The party was riven by factional infighting, and Drew, a man with no enemies, was acceptable to all factions.[40] He was elected with forty-seven percent of the vote in a three-way election. In a letter to a friend, he describes himself as merely "the humble instrument to save [the party]."[41]

Drew's achievements as governor, in contrast to those of his more flamboyant predecessors, were so obscure that the few historians who bother to mention him find hardly anything to say. He advocated for a series of badly needed measures—schools, improvements in roads and bridges, the establishment of a state college—but the legislature ignored him, as it had his predecessors. He signed a bill, previously vetoed by his predecessor Governor Yell, that echoed the French system for protecting a married woman's property, allowing a woman to register her property at the local courthouse to prevent it from being taken to pay debts incurred by her husband after the marriage. Cinderella, no fool, quickly took advantage of this law.

But historians fail to comment on what was perhaps Drew's most significant achievement. In 1846, he told the legislature the truth about the state banks and state finances, clearly, in convincing detail, and without pontificating or laying blame. He proposed the harsh remedy of doubling property taxes to their original value of half a percent. Astonishingly, the legislature listened.[42] The state property tax was increased to its original value, a measure that solved the current problems but did nothing to pay off the state's debts.

At the same time, Drew's financial problems deepened. By February of 1846, a little more than a year after his election, he had sold most or all of his agricultural land and was borrowing money from his mother-in-law, Mary Bettis.[43] Pocahontas historians tend to blame his troubles on Cinderella. Attorney John W. Meeks, who was largely responsible for the erection of a monument on Drew's grave, described her slightingly in a 1924 letter to my grandmother as "a petted and spoilt child who never knew what it was to want" and who once came home from a shopping expedition with a piece of jewelry worth the governor's entire annual salary. He added, however, that she spent much money on charity work and that "at Christmas time—she never allowed any poor people here to go without a feast if she could find them."[44]

A more sympathetic portrait is found in *First Ladies of Arkansas*, by Peggy Jacoway:

> Among the "great ladies" . . . of vivid, fine physical appearance, having coal black hair and lustrous dark eyes. She was largely proportioned, had a commanding dignity which could have been taken for hauteur. Though in the way she had been obliged to spend her youth, distant from superior educational sources and in a day when formal schooling for girls was negligible, Mrs. Drew delighted in flowery verbiage; to her taste was the use of superlative, rich words.[45]

A woman, in short, with something to prove, determined to establish her worth in the highest society available to her. Her superlative, rich words were probably drawn from the romantic novels then crowding into the stores.[46] It seems likely that her generosity and her extravagant spending did in fact make a contribution to Thomas's mounting pile of debt.

Drew's tenure as governor was also marred by an increasingly acrimonious relationship with the ambitious speculator/politician Chester Ashley. By 1846, Drew had come to detest Ashley, perhaps less for his ambition than for his attempts to manipulate Drew into serving it. The clique that had dominated the Arkansas Democratic Party since its beginning was by that time badly split. On one side was the interrelated Family or Dynasty, consisting of members of the Conway, Sevier, and Johnson families, with whom Drew was associated and who appear to have furthered his political career. They, in turn, were supported by the *Arkansas Banner*, a newspaper established as the voice of the Democrats after the *Arkansas Gazette* was sold to a member of the minority Whig party. The editor of the *Banner* was the pugnacious "fightist" Solon Borland. On the other side of the divide were disaffected ex-Family allies like Ashley and William Woodruff, the former publisher of the *Arkansas Gazette*, who had been a strong supporter of Drew in his first gubernatorial race.[47]

As Drew told it, he did his best to remain neutral in the conflict between the two factions. But then Ashley decided to run for the US Senate against former governor and Family associate Archibald Yell and tried to enlist Drew's support by offering what Drew saw as "an unholy proposition" for "a corrupt alliance . . . to defeat Yell and supersede [US Senator Ambrose] Sevier [as the head of the Arkansas Democratic Party.]" A letter to a friend, describing the incident, provides one of our first glimpses into Drew's mind and our first three examples of what would prove to be his most characteristic word: "principle."[48] It was not merely Ashley's manipulations that offended him but Ashley's planned betrayal of a friend. Although it is not clear whether the friend to whom Drew was referring was Yell or Sevier, in any case Drew considered him to be "the most distinguished man in the state." Ashley, on the other hand, he described as "the most unsafe man in the state," whose "reckless indifference to the welfare of all else when clashing with his interest" and whose "exorbitant conceptions of self and puny views of others, totally disqualify him to represent a free people, who recognize the principle of equality as paramount." Drew also believed that, in retaliation for his refusal of support, Ashley had persuaded his own lackeys in the Democratic press to publish a series of "ill-natured Phillipics" against him, accusing Drew of improper meddling in the Senatorial election. With more than a whiff of self-pity, Drew describes his desire to abandon politics and return to private life, "leaving the business of political juggling, corruption bargain and intrigue, to those whose habits of life, disposition and taste better fitted them to encounter the thorny mazes of political strife."

At that time, US senators were still elected by the legislatures of the various states rather than directly by the people. In a slightly earlier letter, written in August of the same year, Drew discussed the probable vote counts in the contest between Yell and Ashley and claimed to have resisted entreaties to join the Senatorial race as a third candidate on the grounds that it "would rather injure than benefit the project of Ashley's defeat."[49] Ashley was elected in a landslide in spite of Drew's opposition. The influence of the Family was declining as voters and legislators became disillusioned by repeated revelations of corruption involving Family members.

Subsequently, both Yell and the fighting newspaper editor Solon Borland enlisted in the Mexican War, in the course of which they got into a quarrel that was unresolved when Yell was killed in battle. Then, on his return home, Borland switched sides, abandoning the Family and casting his lot with Woodruff and Ashley.[50]

No flow chart can explain what happened next. At the conclusion of the Mexican War, President Polk appointed Ambrose Sevier as peace commissioner to Mexico, a job that required Sevier's resignation from the Senate. Sevier wanted his seat to be filled temporarily by the appointment of a relative, who would agree to step aside when Sevier returned from Mexico. Borland also wanted the job, and his animosity towards the deceased Yell had expanded to include Sevier and others of his former allies. Inexplicably, Drew—who admired Sevier and was beholden to the Family—appointed Borland. Then, even though Ashley's sudden death had left another Senate seat to be filled, Borland insisted on running against Sevier for the remainder of Sevier's unexpired term—and won. Drew's decision in this case is usually attributed to some kind of bargain with Borland, but no Arkansas historian has been able to say what that bargain involved or what, indeed, Borland had to offer in exchange for the appointment.[51] In addition, we have already seen how Drew felt on the subject of political bargains.

In 1847, Drew was nominated for a second term as governor. Because of his ongoing financial problems, he was reluctant to accept the nomination. He ultimately did so only on the assurance of unidentified "friends" in the legislature that, before he took office, they would increase the governor's salary to a point sufficient at least to pay my expenses with my family at the seat of government, which the constitution of the state makes it imperative that the Executive shall reside.[52]

With no significant opposition, Drew was re-elected by a huge majority; but his "friends" did not come through. Unable to meet the expenses of acting as governor while supporting a growing family, he resigned on January 10, 1849, a few weeks after his second inauguration.[53] Perhaps the Family clique abandoned him because of his appointment of Borland to the Senate. Perhaps the anti-Family party was disinclined to reward someone still so closely associated with the Family and its record of corruption. Or perhaps Drew's stubborn refusal to go with the political flow had simply ended up exasperating both sides.

His resignation was delayed by a final project. By the 1840s, railroads were being constructed at breakneck speed throughout the northern states. But in Arkansas, there was nothing—not a mile of railroad, not even any really passable road. Everywhere there was talk of the need for a transcontinental railroad, with its western terminus at San Francisco or San Diego and its eastern one somewhere on the Mississippi. Several proposals for that railroad were floated, each one reflecting the local interests of the state or states proposing it. In 1849, the states of the South finally joined the contest for the transcontinental route, which its proponents hoped would lead to the economic regeneration of their region.

On January 6, Drew chaired a meeting at Little Rock to draw up a petition to Congress for a transcontinental military road. By the meeting's end, its goal had changed from a military road to a southern route for the transcontinental railroad, and a convention was planned for the Fourth of July in Memphis to promote the idea.[54] Two days later, Drew resigned as governor.

Nothing ever came of the proposed southern railroad route. A few years later, the focus of its Arkansas promoters had shifted to a system of railroads within the state, in the hopes that their existence would secure the state's place as part of the transcontinental route. But even that plan ran aground on the squabbling between local interests.[55] Among the reasons given for its failure by an anonymous correspondent to the *Little Rock Whig* in 1854, three stand out: the refusal of southern states to cooperate with each other, the disadvantages caused by the South's "peculiar institution," and the destructive effects of "chivalry."[56] By "chivalry," the writer most likely meant the competition for reputation among ambitious politicians, which made cooperation difficult or impossible. It is hard to know which of the many ill effects of slavery he had in mind, but the scarcity of skilled free labor, and the fact that so much of the South's capital was tied up in land and slaves, were probably among them.

In the meantime, the pace of Drew's ruin accelerated. In 1850, he deeded much of his remaining land to his mother-in-law to satisfy the 1846 debt,[57] and then, ever hopeful, embarked on an attempt to establish a cotton plantation, in the rich delta soil of Desha County. The cotton boom in the delta counties was just beginning. The virgin forests and malarial swamps of the lands near the Mississippi were slowly being cleared by the labor of the hundreds of slaves who cleared the underbrush, felled the giant trees, hauled their intertwined roots out of the thick wet soil, and dug the ditches to drain the swamps.

The white population of Desha County would increase by fifty-seven percent in the next ten years, and the enslaved population would more than triple.[58] The slaves who created the new plantations were driven mercilessly. Their work was much harder and far more regimented than on the smaller farms of the uplands and more often carried out by the gang system under the supervision of an overseer.[59] Many plantation owners made sizable fortunes during those years. Many others, particularly those with few or no slaves, failed and gave up.[60]

Some slaveholders in this situation would send a group of slaves and an overseer ahead to do the hard and dangerous work while the white family remained in the healthier uplands until the land was cleared and the plantation established. Thomas and Cinderella seem to have taken this approach. Although they themselves do not appear anywhere in the 1850 census, the federal slave census for Desha County shows Thomas as the owner of twenty-eight slaves. The Drews, however, spent at least some time in Desha, since the Arkansas Mortality Schedule for 1850 shows a Bennett Drew, age seven, who died there in that year.[61] It was the second time that Thomas and Cinderella needed to work together to establish a plantation, and this time they did not succeed.

Only a year later, Thomas gave up, selling thirteen of those slaves and all of his livestock and farming tools to his rich brother James for $7,205 and James's assumption of a $3,455 debt.[62] It is worth taking a look at those two documents, the census list and the deed of sale, because together they offer one of the few opportunities in this history to see enslaved people as individuals with names and to guess at some of the details of their lives. More than half of the twenty-eight slaves listed in the slave census are children and young teenagers from one month to fifteen years old, perhaps not the most productive labor force for an aspiring cotton planter. The deed of sale from Thomas to James, which itemizes its merchandise by name and age, suggests an attempt to keep family members together at least to some extent. There appear to be two adult couples, Fanny and an unnamed man, both in their forties, and Reuben and Elsy, both in their thirties, as well as six children between the ages of nine and thirteen, plus Sarah and her eighteen-month-old twins, George and Fanny, who may be the grandchildren of the older Fanny.

Of the fifteen slaves included in the census listing but not in the deed, the majority were in their late teens and twenties, prime ages for field hands. Since Thomas was abandoning his attempt at a plantation, he may have reserved these young adults—many of them perhaps siblings of the children that he sold to his brother—to be sold or rented out to more determined planters or to slave traders. Among the others not included in the deed were a girl of thirteen and a boy of fourteen, the only two on either list identified as mulatto; the girl may be the same as the mulatto woman who appears in Thomas's much reduced household ten years later, at the age of twenty-three. By 1852, the white family, consisting of Thomas, Cinderella, six children, and Cinderella's mother, Mary Bettis, was apparently living on one of James's properties in Lake Providence, Louisiana, where Mary died on June 23.[63]

Their oldest son, Ranson Drew, had left Arkansas at the age of nineteen in pursuit of California gold. The Gold Rush struck

Arkansas hard, and thousands of men set out in wagon trains for the promise of riches in the West. Few returned with the fortunes they had sought; Ranson was not among them. Failing to find gold, he signed on for the harebrained 1855 invasion of Nicaragua, led by the adventurer William Walker.

The exuberant optimism of the age had given rise to extravagant fantasies, many of them having to do with the expansion of slavery. In Texas, Sam Houston was calling for the establishment of a "protectorate" over all of Mexico and Central America. An organization calling itself the Knights of the Golden Circle, organized in quasi-Masonic fashion into secret lodges or "castles" with mysterious rituals, aimed at the establishment of a Golden Circle, a slaveholding empire stretching from Brazil to the Mason-Dixon line. If contemporary drawings of their costumes and rituals are to be believed, they even dressed up as medieval knights, so fully had they absorbed the romantic mythology popular among their Southern contemporaries.[64]

There was also a crowd of freelance adventurers known as filibusters, whose ambition was not only the acquisition of new territory for the expansion of slavery but sometimes a small country for themselves—Cuba, say, or Costa Rica. Walker, the most famous of them, made three attempts to carve out a country of his own. In 1853, with a force of fifty-three men, he tried and failed to capture the Mexican territories of Sonora and Baja Caifornia. In 1855, with sixty men and a little more than a hundred locals, he intervened in a Nicaraguan civil war, defeated the opposing Legitimist army, and occupied the capital, managing to become President of Nicaragua in 1856 before being driven out by the combined armies of four neighboring countries. He returned to New York, where he was greeted as a hero. In 1860, he tried yet again at the invitation of some British colonists in Honduras. He was captured by the British Navy, turned over to the Honduran authorities, and executed by firing squad.[65] According to Ranson's 1913 obituary, he too was captured on the high seas by the British, put ashore in California, and then traveled through Nevada, Idaho, and Alaska for the next forty years before finally reuniting with his family at the end of his life.[66]

Governor Thomas Drew in his mid forties. The row of army tents on the painted backdrop suggests that the photograph was taken at the time of the Mexican War.

25. Border Worlds

In 1838, a desolate caravan passed over the Elevenpoint River at Pitman's Ferry: Cherokees forcibly uprooted from their homeland and moved to the territory that later became Oklahoma by way of the Trail of Tears. Fifteen years later, Thomas Drew would follow them west.

In April of 1853, he secured an appointment as Superintendent of Indian Affairs for the Southern Superintendency. His office, originally headquartered in the town of Van Buren, Arkansas, was subsequently moved to Fort Smith, on the border of Indian Territory. His responsibilities covered all of the Indian nations involuntarily resettled in that territory, in particular those known as the Five Civilized Tribes—Cherokees, Creeks, Chickasaws, Choctaws, and Seminoles, those who had made the greatest effort to adapt to the customs of the whites. Turnover was high in that position: the eight-year period from 1849 to 1857 saw no fewer than five southern superintendents, each with a different degree of sympathy towards the Indian nations and a different degree of willingness to speak his mind.[1] Cinderella and the children returned to Pocahontas, where Thomas occasionally visited them for a month at a time.[2]

Among the nations for whose welfare Drew was responsible, the political situation of the Cherokees was the most complex and daunting. The Cherokee Nation was composed of three factions, two of them violently hostile to each other. The earliest arrivals had been the Old Settlers, Cherokees who had moved to Arkansas in the eighteen-teens in search of a place where they could preserve their traditional way of life and who had been forced to move west again only ten years later. The second group had arrived from North Carolina in 1835, led by a small group of men who recognized the inevitability of removal and who had signed the Treaty of New Echota in an attempt to gain the maximum advantage for their people from the surrender of their land. The treaty was illegal under Cherokee law, which prescribed the death penalty for anyone who sold tribal land to whites. The signers, known as the Treaty Party, were regarded as traitors by those who stayed on, trusting in the assurances of Chief John Ross that they would be able to remain on their ancestral land. It was those last holdouts who were finally evicted from their homes at gunpoint in 1838 and who endured the agonies of the Trail of Tears on their grueling journey west. In numbers, their group was about twice as large as the other two combined.[3]

The arrival of the Ross party precipitated a struggle for control of the Cherokee Nation between the Old Settlers, whose laws and constitution reflected traditional norms, and the Ross party, which had drafted a constitution and a set of laws modeled on those of the United States. It also precipitated a series of revenge killings, house burnings, terrorism, and banditry that began with the assassinations of several Treaty Party leaders and lasted for another seven years. In 1846, the period of terror was finally ended by a new treaty that involved painful compromises by all sides but left Ross firmly in control. Nevertheless, old hatreds continued to fester.

The next ten years were a period of unprecedented peace and prosperity for the Cherokees, during which Ross fought tirelessly to maintain the independence of the Nation in the face of constant violations of its sovereignty by the United States and by the settlers who coveted its land. Among his major concerns as Principal Chief were the massive cattle drives across Cherokee land, north from Texas to St. Louis and west from Arkansas to California. The drives were slow-moving tides of destruction during which the American cattle not only ate up the grass on the "vacant" tribal land but also spread diseases to the Cherokee cattle. Ross exerted every effort to end them or at least to secure payment for the damages they caused, but to no avail. He also fought in vain to establish the right of Cherokee courts to try crimes occurring in the Cherokee Nation and involving both whites and Indians.[4]

Somewhat more successful was his plan to establish a nationwide system of primary schools, which he hoped would assist in the acculturation of the Nation. By 1860 there were thirty of these schools, serving fifteen hundred children out of a probable total of from three to four thousand. Their success, however, was undermined by another fissure within the Cherokee Nation, a division of race and class that cut across the party divisions that already weakened it. The large majority of the population were Cherokee-speaking full-bloods, often desperately poor. The mixed-blood elite, most of whom spoke only English, were far richer, many of them merchants or large planters and slaveholders who lived like wealthy whites. Although supported by the full-bloods, Ross himself was only one-eighth Cherokee and spoke only a few words of the language. His Rose Cottage was a porticoed mansion that would not have been out of place in *Gone with the Wind*.

The primary schools were taught exclusively in English. The full-blood children, most of whom spoke only Cherokee, were ridiculed as "stupid" by their mixed-blood classmates, often missed school because they were needed on their parents' farms, and generally ended by dropping out. These divisions were heightened in 1847, when Ross persuaded the Cherokee National Council to provide for the establishment of two free seminaries, one for males and one for females. The purpose of the seminaries was to provide a corps of Cherokee teachers for the Nation's schools, ending their reliance on missionaries and idealistic young Easterners who knew nothing about Cherokee culture. But the seminaries, too, were taught in English, and most of the students were English-speaking mixed-bloods whose ability to communicate with the children of their Cherokee-speaking neighbors was only slightly greater than that of the whites.[5]

Soon after Drew's appointment as superintendent, Chief Ross invited him to attend the next session of the national council at the Cherokee capital of Tahlequah, "that you might see for yourself the progress of improvements in the country."[6] There are indications in surviving documents that the visit took place and may even have given rise to a friendship between the two men. In February of 1854, Drew relayed Ross's concerns about the cattle drives to George Manypenny, the United States Commissioner of Indian Affairs in Washington, in terms sympathetic to the Indians, referring to laws and regulations of the United States that appeared to cover the issue. Manypenny swatted down the protest and ordered Drew to issue passports to cattle drovers. Nearly a year later, Drew wrote to his subordinate George Butler, the agent to the Cherokees, supporting Manypenny's decision with what seems like unnecessarily defensive rhetoric:

... the right however of free passage ... is a right too sacred to be called into question, and that will at all times command the protection of the strong arm of the Government ... wherever she is represented by Officers or Agents who understand and appreciate the blessing and high privileges of an American Citizen.[7]

Drew's 1854 annual report to the commissioner of Indian affairs contains only a few words about the Cherokee schools, but they are Ross's words:

The system adopted by the Cherokee council of giving employment to the highly-educated natives, as teachers in their primary schools, appears from experience to be founded in wisdom, and has proven eminently successful.[8]

We may wonder whether Drew's investigation of the subject ever went further than Ross's front parlor. At the time of Drew's report, the first class of prospective Cherokee teachers had just graduated, most of them mixed-bloods who spoke only English. Nearly all of the Cherokee schools were still run by white missionaries and teachers imported from the East. In 1856, the seminaries, never popular with the full-blood majority, were forced to close for lack of funds.[9]

This annual report and its 1853 predecessor provide us with a vivid picture of Drew as a person. His reports differ sharply from those of five of the six other regional superintendents, each of whom seems to have seen his role as that of a schoolmaster or overseer of his Indian charges. As Minnesota Superintendent Willis A. Gorman put it, "A report of this kind should be confined properly to a history of their advance towards civilization." Even the most sympathetic of them, Oregon Superintendent Joel Palmer, a poetical soul who filled pages with dramatic descriptions of scenery, geography, and the sufferings of unfortunate tribes, advocated concentrating the more warlike tribes at convenient points "where the agents of the government can watch over, instruct, and protect them." The only exception was the brief tenure of California Superintendent Beale, who lived with the local Indians, praised their "docility and energy," and taught them agriculture by working alongside them in the fields. He was quickly replaced by a harsh authoritarian who seems to have believed that his only responsibility to the Indians was to get them out of the way of white settlers and put them to work profitably in the mines.[10]

Drew, on the other hand, consistently wrote as an ally and advocate of the Indians in his district. In both his 1853 and 1854 reports, he spoke out against the political arrangements that had been forced upon the Chickasaws and the Seminoles. The two tribes had been required to place themselves under the jurisdiction, respectively, of the numerically superior Choctaws and Creeks, and deeply resented what they felt to be the injustices imposed upon them by the dominant groups.[11] In 1853, Drew also went into passionate detail about the injustice of trying Indians in United States courts for the crime of selling liquor when they had already been tried, convicted, and punished under their own law. Characteristically, he referred to the principles of the Declaration of Independence and the United States Constitution, specifically invoking the Bill of Rights. He reported that one of the Creek chiefs, Benjamin Marshall, had promised his people that if liquor sellers were prosecuted under their own law, they would not be subject to any further jeopardy and that, as a result, several hundred men had sworn to execute Marshall if United States officials initiated further criminal proceedings. And he went on:

> *I conceive it important to save this good man's life. . . .* Therefore I shall, as I deem it my solemn duty, insist upon an amnesty. . . until further information can be obtained in reference thereto from the commissioner of Indian affairs and the Secretary of the Interior, and to this end will await the action of the proper authorities with great interest.[12]

Coming from the mild-mannered, conciliatory Drew, the boldness of this assertion is startling. More interesting is the fact that his superior, Commissioner Manypenny, supported his recommendations on this and at least two other issues, mentioning him by name in his own report and sometimes adopting his arguments nearly word for word.[13] Although the policy on sales of liquor did not change, Benjamin Marshall survived for another eleven years.

Manypenny, however, declined to comment on Drew's opinion, voiced in his 1854 report, of a bill recently introduced in the United States Senate by Senator Robert W. Johnson, a powerful member of the Arkansas Family. The bill would have abolished the sovereignty of all of the nations in Indian Territory by merging them into one and converting their land—only recently granted to them in perpetuity by the United States—into an American territory.[14] The bill, said Drew, "although extremely liberal in its provisions . . . does not appear to have been received with much favor" by the nations concerned. Part of the reason for this disfavor was the form of the bill, which demanded that the Indians assent to its general outline before the final wording was determined. According to Drew, the Indians did not trust the Senate not to change the bill after they had assented. Perhaps if Congress passed a final bill with the provision that it would go into effect only if the Indians voted to approve it and then gave them

> some reasonable time to determine for themselves either to accept
> or reject it, I entertain the opinion that, with all their prejudices
> against change and their prepossessions in favor of ancient
> customs, the intelligent portion of those Nations would be able in
> one or two years to remove every serious objection.[15]

Drew's hopeful conclusion was hopelessly wrong, and he must have known it. Opposition to the bill was passionate and nearly unanimous. In his cautious and deferential criticism of Johnson's bill, Drew was treading the fine line between voicing his own beliefs and maintaining the goodwill of his state's most powerful politician. He may have been unsuccessful in keeping to that line.

Even as Drew sat down to write the 1854 report, the train wreck of his newest career was already underway. It had been set in motion twenty-two years earlier, and by the time it smashed into Drew, it had involved at least seventy people in an epic of greed, betrayal, pursuit, and defense spanning an entire generation. Three secretaries of war, a secretary of the interior, two United States Attorneys General, three commissioners of Indian affairs, a couple of generations of Choctaw chiefs, and three southern superintendents were involved in it before it finally ended.

The story, told in lengthy and fascinating detail in an article by Daniel F. Littlefield Jr. and Mary Ann Littlefield,[16] takes place against a background of changing attitudes towards slaves and free people of color among the Indian nations. The severity of the laws dealing with slavery varied widely among the Five Civilized Tribes: Seminole slaves enjoyed a great deal of autonomy and free people of color were treated like any other Seminole citizens, while the far more restrictive Cherokee laws closely paralleled those of their white neighbors. In the early years of the nineteenth century, Creek and Choctaw laws and customs held a place between those two extremes.

After the Removal, however, the views of the slaveholding elites in Indian Territory increasingly converged with those of whites, and the teachings of pro-slavery missionaries reinforced this trend. Among the Creeks, slaves lost their right to own property, and free people of color were made subject to a property tax. In the somewhat more lenient Choctaw Nation after 1838, a slave owner could teach his or her slaves to read and write, but no one else could do it without the owner's consent. After 1844, no free person of color unconnected to Choctaw blood could receive any money from the Choctaw annuity. The kidnapping and enslavement of free people of color was a highly lucrative business in the mid nineteenth century, and as their status declined and the protection of their neighbors disappeared, free people of color in the Choctaw Nation became attractive targets.

In 1823, a white man named William Beams, a citizen of the Choctaw Nation by virtue of his previous marriage to a Choctaw woman, took his enslaved African-American second wife, Nelly, and a dozen of their children and grandchildren from Mississippi to Illinois to set them free. They then returned to the Choctaw Nation, where Beams announced the emancipation of his African-American family. Nelly and her children lived there as free people for the next five years, until Beams divided his estate among his four Choctaw children and returned with the rest of his family to Illinois. After his death, his African-American family made the mistake of returning home. In 1832, although Nelly and all of her children had been registered as free by the Mississippi courts, their Choctaw half-siblings decided to sell them.

It is here that John B. Davis first appears, at the beginning of his obsessive, decades-long struggle for ownership of the African-American Beams. The Choctaw Beams siblings either sold their African-American siblings to him or contracted with him to sell them in any way he could in exchange for half the profits. He and an associate rounded up the entire family and kept them captive for a year until the Choctaw chief finally intervened and ordered them released. Seven years later, when the number of African-American Beams descendants had grown to between twenty-five and thirty, all living in Indian Territory since the Removal, Davis tried again. By misrepresenting the true status of the Beams family, he succeeded in manipulating the United States Attorney General, the commissioner of Indian affairs, the secretary of war, and the brigadier general in command of Fort Gibson into ordering their capture. The family was protected, however, by lower-level federal officers and by then-Southern Superintendent Armstrong, who knew that they were free and who dodged and delayed until the commissioner finally allowed him to use his discretion and send Davis packing.

In 1840, Davis sold his claim to the family to a man named Fowler, who didn't bother with politicians but simply hired kidnappers. The kidnappers succeeded in capturing four family members and killing one. Fowler was tried for kidnapping but acquitted, and the four captured women were sold into slavery and never recovered. In 1844, after Davis's claim had been sold and resold several times, a third buyer captured a few more, was arrested by federal troops, tried, and also acquitted. The decline in the status of free people of color within the Choctaw Nation in the preceding twelve years can be seen in the fact that this time, instead of helping the Beams family members, the Choctaw authorities actually assisted in their capture.

Two years after that, Chester Ashley, then a US senator, took the third man's claim to a second secretary of war. At the same time, Davis himself appealed to the same secretary, having decided that the Beams were still his. The second secretary of war and a second commissioner ordered a second southern superintendent to give up the Beams family, but the claimants got nowhere. The family, by then numbering about fifty people and representing a sizable fortune to anyone who could capture them, decided that they would be safer if they separated, and several of them settled in the Creek Nation, where they lived in safety for a while.

In the summer of 1854, the pursuers arrived at Thomas Drew's door. Davis, still carrying on his obsessive pursuit of the family, had appealed to a third secretary of war, Jefferson Davis, who referred the matter to a second United States Attorney General. Once again, Davis lied, misrepresenting the issue as one of the applicability of the Fugitive Slave Law in Indian Territory while ignoring the fact that the Beams family members were neither fugitives nor slaves. The attorney general ruled that Davis or his agents had the right, under the Fugitive Slave Law, to enter the Choctaw Nation to retrieve *any slaves who belonged to him.*

Drew, the third southern superintendent to have dealt with this problem, refused to assist him without instructions from his superiors. But then he fumbled. On July 23 the Choctaw agent, Douglas Cooper, requested instructions from the secretary of the interior. The secretary did not answer until September 11, when he told Cooper to take no action until the facts were investigated and definitive instructions received. By then it was too late. On July 27, Davis's agent, a man named Houser, had returned to pester Drew again and found him preparing to leave for a month's visit with his family, some of whom were ill.[17] Since the Creek agent was also unavailable for an unspecified amount of time, any order arriving from Washington during Drew's and the agent's absence would simply have warned the family members to flee. The harried Drew agreed to give Houser a letter ordering the Creek chiefs to assist Davis in capturing those members of the family who were living in the Creek Nation. When questioned about the letter later, Drew first denied having written it, then said that it had been given to Houser with the oral understanding that it was not to be used until approval for the action was received from Washington. That understanding, however, had not been stated in the document, and no copy had been kept. Davis and his agents had finally found the weak link in the chain of protection that had maintained the family's freedom for so long.

Houser took the order to Choctaw agent Cooper along with a copy of a letter from Secretary of War Jefferson Davis saying that the attorney general had ruled that the Fugitive Slave Law applied. Cooper, who knew that the family was free and that the law was therefore irrelevant, refused to act. Houser then went to the Choctaw chiefs and lied again, telling them that Jefferson Davis had said that the attorney general had ruled that the Beams were slaves and that Cooper had promised to have those in the Choctaw Nation rounded up and delivered to the superintendent in Van Buren. The lie succeeded in gaining him possession of five family members from the Choctaw Nation plus two from the Creeks. He took them to the Cherokee Nation to sell them, but there, finally, his luck turned. A missionary named Worcester recognized the family members and intervened. Worcester appealed to the secretary of the interior and to Jefferson Davis, who responded indignantly that he would "abhor any act that deprives a Freeman of his rights and perverts a constitutional law to such base purposes." By this time, however, the captured family members had been sold.

As soon as they heard of their capture, friends of the Beams family went to court to sue for their freedom. Drew was called on the carpet for acting without authorization and directed to hire counsel in the Arkansas courts, to make every effort to have them freed, and to "have the most vigorous search made for those members of the family that have been sold and carried away—to enable the Department to institute proceedings for their release."[18] In yet another bizarre wrinkle, the sole survivor of the Choctaw Beams children joined the suit, claiming that Davis had never paid them the agreed-upon price for their stepmother, siblings, nieces, and nephews and that, as a result, all of them still belonged to her.

The captured family members were released until the conclusion of the two trials, which did not come for another year and a half. In both cases, the Arkansas juries immediately decided that they were free. Such quick decisions seem surprising, given the animosity against free people of color that was gathering force in Arkansas at the time. They may reflect the fact that northwest Arkansas, where the trial would have been held, still had very few slaves and, only three years later, a high level of pro-Union sentiment.

The outcome was not so happy for Thomas Drew, who had been fired in April of 1855. His former supporter, Commissioner Manypenny, wrote to the secretary of the interior on February 2, 1855, that

> in my opinion the facts developed in the papers emanating from Mr. Drew himself are sufficient to justify his removal from office without any further investigation.[19]

It is possible that Drew's earlier opposition to the Johnson bill or his cautious advocacy for the concerns of the nations for which he was responsible may already have weakened his position. In any case, his misstep in the Beams matter was the final straw.

Dismissed as superintendent, Drew rejoined his family. He brought them to Fort Smith, where he set up a law practice, drawing in part on the connections he had made in the Cherokee Nation during his brief tenure as superintendent.[20] By this time, he had spent so much of his life on borders of one sort or another, always seeing both sides and attempting to reconcile them, that this new location must have seemed like his natural home. Half a dozen of Cinderella's first cousins were living on or near the Arkansas River, chasing the border as generations of Bettises had done before them.[21] As far back as 1838, Elijah Alston, Sally's son, had been living at Spadra Bluff, near Clarksville, where he had discovered large deposits of high-quality anthracite coal. Following family tradition, he immediately subdivided his land and started selling off lots in the new town that he named Spadra.[22] For about ten years, he was joined there by William Wiley Rubottom, the most adventurous of all Cinderella's cousins.[23]

In the 1860 census for Fort Smith, the Drews appear with five of their children: James, 20; Saidee, 18; Thomas, 16; Emma Cinderella, 14; and Joseph, 10. Their older sister, Mollie, had died of consumption at the age of 22 in April of that year.[24] Just as none of Newit Drew's children had been named for his father, Jeremiah, none of Thomas's children were named for Newit. Although Thomas claims personal property worth $17,000, they own no real estate in Fort Smith and only three slaves, one of them a child of seven. One of the slaves, a mulatto woman of 23, can perhaps be matched with the 13-year-old mulatto girl in the 1850 census. The high valuation for personal property may indicate that Drew, in addition to practicing law, was involved in purchasing goods for transshipment into Indian Territory, a line of commerce whose importance to the economy of Fort Smith is indicated by the extraordinarily high number of "wagon conductors," "teamsters," and "drivers" listed on the census in the Drews' immediate neighborhood.

26. Worlds Destroyed

The late 1850s were a period of chaos in national politics. The majority Democrats and the minority Whigs each split apart along regional lines on the question of slavery, and many from both parties jumped ship to the American or "Know-Nothing" Party. Drew was among this group, and in 1858, he was briefly a candidate for Congress, a project that he abandoned almost as soon as he began.[1] The Know-Nothings were nativists. Their goal was to build a national party strong enough to save the Union, and they tried to achieve that end by unifying Americans around anti-Catholicism and hostility to immigrants. Like the Knights of the Golden Circle, they were organized as a quasi-Masonic order with degrees, secret rituals, secret handshakes, and secret passwords. Their popular name was derived from the words "I know nothing," supposedly uttered by members in response to any questions about those secrets. Shortly after Drew's brief flirtation with it, however, the party came apart at a convention where Northern abolitionists tried and failed to seize control.[2]

At some time after the 1860 census listing, the Drew family moved again, this time back down the Arkansas River to Clarksville where Elijah Bettis Alston had established himself as a merchant.[3] In the fall of that year, we find Thomas once again engaged in a search for compromise. As secession and war drew ever closer, he wrote a lengthy letter to an unnamed Arkansas newspaper, supporting Stephen Douglas, the Democratic candidate for President.[4] The national Democratic Party had nominated Douglas over the objections of the southern Democrats; the nomination led to a southern walkout, which six of the eight Arkansas delegates joined. The leading Arkansas politicians were working hard for the election of the southern candidate, John C. Breckenridge. Drew did not agree. A draft of his letter, running to eighteen handwritten pages, offers a reasoned, low-key, lawyerly argument strikingly different from the fire-breathing oratory of most southern politicians at that moment of crisis. The letter reveals an aspect of the Thomas Drew that we already know: a conciliator, always seeking the middle ground, stubbornly rational at that most irrational of historical moments. The key word of the piece, not only the actual final word but one repeated at least once on every page, is "principle."

The southern walkout grew out of the violent events that had taken place in Kansas over the previous six years. Douglas's principle of "popular sovereignty," embodied in the Kansas-Nebraska Act of 1854, had dynamited the fragile truce between North and South achieved by the Missouri Compromise and the Compromise of 1850. The Missouri Compromise involved the simultaneous admission of Missouri as a slave state and Maine as a free one along with a provision whereby slavery was to be permanently banned in any new states north of latitude 36 degrees, 30 minutes. The Kansas-Nebraska Act, however, replaced that ban with a free-for-all by allowing voters of each new state to decide for themselves whether or not to allow slavery. The sudden possibility of extending slavery to Kansas, where it had previously been forbidden, seemed to Missouri slaveholders like an unexpected gift, a gift that they named the "Christmas Goose."[5] And as soon as the gift was received, the extension of slavery to the new state began to be seen as a matter of survival in the old, since the existence of a free Kansas on the Missouri border would have offered an immediate haven to runaway slaves.

Believing that Kansas was rightfully theirs, parties of slaveholding emigrants began moving in. So, however, did groups of anti-slavery northerners. Some were simply attracted by the prospect of free land, but others were funded and armed by anti-slavery activists like Amos Lawrence, an heir to the textile fortune that had created Lawrence, Massachusetts. Missouri "border ruffians" quickly resorted to violence in an attempt to blockade the northerners or to drive them out.

The principle of democratic self-government in the territories, at first welcomed so eagerly by the slave states, was immediately overruled by the self-interest of the slaveholders. A combination of violence and massive voter fraud in the 1855 territorial elections gave control of the Kansas territorial legislature to the pro-slavery party, causing the free-state immigrants to organize their own party and elect their own, unsanctioned, legislature. The pro-slavery legislature responded by accusing the dissident legislators, and anyone else who agreed with them on the issue of slavery, of treason.[6] There were outbreaks of violence, at first sporadic and disorganized, and armed militias began forming on both sides.

In May of 1856, a pro-slavery judge ordered the indictment of all free-state leaders and the closing of free-state newspapers. The free-state stronghold of Lawrence was attacked, the headquarters of the Free State party and several houses burned, and the printing presses of the newspapers destroyed. Not long afterward, the murder of unarmed pro-slavery civilians at Pottawatomie Creek by anti-slavery terrorist John Brown touched off a bloody guerilla war in which murder, arson, and terror were the weapons of choice.

Meanwhile, the influx of anti-slavery settlers from the northern states was quickly overwhelming the influx from the South. In 1857, a blatantly rigged Kansas constitutional convention produced the pro-slavery Lecompton Constitution, but the delegates refused to submit the document to voters for ratification as they had pledged to do. The vastly greater numbers of anti-slavery settlers then elected a new territorial legislature controlled by the anti-slavery party, and that new legislature did schedule a ratification vote. Anti-slavery voters defeated the proposed constitution by a vote of ten thousand to two hundred.

Anxious to preserve the support of the South for the Democrats, President James Buchanan attempted to force the rejected pro-slavery constitution through Congress anyway. Douglas broke with his fellow Democrats to oppose it, based on the flagrant violations of popular sovereignty by which it had been produced. His consistent adherence to his own principle was the reason for the southern rejection of his candidacy for the Democratic presidential nomination in 1860.

It is easy to see how Douglas's devotion to principle, at considerable political cost, must have impressed Thomas Drew.[7] Drew's letter minimizes the danger to the institution of slavery resulting from that principle, describing the fears of his fellow Southerners as involving "some imaginary danger to the slave interest." Even if the existence of a free Kansas involves some danger to the private rights of slaveholders, he argues, it "does not involve our equality in the Union, our honor as a people, . . . [or any] principle essential to present security, or future safety." He dissects the hypocrisy of the Breckenridge supporters, who strongly opposed Congressional interference with the laws or constitutions of the individual states except when such interference promoted the interests of slavery. In the middle of the letter, he spends several pages carefully refuting the view that the Constitution allows for any right of secession "on any political pretext, short of despotic rule of the agents of government, such as to justify revolution." He then goes on to argue that even if Douglas is not intransigent enough to please the South, he should still be supported because he is the only Democratic candidate who could attract any northern votes and thus the only one with a chance of defeating "the Black Republican Lincoln."

Drew was far from alone in these opinions, especially in the northwest part of Arkansas where he was then living. When a state convention was called in February of 1861 to consider the question of secession, Arkansas voters elected a majority of Unionist delegates. When the convention took place in March, those delegates voted to remain in the Union, thirty-nine to thirty-five.[8]

From our perspective, however, Drew's argument seems naively optimistic. He had failed to grasp the degree to which both self-interest and moral passion could overwhelm reason. The violence and suffering of "Bleeding Kansas" had radicalized both sides, igniting a firestorm of outrage across the North and ultimately causing northern voters to regroup around the newly formed Republican Party.[9] The growth of abolitionism in the North, in turn, had raised in southern minds the terrifying spectacle of the total collapse of their social order and of the violent revenge that they believed would be taken upon them by newly freed slaves. In spite of the hopes of Arkansas Unionists, there was no longer a sustainable middle ground between slave and anti-slavery states. Breckenridge won the Arkansas primary in a three-way election with fifty-three percent of the vote. John Bell, the candidate of the Constitutional Unionist Party, got thirty-seven percent. Douglas received ten percent.[10] Drew the conciliator, the eternally, irrationally hopeful, had been doing his best for another lost cause.

When all hopes for peace were shattered in the Confederate bombardment of Fort Sumter, Drew went with his state. A letter written from Clarksville about a year later shows him trying to cajole his way into a colonel's commission in the Confederate army with an almost touching series of boasts and self-delusions. "Since the days of DeSoto," he writes,

> I am doubtless the first civilized man that ever mustered a Company in Arkansas, which I had the honor of doing forty-two years ago last Spring. I was fifty-nine years old the other day— incapable of going on foot or I would take a Captain's place. I was taught military tactics by a master of his profession [his uncle, Harmon Atkins Hays, whom he had known as a boy in Tennessee] who had served as adjt. during the War of 1812, and have subsequently practiced it in the capacity of . . . Sergeant, Major, and Brig. Gen. of Militia—and have [illegible] that I would have received of Mr. Polk the appt. of Brig. Genl. in the US Service during the Mexican War, had the second Regmt been called into that service from this State.[11]

Two of his sons, James and Thomas, enlisted in the Arkansas infantry in 1862.[12]

The outbreak of war did nothing to end the divisions among Arkansas citizens. As in many other southern states, there were pockets of Unionist resistance, particularly in the northwestern hills where farms were small, slaves few, and the white inhabitants stubbornly independent. In Searcy County and neighboring areas, the clandestine Arkansas Peace Society may have numbered as many as seventeen hundred members. The society created a network whose members recognized each other by codes: a yellow ribbon on a fencepost or the phrase "It's a dark night" with the response "Not so dark as it will be before morning." In December of 1861, the Confederate authorities arrested seventy-eight of those unionists and marched them in chains to Little Rock along with sympathizers from several neighboring counties. Most enlisted in the Confederate Army in order to avoid being tried and presumably hanged for treason, but they somehow failed to gain the trust of the officers under whom they served. As it turned out, the distrust was justified: many quickly deserted, and sometimes followed up by heading north and enlisting in the Union Army. Meanwhile, the men who had refused to enlist were never tried because a grand jury refused to indict them.[13]

From the beginning, the experience of civilians in northern Arkansas was fated to be one of drawn-out agony. As in Moore County, North Carolina, during the Revolution, people of opposing loyalties lived side by side in many areas, adding a touch of personal ferocity to the political and military struggle. The situation worsened dramatically in 1862 when the Union Army of the Southwest under General Samuel Curtis, stranded at Batesville and cut off from its supply lines, was forced to provision itself by plundering civilians. More brutal than the North Carolina militias of a century earlier, Curtis's troops laid waste to the countryside, taking what they wanted and burning what remained. In response, Confederate General Thomas Hindman ordered a scorched earth policy of his own, directing civilians to destroy all food, fodder, and crops that could be useful to advancing Federals. Whatever was left was taken or destroyed by roving gangs of Confederate guerrillas, by enemies settling old scores, or by the predators who appear in any society when the glue that holds it together has disintegrated.[14]

As Union and Confederate troops pursued each other across northern Arkansas, the Drew family moved further down the Arkansas River to the town of Dardanelle. But they could not move far enough to avoid the war. On September 1,1863, a division of the Union Army of the Frontier under General James G. Blunt marched in from Kansas to capture Fort Smith. Nine days later Union forces under General Frederick Steele, commander of the Union Army of Arkansas, and General John Davidson, commander of General Steele's first division, captured Little Rock. On September 12 all of Drew's papers were scattered and most of them burned, as federal forces captured Dardanelle.[15] It is likely that most of the family's other possessions were lost as well in the course of three major Confederate attempts to retake the town. Throughout northern Arkansas, the structures of normal community life were collapsing. Local government shut down, jails were opened and prisoners freed, crops went unharvested, and economic activity vanished.[16] The civilian population of Dardanelle fled to escape the starvation resulting from the ongoing battles, and, later, the terrorism of the guerilla forces that filled the area after the withdrawal of the Confederate troops.[17]

In and around Pocahontas, there were ongoing engagements between 1862 and 1864 with control of the area switching back and forth repeatedly between the two armies. Military activity continued until General Sterling Price's doomed effort to recapture Missouri for the Confederacy, known to history as Price's Raid, set off from Pocahontas in September of 1864. At some point during those two years of chaos, the Drew home was destroyed, perhaps when the town was burned in a Union raid in May of 1863. Colonel J. B. Rogers, commanding officer of the Missouri State [Union] Militia Cavalry, reported in 1865 that he "found the country infested by small bands of guerrillas, who will not stand and fight, but subsist by plundering the inhabitants, and the swamps and canebreaks of the region afford them secure shelter."[18] A low mound in the middle of a field, near the present-day town of Biggers, is still pointed out to visitors as the place where the Drew home once stood.

Wherever the family was living at the tail end of the war, Union Army officers were quartered in their house. One of them was a sutler, Captain Guy Coryell Bennett, an officer responsible for supplying the army with provisions. When Bennett returned home, Saidee Drew went with him. On July 17, 1865, only weeks after the end of the war, she was married to him at his parents' home in Illinois.[19] Saidee's sister Emma also married a Union officer.[20] Emma, however, apparently thought better of it, since she divorced him after a year or two and returned to Pocahontas to marry her second cousin William Marr, the son of T. O. Marr, the ferry owner. Joe, the youngest of the Drew children, married Algenora

Brimmage, daughter of a Pocahontas neighbor.[21] The name Brimmage appears on the Cherokee Rolls, and a surviving photo of Algenora strongly suggests that she was at least half-Indian.[22]

By 1866, the white population of Arkansas may have been reduced by as much as half.[23] Drew was working as a bookkeeper in Green Jones's general store with part of his two hundred dollar monthly salary being credited to his family's account at the same store. After a while, he quit his job at the store to set up another law practice, once acting as co-counsel in the unsuccessful defense of a notorious murderer.[24] When William Jarrett was hired to replace him, it was with the stipulation that Jarrett was to board with the Drew family and that twenty-five dollars of his monthly salary would be credited to the same account. Jarrett lived with the Drews for four years. In his old age, he remembered that although the family's finances were tight, both daughters were musical and the family full of warmth. He said of Thomas that he was "small in stature, had a kindly, friendly smile, and was one of the gentlest, most patient men you ever saw."[25]

The war was even more devastating for the nations of Indian Territory than it was for white Arkansas. Most of them, particularly the Creeks and Seminoles, faced the same divisions as the Cherokees: between mixed-bloods and full-bloods, between those who had accepted removal and those who had resisted till the end. The war brought those old resentments to a boil, and the result, in many cases, was the total destruction of the Indians' painstakingly rebuilt societies.

In the face of unrelenting pressure from Arkansas officials, both military and civilian, Cherokee Principal Chief John Ross tried desperately to maintain the unity of his nation by keeping it out of the conflict. But his efforts were undercut by the Southern Rights party led by Stand Watie, the last surviving member of the original group of Treaty Party leaders. Shortly after Arkansas seceded, members of this party met secretly with Confederate military leaders to ask for the protection of the Confederate Army if they should take up arms on the side of the South. In spite of Ross's refusal to permit such activity, Watie was given a colonel's commission and proceeded to raise a regiment of three hundred men.[26] Shortly thereafter, all four of the other Civilized Tribes signed treaties with the Confederacy.

Boxed in on all sides, Ross gave in, called a national convention, and obtained the authority to negotiate with the Confederacy. He managed to obtain a treaty that, on its face, gave the Cherokees almost everything they had failed to get from the United States, in addition to stipulating that no Cherokee troops would be required to serve outside of the Cherokee Nation. John Drew, a wealthy mixed-blood merchant and confidant of Ross, was commissioned a colonel and authorized to raise a regiment composed primarily of full-blood Ross supporters, known as Pins from the insignia they wore on their lapels.

Everywhere in Indian Territory, old feuds and hatreds were resurfacing. When the Creek government, dominated by slaveholding mixed-bloods, signed its treaty with the Confederacy, thousands of full-blood followers of the traditionalist Chief Opothleyoholo gathered around him in search of protection from their fellow tribesmen. From there they fled north towards Kansas with their women and children, their livestock, and their household

366

possessions, pursued by a Confederate force that included the mutually antagonistic Cherokee regiments of Watie and Drew. The Confederates caught them three times. In the first two engagements, the pro-Union Indians fought back successfully and escaped. The second time, most of Drew's Pins deserted, either joining the pro-Union refugees or heading home to their farms. The third time, however, a force of Texas and Arkansas cavalrymen crushed the refugees, driving them north in a panicked rout and forcing them to abandon all of the supplies that they needed to survive. They reached Kansas, where ten thousand other refugees were already encamped, in midwinter, without food, clothing, or shelter. Many died of starvation and exposure before the spring.[27]

All of the promises made to the Indians by their Confederate allies were immediately broken. Throughout the rest of the war, both Confederate and Union armies used their Indian troops as convenient, both inside and outside of Indian Territory, only to desert them when more pressing matters arose. Many of the shipments of arms, ammunition, and clothing that had been promised to the Confederate Indians were commandeered by the white troops.[28] In the course of a Union incursion in July of 1862, Ross was taken prisoner and ultimately shipped off to Washington to explain himself to Lincoln, leaving the Confederate Colonel Watie and his troops in charge. A year later, Union General Blunt decided to return the pro-Union Indian women and children to their homes. The small Union force at Fort Gibson, however, was unable to protect them from Watie's guerillas, who had retreated across the Arkansas River but were able to return, ambush the supply trains coming from

Kansas, and raid the country at will. Back in their devastated country, the former refugees continued to die.[29]

Finally, abandoned by both Union and Confederate armies, the Cherokees were left to destroy each other. The carnage was similar to that experienced in Cumberland County, North Carolina, during the Revolution, only far, far worse. Hundreds of people were killed for being "traitors" to one side or the other. Houses, barns, and crops were pillaged and burned by both sides, gangs of freelance bandits robbed and murdered at will, and whatever livestock was left was stolen by white settlers coming over the border from Arkansas. By the end of the war, only a wasteland was left where once there had been a flourishing nation.

Cinderella at Breakfast

Fort Smith, Arkansas • 1858

In the dining room of the rented house in Fort Smith, Cinderella and
Saidee are lingering over the remains of breakfast. Mollie sits in a chair
by the window, mending a hoop skirt. James has gone off to the office
with Thomas, and the younger children are already at school.

Mollie has hardly been coughing at all lately. Both she and Saidee
can sew superbly; if need be, they can look as soignée as any of the girls
in Little Rock. Mollie, the eldest, is sweet and tractable, the epitome of a
well-bred young lady. Emma is demonstrating exceptional proficiency at
her piano lessons. And Saidee—well, at least she has the Bettis spirit.

By now Cinderella is an old hand at moving. Even with only two
servants to help her, she can manage her family and her possessions.
They've managed to keep the piano, the good china, Thomas's books,
and the best of the furniture. No one suspects the little economies that
they must practice in order to keep up appearances. This is not a genteel
neighborhood, what with the teamsters and drivers shouting at each
other day and night outside the windows. But there is nothing left for
them in Pocahontas. The only cousin still there is that snippy little
Cousin Amy, and now that her family owns the whole town she thinks
she's above everyone.

It was not until she was forty that Cinderella discovered her own
strength. Before that she was merely a spoiled young girl, berating her
husband, slapping the servants and twisting their ears, luxuriating
in her own anger. And later—for oh, how brief a moment!—finding
recompense in her wealth and her preeminence, as the Governor's wife.
But at the bottom of the dark valley, when they had lost everything,

when little Bennett had died and she and Thomas and six small children and her mother had all had to depend on the charity of his brother James, she found that her family's survival depended upon her, and that only she could bring them through. Only she could surround them with affection, and give them the courage they needed to go on.

In that dark time, the person who helped her most was old Mrs. Drew. A woman of no education, no refinement, but tough as nails, and kind to them when they needed it most. She taught Cinderella about the kind of character it takes to get through life.

Mollie will get better.

Thomas will once again be important and respected. She is sure she can persuade him to run for Congress in the new 2nd District.

Hold your heads up, she tells her children. We are people who count.

The mulatto girl brings in the coffee. The one Thomas insisted on keeping when they had to sell all the others. A year older than Mollie. Patsie was barely out the door. We spend our lives surrounded by them, and the men think we don't know. In the end, what can one do with one's life but bear it, with whatever dignity—and generosity, if at all possible—one can manage?

Saidee is complaining that her new dress will not have the lace collar she wants. Cinderella, distracted, reaches for the small silver salt dish instead of the sugar bowl, and pours a spoonful of salt into her coffee. Saidee falls silent. As Cinderella takes the first sip of coffee, she looks up and sees Saidee watching her, saying nothing. She looks Saidee straight in the eye and drinks the entire cup.

27. The Wilder West

Cinderella died in 1872 at the age of sixty-two. Thomas, a seventy-year-old widower, could easily have settled down in Pocahontas to live out a quiet old age. Instead, he and his unmarried son James set off for California. Cinderella's cousin William Wiley Rubottom, then and thereafter known to everyone as Uncle Billy, had been living in the Pomona Valley near the present-day town of El Monte, on the stagecoach route between Los Angeles and San Bernardino, for the previous twenty years. In true Bettis style he had founded the town of Spadra, named it after his former home on the Arkansas River, established a well-known hotel and stagecoach stop, and become one of the town's leading citizens.[1] As the son of Ezekiel Rubottom's second wife, he was not, strictly speaking, a cousin. But he had grown up with the Bettis cousins in the tight little community of Greenville and remained close to several of them. Elijah Bettis IV followed him to California and married his daughter.[2]

In the course of Billy's life, stories accumulated around him, some of them with a basis in fact. His career was typical of many frontier entrepreneurs: a series of bold initiatives, repeated failures, and repeated restarts. He was tough, determined, and resilient, and you would not have wanted to cross him. He was not, however, a rugged individualist. Like his father, Ezekiel, he was a high-ranking Mason and is said by Rubottom expert Anne Collier to have restricted his most profitable business deals to a circle of family members and fellow Masons.[3] Linking his entrepreneurial energy to the support of a small, powerful, and close-knit group, he embodied one version of the American dream, as it was coming into being in the American West.

In 1849, Billy and his brother Ezekiel set off for the California gold fields, as did their cousin, the nineteen-year-old Ranson Drew. The story goes that Billy made a lot of money mining but lost it when a dam burst upstream from his mine and washed away the mine works, along with his pouch of gold. He then went to work on a Sacramento River boat carrying flour down to San Francisco. The boat sank, but Billy managed to salvage the sacks of flour, put them out in the sun to dry until the outer layer of flour was baked hard, and then took advantage of a flour shortage to sell the dry flour inside the crust at a large profit. Inspired by a vision of the opportunities available in the beautiful new land, he returned to Johnson County, Arkansas, organized a wagon train of somewhere between a dozen and a hundred families, and headed for the Pomona Valley.[4]

Some of the stories told about him appear in more than one version, providing amusing examples of the evolution of a western legend. Horace Bell, a Los Angeles Ranger, member of William Walker's filibustering expedition, scout in the Union Army during the Civil War, lawyer, journalist, and author of two books of lively anecdotes about early California history, provides us with one of them. According to Bell, who claimed to have known Billy well, during his first visit to California Billy was a resident of a mining camp where one of the other residents was a slave boy named Harry. Harry was traded around among the miners in a weekly card game, with each week's winner gaining the right to his services for the following week. In one of these games, he was won by a Mr. McGullion. At that point, however, Billy dropped in on the game, declared that it had gone on long enough, and told the gamblers that Harry was free under California law. He then offered Harry four dollars a week if Harry would agree to work for him. Since Billy was the dominant figure in the camp, none of the miners dared to disagree, and Harry worked for Billy until Billy decided to return to Arkansas, leaving him in the care of a local judge. McGullion, however, got to Arkansas first, told everyone that Billy had become an abolitionist and had stolen McGullion's slave, and procured a warrant for Billy's arrest.

McGullion took no further action until Billy returned home and organized his party of relatives to return to California with him. Just beyond the edge of Indian Territory, McGullion and two deputies caught up with them and announced that Billy was under arrest. In recounting the story to Bell, Billy said that he had had no weapons but that the next thing he remembered was coming to in his family's wagon, covered with blood, and being told that he had killed McGullion and both of the deputies. Bell's book, *On the Old West Coast*, written in the last years of the nineteenth century but not published for another thirty years, also includes an account of Billy saving a man named Mexican Joe from a lynching by cursing the lynch mob "so scathingly that the bark peeled off the big oak tree . . . one of the listeners' hair turned grey and three others were stricken baldheaded." He describes Billy as "honest, generous and just, a lover of right and a hater of wrong."[5]

In Frank Parkhurst Brackett's imaginative and highly romanticized *History of Pomona Valley*—published in 1923, at the height of the Jim Crow era—the story of the young slave Harry has changed dramatically. In Brackett's version, there are nine slaves, and they all "emancipate themselves" rather than being liberated by Billy. When Billy returns to Arkansas without the slaves, their former owner and another man meet Billy on the street and accuse him of selling them and keeping the profits. In the course of the heated discussion that follows, the slaveowner draws a gun and shoots at Billy, wounding him in the hand. As Brackett tells it:

> With incredible stamina he drew a silk handkerchief through the bullet hole to stanch the flow of blood, and then in a frenzy of rage he dashed after the two men. With his whole hand he drew his knife from his belt and pulled off the sheath with his teeth.

He then chases his assailants into a nearby tavern and stabs them both to death. Thirty years later, when a Johnson County sheriff finally arrives in California to arrest him, the seventy-year-old Billy, sitting on his porch with a knife and a shotgun, scares him back to Johnson County.[6] Whereas Bell's stories about Billy consistently emphasize his human decency and his aversion to slavery, Brackett prefers to celebrate an ideal of reckless courage and homicidal rage.

Another killing, this one verified, was closer to home. Before the family moved from El Monte to the future town of Spadra, Billy's daughter Civility had married a southern officer named Hilliard Dorsey, like Billy a prominent Mason and community leader. Dorsey had a reputation as a street fighter and was said to have once bitten off an opponent's nose.[7] Anne Collier, the Rubottom researcher, adds that he was also an alcoholic and a womanizer. Horace Bell, purporting to quote Billy's actual words, has him describing Dorsey as "the bravest man I ever faced" but also an "overbearing bully" who "didn't know how to treat a woman." At some point, Civility was compelled to take the couple's small son and flee to her father's house. Dorsey followed, announcing that he was there to take back his son. He was met at the front door by Billy sitting on the porch with a shotgun across his knees. Both men drew their guns; Dorsey died. "I hated to shoot him," says Billy in Bell's telling. "I begged him to stop, but on he came."[8] Brackett's *History of Pomona Valley* says nothing about Dorsey's reputed faults but goes on at length about his "many sterling qualities, frankness, sincerity and winsomeness and energy," presenting the incident as a tragic conflict between two southern gentlemen forced by circumstance to defend their honor and implicitly casting the blame on Civility for disrupting her happy home.[9]

Uncle Billy's hotel and stagecoach stop was the center of activity for the surrounding community. And for two or three years, it looked as if it might be more. In 1872, bandits hiding out in Surprise Canyon, three hundred miles to the north in what later became Death Valley National Park, accidentally discovered a lode of silver ore. In short order, two Nevada senators were informed of the discovery, charges against the discoverers were dropped, and the Panamint Mining District was formed with the two senators as principal investors.[10] Miners swarmed into the mountains. Wagonloads of silver ore, cast into giant four-hundred-pound cannonballs in order to foil bandits on horseback, began arriving at Billy's stagecoach stop just as the tracks for the Southern Pacific Railroad were being laid into the area from the west. Somehow Billy persuaded the railroad's owners to make Spadra the eastern terminus of the line so that silver ore could be loaded onto its trains from there.

Rubottom Inn, 1866

It was at this point that Thomas Drew arrived in California. Fifty years later, in a letter to the editor of the *Dallas News*, an old acquaintance of his reported that Drew had been given money for the trip by his first cousin John Coffee Hays, who had won fame as a Texas Ranger and later as Sheriff of San Francisco and the founder of the city of Oakland.[11] He expected to repair his fortune through land speculation, but luck deserted him once again. By 1875, the Panamint mines were already played out, and later that year, the Southern Pacific Railroad reconsidered its proposed route and moved the line north to the town of Colton.[12]

A letter to Drew's daughter Emma, written from San Bernardino in February of 1875, describes his undiminished hopes. Emma was by then a widow with two young sons and embroiled in a series of lawsuits as she attempted to hold on to her father-in-law's ferry. "I do not know if it will avail you anything," Drew wrote,

> but I might possibly make a large sale of land in time to come to your relief. The town of San Bernardino is destined, although

far out from the seacoast (eighty miles) to become a great Rail Road Center!

Neither the exhaustion of the Panamint mines nor the change in the plans of the Southern Pacific Railroad was yet on his horizon; all he could see was the prospect of more and more railroads and the "hundreds of rich mines recently discovered." Emma's brother James was running a wagon yard and boarding house ten miles south of the Panamint mines and was "stout and healthy and well situated." Land was available at unbelievably low prices and appreciating rapidly in value. Emma should be telling all their old friends in Randolph County to sell out and come west. "If money is not so plentiful now as desired, it soon will be abundant."

Although Pocahontas was then at the peak of its prosperity, Thomas's memories of it were not fond. San Bernardino, he writes,

> is a better country than that sickly region that has gained in living population but little during the last forty years of my acquaintance with it. If I had [Joe's] and your little families out of that country I would not remain in constant dread on account of sickness and death.[13]

The 1923 letter to the *Dallas News* states that Drew actually did make a fortune in California only to lose it almost immediately. According to the writer, who claimed an intimate knowledge of the Drew family, John Coffee Hays was able to direct a profitable piece of litigation Drew's way, from which Drew netted a fee of thirty thousand dollars. He was bringing that money to Hood County, Texas, where his son Joe and his daughter Emma were later to join him, when the stagecoach he was traveling in was robbed. Drew lost all of his silver in the robbery except for three thousand dollars that he managed to hide.[14] For the next few years, he remained in Hood County, buying a few scattered parcels of land. During the whole of his long life, he had left no evidence of any connection to the Baptist faith of his father, but in 1877 he was "saved" in Lipan and joined the Baptist church there.[15]

What impelled him to keep moving right up to the end of his life? Perhaps his health had something to do with it: in his letter to Emma he speaks of having saved his own life by the move to California. Perhaps his incurable hopefulness simply would not let him rest. Perhaps, like many pioneers, he could not bear the restraints and predictability of settled community life. Or perhaps he could not bear being poor in Pocahontas in his old age after having been the town's founder, benefactor, and leading citizen in his thirties.

Seven of his eleven children survived to adulthood: Ranson, James, Thomas, Saidee, Emma, Joseph, and his illegitimate son, Drew Bettis. Joe, like his older brother Ranson, seems to have inherited their family's adventurous streak. His obituary in an unidentified Prescott, Arizona, newspaper says that

> ... for the 45 years during which Mr. Drew dwelt in this section
> he was most of the time engaged in lion and other big game
> hunting .... He dressed like a hunter of old days and wore long
> curls which hung clear to his shoulders.

He was a member of the Ku Klux Klan and, according to his obituary, was buried with "full Klan honors."[16] A few years before his death, he had gone to Claifornia to bring the ailing Ranson back to Arizona with him. Their sister Saidee Drew Bennett settled in Phoenix, with a ranch in Prescott where the family spent its summers. It seems somehow appropriate that so many members of this restless family wound up in the very last of the lower forty-eight states to abandon its territorial status.

Thomas Drew died in Texas in 1879. In 1923, his remains were dug up and returned to Pocahontas, where they were reburied with great ceremony in the presence of twenty-five thousand people.[17] Although it was not publicized at the time, the only thing found in his grave—and transported to and reburied in Pocahontas—was a single gold tooth.[18]

Part VII

Citizens of a Free Nation

LEAVENWORTH

5

KANSAS CITY

KANSAS

JOURNEYS OF MARTHA BETTIS COOPER AND HER CHILDREN

INDIAN TERRITORY

KEY

1. GREENVILLE MISSOURI : 1806
2. POCAHONTAS ARKANSAS : 1832 - 1837
3. JACKSONPORT ARKANSAS : 1854
4. LEAVENWORTH KANSAS : 1860
5. NICODEMUS KANSAS : 1880 - 1885
   [MARTIN BETTIS, MARY JANE BETTIS KELLY, WILLIAM KELLY]

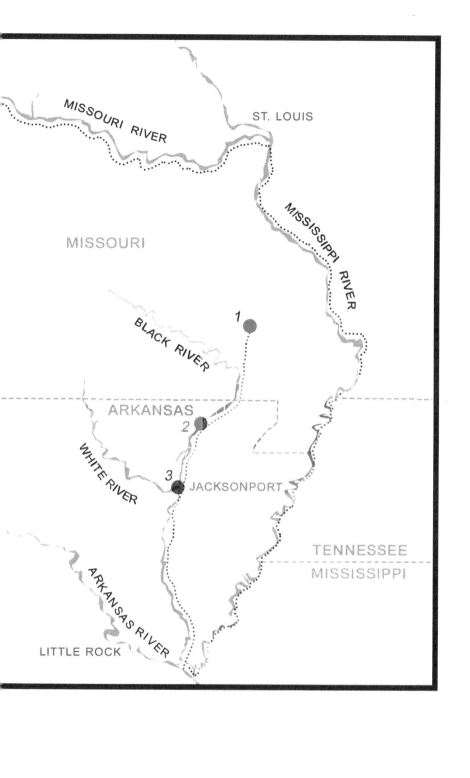

28. A Free Woman of Color in Jacksonport

When Elijah Bettis's enslaved daughters gained their freedom, several of them abandoned their childish nicknames and reclaimed their adult names. Haley became Mahala, and Litty, Elizabeth. When we meet Patsie again on March 15, 1849, she is Martha Cooper, buying a house lot in Jacksonport, Arkansas, a bustling steamboat town at the confluence of the White and Black Rivers, for fifty dollars.[1] Land was appreciating rapidly in Jacksonport, but not as rapidly as the price of that lot: seven years later, in January of 1856, she resold it for a thousand dollars to a rich and influential lawyer named James Robinson.[2]

A month before that sale, on December 18, 1855, she had signed, with an *X*, a deed by which

> from motives of benevolence, humanity and natural affection I
> have manumitted and emancipated and hereby do manumit and
> emancipate and set free from slavery my son and negro man slave
> Drew aged about twenty-five years and of copper color and I do
> hereby give, grant and release unto the said Drew all my right, title
> and claim of in and to his person labor and service and of in and to
> the estate and property which he may hereafter acquire or obtain.

Two prominent white men, Richard Searcy and Publius Wisdom, were witnesses to the deed, which was then presented to the local court, and "it is therefore considered by the court that the said Drew be considered and declared a free person of color."[3] It is not clear whether there was any connection between Martha's purchase of Drew and the sale of her lot. Buying her son's freedom would have cost her a considerable fraction of that thousand dollars—but the money, presumably, had not yet been paid to her.

The story behind the exceptionally high price of the land remains a mystery.

Richard Searcy, who witnessed the deed of emancipation, was the nephew of an earlier Richard Searcy, a prominent early settler of Davidsonville, where Cinderella's relatives Isaac and Charles Kelly had also settled. Like Thomas Drew, this earlier Richard had been a judge of the Lawrence County Circuit Court,[4] and later, he was also a judge of the Superior Court of Arkansas Territory. When this Richard Searcy died in 1832, he left a great deal of property in Independence County, Arkansas, across the Black River from Jacksonport. The Searcy family, then, most likely had a connection with the Drew and Bettis families spanning nearly thirty years.[5] Publius Wisdom, a wealthy merchant in Jacksonport, was unmarried at the time of the deed, and, interestingly, owned no slaves.[6] Martha was pursuing a common strategy for free people of color in that era: maintaining connections with powerful white citizens who could attest to her freedom, vouch for her in court if necessary, and offer her protection from unscrupulous people who might cheat and rob her and her son, or even kidnap them in order to sell them back into slavery.[7] The story of the Beams family, whom we met earlier, offers an example both of the dangers she faced and of the usefulness of such protectors.

Little by little, the status of free people of color continued to deteriorate. In 1840, the Arkansas legislature passed a law that relieved employers of African-American apprentices from the obligation of providing them with an education and at the same time mandated more generous treatment of white apprentices. In 1844, the legislature passed a resolution declaring that free people of color were not citizens of the US "within the meaning of the constitutional guarantee of the privileges and immunities of the citizens of one state in the other states."[8]

Six months after Martha freed her son, Mahala (formerly Haley) Bettis, also of Jacksonport but with a less eloquent lawyer, emancipated

> for divers good and sufficient reasons ... my negro girl named Evalina Bettis who shall and after the time above mentioned be free from the bonds of slavery from me my heirs executors administrators and assigns forever.[9]

It looks very much as if Martha had made enough money from the January sale and whatever savings she had accumulated previously to buy and free not only her son but another young family member as well.[10] In November of 1857, she bought another lot, and a year after that, her son Drew did the same.[11] On May 18, 1859, both of them sold their lots to Publius Wisdom and another man for the same price they had paid for them.[12]

The only clue we have about Martha's presumed husband, Mr. Cooper, is a statement in a 1976 letter from her descendant, the imaginative family historian Bettie Hurd, to the effect that Martha was "the widow of a steamboat captain."[13] But since this is the same letter in which Ms. Hurd identifies Elijah Bettis III as a refugee French aristocrat rather than the son of a backwoods North Carolina farmer, we need to take her statement with several grains of salt. If Cooper was a steamboat captain, he would almost undoubtedly have been white, since men of color were normally barred from all positions as steamboat officers.[14] Interracial marriage, however, was illegal in every southern state. Whoever he was, Martha kept his name, Cooper, for the rest of her life, while her son Drew and the rest of her family held fast to Bettis.

The river offered a wide variety of opportunities to free people of color. At the top of the occupational pyramid was the position of steamboat steward, a role that involved an extensive list of responsibilities and a high level of personal and intellectual skills, the most prestigious and one of the most lucrative jobs available to a free man of color in the antebellum South. Steamboats had evolved since the days when Mrs. Trollope complained so vehemently about them: by the late 1840s the main cabins had become luxurious places where men and women socialized and even ate together. Stewards were responsible for purchasing supplies at every stop; supervising the cooks, waiters, and cabin crew; planning activities and entertainments for the passengers; and sometimes even making sure that passengers obeyed the rules—an extremely delicate undertaking. A steward had to be well-dressed and well-spoken, possessing not only managerial ability but tact, diplomacy, and an in-depth understanding of the quirks of the passengers he served.[15]

In addition to a salary of fifty dollars per month, a steward often received tips from passengers and might also engage in business on the side, selling and trading supplies on his own account as well as for the steamboat owners.[16] Waiters and deckhands, the lower ranks of steamboat workers, also engaged in such trading and were admired and envied by plantation slaves for their independence, knowledge of the world, and possession of that priceless resource, information. They knew what was going on in distant cities and could sometimes transmit messages between separated family members up and down the rivers.[17] However exhausting their work, steamboat crews enjoyed a degree of independence and autonomy that most enslaved people could only dream of, and some made enough money on the river to buy both their own freedom and that of their families.

But perhaps we do not need a rich Mr. Cooper to account for Martha's financial success. He may have been plain Willis Cooper, an otherwise unknown resident of Jacksonport who was paid small amounts by the Jacksonport Circuit Court in 1855 and 1856 for guarding prisoners.[18] Jacksonport offered many opportunities for an enterprising woman, married or single, to build up her savings. In the 1840s and '50s, hundreds of steamboats plied the rivers, with ten or more tied up at the Jacksonport wharves at any one time. Downstream came furs, timber, cotton, and rendered bear fat, the latter prized both as lamp fuel and as a tasty cooking ingredient. Upstream came manufactured goods, staples such as coffee, tea, and sugar, and boatloads of westward-bound emigrants. The town's main street was lined with inns, saloons, and stores. Steamboat captains could make enormous fortunes, from $50,000 to $250,000 in a single year, and they gambled them away with abandon. At each port, the boat's steward had to see to supplies of food and lumber. At the same time, the crew and passengers, longing for fresh food after days of steamboat fare, were willing to pay high prices for whatever was offered on the shore. Fresh baked goods were in particular demand, and one of Jacksonport's booming industries was cooking and baking for steamboat passengers and crews.[19] Martha may have accumulated some savings by establishing a successful business and then, like many of her Bettis relatives, moved into real estate.

Or perhaps Martha herself worked on the river, at least for the first few years after she was freed. Every large steamboat had one or two chambermaids who kept the cabins clean and looked after the needs of the ladies. Like the stewards, chambermaids had to be well-dressed, well-spoken, and constantly attentive. The job was exhausting. It was also dangerous, because of the constant threat of sexual abuse by passengers or crew members. Few women held it for long. But it offered opportunities for generous tips, particularly if a chambermaid took on extra work like washing ladies' clothes.[20] In a couple of years, a job as a steamboat chambermaid might have allowed Martha to accumulate enough savings and enough connections to set up her own small business in Jacksonport. It might also have helped her to accomplish something even more significant: assisting in the escape of her brother and her second son.

According to the censuses of 1870 and 1880, Martin Bettis was born in 1835 or 1836 while his mother was still a slave. He appears in an 1839 document along with his older brother Drew as one of the enslaved grandchildren bequeathed to Elijah's legitimate daughters, Amy and Charnelsea, after their mothers were freed.[21] Family legend as transmitted by Bettie Hurd, herself a descendant of Martin,[22] says that Martha was riding in the woods one day when her horse balked and she could not get him to move.

> A little man dressed in a breech cloth and who could speak
> no English came out of the brush. He cleaned a switch of bark
> and gave the horse a . . . lick and the horse and Martha took off .

... Anyway she must have liked what she saw because she went back and he showed up. He was a short man. She must have been at least 5'7"....His father was a French trader and his mother was a Cherokee Indian .... Anyway Martin was born of this alliance ....At the age of two years he was taken to Canada, London, Ontario, by an uncle."[23]

In an earlier letter Ms. Hurd says that Martha's brother James

saw Martin as a little boy two years old and as he and his family were moving to Canada he asked his sister Martha if he could take him. She consented and Martin was raised with his children until he was 21 at which time his mother prevailed upon him to return.[24]

We can discount the part about the breech cloth. Any mixed-blood Cherokees still in Arkansas in 1835 would have been wearing European clothes, as Cherokees had been doing for decades. The census and court documents also indicate that Martin was at least four by the time of his journey north. James Bettis may have been not Martha's brother but her oldest nephew, since a slave named "Jim" appears at the head of the list of Elijah's bequeathed grandchildren.[25] The only point on which there is no doubt is that James took the young Martin with him to Ontario. None of Bettie Hurd's letters contains a hint that her ancestors were enslaved; in one of them she describes the illiterate Martha as having been "educated like any wealthy girl of her time." By the time those letters were written, Ms. Hurd and her branch of the family had crossed the line into the white community. But there is also not much question about what James was doing: he was escaping from slavery. Central Ontario was a major northern terminus of the underground railroad and an obvious destination for a fugitive.

The more difficult question is how James could have made that dangerous journey with a small child in tow. That is where Martha's river contacts might have been useful. If she was working on a steamboat or was already established in Jacksonport, the busy and highly mobile river society would have allowed her to do such things as obtain forged freedom papers for James or buy or make him a good suit of clothes so that he looked like someone with an unquestionable right to travel. Family photographs shared with me by William Gary Hildebrandt and labeled "Great Great Great Great Uncle James Bettis (Beatty) taken in London, Ontario, Canada" suggest that James was white enough so that he may have had no great difficulty in that attempt. Martin himself is listed as "white" in both the 1880 federal census for Kansas and the 1885 Kansas state census. If any problems arose, Martha may have had friends who could vouch for his freedom. She may have had information about safe houses on the Underground Railroad once James and Martin left the river. In any case, with or without her help, they made it to Ontario where James and his family settled down as free citizens. Martha, unable to read or write, would have had little or no news of her son for at least thirty years, but she would have known that he was free.

For several years after her emancipation of Drew, Martha continued to prosper. By 1859, however, their position, like that of free people of color everywhere in the South, was becoming more precarious. With the approach of war, the southern defense of slavery was becoming ever more hysterical. Because the self-justification of the slaveholders was based on a belief in the hopeless inferiority, the naïve, childlike, lazy, and savage character of all people of African descent, the existence of industrious, successful free people of color like Martha posed a threat to their whole conception of their world. As a result, some supporters of slavery felt forced to defend that world with increasingly irrational rhetoric. A circular published in 1858 described free people of color as

> lazy, worthless, immoral, impudent and unprincipled ... intentionally exerting the worst influence on slaves, encouraging them in all their evil habits and inclinations, hating us who deny them equal privileges with ourselves; ever ready to receive stolen wares and harbor the fugitive; and wholly *unfit* to be free.[26]

Another circular in the same year referred to "the free Negro so worthless and depraved an animal," and "the laziness and bestiality of a degraded race." [27] There was, of course, some quite rational concern about the assistance offered by those free people to slaves who wished to escape, but it was their threat to the slaveholders' sense of themselves that prompted the most extreme response.

Throughout the 1850s, there were attempts in the Arkansas legislature to pass laws expelling free people of color from the state. In 1859 one such attempt finally succeeded. Under this law, if Martha and Drew did not leave by January, 1860, they could be seized and hired out for a year, after which they would be given the choice of leaving or "voluntarily" re-enslaving themselves. Manumission was also banned. In a provision of particular viciousness, children between the ages of seven and twenty-one were not allowed to leave the state with their parents but were required to be hired out to the highest bidder until the age of twenty-one, when they would receive their back pay and be driven out. The law was not well enforced, and in 1861, it was suspended for two years. By the end of that time, it had become irrelevant.[28] Nevertheless, it seems likely that its passage was the reason for Martha and Drew's decision to sell their remaining Jacksonport property and move to Kansas.

A year earlier, Martha's sister Charity Bettis had sold her house in Pocahontas, presumably also intending to move. The buyer, interestingly, was Thomas Drew's rich brother, James Cloyd Drew.[29] Since there was no reason for James to want a small house in a remote small town, even for the sake of speculation, he must have made the purchase at Thomas's request, to help out a woman who was regarded as a family connection.

At some point in 1859, Martha and Drew traveled up the Mississippi and Missouri Rivers to Leavenworth, Kansas, the first town of any size that they would have encountered on free soil. With them was a ten-year-old boy who appears in later censuses as John P. or John V. Bettis and is sometimes identified by Martha's descendants as her youngest son. There is no documentation to support that characterization of the relationship. According to the 1860 and 1870 United States Census, he was born in Louisiana at a date that would have made Martha over forty at the time of his birth.[30] He lived with Martha or Drew for the next ten years, finally moving to Abilene with his sixteen-year-old wife. Whether or not he was Martha's son, his story is one example of her determination to gather together the pieces of her scattered family.

No free person of color, however rich and respectable, could travel in the upper cabin of a steamboat with the whites. Martha and Drew traveled on the lower deck amid the roar of the great boilers with the deckhands, the cabin crew, the slaves, the merchandise, and those who could not afford a stateroom. And whether or not they knew it, they were traveling upriver during a short window of comparative safety, perhaps less than two years, between random chaos and total destruction.

29. Into the Whirlwind

With the election of a strongly anti-slavery legislature and the overwhelming defeat of the pro-slavery Lecompton Constitution in 1858, the question of slavery in Kansas had finally been settled. But the conflict had radicalized both sides, not only in Kansas but on the national stage. Settlers from the North, at first indifferent to or even supportive of their neighbors' right to own human beings, were openly rejecting that right. In October of 1859, at about the time that Martha and Drew arrived, the new Wyandotte Constitution was ratified, not only outlawing slavery but also, unlike the constitutions of many northern states, allowing immigration by free people of color and even granting them limited voting rights.[1] By this time, however, the habit of violence had become addictive among both groups of Kansans. In May of 1858, the pro-slavery guerilla Charles Hamilton attempted to ignite a war of extermination against free-state settlers by murdering five of them at Marais des Cygnes.[2] Meanwhile, the anti-slavery guerilla James Montgomery was terrorizing pro-slavery settlers, John Brown and his followers were crossing from Kansas into Missouri to liberate Missouri slaves, and mobs of free-state settlers were joining together to rescue runaways who had been recaptured.[3]

Why would Martha and Drew have chosen to settle in such a dangerous place? Simply put, it was more welcoming to them than any other state within easy reach. Until after the Civil War, Illinois and Indiana maintained their black codes, forbidding free people of color from entering their states without official certificates of their freedom or, in the case of Illinois, from entering at all. Under

Illinois law, the most repressive in the nation, a free person of color who remained in the state for more than ten days could be arrested, jailed, and fined fifty dollars. Free men of color who already resided in either Illinois or Indiana could not vote, testify in court, or serve on juries. Although seldom enforced, these laws reflected the attitudes of the majority of the inhabitants of those states.[4]

In Missouri, things were even worse. Free people of color were required to choose white guardians to handle all their business transactions and could not buy land, sell a crop, or even travel to another town to visit friends without the guardian's permission.[5] Kansas, on the other hand, not only recognized African-Americans as citizens—second-class citizens, but citizens nonetheless—but still had an abundance of land available to enterprising settlers. You needed courage to settle there, but courage was what they had.

With the outbreak of war, the violence escalated, and continued to escalate over the next three years into the most savage of all the local civil wars that we have encountered in this history, perhaps the most savage ever fought on American soil. As in backwoods North Carolina eighty-five years earlier and as in Indian Territory just to the south, the two regular armies had few troops to spare for remote border conflicts. The inhabitants, organized into local militias, irregular guerilla bands, and gangs of freelance bandits, were left to settle their own accounts, and, as in the divided nations of Indian Territory, those accounts were based on old hatreds and the lust for revenge. "I am here for revenge," said one pro-southern guerilla, "and I have got it."[6]

The first year of the war saw troops of Kansas jayhawkers crossing into Missouri to wreak vengeance on the pro-slavery

Missourians who had tried to steal their state. At first, they merely burned and looted stores, making little distinction between pro-slavery and pro-Union inhabitants, but soon the Independent Mounted Kansas Jayhawkers were looting and burning farmhouses and even entire towns, stealing every horse they found, preying on the women, children, and old men who had been left behind when their sons and husbands went off to war, and leaving their victims without food, clothing, or shelter in the winter snow.[7] The loot from the pillaged farms was hauled off in wagons, sometimes in convoys many miles long, to be sold at auction on the streets of border towns like Leavenworth. The indiscriminate plundering of pro-Confederacy and pro-Union families drove many former Union supporters to change sides and fight for the Confederacy.[8]

Wherever the jayhawkers appeared, Missouri slaves left with them. Hundreds of others simply crossed to freedom on their own. Lawrence and Leavenworth were particularly popular destinations for runaways, and Kansans, formerly hostile, were proud to assist them. In the depth of winter, when the Missouri River froze over, Kansans watching from the Leavenworth shore could see the ice black with fugitives, crossing with "sparkling eyes, happy grins, and elastic steps."[9] Some brought with them the family goods, wagons, and horses of their former owners or crossed back over the border to do some jayhawking of their own.

Eager for an opportunity to assist in the destruction of slavery, others enlisted in the First Kansas Colored Volunteers. In their blue uniforms, shouldering the rifles they had never before been allowed to carry, they could experience themselves for the first time as *men*, rather than as slaves or "boys." The exhilaration of that experience rings out again and again in the speeches, songs, and writings of African-American soldiers who fought in the Union army. In the words of one such song,

> *They look like men,*
> *they look like men,*
> *they look like men of war.*
> *All arm'd and dressed in uniform,*
> *they look like men of war.[10]*

July, 1862, saw the passage of the first federal law allowing recruitment of African-American soldiers, and Kansas was the first state to put the provisions of that law into practice.[11]

The revenge exacted by the Kansas jayhawkers soon generated an even more brutal retaliation. A young man named William Quantrill, described by one observer as "modest, quiet, . . . gentle and courteous,"[12] was its instrument. A Northerner and former free-state supporter, Quantrill switched sides at the beginning of the war, and quickly attracted a following of ruthless young men, many of them seeking revenge for the suffering and death of family members at the hands of the jayhawkers.[13] Beginning with small-scale raids, in which stores and houses were looted and a few of the inhabitants killed, Quantrill and his "bushwhackers" soon established a reputation as

> braver and more dangerous than the Apache or Comanche
> Indians [and] better riders . . . industrious, bloodthirsty devils,
> who apparently never slept.[14]

By 1863, they had brought the war back to Kansas in earnest. In the spring and summer of that year, small bands of Quantrill's men staged repeated raids into Kansas. By August, he had raised his sights to Lawrence.

In the town that Quantrill called "the great hot-bed of abolitionism," where artillery exercises and mounted defense patrols had been part of daily life for the previous two years, the state of constant vigilance was beginning to relax. Union victories at Gettysburg and Vicksburg a month earlier had persuaded the population that the war was coming to an end. So when Quantrill and four hundred of his men arrived in the early morning of August 21, the town was undefended. The bushwhackers were well-informed about the town. Some of them carried lists of the men who were their primary targets while others knew whose house held the key to the safe in each store. By the time they left only a few hours later, nearly two hundred men and boys had been murdered in cold blood and more than two hundred homes and businesses burned to the ground.[15]

Quantrill and his men got away. Pursued by a hastily-assembled force of thousands of men, they headed back to the Missouri border, burning and pillaging farms along the way. And within less than three weeks, twenty thousand residents of four Missouri border counties were made to suffer for Quantrill's crimes. Lacking any other way to protect the Kansas border, Union General Thomas Ewing decided to sterilize it on the Missouri side. Under General Order #11, all residents of those counties were ordered to leave their homes within fifteen days. Farm by farm, town by town, the Union troops drove out the inhabitants, sometimes allowing them to take a wagon and a few of their possessions and sometimes not. The houses they left behind were often not even robbed but simply burned with everything in them. A month after Quantrill's raid, nothing was left in those thousands of square miles but blackened chimneys and hungry, wandering stock. Years after the war ended, the area was still known as "the burnt district."[16]

Hunted and hiding, Quantrill and his men continued their raids into Kansas. In that state, meanwhile, equally savage retribution was inflicted on Kansans suspected of pro-southern sympathies. Civilians in both states lived in constant terror until the end of the war and even after. The towns were somewhat safer than the countryside, where roving gangs of horse thieves pillaged and burned without restraint, but even in the towns, everyone went armed, and the inhabitants, perhaps including Martha and Drew, slept fully clothed, with loaded guns by their beds.[17] In the bitter final days of the war, in the no-man's-land of central Missouri, the descent into savagery reached previously undreamed-of depths, with irregular fighters on both sides murdering their captives in gruesome ways, then mutilating their bodies and using their scalps and other body parts as trophies.[18]

Although the town of Leavenworth was spared the worst of the carnage, the backwash of the war flooded its streets, bringing with it all the debris of the disintegrating society on the other side of the border. The household goods of plundered farms were sold by the roadside, where thieves, gamblers, and prostitutes also plied their trades. Public drunkenness was endemic. Bodies of animals and men were sometimes left lying in plain sight for days.[19] Union soldiers themselves were among the worst offenders: military discipline had collapsed, and drinking, theft, and assaults on civilians were commonplace.[20] Lacking any other means of restoring order, General Ewing declared martial law in 1863.[21] In spite of the general anarchy, however, some attempts were made to carry on normal life. Circuses came to town, and the Union Theater witnessed some memorable performances, including one by John Wilkes Booth as Richard III.[22]

Another complication was added by the hundreds of escaped slaves pouring across the border from Missouri. Unlike Martha and her family, many came without resources and with no experience of the responsibilities of freedom. But like Martha, the newcomers knew how to work, and by means of effort and diligence many managed to save enough to buy themselves small houses or start their own small businesses. With its large population of newly free African-Americans, Leavenworth County supplied more recruits for the Union Army than any other county in Kansas.[23] None of it was easy, and neither whites nor blacks were free from the pervasive terror, but they persevered. They had no choice. General Ewing claimed that there was "not a negro pauper in the State."[24]

30. Claiming a Place as Citizens

In the 1860 United States Census taken a few months after they arrived, Martha Cooper is listed as living with the white Duffey family with her son Drew and John P. Bettis living next door.[1] She owns a cow worth $50. Drew is not yet employed; John is attending school. By November 27 of that year, Martha has bought a house lot in Leavenworth for $120.[2]

In the 1865 Kansas state census, taken only five years later immediately after the end of the terrible war, Martha is living with sixteen-year-old John. She owns real estate worth eight hundred dollars, probably including a house, and personal property worth a hundred dollars. Drew is listed as a farmer; he does not own the land he is farming but does own a cow. His household includes his wife, Leanna Robinson, and their two children, plus his aunt Celia Bettis, her daughter Elizabeth Bettis Ward, and Elizabeth's husband, Perry Ward. In this census, as in nearly all subsequent ones, both Drew and Leanna are listed as able to read and write, although on an 1881 deed both of their names are signed with an X.[3] This census and subsequent ones listing this family provide a lesson in why one should be cautious in relying on nineteenth-century records. Not only names, ages, and literacy status but race and even gender can change randomly from census to census. Drew's three-year-old daughter Martha appears here as a boy of the same age named Matthew, while fifty-three-year-old Celia appears as a man of the same age named Silas.

In 1867, Martha Cooper sold her $120 house lot for $500.[4] And within three years, there was a long-awaited reunion. In the

1870 federal census, her younger son Martin, whom she had not seen since he was a small child 30 years earlier, has arrived from Canada. Martha is living with him, 21-year-old John, and John's 16-year-old wife. Their neighborhood is about equally mixed between black and white families. Roughly three-quarters of the school-age children of both races are in school, including Drew's oldest daughter Martha, age eight. Things are going well for the family: Martha Cooper owns real estate worth $577 while Drew is listed as a grocer with personal property worth $200. Martha's sister Celia is living with her daughter and son-in-law and their children along with another sister, Elizabeth Bettis, at 70 the oldest of Elijah Bettis's seven enslaved daughters. Her namesake Elizabeth Ward, at thirty, appears in this census as a year younger than she was five years earlier, while her husband has aged eight years in the same time period. Five years later, Drew has been able to establish himself as a farmer in the outlying area that later became Lansing, Kansas. Nearby is the mixed-race Hildebrandt family, one of whose sons later married one of Drew's daughters.[5]

Two things stand out about these census listings. One is Martha's real estate savvy. Unlike Thomas Drew, she seems to have adopted a cautious and disciplined approach to her land dealings, which, though smaller than his, appear considerably more successful. The other is the central role that she has played in reuniting as many of her family members as possible. Her efforts echoed those of many African-American mothers in the first years after the war, when families destroyed by slavery could finally be reestablished.

The new arrivals in Kansas did not have to depend solely on their own efforts. In the early years, whites and blacks organized to provide schools and medical care for the immigrants. In Lawrence as early as 1862, there was a night school for "contrabands"—a name for escaped slaves that suggests stolen property—attended by ninety people of all ages, and by 1864 the Ladies' Refugee Aid Society had organized to provide medical care.[6] In Leavenworth and other communities, free schools were established for the children of former slaves.

Black churches, too, played a key role in building communities, providing not only spiritual but also social and, when needed, material support.[7] According to Martha's obituary, she was a member of the AME Methodist Church on Kiowa Street for thirty-five years, and her son Drew sang in the choir of the same church.[8] Martin Bettis was a member of the Mount Olive Lodge of the Ancient Free and Accepted Masons.[9] For the Bettises, as for their white ancestors, there was also the support of a large and close extended family. An examination of federal and Kansas census records from 1870 to 1885 shows Drew's daughters and their husbands living near or next door to him and Leanna and repeatedly naming their children after their grandmother and great-aunts, Elijah Bettis's daughters, Martha, Elizabeth, Celia, Mary, and Jane.[10]

Although slavery had been abolished by the Thirteenth Amendment to the United States Constitution in 1865, it took another five years for African-Americans to attain full citizenship. Even in Kansas, support, welcome, and tolerance were far from universal. In 1867, the Kansas legislature voted to deny the vote to African-Americans and passed a law allowing cities like Leavenworth to provide separate schools for black and white children.[11]

The Fourteenth Amendment, ratified in 1866, provided, for the first time, a comprehensive definition of citizenship: *"All persons born or naturalized in the United States are citizens of the United States and of the state in which they reside."* The federal Civil Rights Act, passed in the same year, provided, for the first time, a list of the rights of American citizens: the rights to

> make and enforce contracts, to sue, be parties, and give evidence, to inherit, purchase, lease, sell, hold, and convey real and personal property, and to full and equal benefit of all laws and proceedings for the security of person and property.

The Civil Rights Act, however, did not mention the vote—the sole means by which the other rights could be protected. Historian Christian Samito argues that it was the unrelenting effort of blacks themselves, led by the veterans who had helped to save the Union, that finally resulted in the passage of the Fifteenth Amendment, guaranteeing all citizens the right to vote, in 1870. These efforts finally solidified the concept of a national citizenship in place of a loosely defined local citizenship dependent on the generosity of individual states.[12] After 250 years, African-Americans were finally defined as fully American, at least in the eyes of the Constitution. But of course, the story was not over.

The autobiography of Henry Clay Bruce, who arrived in Leavenworth with his wife before the war after escaping from slavery in Missouri, describes the difficulties faced by the newly free and the hard work and perseverance that they needed to overcome those difficulties. Even with the advantage of literacy, Bruce was repeatedly cheated by white men pretending to be his friends. Nevertheless, he succeeded first in buying a house and then, by 1868, in establishing a small business. He lost most of that investment when the building where the business was located burned to the ground six months after it opened. He tried again, paying off his debts, re-establishing the business, and running it successfully for seven years until it too was destroyed by fire. He re-opened it a third time and ran it for another three years, until he was finally forced to close in 1878 because a harsh winter and a dry summer had destroyed the crops of local farmers and left them unable to pay their bills.[13] Then, with money borrowed from a friend, he bought two express wagon teams, driving one himself and renting the other out for a portion of the earnings until another harsh winter and an ill-advised political campaign intervened and left him unable to afford food for his mules. Ultimately the assistance of white politicians and of his brother, who held a government position, led to a series of government jobs of increasing responsibility, ending with a well-paid position in the pension office.[14]

Although he had learned to read before his escape from slavery, Bruce was ill-prepared for the challenges of freedom. Looking back on that period, he remembered that

> I had to make my own bargains for whatever necessaries we needed, and to provide for a rainy day, all of which experiences were new to me, yes, very new, and were a source of annoyance for a long time, because it taxed my mind each day to provide the necessaries for the next week and from week to week. I had lived to be twenty-eight years old, and had never been placed in a position where I had occasion to give this matter a single thought, for the reason that my master had it to attend to I

found myself almost as helpless as a child, so far as managing and providing for personal welfare and the future was concerned.[15]

Having been taught from childhood that a white man would never lie, Bruce was astonished and distressed to find that his new neighbors frequently lied to him in order to take advantage of him. Like many other former slaves in Leavenworth, he bought a small house on the assurance of the seller that the purchase included both the house and the land, only to find that the land on which it stood was still owned by someone else, who demanded rent for letting him live there.[16] His experiences led him to conclude that northern whites were morally inferior to the older generation of aristocratic southerners, who, he believed, felt themselves bound to behave honorably towards their slaves.

In spite of hopeful beginnings, conditions seem to have become more difficult for Leavenworth's black community over time. In the Kansas census of 1875, none of Drew Bettis's three school-age daughters is listed as attending school. That census, based on districts drawn differently from those in the federal census, shows something else as well: a nearby neighborhood of totally illiterate black families where none of the children are in school and several households contain two or more people unrelated to the listed family. There has been an influx of people much poorer and less self-sufficient than early arrivals like Martha and Drew, and the community is struggling to absorb them. Drew and Leanna themselves are sharing their home with no fewer than five unrelated teenagers plus one toddler. We are seeing the beginning of the rising wave of black emigration from the South, a wave that would overwhelm Kansas in the next five years.

Conditions worsened dramatically in 1879 when thousands of new arrivals flooded into Kansas, migrants from the former Confederate states who referred to themselves in Biblical terms as Exodusters. The attention of northern whites had shifted from establishing and defending the rights of freed slaves to promoting reconciliation between northern and southern whites. The era of Reconstruction had ended in 1877 when President Rutherford B. Hayes ordered the withdrawal of all federal troops from the South. Former slaves had lost all protection from the ensuing outbreak of mob violence, arson, lynching, and rape. Fleeing the terror around them, thousands of black southerners packed up and traveled north and west, most of them without money, farm equipment, winter clothing, or anything else that they needed to survive. Arriving destitute, sick, and starving in Kansas, they overwhelmed the resources of local communities. The same terrible winter and drought of 1877-78 that caused Henry Clay Bruce's business to fail made their condition even more desperate. The flood of migrants, however, continued to grow.

In a letter published in Topeka's *Commonwealth* in April of 1879, the mayor of Wyandotte, Kansas, described the plight of his city, where he had just issued a proclamation banning all steamboats carrying Exodusters from landing at the docks.

> Our city is filled with colored refugees, utterly destitute. Large numbers have died and many are now sick. The city has struggled to stem this terrible tide of pauperism, hoping to open up a way for forwarding these destitute emigrants to western homes.

He reported that all normal business in Wyandotte was at a standstill as the population attempted to provide food and shelter for the emigrants.[17]

In May of that year, the Kansas Freedmen's Relief Association was formed, under the direction of two doughty Quaker ladies, Elizabeth Comstock and Laura S. Haviland, to solicit and distribute donations of food and clothing to those most in need. Donations came in from all over the country. Railroad magnate Jay Gould pitched in as well, donating 1,000 pounds of flour, 1,800 pounds of cornmeal, 1,323 pounds of bacon, and 400 pounds of beef.[18] Slowly the crisis subsided, as some migrants gave up and returned home, others found jobs or learned how to wrest a living from the Kansas plains, and white and black leaders squabbled among themselves over the desirability of injuring Kansas's reputation by asking for aid from other states.

In 1880, Leavenworth had the largest African-American population of any Kansas city but Topeka, about 5000 people out of a total population of 16,500.[19] That population, however, also included a large number of former slaveholders from Missouri as well as a substantial group of Irish immigrants who competed fiercely with the African-Americans for the available jobs. There were instances of racist violence. In one such incident, described by Henry Clay Bruce, a group of Irishmen gathered for an attack on a Baptist church. Forewarned of the attack, 50 armed black men hid around the area, prepared to defend the church. Violence was only averted because a local leader known to be a friend of both the blacks and the Irish intervened and persuaded the would-be attackers to go home.[20]

The 1880 census finds the Bettis family surviving, but not prospering. Drew's daughter Martha, eighteen, is married and living next door with her husband. Her younger sister Jennie (Mary Jane), sixteen, and Drew's "adopted daughter" Lizzie are listed as "servants." None of the younger children is in school. With jobs, family support, and a roof over their heads, they were doing better than the new arrivals, but it was not until 1885 that the youngest daughters, Celia, then sixteen, and Bertie, thirteen, were finally listed as having attended school in the previous year.

At some point between 1880 and 1885, Mary Jane and her husband William Kelly set out for the treeless plains of western Kansas to the all-black town of Nicodemus, to establish a farm.[21] Drew's brother Martin Bettis followed them in 1885. Founded in 1878 by men not unlike Martin himself—light-skinned, literate, and raised in freedom[22]—Nicodemus was a symbol of black hope and self-respect, an announcement to the world that African-Americans could build and maintain a thriving community of their own with no need for dependence on whites. Ten years after it was founded, it had grown from a straggling expanse of sod-roofed dugouts sticking up like anthills from the plain to a small community with stores, a bank, two hotels, several churches, two newspapers, a literary society, an ice-cream parlor, a baseball team, and a band.[23]

As it turned out, however, the move to Nicodemus was fatal to both men. William Kelly was shot and killed by a racist thug during a pool hall brawl in 1886.[24] Martin Bettis, whose farm was apparently flourishing, died three years later in the collapse of an unoccupied sod dugout where he had taken shelter from a heavy rainstorm.[25] He was buried in Leavenworth, under the auspices of Mount Olive Lodge #3 of the Ancient Free and Accepted Masons; both a Baptist and an AME pastor presided at the ceremony.[26] The year before his death Nicodemus's good fortune had already reached its peak and was starting on its long, slow, irreversible decline, beginning when the Union Pacific Railroad refused to run an extension line to the town and instead located it six miles to the south.[27]

In spite of hardship and tragedy, the Bettis family hung together and survived. Like all of their pioneer ancestors, they were supported by a network of kinfolk and churches, and in Martin's case, by the Masonic network as well. Martha Bettis Cooper's evident intelligence, determination, and devotion to her family provided them with the foundation on which to build their future and claim the place denied them for so long, as citizens of a free nation. When she died in 1890, her obituary described her as a woman who

> by her conduct, upright life, and by her talk [had] been a teacher of the principles of Christianity. She died as she lived a Christian .... Her last words to her weeping friends were those of comfort; and her spirit is now at rest.[28]

In July 2018, in Kansas City, Missouri, one hundred of her descendants and their spouses—fourth, fifth, and sixth cousins from at least four different branches; lawyers, ministers, veterans, teachers, therapists, an architect, a judge, and a retired state senator—celebrated the ninety-fourth in an uninterrupted series of family reunions.

Martha, Bound for Kansas

Somewhere on the Mississippi River · 1859

She has dressed in her best for the trip, an imposing woman in a silk dress and a fine new hat, with two handsome young men beside her. As she leans on the railing of the lower deck, watching the familiar bluffs and islands, the great trees and the river eating away at the earth around their roots, the crowd of boats heading upriver for Cincinnati or down from St. Louis, she remembers the long-ago journeys when all that kept her going was the thought of her sons, and the fierce determination to someday be where she is today. She remembers the blows and the insults, along with the occasional kindness, and the respect that she earned by hard work and attention. She remembers the hostility of the Irish and German deckhands, and the fear in the eyes of the disguised fugitives. There is more than one runaway on this boat today, heading north; she can see the tension in the face of a deckhand, and guess the place where another man is hiding. Brother James was one of those runaways once, and her baby Martin, whom she hasn't seen in twenty years. She has news of them sometimes. Mr. Wisdom used to read the letters to her.

We sure do frighten them, she thinks. We're so scary they had to kick us right out of Arkansas. Colored people can't get off a boat anywhere in Missouri, except in some towns where they're packed off to spend the night in jail, so they won't be causing any ruckus among the local slaves. But none of that's going to happen on this trip. The captain knows me well, and he does what he wants on the river no matter what the laws say.

And maybe they have reasons to be afraid. The Lord's justice is waiting to fall on them. They tried to bring slavery to Kansas, and they failed; the Free Staters sent them home with their tails between their legs.

The abolitionists watered that ground with their blood, so that people like us could hold our heads up like anybody else. They say that if a free colored person is kidnapped up there, the white folks will form up a posse to get him back. They say it's still dangerous on the Missouri past Kansas City, that there are men on the banks shooting at you as you go by. But we'll get there. The Lord has been good to us so far, and He won't abandon us now.

She is blessed to have Drew with her. A fine son, sober, industrious, and dutiful. The Lord's been good to him too, keeping him in the circle of a family where he was well-treated, when so many others were torn away from everyone they loved. She shudders as she remembers the horror on the lower decks of the southbound boats, the men and women chained up in their own filth like animals. The Lord's justice is waiting.

When she was a girl, back in Missouri, she had a family. All of them sisters and brothers grew up together, played together, worked together, took care of each other. They belonged together. Now they're all scattered. But she has Drew now, and John. Haley has Evalina back. Once they get settled in Kansas, maybe the others will join them. Maybe even Martin, her lost baby. The way it's supposed to be. The way it will be again.

Threads in a Tapestry

an afterword by Carla Rabinowitz

Certain traits of Newit and Thomas Drew—the restlessness, the love of words, the attachment to principle, the inability to feel comfortable in the community into which one was born, and the need to find or create a new one—run through my family like distinctively colored threads in a complex tapestry, along with Cinderella's coal black hair and flashing black eyes. At times they disappear entirely only to reappear in another generation or another cousin. Tracing these threads back is one way, for me, of understanding how we as a family came to be who we are. It is also a way of understanding at least one small part of the story of how we as Americans grew into the distinctive people we are today.

I wanted to know who these ancestors were. They were not who I thought they were, but in the course of my search, I found out a lot about them—and a lot more about America than I knew before. Their experiences as they travelled west along the southern border were typical of those of thousands of others, and those experiences have helped to form their descendants for good or for ill.

The transformation of the backwoods farmers of the colonial era into Americans was not something that occurred overnight, with the success of a Revolution or the ratification of a Constitution. It was a process that, by the time of the Revolution, had been underway for more than a hundred years, one that has taken nearly two and a half centuries since then, and one that is not yet finished. In tracing the journeys of the Drews and the Bettises, I became aware of five major strands in the experiences that shaped them:

+ the emergence of traits that are often thought of as distinctively American

+ the development of the trust and the skills necessary for effective participation in a democratic society

+ the slow accumulation of the legal rights that we consider essential to that society

+ the development of an inclusive national identity that could override regional, ethnic, and even ideological loyalties, and

+ the ways in which the institution of slavery undermined that national identity and distorted their understanding of those rights

From the very beginning, long before we were a nation, these southern borderers were different from their European and African ancestors as well as from the inhabitants of the coastal cities. William Byrd II noticed the difference on the Carolina border, where inhabitants rejected all order and government and every one preferred to do "what seemed best in his own Eyes." Two generations later, the accomplished con man who called himself John Ferdinand Dalziel Smyth was amazed at the borderers' "total want of proper subordination" and their "insolence, folly, and ridiculous pride." The French-speaking inhabitants of the Mississippi Valley were appalled by the rudeness of the newly arrived Americans as well as their propensity for violence and litigation.

The litany of complaints continued in a different key in the nineteenth century when Frances Trollope, traveling in the new states of the West, commented on the dreadful manners of Americans and the shocking familiarity with which ordinary people would address an English lady. Numerous European observers were also surprised about Americans' single-minded preoccupation with making money.

Yet along with the borderers' rude manners and egalitarian ideology came an independence and self-confidence that ordinary Europeans lacked, an enterprising spirit based on a sense of limitless resources, an optimism untarnished by experience, and a refusal to accept any failure as final. True, the optimism has its dark side, one that we have come to appreciate all too well in our own generation— the denial of limits, the refusal to come to terms with reality when it gets in the way of our desires. But since the founding of the nation, these most American of all traits have propelled us forward. The immense westward migration after the Louisiana Purchase gave them added strength as new opportunities unleashed new energies and gave rise to new ambitions. The Drew and Bettis families, who on the other side of the mountains had struggled to rise to or remain in the ranks of the gentry, seized those opportunities to become leading citizens of communities they themselves had founded. For these families and for thousands of others, the vast new lands across the Mississippi provided a chance to discover a broad range of talents that had gone unused before and a sense that if one project failed, there was always another just over the horizon.

The individualism that came to be seen as characteristic of Americans was accompanied by a self-assertion that too often resulted in violence. It might well have degenerated into chaos and stagnation had it not been for a countervailing force: the religious and quasi-religious organizations that acted to train inhabitants of the new nation in the skills of citizenship and the habits of mind necessary to maintain a free society. Responding to the self-reliance of the borderers no less than to the Enlightenment ideal of the dignity of the individual soul, Baptists and Quakers developed models of self-governing communities based not on the dictates of authority but on the voluntary consent of their members. These communities helped to establish a new form of authority, appropriate for citizens of a new republic. They provided their members with experience in respectful discussion and in thinking through difficult questions of faith and discipline along with bonds of fellowship that fostered trust and collaboration.

The Freemasons set out more deliberately to create a cohesive group of local and national leaders, teaching them to deal with each other with courtesy, to respect differing opinions, and to adopt an ethic of service focusing on the advancement of religion and education. In the following century, Methodist classes even extended leadership opportunities to women, providing a training ground for the social welfare movements that would change society in so many ways in the years after the Civil War.

Newit, Sally, and Thomas Drew; Elijah Bettis III; Ezekiel and Billy Rubottom; and Martha, Drew and Martin Bettis were all touched in one way or another by these institutions. When Newit Drew chose the Baptist faith of his guardian, he was choosing a future in which an individual was free to follow the dictates of his own conscience, sustained by a close-knit community that could reproduce itself wherever its members traveled. In the devastated society of the upper Cape Fear Valley, after the chaos of the Revolution, the Masons worked to re-weave the bonds of fellowship among former enemies, helping them to accept each other as fellow citizens. In the lives of Elijah Bettis III, his brother-in-law Ezekiel Rubottom, his nephew Billy Rubottom and his grandson Martin Bettis, we can see the Masons from another angle, supporting the economic and political interests of Masonic brothers by linking them with a network of trusted associates in whatever community they found themselves.

Enslaved African-Americas were denied the independence, the opportunities, the supports, and the chances to develop citizenship skills that were available to their white owners. When they emerged into freedom in the aftermath of the Civil War, they were faced with the necessity of creating lives and communities for themselves without access to the land or other resources that had been available to the white borderers. Their families and their churches were their primary supports in that often harsh new world. In Leavenworth during and after the Civil War, Martha Bettis Cooper and her son Drew Bettis drew support from their Methodist church as they struggled to establish their new lives. Martha's son Martin relied on his Masonic lodge as he participated, however briefly, in the building of the new town of Nicodemus, a town that its founders hoped would provide the chance for independence and self-government.

All of these forces went into creating Thomas Stevenson Drew. Although he lacked the impulses towards violence and litigation that characterized the border society of his day, his story is rooted in the distinctively American stories that shaped his ancestors and his in-laws. The constant, restless motion that characterized his life mirrored the restless mobility of his society. His inclination to act as a reconciler of conflicts may have arisen naturally from his person- ality or from his position as the second son, the one in the middle when his strong-willed family members were at odds. But it was strengthened by his experience in his parents' Baptist congregations, where forgiveness and reconciliation were the guiding principles of community life.

Those same congregations may have honed his skill at navigating political groups, developing compromises and avoiding personal quarrels—without, however, protecting him from costly mistakes. Like his Bettis in-laws and his rich older brother, he acquired the taste for large endeavors and for risk-taking in the pursuit of wealth, although he apparently lacked their ability to make wise choices about those risks. When one of his many projects failed, he apparently responded—with what degree of regret we can never know—by selling a dozen young adults away from their families and into the most brutal form of bondage. The most impressive aspects of his personality, however, appeared in the moments when he held out against the dominant currents of his society: his unusually sympathetic and humane relationship with the Indian nations for whose welfare he was briefly responsible and his devotion to principle in the face of the mounting hysteria that preceded the Civil War. Ultimately, the most American thing about him may have been his inexhaustible hope.

The process of becoming Americans has had other strands as well. Above all else, Americans have seen their country as one defined by rights, rights laid out in laws and constitutions and protected by the courts. But these rights, too, have been acquired gradually, and often in the aftermath of great upheavals. In the wake of populist uprisings like the Regulator Rebellion, the coastal elites saw the necessity of responding to the concerns of the alienated backwoodsmen. The first declarations of rights by many of the future states enshrined some of the rights demanded by those rebels: the right of the people to assemble together and to "instruct their Representatives," the right to bear arms for the defense of the state, and a ban on the enactment of ex post facto laws—all provisions that eventually found their way into the Bill of Rights of the United States Constitution. The persecutions of the Virginia Baptists and the ultimate Baptist victory were responsible, in part, for the inclusion of the First Amendment at the very head of that Bill of Rights.

As the country expanded westward in the following century, the new states extended the right to vote, previously granted only to property owners, to all white males. At the same time, another change was taking place: the ongoing development of a broader, more democratic national identity. The new states of the West were governed by the "sovereign people" as a whole rather than by a small elite, and the new rulers grasped that opportunity with passionate enthusiasm. Improvements in transportation accompanied by the explosive growth of newspapers broke down barriers of distance, allowing ordinary people to participate in discussions of large national issues and to begin to understand themselves as members of a national community.

In the course of their journeys, borderers like the Drews and Bettises encountered a variety of peoples, peoples with different cultures, religions, and ideas. From some of them they learned valuable new skills; with others they made profitable commercial connections. Most important, exposure to this type of diversity increased the flexibility of their minds and their ability to accommodate themselves to different situations. The wandering clergyman Timothy Flint commented on this intellectual growth, observing that it created a society "more free from prejudices, and in some respects more pleasant, than in those older countries." Over time, most of the descendants of these diverse groups acquired the ability to see each other as fellow citizens bound together by voluntary allegiance to their nation and to the ideals on which it was founded.

This broader national identity was not achieved without a cost—the cost of casting out the races and the cultures identified as "not us." The new states that extended the vote to all white males in the early nineteenth century also stripped it from free people of color and expelled their remaining Indian residents. By the 1820s, Newit Drew's Big Cedar Lick Church was unable to maintain the limited equality originally allowed to its African-American members. By 1830, the Indians with whom the Bettises had traded had been forced out of Missouri and Arkansas. The mixed-race descendants of Joseph and Roddé Labbé, accepted as equals in their original French community, eventually moved to Illinois to escape Missouri's increasingly harsh restrictions.

The harm done by the marginalization of non-white peoples was not confined to those marginalized. The enforced removal of the Indians required self-justification by means of exaggerated and sometimes hysterical rhetoric. The growth of plantation slavery made otherwise decent people capable of inflicting terrible suffering. It inspired apocalyptic fears among slaveholders, fears that were normally suppressed by self-delusion but that sometimes expressed themselves in eruptions of racial hatred and paranoid fantasy, making thought more rigid and dissent akin to treason. Ultimately, the perceived threat to the slaveholders' society from the creation of new free states on their borders proved powerful enough to overcome their identification with their nation.

It took the cataclysm of the Civil War to ensure that the Union would never again be divided, and that *all* of its people were indeed Americans. It was only in the aftermath of that war that the basic rights of American citizens—rights that could not be infringed by the states—were codified in the Constitution and the Civil Rights Act of 1866, and extended to "all persons born or naturalized in the United States." And even then it took another four years for the country to extend the right to vote, the most fundamental of all rights in a democratic society, to African-Americans and another hundred to make that right a living reality.

The process of becoming Americans is an ongoing one, and it is not finished yet. It has continued for a century and a quarter since the end of this narrative as millions of immigrants from every inhabited continent have arrived to begin new lives and have changed the country in doing so. It has continued, as well, in the expansion of rights: after the First World War, when women finally gained the right to vote; during the Great Depression, when the foundations of the social safety net were established; and during the 1960s, when the turmoil of the civil rights movement resulted in the passage of the Civil Rights Act of 1965 and the Voting Rights Act of 1965, turning a collection of largely theoretical rights into realities. Even as this is written, new groups of people are being recognized as citizens with the same rights as any others. At times, these rights have been threatened.

At times—perhaps even today—the communities and institutions that bind us together have appeared to be crumbling under the pressure of our rampant individualism. But up till now, the long-term movement has always been forward, in the direction of a more just society and a more inclusive nation. That this progress will continue is the American hope.

Acknowledgments

The soil in which this book was planted was laid down by the members of the grand fraternity of obsessive family researchers who have generously shared their findings with me. Among these the most important was Lou Poole, with his hundred-page files of carefully researched documents on the Drew, Maxwell, Parker, Purcell and Reed families. Tim Hashaw, later the author of *The Birth of Black America: The First African Americans and the Pursuit of Freedom in Jamestown,* shared the early days of my search and helped me to clarify its goals. Nevel Overton-Slack, one of the creators of the overtonsonly website, not only guided me through the complicated relationships of that family but also introduced me to the fascinating history of the Jewish pirates, a family legend handed down for over five hundred years and still astonishingly accurate. Tony Vagnone with his rooms full of documents many of which he transferred to DVD for me, Terry Goode with his dozens or perhaps hundreds of family history postings on ancestry.com, Ron Thompson, Jerry Scott, Thomas and Richard Drew Carey, Donna Goodwin, Anne Collier, Frances Baggett, Anne Graff, Connee Kroeger, and Alice Martin, have all contributed to my story. And of course there is also the late Adele Cobb Kerrigan, whose hundred-page unpublished manuscript, "The Bettes: England to America," a glorious mess of errors, fantasies, fictions, and actual documented facts, not to mention the information provided by a psychic horse, was the indispensable starting point for my Bettis discoveries.

Royalston librarian Kathy Morris first showed me the magic power of librarians by obtaining an obscure and long out-of-print book called *First Ladies of Arkansas,* which provided me with one of my only two word pictures of Cinderella Bettis Drew. As my narrative took shape and I began to travel to the places where my characters had lived, I also learned from the staffs of museums, historical sites and nature preserves, including Kim Hyre of the Weymouth Woods Sandhills Nature Preserve; Jim Apple, a presenter at Historic Mansker's Station; Matt Manos, a park interpreter at Jacksonport State Park; Russell Weisman, Senior Historic Presentation Specialist for the Missouri DOT Environmental and Historic Preservation Station; and Russell Baker of the Arkansas History Commission, subsequently renamed the Arkansas State Archives. Steve Pledger of the Cape Girardeau County Archives was helpful in unearthing the ancient boxed records of the Bettis lawsuits. I owe special thanks to Kay K. Moss, director of the Backcountry Lifeways Studies Program at the Schiele Museum of Natural History in Gastonia, North Carolina and author of *Journey to the Piedmont Past,* who spent several hours showing me around and explaining the museum's recreated 18th-century backcountry house and farm. Thanks also to Judge Phil Smith of Randolph County, Arkansas, who offered me my first chance to tell a part of the story to a live audience at the Pocahontas Sesquicentennial in 2006.

One of the great gifts of this journey has been the discovery of a whole new tribe of third cousins, the Kansas descendants of Martha Bettis Cooper and Drew Bettis. Gary Hildebrandt and I first connected on a genealogy website, and little by little a new chapter of our shared family history was revealed, providing a new dimension and depth to this book. The enthusiasm with which these cousins have welcomed the project is a much-appreciated reward.

The imagined anecdote of the salted coffee is based on a real event described to me by another cousin, Margaret Chew Barringer. The coffee drinker was our grandmother, Margaret Bennett Barringer, whose life paralleled that of her grandmother Cinderella in several respects. The watching child was Margot herself, then five or six years old.

The readers who have enjoyed, encouraged and not often enough criticized the book have provided a lifeline that kept the project going for over a decade since I started writing in earnest. I am deeply grateful to Sheila Paige, Bill Madeira, Phyllis Nahman, Jane Taubman, Mark Mancall, and Felicity Barringer Taubman. Mark Wright, who seemed to genuinely enjoy designing the maps and genealogies, has been a pleasure to work with. Finally, heartfelt thanks to the three people who have contributed the most to shaping the book. To my editor and publisher Marcia Gagliardi, who helped to dig new understanding out of my brain, forcing me to clarify my thinking where it was muddled and to add where an addition would be valuable, and to my best readers and severest critics, my son Adam Rabinowitz and especially my husband Phil Rabinowitz, whose constant support, encouragement and belief in the book provided the air, sunlight and nourishment that it needed to grow: I could never have done it without you.

Endnotes

When referring to old documents, citations retain original, often colloquial, spellings

Notes to Chapter 1, William Byrd Surveys the Border

1. Jack Temple Kirby, *Poquosin: A Study of Rural Landscape and Society* (Chapel Hill: The University of North Carolina Press, 1995), 13.

2. William K. Boyd, ed., "History," in *William Byrd's Histories of the Dividing Line betwixt Virginia and North Carolina* (New York: Dover Publications, Inc., 1967), 94. The "Secret History" was the name given to Byrd's private journal of the expedition by its first editor, William K. Boyd. Although the manuscript of the "Secret History" was known to some of Byrd's contemporaries, it was not published until 1929 because the content was considered too shocking.

3. Ibid., 72-74.

4. The sexual content of these diaries is discussed in Percy G. Adams, "Introduction to the Dover Edition," in Boyd, ed., *William Byrd's Histories*, xvii-xix.

5. Boyd, ed., "History," *William Byrd's Histories*, 116.

6. Boyd, ed., "Secret History," *William Byrd's Histories,* 179.

7. Boyd, ed., "History," *William Byrd's Histories*, 238.

Notes to Chapter 2, People of the Border

1. Jack Temple Kirby, *Poquosin: A Study of Rural Landscape and Society* (Chapel Hill: University of North Carolina Press, 1995), 11.

2. David Hackett Fischer, *Albion's Seed: Four British Folkways in America* (New York: Oxford University Press, 1989), 210-225; David Hackett Fischer and James C. Kelly, *Bound Away: Virginia and the Westward Movement* (Charlottesville: University of Virginia Press, 2000), 32-37.

3. Fishcher, *Albion's Seed,* 347.

4. J. Leitch Wright Jr., *The Only Land They Knew: The Tragic Story of the American Indians in the Old South* (New York: The Free Press, 1981), 148, 258.

5. Fischer and Kelly, *Bound Away,* 43; Alan Taylor, *American Colonies: The Settling of North America* (New York: Penguin Books, 2001), 142.

6. Peter Kolchin, *American Slavery, 1619-1877* (New York: Hill and Wang, 1993), 9; Fischer and Kelly, *Bound Away,* 44, 53. Bernard Bailyn, *The Peopling of British North America: An Introduction* (New York: Vintage Books, 1986), 100, gives a male-female ratio of 6:1.

7. Edmund S. Morgan, *American Slavery, American Freedom: The Ordeal of Colonial Virginia* (New York: W. W. Norton & Company, 1975), 183.

8. Anthony S. Parent Jr., *Foul Means: The Formation of a Slave Society in Virginia, 1660-1740* (Chapel Hill: University of North Carolina Press, 2003), 36; T.H. Breen and Stephen Innes, *"Myne Owne Ground": Race and Freedom on Virginia's Eastern Shore, 1640-1676* (New York: Oxford University Press, 1980), 61, citing Susie M. Ames, ed., *County Court Records of Accomack-Northampton, 1640-1645,* 184, 453.

9. Tim Hashaw, *The Birth of Black America: The First African-Americans and the Pursuit of Freedom in Jamestown* (New York: Carroll and Graf Publishers, 2007), Chapters 4 and 5, tells the story in fascinating detail.

10. Wright, *The Only Land They Knew*, 258.

11. Breen and Innes, *"Myne Owne Ground,"* 73, 83.

12. Ibid., 83, 101, 105; Hashaw, *The Birth of Black America*, 192-193.

13. Hashaw, *The Birth of Black America*, 164-166, 188, 190.

14. Russell, John H., "Colored Freemen as Slave Owners in Virginia," *Journal of Negro History 1* (June 1916), 233-42; Paul Heinegg, *Free African Americans of North Carolina, Virginia, and South Carolina*, Vol. 2, fifth edition (Baltimore: Genealogical Publishing Company, 2007), 705, citing *Northampton County, VA Order Book 1651-54*, 226 and *Northampton County, VA Order Book 1655-58*, 10; Tim Hashaw, *The Birth of Black America*, 215.

15. Heinegg, *Free African-Americans*, Introduction, 1-5.

16. Fischer and Kelly, *Bound Away*, 37-42. For an in-depth discussion of this process, see Parent, *Foul Means*, 28-40.

17. Morgan, *American Slavery*, 218-219.

18. Fischer, *Albion's Seed*, 377; Parent, *Foul Means*, 34.

19. Percy G. Adams, "Introduction to the Dover Edition," v, and William K. Boyd, Introduction, xxxviii, in William K. Boyd, ed., *William Byrd's Histories of the Dividing Line betwixt Virginia and North Carolina* (New York: Dover Publications, Inc., 1967).

20. Taylor, *American Colonies*, 146.

21. Fischer and Kelly, *Bound Away*, 42.

22. Fischer, *Albion's Seed*, 374.

23. Fischer and Kelly, *Bound Away*, 47; Parent, *Foul Means*, 56.

24. Morgan, *American Slavery*, 228-230.

25. Morgan, *American Slavery*, 254.

26. The story is told in fascinating detail by Morgan, 254-270.

27. Parent, *Foul Means*, 146-47; Morgan, *American Slavery*, 328-337.

28. William Waller Hening, *The Statutes at Large, Being a Collection of all the Laws of Virginia from the First Session of the Legislature, in the Year 1619*, Vol. 2, transcribed for the internet by Freddie L. Spradlin, Torrance, California, accessed January 19, 2017, vagenweb.org/hening/, 481 .

29. A. Leon Higginbotham Jr. and Barbara K. Kopytoff, "Racial Purity and Interracial Sex in the Law of Colonial and Antebellum Virginia," *Georgetown Law Journal 77.6* (August 1989), 1967-2029, in Werner Sollors, *Interracialism* (Oxford University Press, 2000), 118.

30. Hening, *Statutes at Large*, Vol. 3, 87-88.

31. Higginbotham et al., "Racial Purity," 97-98.

32. Hening, *Statutes at Large*, Vol. 3, 251.

33. Ibid., 448.

34. Higginbotham et al., "Racial Purity," 108.

35. Hening, *Statutes at Large*, Vol. 4, 126, 132, 133-34.

36. Stephen B. Weeks, *Southern Quakers and Slavery* (Baltimore: The Johns Hopkins Press, 1895), 74-75.

37. Fischer, *Albion's Seed*, 574-577.

38. Weeks, *Southern Quakers*, 150.

39. Ibid., 17-22; Fischer, *Albion's Seed*, 234.

40. Fischer, *Albion's Seed*, 234.

41. Miles White Jr., *Early Quaker Records in Virginia* (Baltimore: Genealogical Publishing Company, 1985), 26.

42. Weeks, *Southern Quakers*, 151-154.

43. Ibid., 8, citing *Colonial Records of North Carolina* Vol. 1, 32, 33.

44. Ibid., 31, 35.

45. Ibid., 37, quoting Fox's *Journal*, Vol. 2, 161, 162.

46. Fischer, *Albion's Seed*, 499, 540, 557; W. A. Bryan, "Some Social Traits of the Quakers of Rich Square" (Durham, N. C.: *Trinity College Historical Society Papers*, Vol. 7, 1905), 64-70, accessed January 23, 2017, Google Books Result.

47. Ellen T. Berry and David A. Berry, *Our Quaker Ancestors: Finding Them in Quaker Records* (Baltimore: Genealogical Publishing Company, 1987), 48.

48. Weeks, *Southern Quakers*, 61.

49. Fischer, *Albion's Seed*, 234.

50. Weeks, *Southern Quakers*, 80-84.

51. Fischer, *Albion's Seed*, 235, quoting George M. Brydon, *Virginia's Mother Church* (New York:1947), Vol. 1, 371-372.

52. A total of about five hundred individuals are listed in Quaker records for Isle of Wight and Nansemond Counties between 1682 and 1733: White, *Early Quaker Records in Virginia*. Quaker-associated surnames make up about twenty percent of those listed on early Isle of Wight land patents north of the Blackwater, ten percent south of it.

53. Henry Wiencek, *An Imperfect God: George Washington, His Slaves, and the Creation of America* (New York: Farrar, Straus & Giroux, 2003), 44.

Notes to Chapter 3, Around Angelica Swamp

1. Allan Kulikoff, *Tobacco and Slaves: the Development of Southern Cultures in the Chesapeake, 1680-1800* (Chapel Hill: University of North Carolina Press, 1986), 95.

2. Claiborne T. Smith Jr., "Drew of Surry County, Virginia," in John Bennett Boddie, *Historical Southern Families*, Vol. 4 (Baltimore: Genealogical Publishing Co., 1968), 238.

3. Will of Richard Drew, dated April 4, 1679, probated May 6, 1679: Smith, "Drew of Surry County, Virginia," in Boddie, *Historical Southern Families*, Vol. 4, 238.

4. Anthony S. Parent Jr., *Foul Means: the Formation of a Slave Society in Virginia, 1600-1740* (Chapel Hill: University of North Carolina Press, 2003), 92-93.

5. Deed of Edward Drew to William Drew, March 15, 1719: Smith, "Drew of Surry County, Virginia," in Boddie, *Historical Southern Families*, Vol. 4, 241.

6. The first mention of Newitt's name in the records is in 1727. At that time, he was already an adult, since he was appointed one of the tellers of tobacco. William Lindsay Hopkins, *Suffolk Parish Vestry Book, 1749-1784, Nansemond County, Virginia, and Newport Parish Vestry Book, 1724-1772, Isle of Wight County, Virginia*, 78.

7. west.stanford.edu/news/blogs/and-the-west-blog/2017/other-words-water, accessed June 19, 2017.

8. William Robertson, "An Account of the Manner of Taking Up and Patenting of Land in Her Majesty's Colony and Dominion of Virginia with Reasons Humbly Offered for the Continuance Thereof," *William and Mary Quarterly*, Series 2 and 3 (1923), 137.

9. Kevin Kelly, "'In dispers'd Country Plantations': Settlement Patterns in Seventeenth-Century Surry County, Virginia," in *The Chesapeake in the Seventeenth Century*, ed. Thad W. Tate and David L. Ammerman (New York: W. W. Norton Company, Inc., 1979), 185.

10. David Hackett Fischer, *Albion's Seed: Four British Folkways in America* (New York: Oxford University Press, 1989), 345-47. Women were less likely than men to receive an education: almost ninety percent in Isle of Wight were illiterate in the late seventeenth century.

11. Ibid., 393.

12. Bland Simpson, *The Great Dismal: A Carolinian's Swamp Memoir* (Chapel Hill: University of North Carolina Press, 1990), 35-36.

13. William K. Boyd, ed., *William Byrd's Histories of the Dividing Line betwixt Virginia and North Carolina* (New York: Dover Publications, Inc., 1967), "History," 108.

14. Robert Beverley, *The History and Present State of Virginia*, 1705, revised 1722 (Chapel Hill: University of North Carolina Press, 1947), 153.

15. Jack Temple Kirby, *Poquosin: A Study of Rural Landscape and Society* (Chapel Hill: University of North Carolina Press, 1995), 7; Beverley, *The History and Present State of Virginia*, 141.

16. Fenn, Elizabeth A., *Natives and Newcomers: The Way We Lived in North Carolina before 1770* (Chapel Hill: University of North Carolina Press, 1983), 30.

17. Kirby, *Poquosin*, 101.

18. Ibid., 204-207.

19. Kulikoff, *Tobacco and Slaves*, 100.

20. Fischer, *Albion's Seed*, 271.

21. Alan Taylor, *American Colonies: The Settling of North America* (New York: Penguin Group, 2001), 145; Fischer, *Albion's Seed*, 271; Mechal Sobel, *The World They Made Together: Black and White Values in Eighteenth-Century Virginia* (Princeton: Princeton University Press, 1987), 100. Sobel has called attention to the resemblance between the lightweight construction of Virginia houses in this era and building techniques imported from Africa by the increasing number of slaves.

22. Bernard Bailyn, *The Peopling of British North America: An Introduction* (New York: Vintage Books, 1988), 104.

23. "Isle of Wight County VA Records," *William and Mary College Quarterly* 7 (April 1899), 4.

24. Inventory of Nathaniel Ridley, filed March 14, 1755, *Southampton County Will Book 1*, 162.

25. *Southampton County Court Order Book, 1749-1754* and *Southampton County Court Order Book, 1754-1759*, accessed January 4, 2017, at www.brantleyassociation.com/southampton_project/southampton

26. Alan Taylor, *American Colonies*, 154; Peter Kolchin, *American Slavery, 1619-1877* (New York: Hill and Wang, 1933), 11.

27. Will of Edward Drew, dated November 24, 1745, filed March 8, 1746; *Southampton County Will Book 1*, 8.

28. Deed of Thomas Drew to his sons, Halifax, North Carolina, Registry, February 1747: Smith, "Drew of Surry County, Virginia," in Boddie, *Historical Southern Families*, Vol. 4, 241.

Notes to 4, The Neighbors

1. Paul Heinegg, *Free African Americans of North Carolina, Virginia, and South Carolina, 5th edition* (Baltimore, Genealogical Publishing Company, 2007), online at www.freeafricanamericans.com.

2. Tim Hashaw, *The Birth of Black America: The First African Americans and the Pursuit of Freedom in Jamestown* (New York: Carroll & Graf, 2007), 213-217; Larry Koger, *Black Slaveowners: Free Black Slave Masters in South Carolina, 1790-1860* (Columbia: University of South Carolina Press, 1985); Michael Johnson and James L. Roark, *Black Masters: A Free Family of Color in the Old South* (New York: W. W. Norton & Company, 1984).

3. Heinegg, *Free African Americans*, Vol. 2, 878.

4. Deed from Thomas and Elizabeth Newsom to Moses Newsom, *Isle of Wight Deed Book 5*, 94.

5. Although there have been vicious arguments on Harris genealogy web pages, most Harris researchers appear to agree that the Edward Harris of Angelica Swamp had siblings named Daniel, Martha, Jacob and Nathan, and an uncle named George. Daniel moved to the Fishing Creek district of Granville County, North Carolina; his descendants are unknown. A generation later Heinegg identifies a mixed-race Edward, Martha (Hawley), George, and Nathan Harris, probably siblings, all born in the 1730s and living in or near the Fishing Creek district. Martha had sons named Jacob and Nathan. The first names Hardy and Claiborne also occur in both white and free colored Harris families, sometimes in the same county. Heinegg, *Free African Americans*, Vol. 1, 611, 613, 614, 627.

6. Heinegg, *Free African Americans*, Vol. 1, 201-204.

7. Will of James Brooks, dated March 5, 1798, filed May 21, 1798, *Southampton County Will Book 5*, 58; Will of William Brooks, dated May 9, 1788, filed October 8, 1789, *Southampton County Will Book 4*, 341, both signed.

8. Estate inventory of of William Brooks, filed October 8, 1789, *Southampton County Will Book 4*, 341. The inventory also includes a punch bowl. One suspects that an evening with William might have been more enjoyable than with many of his neighbors.

9. Library of Virginia, *Index to Virginia Land Office Patents and Grants, Book 20*, 280, accessed March 31, 2017, image.lva.virginia.gov/LONN/LO-1/018/201-300.html.

10. Library of Virginia, *Index to Virginia Land Office Patents and Grants, Book 24*, 620, accessed March 31, 2017; image.lva.virginia.gov/LONN/LO-1/022/601-644.html.

11. Heinegg, *Free African Americans*, Vol. 1, 202-203.

12. Hening, *Virginia Statutes at Large*, Vol. 4, 327; Vol. 5, 245.

13. Heinegg, *Free African Americans*, Vol. 2, 128.

14. Heinegg, *Free African Americans*, Vol. 1, 38-41.

15. Ibid., 38, 239.

16. *Southampton County Court Order Book, 1749-1754*, 159, accessed January 24, 2017, www.brantleyassociation.com/southampton_project/southampton_project_list.htm.

17. *Southampton County Court Order Book, 1749-1754*, 477; *1754-1759*, 392.

18. *Southampton County Court Order Book, 1749-1754*, 477.

19. *Southampton County Court Order Book, 1749-1754*, 500.

20. A. Leon Higginbotham Jr. and Barbara K. Kopytoff, "Racial Purity and Interracial Sex in the Law of Colonial and Antebellum Virginia," *Georgetown Law Journal 77.6* (August 1989), 1967-2029, in Werner Sollors, *Interracialism* (Oxford University Press, 2000), 90-92, 97-99

21. *Southampton County Court Order Book, 1759-1763*, 24.

22. Ibid., 59.

23. Heinegg lists 12, but misses Elisha Milton, whose deed was not recorded: Will of Newitt Drew, dated September 10, 1774, probated August 10, 1775, *Southampton County Will Book 3*, 132

24. Allan Kulikoff, *Tobacco and Slaves: the Development of Southern Cultures in the Chesapeake, 1680-1800* (Chapel Hill: University of North Carolina Press, 1986), 136 and 153-160.

25. See, for instance, the Greensville County VA tax lists for 1782-1820, abstracted by Heinegg at www.freeafricanamericans.com.

Notes to Chapter 5, The Birth of Southampton County

1. Thomas C. Parramore, *Southampton County, Virginia* (Charlottesville: University Press of Virginia, 978), 38-40.

2. Jack Temple Kirby, *Poquosin: A Study of Rural Landscape and Society* (Chapel Hill: University of North Carolina Press, 1995, 51; Susan Dunn, *Dominion of Memories: Jefferson, Madison, and the Decline of Virginia* (New York: Basic Books, 2007), 23; Lewis Cecil Gray, *History of Agriculture in the Southern United States to 1860*, Vol. 1 (Carnegie Institute of Washington, 1933), 446.

3. Kirby, *Poquosin*, 103-104, 110-111.

4. Parramore, *Southampton County, Virginia*, 50-51.

5. Inventory of Newitt Drew, recorded October 9, 1783, *Southampton County Will Book 4*, 36.

6. Will of Joshua Gardner, signed February 4, 1793, probated December 12, 1793, *Southampton County Will Book 4, Part 2*, 586.

7. Parramore, *Southampton County, Virginia*, 38.

8. *Southampton County Court Order Book, 1768-1777*, 213, accessed January 24, 2017, at www.brantleyassociation.com/southampton_project/southampton.

9. *Southampton County Court Order Book, 1777-1784*, 68.

10. *Southampton County Court Order Book, 1768-1772 b*, 519.

11. *Southampton County Court Order Book, 1772-1777 a*, 147.

12. Lewis Cecil Gray, *History of Agriculture in the Southern United States to 1860*, Vol. 1, 162.

13. Daughters of the American Revolution membership application of Mary Glover Brooks, National Number 621978, dated July 27, 1977, citing Public Service Claims, *Commissioner's Book 5*, 175, Virginia State Library.

14. Estate inventory of of Drury Parker, dated June 9, 1791, *Southampton County Will Book 4*, 430. Appraised by William Myrick, account signed by Randolph Newsum.

15. Southampton County tax list, 1782, reprinted in Ulysses Joyner Jr., *They Crossed the Blackwater*, second printing, 2003, 10528 Little Skyline Drive, Orange, Virginia, 22960-2221. Only slaves over the age of sixteen appear on the tax lists, suggesting total enslaved population of around two dozen.

16. Kirby, *Poquosin*, 61.

17. Elizabeth Fox-Genovese, *Within the Plantation Household: Black and White Women of the Old South* (Chapel Hill: University of North Carolina Press, 1988), 138, 142, 159.

18. John Ferdinand Dalziel Smyth, *A Tour in the United States of America*, two volumes, Dublin, 1784, reprinted in *Eyewitness Accounts of the American Revolution* (New York: Arno Press, 1968), 67.

19. On the increasing wealth of small planters in the eighteenth century, see Edmund S. Morgan, *American Slavery, American Freedom: The Ordeal of Colonial Virginia* (New York: W. W. Norton & Co., Inc, 1975), 343. On the emergence of a gentry class, see Rhys Isaac, *The Transformation of Virginia, 1740-1790* (Chapel Hill: University of North Carolina Press, 1982), 73.

20. Gray, *History of Agriculture*, Vol. 1, 443-444.

21. Parramore, *Southampton County, Virginia*, 48, 53.

22. Paul Heinegg, *Free African Americans of North Carolina, Virginia, and South Carolina*, Vol. 2, fifth edition (Baltimore: Genealogical Publishing Company, 2007), 833.

23. On the importance of dancing, see Rhys Isaac, *The Transformation of Virginia*, 81-86.

24. Heinegg, *Free African Americans*, Vol. 1, 480.

25. Will of Jeremiah Drew, dated November 24, 1784, probated July 14, 1785, *Southampton County Will Book 4*, 124; John Frederick Dorman Jr., "Southampton County, Virginia, Guardians' Bonds," *The Virginia Genealogist 25* (July-Sept. 1981), 171.

26. John Frederick Dorman Jr., "Guardians' Bonds," 176.

27. Will of Henry Harris, dated February 6, 1791, probated June 9, 1791, *Southampton County Will Book 4*, 428

Notes to Chapter 6, The Quakers Press On

1. Stephen B. Weeks, *Southern Quakers and Slavery* (Baltimore: The Johns Hopkins Press, 1895), 127-128; W. A. Bryan, "Some Social Traits of the Quakers of Rich Square" (Durham, N. C.: *Trinity College Historical Society Papers*, Vol. 7, 1905), accessed January 23, 2017, Google Books result, 65.

2. Weeks, *Southern Quakers*, 128.

3. Bryan, "Quakers of Rich Square," 69.

4. Weeks, *Southern Quakers*, 184.

5. Ibid., 198-204.

6. Ibid., 210.

7. Ibid., 219.

Notes to Chapter 7, What the Baptists Achieved

1. See Rhys Isaac, *The Transformation of Virginia, 1740-1790* (Chapel Hill: University of North Carolina Press, 1982), 58-65, for a vivid description of the displays of power and status associated with Anglican church services.

2. Mechal Sobel, *The World They Made Together: Black and White Values in Eighteenth-Century Virginia* (Princeton, Princeton University Press, 1987), 182-188; Isaac, *The Transformation of Virginia*, 159.

3. H. Leon McBeth, *The Baptist Heritage: Four Centuries of Baptist Witness* (Nashville: Broadman Press, 1987), 216; Isaac, *The Transformation of Virginia*, 164.

4. Isaac, *The Transformation of Virginia*, 164-167.

5. Sobel, *The World They Made Together*, 180, 189; McBeth, *The Baptist Heritage*, 229-230.

6. McBeth, *The Baptist Heritage*, 233-234.

7. Ibid, 268.

8. Isaac, *The Transformation of Virginia*, 165, 173.

9. Sobel, *The World They Made Together*, 180, 189-190; Jewel L. Spangler, "Becoming Baptists: Conversion in Colonial and Early National Virginia," *The Journal of Southern History 67* (May, 2001), 243-286.

10. Isaac, *The Transformation of Virginia, 1740-1790*, 176.

11. Lewis Peyton Little, *Imprisoned Preachers and Religious Liberty in Virginia* (Lynchburg: J.Bell Co., Inc., 1938).

12. Steven Waldman, *Founding Faith: Providence, Politics, and the Birth of Religious Freedom in America* (New York: Random House, 2008), 100-101.

13. Patrick H. Breen, "Contested Communion: The Limits of White Solidarity in Nat Turner's Virginia," *Journal of the Early Republic* 27 (Winter 2007), 687-690. Most other sources give the founding date of the church as 1786, but there was clearly already a cohesive congregation under Barrow's leadership in 1784, the year of the first petition and the year that Barrow freed his slaves.

14. Little, *Imprisoned Preachers*, 463.

15. Early Quaker families of Isle of Wight and Nansemond Counties, as well as Pasquotank and Perquimans Counties just south of the North Carolina border, can be found in Miles White Jr., *Early Quaker Records in Virginia* (Baltimore: Genealogical Publishing Company, 1995), and Gwen Boyer Bjorkman, *Quaker Marriage Certificates* (Bowie, MD: Heritage Books, 1999, CD-ROM). Quaker families can also be identified in early Isle of Wight wills and deeds by such markers as the use of affirmations rather than oaths, bequests of money for repairing meeting houses, and a collection of other Quaker names as relatives and witnesses to the document.

16. Jewel L. Spangler, "Becoming Baptists," 275.

17. Ibid., 248-98 and 255.

18. *Southampton County Court Order Book, 1777-1784*, 164, 190; *Southampton County Court Order Book 1784-1788*, 14, accessed January 24, 2017, at www.brantleyassociation.com/southampton_project/southampton.

19. Spangler, "Becoming Baptists."

20. Sobel, *The World They Made Together*, 189-190.

21. Ibid., 197.

22. Spangler, "Becoming Baptists," 265.

23. Paul Heinegg, "Virginia Slaves Freed After 1782," in *Free African Americans of Virginia, North Carolina, South Carolina, Maryland, and Delaware*, accessed January 27, 2017, freeafricanamericans.com/virginiafreeafter1782.htm.

24. Spangler, "Becoming Baptists," 247, 259.

25. Sobel, *The World They Made Together*, 209; Patrick H. Breen, "Contested Communion," 685.

26. Isaac, *The Transformation of Virginia*, 284.

27. The originals of many of these petitions are in the collection of the Library of Virginia, accessed January 30, 2017, www.virginiamemory.com/collections/petitions.

28. McBeth, *The Baptist Heritage*, 279-282; Little, *Imprisoned Preachers*, 490.

Notes to Chapter 8, Newit Drew Comes of Age

1. Jewel L. Spangler, "Becoming Baptists: Conversion in Colonial and Early National Virginia," *Journal of Southern History* 67 (May 2001), 261; Paul Heinegg, "Virginia Slaves Freed after 1782" in *Free African Americans of Virginia, North Carolina, South Carolina, Maryland, and Delaware*, accessed January 27, 2017, freeafricanamericans. com/virginiafreeafter1782.htm. Giles Johnson, John Johnson, and Matthew Vick, who appear on this list, were Black Creek members. Matthew Vick apparently persuaded his brothers-in-law to follow suit.

2. Patrick H. Breen, "Contested Communion: The Limits of White Solidarity in Nat Turner's Virginia," *Journal of the Early Republic* 27 (Winter 2007), 685-703.

3. Mechal Sobel, *The World They Made Together: Black and White Values in Eighteenth-Century Virginia* (Princeton: Princeton University Press, 1987), 209.

4. Monica Najar, "'Meddling with Emancipation': Baptists, Authority and the Rift Over Slavery in the Upper South," *Journal of the Early Republic* 25 (Summer 2005), 176.

5. Ibid., 183-185.

6. Heinegg, "Southampton County Personal Property Tax List," *Free African Americans*, accessed January 27, 2017, www.freeafricanamericans.com/virginiatax.htm

7. Ira Berlin, *Slaves Without Masters: The Free Negro in the Antebellum South* (New York: The New Press, 1974), 91-92.

8. Randolph Ferguson Scully, "'I Came Here Before You Did and I Shall Not Go Away': Race, Gender and Evangelical Community on the Eve of the Nat Turner Rebellion," *Journal of the Early Republic* 27 (Winter 2007), 667-668.

9. David Hackett Fischer and James C. Kelly, *Bound Away: Virginia and the Westward Movement* (Charlottesville: University of Virginia Press, 2000), 290; Stephen B. Weeks, *Southern Quakers* (Baltimore: The Johns Hopkins Press, 1895), 248.

10. Southampton County Personal Property Tax List, 1790, State Records Collection of the Library of Virginia, microfilm reel 320.

11. Will of Henry Taylor, recorded June 14, 1781, *Southampton County Will Book 3*, 326.

12. Antioch Baptist Church, Minute Books, 1772-1892, Library of Virginia Archives.

13 Jewel L. Spangler, "Becoming Baptists," 249.

14. Antioch Baptist Church, Minute Books, 1772-1892, Library of Virginia Archives.

15. See "Kehukee Baptist Association Abstract of Principles, adopted 1777," in Lemuel Burkitt and Jesse Read, *A Concise History of the Kehukee Baptist Association, From its Original Rise Down to 1803*, accessed January 27, 2017, www.essentialbaptistprinciples. org/confessions/kehukee_1777.htm.

16. See Sobel, *The World They Made Together*, 207-209.

17. Deed of James Drew to Newit Drew and Randolph Newsum, January 7, 1795, *Southampton County Deed Book 8*, 154.

18. Deed of Newit and Lucy Drew to Thomas Ridley, August 19, 1797, *Southampton County Deed Book 8*, 516; deed of Matthew Figures to Barrett, September 20, 1797, *Southampton County Deed Book 8*.

19. See Allan Kulikoff, *Tobacco and Slaves: the Development of Southern Cultures in the Chesapeake, 1680-1800* (Chapel Hill: University of North Carolina Press, 1986), 153-160.

20. Thomas C. Parramore, *Southampton County, Virginia* (Charlottesville: University Press of Virginia, 1978), 51. Land in the Three Creeks area seems to have risen sharply in the period 1795-97, from ten or fifteen shillings per acre to a pound or more. Newit got 600 pounds for his 298 acres and half a mill.

21. I owe this idea to Adam Rabinowitz, Associate Professor of Classics and Archaeology at the University of Texas in Austin and an expert on Greek colonies in the ancient Mediterranean.

22. Records found in ancestry.com give the date of her death as 1796, but this conflicts with the date of the 1797 deed by which she and Newit sold their interest in the mill.

23. Mays et al. v. Parker et al., filed 1816, Southampton County Circuit Court Loose Chancery Papers 1831-3, Box 34. The case involves the final settlement of Drury Parker's estate. Living descendants of Mary Parker Drew, listed in the complaint, include only Newit, his sister Peggy Simmons, his half-sister Nancy Fitzhugh, and the children of his deceased brother James. It is possible that his sister Priscilla may have followed him to Tennessee and died there, since a Priscilla Drew, otherwise unidentified, appears in the membership list of the Big Cedar Lick Baptist Church in Lebanon, Tennessee, of which Newit was a deacon.

24. Will of Susan Drew, November 6, 1800, probated April 20, 1801, *Southampton County Will Book 5*, 252-253.

25. Will of Sarah Jones, September 21, 1798, *Southampton County Will Book 5*, 77.

26. David Hackett Fischer and James C. Kelly, *Bound Away: Virginia and the Westward Movement* (Charlottesville: University of Virginia Press, 2000), 224.

27. Ibid., 141, 216, 223.

Notes to Chapter 9, The Enterprising Bettises

1. Edmund S. Morgan, *American Slavery, American Freedom: The Ordeal of Colonial Virginia* (New York: W.W. Norton & Company, 1975), 239.

2. Harry Roy Merrens, *Colonial North Carolina in the Eighteenth Century: A Study in Historical Geography* (Chapel Hill: University of North Carolina Press, 1964), 33.

3. Map: "Quaker Settlements in Pasquotank and Perquimans Counties in Late 1600s," accessed January 24, 2017, www.carolana.com/NC/Counties/pasquotank_county_nc.html.

4. Quaker marriage records from these counties include a couple of dozen Griffins plus a few Evanses and Wilsons, all surnames of people who married Bettises. Ephraim Blanchard/Blansherd, whose family also intermarried with the Bettises, appears as a witness at a Quaker wedding in 1734. Gwen Boyer Bjorkman, *Quaker Marriage Certificates* (Bowie MD: Heritage Books, 1991,CD-ROM).

5. See Blackwell Robinson, *A History of Moore County, North Carolina, 1747-1847* (Southern Pines NC: Moore County Historical Association, 1956), 14, and deeds cited in endnote 15, following.

6. Harry L. Watson, *An Independent People: The Way We Lived in North Carolina, 1770-1820* (Chapel Hill: University of North Carolina Press, 1983), 5.

7. "The Longleaf Pine-Wiregrass Ecosystem," published by the Endangered Species Branch, Directorate of Public Works, Fort Bragg, North Carolina; personal conversation, Kim Hyre, Weymouth Woods Sandhills Nature Preserve, Southern Pines, North Carolina, 2013.

8. John Ferdinand Dalziel Smyth, *A Tour in the United States of America,* 2 vols (Dublin:1784), in *Eyewitness Accounts of the American Revolution* (New York: Arno Press, 1968), 95.

9. Ibid., 96

10. Watson, *An Independent People,* 6.

11. Harry Roy Merrens, *Colonial North Carolina,* 86.

12. Mark Van Doren, ed., *Travels of William Bartram* (New York: Dover Publications, 1955), 376.

13. Margaret M. Hoffman, *Abstracts of Deeds Edgecombe Precinct and Edgecombe County as found in Halifax County, NC Deed Books 1-6*: deed from John Green to Francis Bettis, August 10, 1732, registered Albemarle County, August Court Term, 1732, 4; deed from Francis Betters to Charles Evans, both of Albemarle County, January 13, 1734, 119; deed from Francis Bettis to Jacob Johnson, July 10, 1757, registered Edgecombe County, August Court Term, 1757, 209, *Deed Book 6, Halifax County,* 298; patent to Francis Bettis, March 25, 1749, registered Edgecombe County, June Court Term, 1758.

14. Merrens, *Colonial North Carolina,* 88.

15. Deed from Charles Evans to Francis Bettis, 4 December 1758, *Cumberland County Deed Book 1,* 339; deed from Francis Bettis to Elijah Bettis, land patented by Charles Evans, August 21, 1760, *Cumberland County Deed Book 1,* 364; deed from Francis Bettis to Elisha Bettis, November 4, 1763, *Cumberland County Deed Book 2,* 281, accessed January 25, 2017, www.ccrodinternet.org/BookAndPage.asp.

16. Van Doren, ed., *Travels of William Bartram,* 377.

17. Adele Cobb Kerrigan, "The Bettes—England to America," (unpublished manuscript, 1951), 52-53, 63, 65.

18. Deed from John Overton to Elijah Bettis dated July 22, 1769, *Cumberland County Deed Book 3,* 409; deed from John Overton to Elijah Bettis dated July 24, 1769, *Cumberland County Deed Book 3,* 411.

19. Dowd is usually described as Irish, but his Ulster origins and his family's involvement in the linen trade mark him as a descendant of the Protestant North British borderers usually referred to as "Scots-Irish."

20. Robinson, *A History of Moore County,* 41; Rassie E. Wicker, *Miscellaneous Ancient Records of Moore County, North Carolina* (Moore County Historical Association, 1972), 382

21. The map, based on the research of R. E. Wicker, is included in Robinson, *A History of Moore County.*

22. North Carolina State Archives, Secretary of State Records Group, Land Office, Cumberland County : grant #218, Elijah Bettis, April 25, 1767, *Book 17*, 421, File #2377, call #S.108. 401; grant #218, Elijah Bettis, April 25, 1767, *Book 18*, 383, File #2436, call #S.108.401; grant #152, Elijah Bettis, December 11, 1770, *Book 20*, 601, File #994, call #S.108.652; grant #195, Elijah Bettis, December 11, 1770, *Book 20, 609*, File #609, call #S.108.652; grant # 857, Elijah Bettis, July 25, 1774, *Book 26*, 81, File #1663, call #S.108.653; grant #858, Elijah Bettis, July 25, 1774, *Book 26, 81*, File #1664, call #S.108.653; grant # 1119, Elijah Bettis, July 25, 1774, *Book 26, 150*, File #1727, call #S.108.653; accessed January 25, 2017, mars.archives.ncdcr.gov.

23. Joseph Dodderidge, *Notes on the Settlement and Indian Wars of the Western Parts of Virginia and Pennsylvania from 1763 to 1783* (Pittsburg: John S. Titenour and William T. Lindsey, 1912), in Kay Moss et al., *Journey to the Piedmont Past* (Gastonia, North Carolina: Schiele Museum of Natural History, 2001), 99-100.

24. A replica of such a house, complete with barns and a garden, stands on the grounds of the Schiele Museum.

25. Moss et al., *Journey to the Piedmont Past*, 108.

26. Details of backcountry life provided by Kay Moss, Adjunct Curator of Backcountry Lifeways, Schiele Museum, Gastonia, NC, personal conversation, June 5, 2013.

Notes to Chapter 10, "This Total Want of Subordination"

1. John Ferdinand Dalziel Smyth, *A Tour in the United States of America*, two volumes (Dublin: 1784), in *Eyewitness Accounts of the American Revolution* (New York: Arno Press, 1968).

2. Ibid., 251.

3. Ibid., 329.

4. Ibid., 356.

5. Quoted in Harry L. Watson, *An Independent People: The Way We Lived in North Carolina, 1770-1820* (Chapel Hill: University of North Carolina Press, 1983), 83.

6. Jedidiah Morse, *The American Geography, 1789*, in Watson, *An Independent People*, 77.

7. Rhys Isaac, *The Transformation of Virginia, 1740-1790* (Chapel Hill: University of North Carolina Press, 1999), 95-98, 99-104; Watson, *An Independent People*, 77.

8. David Hackett Fischer, *Albion's Seed: Four British Folkways in America* (New York: Oxford University Press, 1989), 363.

9. Mark Van Doren, ed., *Travels of William Bartram* (New York: Dover Publications, 1955), 377.

10. Smyth, *A Tour in the United States of America*, 162.

11. Thomas C. Parramore, *Launching the Craft: The First Half-Century of Freemasonry in North Carolina* (Raleigh: Grand Lodge of North Carolina, A.F. and A.M., 1975).

12. Harold Hancock, "John Ferdinand Dalziel Smyth," *Maryland Historical Magazine 65* (1960), 350-357, cited in Parramore, *Launching the Craft*.

Notes to Chapter 11, Herman Husband's Lessons in Citizenship

1. Marjoleine Kars, *Breaking Loose Together: The Regulator Rebellion in Pre-Revolutionary North Carolina* (Chapel Hill: The University of North Carolina Press, 2002), 16-17, 23.

2. Fenn, Elizabeth A., *Natives and Newcomers: The Way We Lived in North Carolina before 1770*, University of North Carolina Press, 1983, 77-82; Kars, *Breaking Loose Together*, 32-33.

3. William S. Powell, James K. Huhta, and Thomas J. Farnham, eds., *The Regulators in North Carolina: A Documentary History, 1759-1776* (Raleigh: State Department of Archives and History, 1971), 27.

4. "Petition of Citizens of Rowan and Orange Counties to the Worshipful House of Representatives of North Carolina, 10/4/1768," in Powell, et al., eds., *The Regulators in North Carolina*, 187.

5. George Sims, "An Address to the People of Granville County," 1765, in William K. Boyd, ed., *Some Eighteenth Century Tracts Concerning North Carolina* (Raleigh: Edwards & Broughton Co., 1927), 188-190.

6. Kars, *Breaking Loose Together*, 73.

7. Ibid., 40-47.

8. Charles Woodmason, "A Remonstrance Presented to the Commons House of Assembly of South Carolina, by the Upper Inhabitants of the said Province Nov. 1767," in Richard J. Hooker, ed., *The Carolina Backcountry on the Eve of the Revolution: The Journal and Other Writings of Charles Woodmason, Anglican Itinerant* (Chapel Hill: The University of North Carolina Press, 1953), 240-241.

9. Kars, *Breaking Loose Together*, 95-98.

10. Herman Husband, "Some Remarks on Religion, with the Author's Experiences in Pursuit thereof," written 1750, published 1761, in Boyd, ed., *Some Eighteenth Century Tracts*, 202.

11. The offense for which Rachel Wright was almost denied her certificate was apparently that of not repenting sincerely enough for speaking out against a judgment of the Quarterly Meeting. A young man, Jehu Stuart, had boasted of his sexual activities with several young women, including Rachel's fifteen-year-old daughter Charity. Charity denied the accusation but was disowned by the women's meeting. Rachel appealed the decision to the Quarterly Meeting, which responded by finding Charity guilty of "want of Resistance to the Utmost of her Power." Herman Husband was among the minority who wanted to deny Rachel the certificate for intemperately speaking her mind. Kars, *Breaking Loose Together*, 114-115. Not all heroes are flawless.

12. Kars, *Breaking Loose Together*, 116.

13. Quoted in Boyd, ed., *Some Eighteenth Century Tracts*, 308.

14. Sermon by Husband, quoted in Boyd, ed., *Some Eighteenth Century Tracts*, 324.

15. Kars, *Breaking Loose Together*, 135-136.

16. Herman Husband, "An Impartial Relation of the First Rise and Causes of the Recent Differences in Public Affairs etc.," 1776, in Boyd, ed., *Some Eighteenth Century Tracts*, 263.

17. Steven Waldman, *Founding Faith: Providence, Politics and the Birth of Religious Freedom in America* (New York: Random House, 2008), 31, quoting Frank Lambert, *Inventing the "Great Awakening"* (Princeton: Princeton University Press, 1999).

18. See Rhys Isaac, *The Transformation of Virginia, 1740-1790* (Chapel Hill: The University of North Carolina Press, 1982), 173.

19. Husband, "An Impartial Relation," in Boyd, ed., *Some Eighteenth Century Tracts*, 266.

20. Fanning to Tryon, April 23, 1768, in Powell, et al., eds., *The Regulators in North Carolina*, 84.

21. Husband, "An Impartial Relation," in Boyd, ed., *Some Eighteenth Century Tracts*, 283.

22. Ibid., 283-300.

23. Kars, *Breaking Loose Together*, 171-175.

24. Ibid., 179-193.

25. Ibid., 196-198.

26. Ibid., 199-206.

27. Ibid., 210-213

28. North Carolina Declaration of Rights, adopted December 17, 1776, in Powell, et al., eds., *The Regulators in North Carolina*, 551.

29. North Carolina State Constitution, adopted December 18, 1776, in Powell, et al., eds., *The Regulators in North Carolina*, 559 -560.

Notes to Chapter 12, The Journey of the Highland Scots

1. Duane Meyer, *The Highland Scots of North Carolina, 1732-1776* (Chapel Hill: The University of North Carolina Press, 1961), 77.

2. Ruairidh H. MacLeod, *Flora MacDonald: The Jacobite Heroine in Scotland and North America* (London: Shepheard-Walwyn Ltd., 1995), 131, citing Samuel Johnson, *Journey to the Western Isles of Scotland*, 1775.

3. Letter from James Hogg regarding the reasons for his family's emigration, *Scots Magazine*, July 1774, 345-346, North Carolina Department of Archives and History Colonial Records Project, accessed July 11, 2018, www.ncpublications.com/colonial/bookshelf/Tracts/Informations/Default.htm#5.

4. Boyd, ed., *Some Eighteenth-Century Tracts*, 421.

5. Meyer, *The Highland Scots*, 54-57.

6. Ibid., 61-64.

7. MacLeod, *Flora MacDonald*, 112-113; James Boswell, *Tour of the Hebrides*, in MacLeod, *Flora MacDonald*, 129.

8. James Boswell, *Tour of the Hebrides*, in MacLeod, *Flora MacDonald*, 128.

9. Meyer, *The Highland Scots*, 55.

10. Ibid., maps, 98-101

11. Ibid., 129.

12. Harry Roy Merrens, *Colonial North Carolina in the Eighteenth Century: A Study in Historical Geography* (Chapel Hill: The University of North Carolina Press, 1964), 100.

13. For a contemporary comment on this system, see "Scotus Americanus," "Informations Concerning the Province of North Carolina Etc.," in Boyd, ed., *Some Eighteenth-Century Tracts*.

14. Meyer, *The Highland Scots*, maps, 98-101

15. MacLeod, *Flora MacDonald*, 141.

16. Deed of John Overton to Alexander Morrison, December 15, 1773, *Cumberland County Deed Book 6*, 89, 150 acres on Richland Creek; deed of James Muse to Alexander Morrison, April 28 1774, *Cumberland County Deed Book 6*, 308, 200 acres on wagon road near McClendon's Creek. Blackwell Robinson describes the second of these parcels as "about a mile from present-day Carthage." A historical marker marks the site.

17. Rassie E. Wicker, *Miscellaneous Ancient Records of Moore County, North Carolina* (Southern Pines: Moore County Historical Association, 1971), 416.

18. Minutes, Cumberland County Court of Pleas and Common Sessions, April 27, 1784.

19. Arthur Herman, *How the Scots Invented the Modern World* (New York: Three Rivers Press, 2001).

20. Ibid., 324-329.

21. Claim of Alexander Morrison addressed to the commission deciding the claims of American Loyalists, December 9, 1783, in Rassie E. Wicker, *Miscellaneous Ancient Records of Moore County*, 415.

Notes to Chapter 13, "The Most Relentless Fury"

1. Peter Force, ed., *American Archives*, Fourth Series (Washington, DC: M. St. Clair Clarke, 1848-1853), II, 974, in Duane Meyer, *The Highland Scots of North Carolina, 1732-1776* (Chapel Hill: The University of North Carolina Press, 1987), 140.

2. Meyer, *The Highland Scots*, 72-74; Blackwell Robinson, *A History of Moore County, North Carolina, 1747-1847* (Southern Pines: Moore County Historical Association, 1956), 42.

3. Charles Woodmason, "A Remonstrance Presented to the Commons House of Assembly of South Carolina, by the Upper Inhabitants of the said Province Nov. 1767," in Richard J. Hooker, ed., *The Carolina Backcountry on the Eve of the Revolution: The Journal and Other Writings of Charles Woodmason, Anglican Itinerant* (Chapel Hill: The University of North Carolina Press, 1953), 240 -241.

4. MacLeod, *Flora MacDonald*, 150, citing Alexander MacAlester, "Letter Book," in Paul Green, *The Highland Call*, ed. D.S. Clark, 1976.

5. *Colonial Records of North Carolina*, Vol. 10, 266-67.

6. MacLeod, *Flora MacDonald*, 162-168.

7. *Colonial Records of North Carolina*, Vol. 10, 467-68, cited in Meyer, *The Highland Scots*, 158; MacLeod, *Flora MacDonald*, 183.

8. MacLeod, *Flora MacDonald*, 169.

9. Ibid. 172

10. Ibid., 185-187, citing documents in North Carolina Department of Archives and History.

11. Robert O. DeMond, *The Loyalists in North Carolina during the Revolution* (Hamden, CT: Archon Books, 1964), 95.

12. *Colonial Records of North Carolina*, Vol. 10, 594-603.

13. James Boswell described MacDonald's Highland costume at the time of a visit he and Samuel Johnson paid to him in Skye in 1773: MacLeod, *Flora MacDonald*, 128.

14. MacLeod, *Flora MacDonald*, 183.

15. *Colonial Records of North Carolina*, Vol. 10, 548.

16. Jeffrey J. Crow, "Liberty Men and Loyalists: Disorder and Disaffection in the North Carolina Backcountry," in Ronald Hoffman, Thad W. Tate, and Peter J. Albert, eds., *An Uncivil War: The Southern Backcountry During the American Revolution* (Charlottesville: University Press of Virginia, 1985), 144, citing AO 13/118, English Records Collection, Box 11, NC Division of Archives and History.

17. General Stephen Drayton to Governor Thomas Burke, July 06, 1781, *State Records of North Carolina*, Vol. 15, 511-514.

18. Claim of Alexander Morrison addressed to the commission deciding the claims of American Loyalists, December 9, 1783, in Rassie E. Wicker, *Miscellaneous Ancient Records of Moore County, N.C* (Southern Pines: Moore County Historical Association, 1971), 414.

19. Loyalist claim of Connor Doud, North Carolina State Archives, Raleigh, North Carolina, Series 2, AO 13: Box Claims, North Carolina, C,D,F,G Location 388-432b, bundle 118. Z5.110N, reproduced in Wicker, *Records*, 380.

20. Crow, "Liberty Men and Loyalists," in Hoffman et al., eds., *An Uncivil War*, 133-134.

21. DeMond, *The Loyalists in North Carolina*, 103.

22. Cumberland County Court of Pleas and Quarter Sessions, 1776-78: July Term 1777 and July Term 1778, North Carolina State Archives, Raleigh, North Carolina.

23. Crow, "Liberty Men and Loyalists," in Hoffman et al., eds., *An Uncivil War*, 169-170.

24. DeMond, *The Loyalists in North Carolina*, 153.

25. *State Records of North Carolina*, Vol. 15, 511-514.

26. Robert Rowan to Richard Caswell, September 18, 1777, *State Records of North Carolina*, Vol. 11, 626-631.

27. Lindley S. Butler, "David Fanning's Militia: A Roving Partisan Community," in Robert M. Calhoon, Timothy M. Barnes, and George A. Rawlyk, eds., *Loyalists and Community in North America* (Westport, CT: Greenwood Press, 1994), 151; DeMond, *The Loyalists in North Carolina*, 102.

28. Crow, "Liberty Men and Loyalists," in Hoffman et al., eds., *An Uncivil War*, 159; DeMond, *The Loyalists in North Carolina*, 107.

29. Crow, "Liberty Men and Loyalists," in Hoffman et al., eds., *An Uncivil War*, 167.

30. DeMond, *The Loyalists in North Carolina*, 138-140.

31. Petition of Rowan County Inhabitants, December 30, 1781, quoted in A. Roger Ekrich, "Whig Authority and Public Order in the Backcountry North Carolina," in Hoffman et al., eds., *An Uncivil War*, 108-111.

32. Nathanael Greene to General Robert Howe, December 29, 1780, Greene Papers, Library of Congress, quoted in Ronald Hoffman, "The 'Disaffected' in the Revolutionary South," in Alfred E. Young, ed., *The American Revolution: Explorations in the History of American Radicalism* (DeKalb: Northern Illinois Press, 1976), 294.

33. A.W. Savary, ed., *Colonel David Fanning's Narrative of His Exploits and Adventures as a Loyalist in North Carolina in the American Revolution* (Toronto: The Canadian Magazine, 1908), in the collection of the Cornell University Library, accessed January 26, 2017, archive.org/details/cu31924032742854.

34. Ibid., 18.

35. Loyalist claim of Connor Doud, footnote 19 supra; Blackwell P. Robinson, *Moore County North Carolina, 1747-1846* (Southern Pines, NC: Moore County Historical Association, 1956), 207-208.

36. General Herndon Ramsey et al. to Burke, July 22, 1781, *State Records of North Carolina*, Vol. 22, 550-51.

37. Robinson, *A History of Moore County*, 78.

38. *State Records of North Carolina*, Vol. 16, 1175 and Vol. 17, 194. Aaron Tyson is listed as having enlisted for an eighteen-month term in 1782 and deserting, along with many others, on June 21, 1783. His desertion appears to have had no effect on his future career.

39. Pension application of Connor Dowd, W3664, April 2, 1834, accessed January 26, 2017, revwarapps.org/w3664.pdf ; *World Vital Records, Revolutionary War Pension Records*, accessed January 25, 2017, www.worldvitalrecords.com/SingleIndexIndView. aspx?ix=ft_revwarpensrec&hpp=1&rf=*,z*&qt=i&zdocid=19217694_213_ .

40. Minutes, Cumberland County Court of Pleas and Common Sessions, 1777-1778, North Carolina State Archives, Raleigh, North Carolina.

41. There is general agreement on the birth dates of six of the seven children, three born before the Revolution and three after. Dates given for the oldest son, Elijah III, however, range from 1770 to 1784. The first and last are clearly wrong. In the 1790 census listing for Elijah Jr., there are three males under sixteen, a match for Elijah's three sons if all were born after 1774. Elijah III appears in the 1800 census as a young man between sixteen and twenty-six, living on his own with no dependents; therefore he cannot have been born before 1774, and is not likely to have been born after 1782. A birth date in the middle of the Revolution would make him the only surviving child born to the family in the twelve years between 1772 and 1784, unlikely considering the closely spaced births of his older and younger siblings. A date at the beginning of the Revolution or just before it appears to me to be the most probable.

42. Wicker, *Miscellaneous Ancient Records*, 461. The name of the person listed, an immediate neighbor of John Overton, Connor Dowd, and Philip Alston, is transcribed by Wicker as "Elijah Mealis."

43. Deposition of George G. Miller in the case of Logan v. Bettis, complaint for Trespass on the Case [slander], filed February 1826, Cape Girardeau County Archives, Jackson, Missouri.

44. J. D. Lewis, *North Carolina Patriots in Their Own Words*, 2 (Little River, SC: self-published, 2012), 32, 36, 54, 57, 58.

45. Letter of Ebenezer Folsom, August 7, 1776, Records of the Provincial Assembly, Council of Safety, 443.

46. Ransom Southerland to Cornelius Harnett, Committee of Safety, July 13, 1776, *Colonial Records of North Carolina*, Vol. 10, 663-665.

47. Minutes, Cumberland County Court of Pleas and Common Sessions, January Term 1782.

48. He resigned his commission in December, 1776: www.carolana.com/NC/Revolution/nc_patriot_military_miscellaneous.html, accessed January 26, 2017. By March of 1777 he had already moved to Granville County, and was angling for a government appointment as Register. See Reuben Searcy to Richard Caswell, March 13, 1777, *State Records of North Carolina*, Vol. 11, 426.

Notes to Chapter 14, Healing

1. Jeffrey J. Crow, "Liberty Men and Loyalists: Disorder and Disaffection in the North Carolina Backcountry," in Ronald Hoffman, Thad W. Tate, and Peter J. Albert, eds., *An Uncivil War: The Southern Backcountry During the American Revolution* (Charlottesville: University Press of Virginia, 1985), 175; Alexander Martin to Thomas Owen, October 28, 1782, *State Records of North Carolina*, Vol. 16, 717-718, 720.

2. *State Records of North Carolina*, Vol. 24, 490

3. Jeffery Lucas, "Cooling By Degrees: Reintegration of Loyalists in North Carolina, 1776-1790." (Master's thesis, University of North Carolina, 2007), pdf accessed January 27, 2017, repository.lib.ncsu.edu/ir/bitstream/1840.16/2724/1/etd.pdf

4. Norman Morrison to Alexander Morrison, February 29, 1784, in Rassie E. Wicker, *Miscellaneous Ancient Records of Moore County, North Carolina* (Southern Pines: Moore County Historical Association, 1971), 417.

5. Dugald Crawford to Alexander Morrison, May 2, 1784, in Wicker, *Miscellaneous Ancient Records*, 418.

6. It is not easy to determine whether this is Mary Overton Shields Dowd or a second Mary. Some genealogists say one, some the other.

7. *State Records of North Carolina*, Vol. 24, 638 and Vol. 25, 46.

8. Mary Dowd to Connor Dowd, January 9, 1789, in Wicker, *Miscellaneous Ancient Records*, 387.

9. *State Records of North Carolina*, Vol. 21, 879; Blackwell P. Robinson, *History of Moore County North Carolina 1747-1847* (Southern Pines: Moore County Historical Association, 1956), 108, 109

10. Thomas C. Parramore, *Launching the Craft: The First Half-Century of Freemasonry in North Carolina* (Raleigh: Grand Lodge of North Carolina, A.F. & A.M., 1975), Appendix, 232.

11. North Carolina State Archives, Secretary of State Records Group, Land Office, Cumberland County : grant #1334, Elijah Bettis Jr., September 3, 1799, *Book 103*,118, File #1341, call # S 108.887; grant #1338, Elijah Bettis Jr., September 3, 1799, *Book 103*, 120, File #1345, call #108.887; grant #1706, Elijah Bettis Jr., December 11, 1802, *Book 110*, 170, File #1617, call # S. 108.889, accessed January 27, 2017, mars.archives.ncdcr.gov.

12. Rose Fulton Cramer, *Wayne County, Missouri* (Cape Girardeau: Ramfre Press, 1972), 537.

13. Robinson, *History of Moore County North Carolina 1747-1847*, 120.

14. Ruairidh H. MacLeod, *Flora MacDonald: The Jacobite Heroine in Scotland and North America* (London: Shepheard-Walwyn Ltd., 1995), 195.

15. Paul Starr, *The Social Transformation of American Medicine* (New York: Basic Books, 1982), 40.

16. Kay K. Moss, *Southern Folk Medicine,1750-1820* (Columbia:University of South Carolina Press, 1999), 10–14.

17. Ibid., 229.

18. Ibid., 60.

19. Ibid., 83.

20. Ibid., 132.

21. John Tennent, *Every Man His Own Doctor: Or, the Poor Planter's Physician, 1736*, Facsimile Edition (Williamsburg: Printing Office of Colonial Williamsburg,1984), 55, 64.

22. Ibid., 71.

23. Ibid., 11, 15, 18-19.

24. Starr, *Social Transformation*, 32.

25. Robinson, *A History of Moore County*, 215; incorrectly listed as "Buchan's Family Physician."

26. William Buchan, *Domestic Medicine: Or, A Treatise on the Prevention and Cure of Diseases by Regimen and Simple Medicines: With an Appendix, Containing a Dispensatory for the Use of Private Practitioners*, eleventh edition (Philadelphia: Joseph Cruikshank, Robert Bell, and James Muir, 1790), 135, accessed January 27, 2017, archive.org/details/domesticmedicin00buchgoog.

27. Ibid., 159.

28. Ibid., 319.

29. The treatments described by Buchan were the standard ones for the era. The medicine kit that Meriwether Lewis assembled for his voyage of discovery, after consultation with Benjamin Rush, the most eminent physician in the American colonies, included, in addition to opium and Peruvian bark, eight kinds of laxatives, ranging in strength from harsh to "Rush's thunderbolts;" three kinds of emetics (used to induce vomiting); three medications for venereal disease, including mercury and calomel; three lancets for drawing blood; and a dozen other substances whose use is unclear, including sulfuric acid. Although Lewis himself was vaccinated, his co-captain William Clark was not, and neither were any of their men. Bruce C. Paton, M.D., *Lewis and Clark: Doctors in the Wilderness* (Golden, Colorado, Fulcrum Publishing, 2001), 31, 47.

30. Claim of Alexander Morrison addressed to the commission deciding the claims of American Loyalists, December 9, 1783, in Rassie E. Wicker, *Miscellaneous Ancient Records of Moore County, North Carolina* (Southern Pines: Moore County Historical Association, 1971), 416.

31. Robinson, *A History of Moore County*, 18.

32. Background information on Glascock comes from the archives of the North Carolina DAR, reprinted in the Glascock family tree and numerous others on ancestry.com.

33. *State Records of North Carolina*, Vol. 18, 32.

34. Robinson, *A History of Moore County*, 114-117, Errata and Addenda, 6.

35. Parramore, *Launching the Craft*, 91.

36. Steven C. Bullock, *Revolutionary Brotherhood: Freemasonry and the Transformation of the American Social Order, 1730-1840* (Chapel Hill: The University of North Carolina Press, 1996), 57-59.

37. Ibid., 26, 40, 138-141.

38. Ibid., 202-205.

39. Christopher Hodapp, *Solomon's Builders: Freemasons, Founding Fathers, and the Secrets of Washington, DC* (Berkeley: Ulysses Press, 2007), 116-117.

40. Bullock, *Revolutionary Brotherhood*, 147-150

41. Robinson, *A History of Moore County*, Appendices I and J, 222-227 provides the names of local officials.

42. Robinson, *A History of Moore County*, 158. The five men were Hector McNeill, Neill Smith, Duncan Patterson, William Martin, and Jacob Gaster.

43. Bullock, *Revolutionary Brotherhood*, 147

44. Parramore, *Launching the Craft*, 127.

45. Hector McNeil, Malcolm Smith, John Patterson, Neill McNeill, plus Archibald McNeill as a witness: "Contract with Reverend James Campbell," *Book A*, 349, Recorder's Office, Fayetteville, in Duane Meyer, *The Highland Scots of North Carolina, 1732-1776* (Chapel Hill: The University of North Carolina Press, 1987), 114, footnote 71.

46. Robinson, *A History of Moore County*, 146-153. Robinson's list of Pansophia members, dated 1793, includes John McLeod, John McNeill, and Dugald McMillan. Capsule biographies following the list also include Malcomb Black, and indicate that fathers or brothers of McLeod, McMillan and Black were murdered by Patriot vigilantes. Malcomb's brother Hugh Black appears in Parramore's 1797 list, as does Cornelious Dowd. The family property of John McNeill and Cornelious Dowd was confiscated for Loyalist activities.

47. See Elizabeth Fox-Genovese, *Within the Plantation Household: Black and White Women of the Old South* (Chapel Hill, University of North Carolina Press, 1988), 227-230, for a description of the attitudes of the lowcountry elite towards backcountry yeoman farmers such as the Bettises.

48. Robinson, *A History of Moore County*, 128

49. Cramer, *Wayne County, Missouri*, 35, 52.

50. Will of Elijah Bettis, dated February 25, 1805, copy of handwritten document in the possession of the author.

51. Personal communication, Janet Puckett, a descendant of Lovely and Edward, February 25, 2001. Although Matthews's first name is usually given as Elijah, the marriage license of his daughter Catherine, in possession of Ms. Puckett, states that her parents were Lovey and Edward.

52. The detail about the twenty wagons in given in Adele Cobb Kerrigan, "The Bettes— England to America," (unpublished manuscript, 1951), 57. Kerrigan cannot be trusted for any given name, date, or relationship, except those of her immediate ancestors, but her general outline of the Bettis story, and a few details passed down by descendants, appear to be fairly accurate.

53. In Albert Ray Newsome, ed., "Twelve North Carolina Counties in 1810-1811," *North Carolina Historical Review* 6 (1929), 281-309, cited in Robinson, *A History of Moore County*, 145.

Notes to Chapter 15, Daughter of the Long Hunters

1. David Hackett Fischer, *Albion's Seed: Four British Folkways in America* (New York: Oxford University Press, 1989), 606-614; James Webb, *Born Fighting: How the Scots-Irish Shaped America* (New York: Broadway Books, 2004). Fischer provides an exceptionally detailed and compelling analysis of Scots-Irish culture. Webb's book is a paean to his own Scots-Irish ancestors, more personal and poetic, and decidedly less objective, than Fischer's and capable of transmitting a sympathetic appreciation of his subjects even to an over-educated New England liberal.

2. Fischer, *Albion's Seed*, 663

3. Webb, *Born Fighting,* Chapters 2 and 3.

4. Fischer, *Albion's Seed,* 754; Robert S. Remini, *Andrew Jackson and His Indian Wars* (New York: Penguin Books, 2001), 8, 13; Webb, *Born Fighting,* 19-20, 185-206.

5. Fischer, *Albion's Seed,* 674, 676.

6. Ibid., 642, 774-75; Remini, *Andrew Jackson,* 8, 13;

7. Webb, *Born Fighting,* 163.

8. Marjoleine Kars, *Breaking Loose Together: The Regulator Rebellion in North Carolina* (Chapel Hill: The University of North Carolina Press, 2002), 146.

9. William C. Pendleton, *History of Tazewell County and Southwest Virginia, 1748-1926* (Richmond: W.C. Hill Printing Company, 1920), 233, 432, 515.

10. Ibid., 232-233, 417.

11. Lou Poole, "Maxwell Family," (unpublished manuscript, 2002), Chapter 16, 48.

12. Emory L. Hamilton, "The Long Hunter," *Historical Sketches of Southwest Virginia, Publication 5* (March 1970), accessed January 27, 2017, www.rootsweb.ancestry.com/~vaschs2/long_hunters.htm.

13. Lou Poole, "Maxwell Family," Chapter 16, 48.

14. Harriette Simpson Arnow, *Seedtime on the Cumberland* (New York: MacMillan and Co., 1960), 145, 159.

15. Ibid., 159.

16. Ibid., 159, 170, 171.

17. Pendleton, *History of Tazewell County,* 274-276.

18. Lou Poole, email message to the author, February 5, 2012.

19. Pendleton, *History of Tazewell County,* 277, 445-446; Emory L. Hamilton, "Chapter 46:Capture and Rescue of the Ingles Family and Killing of Captain Thomas Maxwell," and "Chapter 52: Captain James Maxwell's Two Daughters Killed," in "Indian Atrocities Along the Clinch, Powell, and Holston River of Southwest Virginia, 1773-1794," (unpublished manuscript), accessed October 13, 2013, www.rootsweb.ancestry.com/~varussel/indian/ .

20. A replica of Mansker's Station, staffed by historical interpreters, can be found in Moss-Wright Park, Goodlettsville, Tennessee, just outside of Nashville.

21. Remini, *Andrew Jackson,* 26.

22. Ibid.

23. H. W. Brands, *Andrew Jackson: His Life and Times* (New York: Doubleday, 2005), 62.

24. Arnow, *Seedtime on the Cumberland,* 339.

25. *Wilson County Deed Book F,* 347, May 20 1793, State of North Carolina grant #1876.

26. Davidson County Court Records 1783-1790, 385; deed from Andrew Jackson to John Hays, April 1, 1797, *Sumner County Deed Book 1,* 412; deed from Joseph Hendricks to John Hays, January 8, 1798, *Sumner County Deed Book A,* 78.

1. "Narrative of Benjamin Tarver," posted by Robert Powell Carver, accessed October 3, 2016, archiver.rootsweb.ancestry.com/th/read/TNWILSON/1999-01/0916407914.

2. Jim Apple, historical interpreter at Mansker's Station, personal conversation with author, August 25, 2004.

3. Harriette Simpson Arnow, *Seedtime on the Cumberland* (New York: MacMillan & Co., 1960), 249. Arnow's descriptions are based on original manuscripts at the State Historical Society of Wisconsin, Madison, collected by Lyman C. Draper, available on microfilm.

4. Arnow, *Seedtime on the Cumberland*, 381-82; David Hackett Fischer, *Albion's Seed: Four British Folkways in America* (New York: Oxford University Press, 1989), 751.

5. Arnow, *Seedtime on the Cumberland*, 351-361.

6. Ibid., 381.

7. *Wilson County Tennessee Deeds, Marriages, and Wills, 1800-1902* (Southern Historical Press, 1987), Deed of John Brownlee to John Hays, July 7 1803, 256 acres on Cedar Lick Creek, *Wilson County Deed Book A*, 336; deed of John Brownlee to "Newell Dues," July 7 1803, 200 acres on Cedar Lick Creek, *Wilson County Deed book A*, 337; Wilson County Tax list, Captain Crawley's Company, 1806, accessed August 21, 2015, interactive.ancestry.com/49375/FLHG_TaxListsWilsonCntyTN-0081/?backlabel=ReturnBrowsing&dbid=49375&pid=108220&iid=FLHG_TaxListsWilsonCntyTN-0081, entry 112.

8. *The Goodspeed History of Wilson County* (Woodward and Stinson Printing Company, 1886).

9. Eltis N. Brown, Pastor, et al, *History of Mount Olivet Baptist Church, 1801-1976* (Mount Juliet, Tennessee: Mount Olivet Baptist Church, 1976), 130, 141.

10. Barbara Smith, "A Faithful Witness: A History of First Baptist Church of Homer, Claiborne Parish, LA," accessed October 3, 2016, files.usgwarchives.net/la/claiborne/churches/fbchomer.txt .

11. Brown, et al, *History of Mount Olivet Baptist Church*, 141-143; *The Goodspeed History of Wilson County*; J.V. Drake, "A Historical Sketch of Wilson County Tennessee From Its First Settlement to the Present Time," (Nashville: Tavel, Eastman & Howell, 1879), accessed October 3, 2016, www.tngenweb.org/wilson/sketch/htm. John Dew's family was connected with the family of Newit's cousin Matthew Figures in Northampton County, North Carolina. Matthew lost no time in becoming prominent in Wilson County after their arrival. He did not join the church, and there is no official record of further contact between him and Newit.

12. Anna and Tempy Higdon, Higdon Harrington, William Megee. See Richard A. Colbert, "James Logan Colbert of the Chickasaws: The Man and the Myth," *The North Carolina Genealogical Society Journal 20* (May 1994), 82, accessed October 3, 2016, www.angelfire.com/ok3/greybird7/genealogy.html.

13. The others are Mark, Lucy, and John Murry, William Megee, and Wilson C. Davis. Paul Heinegg, *Free African Americans of Virginia, North Carolina, South Carolina, Maryland, and Delaware*, accessed October 3, 2016, freeafricanamericans.com/Stewart_Family.htm.

14. For another instance of the similarity between the organization of Baptist and Quaker congregations, see the story of Rachel Wright, endnote 11 for Chapter 11.

15. In this connection, see Francis Fukuyama, *Trust: The Social Virtues and the Creation of Prosperity*, (Simon and Schuster, 1995), 283-294.

16. Brown, et al, *History of Mount Olivet Baptist Church*.

17. Ibid., 17-18.

18. Ibid., 21: Deed from John McNairy to Newit Drew on behalf of the Baptist Church of Cedar Lick, December 29, 1809, *Wilson County Deed Book H*, 427. A historical marker now indicates the site.

19. "List of Tenants on Doublehead's Reserve," May 25, 1809, abstracted from the correspondence and miscellaneous records of Return J. Meigs, Cherokee Agency in Tennessee, Microcopy M-208, Rolls 1-7, 13 by Janelle Swearingen, accessed May 25, 2013, freepages.genealogy.rootsweb.ancestry.com/~janelle/Intruders.htm, 28, 36.

20. Brown, et al, *History of Mount Olivet Baptist Church*, 9-13.

21. H. Leon McBeth, *The Baptist Heritage: Four Centuries of Baptist Witness* (Nashville: Broadman Press, 1987), 229, 230; Jewel L. Spangler, "Becoming Baptists: Conversion in Colonial and Early National Virginia", *Journal of Southern History* (May, 2001).

22. Brown, et al, *History of Mount Olivet Baptist Church*, 135.

23. See Mechal Sobel, *The World They Made Together: Black and White Values in Eighteenth-Century Virginia* (Princeton: Princeton University Press, 1987), 207-209. Sobel discusses the efforts of Virginia Baptists, a full generation earlier, to limit the emotional expressiveness of black worship within their churches.

24. Anita S. Goodstein, "Black History on the Nashville Frontier, 1780-1810," in Van West, ed., *Trial and Triumph: Essays in Tennessee's African American History* (Tennessee Historical Society, 2002), 16, citing "The Conference Business of the Baptist Church under the Care of James Whitsitt, on Mill Creek, Davidson County," *Record Book, 1797-1814*, Tennessee State Library and Archives, Nashville.

25. Sobel, *The World They Made Together*, 209.

26. Mechal Sobel, "They Can Never Both Prosper Together: Black and White Baptists in Antebellum Nashville," in Van West, ed., *Trial and Triumph*, 57, citing R.B.C. Howell, "A Memorial to the First Baptist Church, Nashville, Tennessee, 1820-1863," manuscript in the Southern Baptist Historical Commission, Nashville.

27. Church covenant, Little Cedar Lick Church, 1821, Tennessee State Library and Archives, Nashville, microfilm roll 329.

28. Ira Berlin, *Slaves Without Masters: The Free Negro in the Antebellum South* (New York: New Press, 1974), 91, 190.

Notes to Chapter 17,
Bear Lard, Parched Acorns, and Hog Potatoes

1. J. V. Drake, "A Historical Sketch of Wilson County, Tennessee From Its First Settlement to the Present Time" (Nashville: Tavel, Eastman and Howell, 1879), accessed August 6, 2014, tngenweb.org/wilson/sketch.htm.

2. J.H. Grime, *History of Middle Tennessee Baptists* (Nashville: 1902), accessed January 27, 2017, archive.org/stream/historyofmiddlet00grim/historyofmiddlet00grim_djvu.txt, 9-10.

3. Eltis N. Brown, Pastor, et al, *History of Mount Olivet Baptist Church, 1801-1976* (Mount Juliet, Tennessee: Mount Olivet Baptist Chiurch, 1976), 26.

4. *Wilson County, Tennessee, Deeds, Marriages, and Wills, 1800-1902* (Southern Historical Press, 1987): Deed of John Hays to Newitt Drew, September 28, 1807, *Wilson County Deed Book C*, 23; Deed of Alexander Ewing to Newet Drew, June 1, 1807, *Wilson County Deed Book C*, 91; Deed of Newet Drew to Isaac Carver, October 12, 1815, *Wilson County Deed Book F*, 62; Deed of Newet Drew to Samuel Steele, May 14, 1816, *Wilson County Deed Book F*, 109; Deed of Newit Drew to Robert Man, November 22, 1816, *Wilson County Deed Book F*, 293.

5. Harriette Simpson Arnow, *Seedtime on the Cumberland* (New York: MacMillan and Co., 1960), 215.

6. John James Audubon, *Delineations of American Scenery and Character* (New York: G.A. Baker and Co, 1926), Kessinger Publishing reprint, 58-59.

7. Timothy Flint, *Recollections of the Last Ten Years in the Valley of the Mississippi, 1826*, facsimile edition (New York: Da Capo Press, 1968), 13-15.

8. Doris Whitaker Tynes, "Biography of James Cloyd Drew," recorded 1942, transcribed 1993. Since neither the dates nor the route described by Tynes make sense given the known facts, I have offered what I think is a more plausible scenario.

9. Personal correspondence, Thomas Carey, January 2014; town history by Thomas Carey and Richard Drew Carey, 2012, accessed November 9, 2017, www.overtonlouisiana.com. The information on the overtonlouisiana website conflicts in multiple details both with the history of the First Baptist Church of Homer by Barbara Smith, cited below, and with official records discovered by Lou Poole in 2002-2003, but the story of the boys' journey downriver is consistent with the Tynes biography.

10. Lou Poole, "Drew Family" (unpublished manuscript, 2002), Chapter 15, 32-33: Court Minutes, Circuit Court of Hempstead County, December 27, 1819; *Arkansas Marriages, Early to 1850* (Bountiful, Utah: Liahona Research, Inc., 1990). Lou Poole and Ron Thompson traced the interrelationships of these families—Berrys, Reeds, and Thompsons—in 2002 and 2003: personal correspondence, Lou Poole, January 2003.

11. Donald McNeilly, *The Old South Frontier: Cotton Plantations and the Formation of Arkansas Society, 1819-1861* (Fayetteville: The University of Arkansas Press, 2000), 19, 49.

12. Rex W. Strickland, "Miller County, Arkansas Territory: the Frontier that Men Forgot," in Oklahoma Historical Society, *Chronicles of Oklahoma*, Vol. 18, 1 (March 1940), 17: accessed March 18, 2018, cdm17279.contentdm.oclc.org/digital/collection/p17279coll4/id/6099/rec/3.

13. Thomas Nutall, *A Journal of Travels into the Arkansa Territory, in the Year 1819: With Occasional Observations of the Manners of the Aborigines; Illustrated by a Map and other Engravings* (London: Forgotten Books, 2015), 159.

14. Nutall, *A Journal of Travels,* and W.B. Dewees, *Letters from an Early Settler of Texas,* both quoted in Strickland, "Miller County, Arkansas Territory," 32-34.

15. McNeilly, *The Old South Frontier,* 15.

16. Ibid., 17

17. Lou Poole, "Drew Family," Chapter 15, 34: Minutes of the Court of Common Pleas of Hempstead County, July 1821.

18. Lynelle Cowan Stevenson, "Moore Stevenson Biography," accessed February 5, 2013, www.rootsweb.ancestry.com/~tnwcogs/bios/steven01.html.

19. Susan T. Herring, "'Father of Claiborne Parish: John Murrell Arrived in August of 1919," *The Guardian-Journal* (April 1999), accessed September 14, 2016, files. usgwarchives.net/la/claiborne/history/parish/murrell.txt; Barbara Smith, "'A Faithful Witness': A History of the first Baptist Church of Homer, Claiborne Parish, Louisiana" (Homer, LA: 1999), accessed February 3, 2013, files.usgwarchives.net/la/claiborne/ churches/fbchomer.txt.

20. D.W. Harris & B.M. Hulse, *The History of Claiborne Parish, Louisiana: From Its Incorporation in 1828 to the Close of the Year 1885, with Sketches of Pioneer Life in North Louisiana* (New Orleans: W.H. Stansbury & Co., 1886), 44,46.

21. Smith, "A Faithful Witness."

22. Harris et al., *The History of Claiborne Parish, Louisiana,* 49.

23. United States federal census for Louisiana, 1830 and 1840.

24. Harris et al., *The History of Claiborne Parish, Louisiana,* 49.

25. Alexis de Tocqueville, *Democracy in America,* trans. and ed. Harvey C. Mansfield and Delba Winthrop (Chicago: University of Chicago Press, 2000), 270.

26. Tynes, "Biography of James Cloyd Drew."

27. Lou Poole is responsible for the extensive research on this topic, which includes a complex land transaction in Walker County Texas in 1855, involving Jane, her third husband, and the adult children of her second husband, as well as a court petition by her brother-in-law in Claiborne Parish LA in 1856, asking the court to order a "family meeting" to consider the "tutorship" (guardianship) of Jane's minor children by her second husband. Personal correspondence, Lou Poole, September 2004.

Notes to Chapter 18, In the Rough Hills

1. One hundred of these ex-slave narratives, representing a vast array of differing experiences, are collected in Norman R. Yetman, ed., *Voices from Slavery: 100 Authentic Slave Narratives* (Mineola, NY: Dover Publications, 2000).

2. Yetman, ed., *Voices from Slavery,* 169.

3. See, e.g., Yetman, ed., *Voices from Slavery,* 62, 76-79,103, 199, 167.

4. The exact location of their first settlement is not known.

5. Walter A. Schroeder, *Opening the Ozarks: A Historical Geography of Missouri's Ste. Genevieve District, 1760-1830* (Columbia: University of Missouri Press, 2002), 220.

6. John James Audubon, *Delineations of American Scenery and Character* (New York: G.A. Baker and Company, 1926), 101-102.

7. Schroeder, *Opening the Ozarks*, 34, 38, 69.

8. Ibid., 88.

9. Rose Fulton Cramer, *Wayne County, Missouri* (Cape Girardeau: The Ramfre Press, 1972), 38.

10. Schroeder, *Opening the Ozarks*, 109-110.

11. Louis Houck, *A History of Missouri from the Earliest Explorations and Settlements Until the Admission of the State into the Union*, Vol. 3 (Chicago: R.R. Donnelley and Sons, 1908; reprint edition Arno Press, 1971), 38-39.

12. Ibid., 50-51.

13. Schroeder, *Opening the Ozarks*, 347.

14. George W. Featherstonehaugh, *Excursion through the Slave States*, Vol. 2 (London: John Murray, Albemarle St., 1844), 3, 31, 68.

15. Cramer, *Wayne County, Missouri*, 84.

16. Research conducted by David Austin on the historic background of Old Greenville, citing *American State Papers 1861*; *Cape Girardeau Deed Book D*, 122, 124; US Surveyor General 1819, 1821. Russell Weisman, Senior Historic Preservation Specialist, MoDOT Environmental and Historic Preservation Section, email messages to author, December 19, 2014-April 15, 2015. The dates and other information compiled by Mr. Austin differ in numerous respects from those offered by Cramer, but are undoubtedly more reliable.

17. Schroeder, *Opening the Ozarks*, 54; Cramer, *Wayne County, Missouri*, 69.

18. Estate inventory of of Elijah Bettis Sr., Cape Girardeau County Archives, Jackson, Missouri, Box 032, Bundle 0628.

19. Cramer identifies Ransom's wife as Isaac's sister "Polly" Kelly. Russell Weisman, however, reports that Isaac's sister's real name was Sarah, and that she was as much as thirteen years older than Ransom. Russell Weisman, email message to author, December 19, 2014. Mr. Weisman believes that the Mary or "Polly" Bettis who shows up in multiple later documents was actually Isaac's daughter.

20. Cramer, *Wayne County, Missouri*, 66.

21. Ibid., 62-63, 249-51, 583.

22. Ibid., 76.

23. Milton D. Rafferty, ed., *Rude Pursuits and Rugged Peaks: Schoolcraft's Ozark Journal. 1818-1819* (Fayetteville: The University of Arkansas Press, 1996), 120; Schroeder, *Opening the Ozarks*, 206.

24. Cramer, *Wayne County, Missouri*, 79.

25. Rafferty, ed., *Rude Pursuits and Rugged Peaks*, 120; Schroeder, *Opening the Ozarks*, 349.

26. Cramer, *Wayne County, Missouri*, 66, 249, 585.

27. Peggy Jacoway, *First Ladies of Arkansas* (Little Rock: Southern Publishers, 1941), 82.

28. Schroeder, *Opening the Ozarks*, 349.

29. Cramer, *Wayne County, Missouri*, 66. Russell Weisman drew my attention to the second Senate term, from 1830 to 1831. Russell Weisman, email to author, December 19, 2014.

30. Cramer, *Wayne County, Missouri*, 96.

31. Ibid., 66.

32. Ibid., 96-98, 584.

33. Cramer, *Wayne County, Missouri*, 65, 67; Bridgehunter.com, map of Wayne County, Missouri, accessed September 5, 2017, bridgehunter.com/mo/wayne/big-map/. The old town of Greenville was located at the north end of what is now Lake Wappapello, where Route 67 crosses the river.

34. 1830 federal census, Wayne County, Missouri; 1850 federal census, Johnson County, Arkansas.

35. Bettie Hurd to Tony Vagnone, July 12, 1976, in the possession of Mr. Vagnone.

36. Tony Vagnone was the first and most diligent researcher of this family history, beginning in the 1980s.

37. Emancipation by Elijah Bettis, *Randolph County Deed Book B*, dated August 20, 1835, recorded April 15, 1839. The deed was discovered by Dr. Jan Fielder Zeigler, the author of the play, "No History Happened Here," written for the Pocahontas 150th anniversary celebration. At the time of the performance, Dr. Ziegler was unaware of the relationship between Elijah and the women he freed. Pocahontas was established and named in 1836; no one connected with the celebration was able to tell me why the celebration calendar places the date of its founding twenty years later.

38. Her height is mentioned in a letter written by a descendant, who describes her as five-feet, seven inches, well above average for a woman at that time: Bettie Hurd to Tony Vagnone, June 30, 1979, in the possession of Mr. Vagnone.

39. 1840 federal census, Randolph County, Arkansas (Charity); 1860 federal census, Leavenworth County, Kansas (Patsie/Martha); 1865 Kansas census, Leavenworth County (Celia); 1870 federal census, Leavenworth County, Kansas (Elizabeth); family data collected by Terry Goode, Saunders/Felder family tree, accessed January 29, 2017, trees.ancestry.com/tree/8842805/family?usePUBJs=true.

40. Bettie Hurd to Tony Vagnone, July 12, 1976, in the possession of Mr. Vagnone.

41. Margaret Jones Bolsterli, ed., *A Remembrance of Eden: Harriet Bailey Bullock Daniel's Memories of a Frontier Plantation in Arkansas, 1849-1872* (Fayetteville: University of Arkansas Press, 1993), in S. Charles Bolton, *Arkansas 1800-1860: Remote and Restless* (Fayetteville: The University of Arkansas Press, 1998), 124.

42. Yetman, ed., *Voices from Slavery*, 171, 200, 259-260.

43. Ibid., 239.

44. Hal Bennett to a Mrs.Williamson, August 2, 1949, in the possession of Tony Vagnone. Hal Bennett also corresponded with Adele Kerrigan on the subject of Bettis history. However, the facts provided in this letter are suspect at best and obviously incorrect in some cases, for instance in the claim that one child of Overton Bettis and Mrs. Timmons eventually married Overton's nephew Billy Rubottom.

45. The original tombstone is on display in the Randolph County History Museum. A more decorous one occupies its former place in the cemetery.

46. Yetman, ed., *Voices from Slavery,* 127, 328. In the former narrative, a child who was the granddaughter of her master and mistress remembered being left alone with the black cook, who slapped her until her nose bled. With no indication of ambivalence, she related that when the master and mistress found out about it, the cook was whipped "so hard that she couldn't walk no more."

47. Yetman, ed., *Voices from Slavery,* 226, 294, 303, 323, 327; Elizabeth Fox-Genovese, *Within the Plantation Household:Black and White Women of the Old South* (Chapel Hill: University of North Carolina Press, 1988), 164, 309.

48. Dorothy Sterling, ed., *We are Your Sisters: Black Women in the Nineteenth Century* (New York: W.W. Norton & Co., 1997), 7, 8; Yetman, ed., *Voices from Slavery,* 20, 40, 42, 109, 131, 163, 200, 222, 257, 281, 291. "Loom house" 60, 163, 200, 267. "Slaves and mistresses weaving together" 163, 267; Fox-Genovese, *Within the Plantation Household,* 121, 127.

49. Donald McNeilly, *The Old South Frontier: Cotton Plantations and the Formation of Arkansas Society, 1819-1861* (Fayetteville: The University of Arkansas Press, 2000), 38.

50. Thomas C. Buchanan, *Black Life on the Mississippi: Slaves, Free Blacks, and the Western Steamboat World* (Chapel Hill: University of North Carolina Press, 2004), 82.

51. Fox-Genovese, *Within the Plantation Household,* Chapter 2, 115-140..

Notes to Chapter 19, The Multicultural Border

1. Stephen Aron, *American Confluence* (Bloomington: Indiana University Press, 2006), 102.

2. Jay Gitlin, *The Bourgeois Frontier: French Towns, French Traders, and American Expansion* (Ann Arbor: Sheridan Books, 2010), 10.

3. Aron, *American Confluence,* 15.

4. Ibid., 94.

5. Carl Ekberg, *Colonial Ste. Genevieve: An Adventure on the Mississippi Frontier* (Gerald, MO: Patrice Press, 1985), 116.

6. Ibid., 226-230; Bonnie Stepenoff, *From French Community to Missouri Town: Ste. Genevieve in the Nineteenth Century* (Columbia: University of Missouri Press, 2006), 24-25, 115.

7. Ekberg, *Colonial Ste. Genevieve,* 215.

8. Henry Brackenridge, *Views of Louisiana: Together with a Journal of a Voyage up the Missouri River in 1811* (Pittsburgh:1814), 135, in Aron, *American Confluence,* 45; Ekberg, *Colonial Ste. Genevieve,* 192.

9. Stepenoff, *From French Community to Missouri Town*, 109.

10. Aron, *American Confluence*, 49, 67, 100; Ekberg, *Colonial Ste. Genevieve*, 318-19, 330-31, 373.

11. Ekberg, *Colonial Ste. Genevieve*, 172, 314-15; Aron, *American Confluence*, 31.

12. Ekberg, *Colonial Ste. Genevieve*, 142.

13. Louis Houck, *A History of Missouri from the Earliest Explorations and Settlements Until the Admission of the State into the Union*, Vol. 3 (Chicago, R.R. Donnelley and Sons, 1908, reprint edition, Arno Press, 1971), 60-69, 186.

14. Ekberg, *Colonial Ste. Genevieve*, 430.

15. Stepenoff, *From French Community to Missouri Town*, 92.

16. Ibid., 91-94.

17. Walter A. Schroeder, *Opening the Ozarks: A Historical Geography of Missouri's Ste. Genevieve District, 1760-1830* (Columbia:University of Missouri Press, 2002), 448; George W. Featherstonehaugh, *Excursion through the Slave States*, Vol. 1 (New York: Harper and brothers, 1844), 249-250.

18. Schroeder, *Opening the Ozarks*, 448.

19. Reverend Timothy Flint, *Recollections of the Last Ten Years in the Valley of the Mississippi, 1826*, facsimile edition (New York: Da Capo Press,1968), 178.

20. Aron, *American Confluence*, 210.

Notes to Chapter 20,
Six Indictments, Four Lawsuits, and Perhaps a Murder

1. Stephen Aron, *American Confluence* (Bloomington: Indiana University Press, 2006), 159.

2. James F. Keefe & Lynn Morrow, eds., *The White River Chronicles of S.C. Turnbo: Man and Wildlife on the Ozarks Frontier* (Fayetteville:University of Arkansas Press, 1999), 5; Rose Fulton Cramer, *Wayne County, Missouri* (Cape Girardeau: The Ramfre Press, 1972), 23.

3. Cramer, *Wayne County, Missouri*, 24.

4. Hal Bennett to Adele Cobb Kerrigan, date unknown, in Kerrigan, "The Bettes— England to America" (unpublished manuscript, 1951), 60.

5. See photographs in Bonnie Stepenoff, *From French Community to Missouri Town: Ste. Genevieve in the Nineteenth Century* (Columbia: University of Missouri Press, 2006), 39 and 163. The "Red House" in Cape Girardeau, a replica of town founder Louis Lorimier's original trading post, is an example of this style. Many images of the Red House are available on the internet.

6. Deposition of Ransom/Ranson Bettis, August 20, 1827, in the case of Jackson v. Labbé, Madison County Court, Madison, MO.

7. Frances Baggett, email message to the author, June 18, 2007.

8. Carl Ekberg, *Colonial Ste. Genevieve: An Adventure on the Mississippi Frontier* (Gerald, MO: Patrice Press, 1985), 230; Walter A. Schroeder, *Opening the Ozarks: A Historical Geography of Missouri's Ste. Genevieve District, 1760-1830* (Columbia:University of Missouri Press, 2002), 277; Frances Baggett, email correspondence with the author, 2007-2016; Indenture between Joseph Labbé and Rhoda Labbé his wife and Antoine Paul Portorique, May 21, 1817, film 32636 f54 roll 4, Ste. Genevieve Archives 002.

9. United States v. Edward and Charles Matthews, Territory of Missouri Court of Common Pleas, Cape Girardeau, March 1814, Cape Girardeau County Archives Box 25, File 18; United States v. Edward H. Matthews and Solomon Bollinger, Territory of Missouri, County of Cape Girardeau, May Term 1816, Cape Girardeau County Archives Box 25, File 16; United States v. Edward H. Matthews, Territory of Missouri, County of Cape Girardeau Circuit Court, August 1816, Box 25, File 60; United States v. Edward H. Matthews, Territory of Missouri, County of Cape Girardeau Circuit Court, September-December Term 1816, Box 25, File 59. Overton Bettis was a member of the grand jury that returned the indictment on his brother-in-law.

10. Cramer, *Wayne County, Missouri*, 65, 238.

11. Janet Puckett, email to the author, February 25, 2001, citing the marriage certificate of her great-great grandmother Catherine Matthews Puckett, which identifies her as a daughter of Edward and Lovely.

12. T.W. Rubottom, "Rubottom Family of America," accessed May 22, 2013, homepages. rootsweb.ancestry.com/~dansgen/bioezfam.htm.

13. Tax lists, Johnson County, Arkansas, "All Arkansas Combined Census and Census Substitutes Index," accessed March 18, 2018, www.ancestry.com.

14. 1840 federal census, Crittenden County, Arkansas. One such line, found in Wilson County Tennessee in the early nineteenth century and later on in Arkansas, included several members of Newit Drew's Big Cedar Lick Church.

15. Blackwell Robinson, *A History of Moore County, North Carolina, 1747-1847* (Southern Pines: Moore County Historical Association, 1956), 78, 110.

16. Claiborne Thweatt Smith Jr., *Smith of Scotland Neck, Planters on the Roanoke* (Baltimore: Gateway Press, 1976), 15.

17. Deposition of George G. Miller in the case of Logan v. Bettis, complaint for Trespass on the Case [slander], filed February 1826, Cape Girardeau County Archives, Box 15, Folder 19; depositions of Isaac Kelly, Thomas Chilton, William Hays and others in the case of Logan v. Bettis, complaint for Trespass and Malicious Prosecution, filed 1827, Cape Girardeau County Archives, Box 15, Folder 20.

18. Deposition of Thomas Chilton in the case of Logan v. Bettis, complaint for Trespass and Malicious Prosecution, filed 1827, Cape Girardeau County Archives Box 15, Folder 20.

19. Stepenoff, *From French Community to Missouri Town*, 59; Jay Gitlin, *The Bourgeois Frontier: French Towns, French Traders, and American Expansion* (Ann Arbor: Sheridan Books, 2010), 17, 187.

20. Questions posed by James Logan in various depositions connected with the case of Logan v. Bettis, complaint for Trespass and Malicious Prosecution, filed 1827, Cape Girardeau County Archives, Box 15, Folder 20.

21. Cramer, *Wayne County, Missouri*, 67.

22. Steven C. Bullock, *Revolutionary Brotherhood: Freemasonry and the Transformation of the American Social Order, 1730-1840* (Chapel Hill:University of North Carolina Press, 1996), 175.

23. Ibid., 222-225.

24. Ibid., 261-62.

25. Ibid., 215.

26. Ibid., 278.

27. Ibid., 283. Bullock gives a full and detailed description of the controversy and its sequels, 277-319.

Notes to Chapter 21, Departures

1. Walter A. Schroeder, *Opening the Ozarks: A Historical Geography of Missouri's Ste. Genevieve District, 1760-1830* (Columbia: University of Missouri Press, 2002), 418.

2. Reverend Timothy Flint, *Recollections of the Last Ten Years in the Valley of the Mississippi,1826*, facsimile edition (New York: Da Capo Press, 1968), 107.

3. Schroeder, *Opening the Ozarks*, 194.

4. Stephen Aron, *American Confluence* (Bloomington: Indiana University Press, 2006), 216.

5. Ibid., 216.

6. Missouri State Archives, "Missouri's Early Slave Laws: A History in Documents," accessed July 16, 2018, www.sos.mo.gov/archives/education/aahi/earlyslavelaws/slavelaws.asp.

7. Tax lists, Johnson County, Arkansas, "All Arkansas Combined Census and Census Substitutes Index," accessed March 18, 2018, www.ancestry.com.

8. Janet Puckett, email to the author, February 25, 2001; 1850 federal census for Washington County, Missouri.

9. Rose Fulton Cramer, *Wayne County, Missouri* (Cape Girardeau: The Ramfre Press, 1972), 485, 495.

10. Lawrence Dalton, *History of Randolph County, Arkansas* (Little Rock: Democrat Printing and Lithographing Company,1946-7), 9.

11. *Arkansas Gazette*, September 14,1824 and September 27,1825; accessed March 16, 2014, www.arkansasties.com/Social/viewforum.php?f+97

12. Flint, *Recollections of the Last Ten Years in the Valley of the Mississippi*, 49.

Notes to Chapter 22, Cherokee Bay

1. Alexis de Tocqueville, *Democracy in America*, trans. Harvey C. Mansfield and Delba Winthrop (Chicago: University of Chicago Press, 2000), footnote 6 on p. 290.

2. Portion of letter from Thomas S. Drew to unidentified recipient, in the Arkansas Archives, Little Rock.

3. Bobby Roberts, "Thomas Stevenson Drew, 1844-1849," in Timothy Donovan, ed., *The Governors of Arkansas: Essays in Political Biography* (Fayetteville: The University of Arkansas Press, 1981), 11; Lawrence Dalton, *History of Randolph County, Arkansas* (Little Rock: Democrat Printing and Lithographing Company,1946-7), 47; Karr Shannon, "The Nebulous Background of Governor Drew," in unknown newspaper, Sunday magazine, October 27, 1957, in the Arkansas Archives, Little Rock.

4. Shannon, "The Nebulous Background of Governor Drew."

5. *Arkansas Gazette,* August 29,1824; September 27,1825, and May 30,1838, accessed March 16, 2014, www.arkansasties.com/Social/viewforum.php?f=97.

6. Bobby Roberts, "Thomas Stevenson Drew," 11.

7. *Arkansas Gazette,* April 30, 1828.

8. *Arkansas Gazette,* February 20, 1827, in "Letters of Dee Powell, 1982 -85, Concerning Thomas S. Drew, Third Governor of Arkansas" compiled for the Arkansas Archives by Tony Vagnone in 1986.

9. See *Randolph County Deed Book B,* 9, and all subsequent deeds involving Ranson.

10. Dalton, *History of Randolph County,* 47.

11. S. Charles Bolton, *Arkansas, 1800-1860: Remote and Restless* (Fayetteville: The University of Arkansas Press, 1998), 99; Orville W. Taylor, *Negro Slavery in Arkansas* (Durham: Duke University Press, 1958), 58. Both of the calculations are based on census figures from 1860, earlier records being unavailable.

12. Thomas A. DeBlack, "'The Rights and Rank to Which We Are Entitled:' Arkansas in the Early Statehood Period," in Jeannie M. Whayne et al., *Arkansas, a Narrative History* (Fayetteville: The University of Arkansas Press, 2002), 122.

13. Milton D. Rafferty, ed., *Rude Pursuits and Rugged Peaks: Schoolcraft's Ozark Journal, 1818-1819* (Fayetteville: The University of Arkansas Press, 1996), 103; William Monks, *A History Of Southern Missouri And Northern Arkansas: Being An Account Of The Early Settlements, The Civil War, The Ku-Klux, And Times Of Peace,* ed. John F. Bradbury and Lou Wehmer (Fayetteville: The University of Arkansas Press, 2003), 6. An advertisement in the *Arkansas Gazette,* dated April 23, 1828, offers clothes, fabrics, sundries, knives, wine, coffee and "seegars" in exchange for "Hides, Tallow, Bear's Oil, Bear, Beaver and Otter Skins, etc. etc."

14. Dalton, *History of Randolph County,* 22.

15. Ibid., 21.

16. Donald McNeilly, *The Old South Frontier: Cotton Plantations and the Formation of Arkansas Society, 1819-1861* (Fayetteville: The University of Arkansas Press, 2000), 104-105.

17. See Elizabeth Fox-Genovese, *Within the Plantation Household: Black and White Women of the Old South* (Chapel Hill: University of North Carolina Press, 1988), 22-23, 110-113, 163-164.

18. Cemetery records, Randolph County courthouse, Pocahontas, Arkansas.

19. Dalton, *History of Randolph County,* 178.

20. Personal communication, William Gary Hildebrandt.

Notes to Chapter 23, "Around You Everything Moves"

1. Kathleen DuVal, *The Native Ground: Indians and Colonists in the Heart of the Continent* (Philadelphia: University of Pennsylvania Press, 2006), 196; James F. Keefe & Lynn Morrow, eds., *The White River Chronicles of S.C. Turnbo: Man and Wildlife on the Ozarks Frontier* (Fayetteville: The University of Arkansas Press, 1999), 5.

2. DuVal, *The Native Ground*, 198, 217.

3. Keefe and Morrow, eds., *The White River Chronicles of S. C. Turnbo*, 7.

4. *Arkansas Gazette*, April 23, 1828.

5. DuVal, *The Native Ground*, 237-238.

6. Jack Larkin, *The Reshaping of Everyday Life,1790-1840* (New York: Harper & Rowe, 1988), 133, 143.

7. Ibid., 190.

8. Ibid., 141.

9. Dorothy Stanley, ed., *The Autobiography of Henry Morton Stanley* (New York: Houghton Mifflin Company, 1909), 148-50, in C. Fred Williams, S. Charles Bolton, Carl H. Moneyhon, and LeRoy T. Williams, *A Documentary History of Arkansas* (Fayetteville: The University of Arkansas Press, 1988), 61.

10. William Monks, *A History Of Southern Missouri And Northern Arkansas: Being An Account Of The Early Settlements, The Civil War, The Ku-Klux, And Times Of Peace*, ed. John F. Bradbury and Lou Wehmer (Fayetteville: The University of Arkansas Press, 2003), 6.

11. Daniel Walker Howe, *What Hath God Wrought: The Transformation of America, 1815-1848* (New York: Oxford University Press, 2007), 227.

12. Frances Trollope, *Domestic Manners of the Americans* (London: Whittaker, Treacher and Co., 1832; Dover Publications edition 2003), 55.

13. Alexis de Tocqueville, *Democracy in America*, trans. Harvey C. Mansfield and Delba Winthrop (Chicago: The University of Chicago Press, 2000), 493.

14. Trollope, *Domestic Manners*, preface,vii.

15. George W. Featherstonehaugh, *Excursion through the Slave States*, Vol. 2 (London: John Murray, Albemarle St., 1844), 49.

16. Trollope, *Domestic Manners*, 55.

17. de Tocqueville, *Democracy in America*, 232, 388.

18. Trollope, *Domestic Manners*, 60.

19. Featherstonehaugh, *Excursion Through the Slave States*, Vol. 1, 281; deTocqueville, *Democracy in America*, 583; Trollope, *Domestic Manners*, 11, 26, 125, 186.

20. Featherstonehaugh, *Excursion through the Slave States*, Vol. 1, 281; Larkin, *The Reshaping of Everyday Life*, 180.

21. de Tocqueville, *Democracy in America*, 565.

22. Trollope, *Domestic Manners*, 10, 11, 35, 41, 90, 91; Featherstonehaugh, *Excursion through the Slave States*, Vol. 1, 276.

23. Trollope, *Domestic Manners*, 46, 76, 98-103, 125-126.

24. Rose Fulton Cramer, *Wayne County, Missouri* (Cape Girardeau: The Ramfre Press, 1972), 464, 481.

25. Howe, *What Hath God Wrought*, 176-179; see also Thomas A. DeBlack, "'The Rights and Rank to Which We Are Entitled': Arkansas in the Early Statehood Period," in Jeannie M. Whayne et al., *Arkansas, a Narrative History* (Fayetteville, University of Arkansas Press, 2002), 120.

26. Howe, *What Hath God Wrought*, 165-66, 178.

27. Ibid., 177.

28. de Tocqueville, *Democracy in America*, 280-283.

29 Dewey A. Stokes, "Public Affairs in Arkansas, 1836-1850" (PhD dissertation, University of Texas, 1966), 311-313.

Notes to Chapter 24,
"An Agglomeration of Adventurers and Speculators"

1. Bobby Roberts, "Thomas Stevenson Drew, 1844-1849," in Timothy Donovan, ed., *The Governors of Arkansas: Essays In Political Biography* (Fayetteville: The University of Arkansas Press, 1981), 12.

2. Personal communication, Ron Thompson, March 2, 2001.

3. Lawrence Dalton, *History of Randolph County, Arkansas* (Little Rock: Democrat Printing and Lithographing Company, 1946-47), 34.

4. Ibid., 15,55.

5. *Randolph County Deed Book B*, 13.

6. *Dalton, History of Randolph County*, 50, 55.

7. Jeannie M. Whayne, "The Turbulent Path to Statehood: Arkansas Territory, 1803-1836," in Jeannie M. Whayne et al., *Arkansas, a Narrative History* (Fayetteville: The University of Arkansas Press, 2002), 106.

8. "Proceedings of the Convention Met to Form a Constitution for the State of Arkansas," collection of the Oppenheimer Library, University of Arkansas at Little Rock, 39, 41, 43.

9. Walter Lee Brown, *A Life of Albert Pike* (Fayetteville: The University of Arkansas Press, 1997), 94-97; Whayne, "The Turbulent Path to Statehood," in Whayne et al., *Arkansas, a Narrative History*, 106; S. Charles Bolton, *Arkansas, 1800-1860: Remote and Restless* (Fayetteville: The University of Arkansas Press, 1998), 46. Brown's account, while not mentioning Drew, is notable for including critical details lacking in the others.

10. *Randolph County Deed Book B*, 137. Out of all the southern states, only Arkansas, Missouri and Delaware still allowed manumission: Ira Berlin, *Slaves Without Masters: The Free Negro in the Antebellum South* (New York: New Press, 1974), 138.

11. *Randolph County Deed Book C*, 398.

12. Roberts, "Thomas Stevenson Drew," 12.

13. Bolton, *Arkansas, 1800-1860*, 170-172; Whayne, "The Turbulent Path to Statehood," 102.

14. Featherstonehaugh, *Excursion through the Slave States*, Vol. 2 (London: John Murray, Albemarle St., 1844), 54; Bolton, *Arkansas, 1800-1860*, 35.

15. Reverend Timothy Flint, *Recollections of the Last Ten Years in the Valley of the Mississippi, 1826*, facsimile edition (New York: Da Capo Press,1968), 178-179.

16. Margaret Ross, *Arkansas Gazette, The Early Years, 1819-1866* (Little Rock, Arkansas Gazette Foundation, 1969), 202, citing Jon Hallum, *Biographical and Pictorial History of Arkansas* (Albany: Weed, Parsons and Co, 1887), 210.

17. Arkansas Constitution, 1836, Article 2.

18. www.arkansasties.com/Social/search.php?keywords=books, accessed March 16, 2014.

19. Mark Twain, *Life on the Mississippi* (New York: Airmont Publishing Company, Inc., 1965), 225.

20. S. Charles Bolton, *Territorial Ambition: Land and Society in Arkansas 1800-1840* (Fayetteville: The University of Arkansas Press, 1993), 67-73; Bolton, *Arkansas, 1800-1860*, 38.

21. Alexis de Tocqueville, *Democracy in America*, trans. Harvey C. Mansfield and Delba Winthrop (Chicago: University of Chicago Press, 2000), 191.

22. Dewey A. Stokes, "Public Affairs in Arkansas, 1836-1850," (PhD diss., University of Texas, 1966), 58; Bolton, *Arkansas, 1800-1860*, 58-59.

23. Message from Governor Thomas S. Drew to the Arkansas Legislature, November 1846, in Stokes, "Public Affairs in Arkansas," 321-322.

24. Ted R. Worley, "The Batesville Branch of the State Bank, 1836-1839," *Arkansas Historical Quarterly* 6 (Autumn, 1947), 296.

25. Stokes, "Public Affairs in Arkansas," 51-53.

26. Thomas A. DeBlack, "'The Rights and Rank to Which We Are Entitled': Arkansas in the Early Statehood Period," in Whayne et al., *Arkansas, a Narrative History*, 111; Bolton, *Arkansas, 1800-1860*, 56.

27. DeBlack, "The Rights and Rank," 111.

28. Brown, *A Life of Albert Pike*, 151.

29. Ibid., 162. Brown's account of the trial is more detailed and convincing than that of Featherstonehaugh, *Excursion through the Slave States*, Vol. 2, 61, although less entertaining. See also DeBlack, "The Rights and Rank," 113; Bolton, *Arkansas, 1800-1860*, 97, 177.

30. Worley, "The Batesville Branch of the State Bank, " 298; Stokes, "Public Affairs in Arkansas," 166.

31. "Randolph County Land Patents," in *Arkansas Land Patents*, Desmond Walls Allen and Bobbie Jones McLane, eds. (Arkansas Research 1991), originals in Eastern States Office, Bureau of Land Management, 350 S. Pickett St., Alexandria, VA 22304.

32. *Randolph County Deed Book B*, 17, 19, 22, and 75.

33. "Randolph County Land Patents" and county maps available in the Randolph County Recorder's office.

34. Stokes, "Public Affairs in Arkansas," 185.

35. DeBlack, "The Rights and Rank," 112-113

36. Stokes, "Public Affairs in Arkansas," 166, 320; Bolton, *Arkansas, 1800-1860*, 60-61.

37. Stokes, "Public Affairs in Arkansas," 318; Worley, "The Batesville Branch of the State Bank," 298.

38. Stokes, "Public Affairs in Arkansas," 321-322.

39. Pocahontas, Arkansas, tax list, 1850.

40. Roberts, "Thomas Stevenson Drew," 13. The process by which Drew was nominated is described in mind-numbing detail in Stokes, "Public Affairs in Arkansas," 279-281.

41. Thomas S. Drew to William Black, Esq., October 1, 1846, Robert W. Trimble manuscript collection, Arkansas Archives, Little Rock, Arkansas.

42. Drew to the Legislators, Little Rock, November 3, 1846, in *Helena Democrat*, November 6, 1846, and *Arkansas Gazette*, November 9, 1846; *Session Laws, 1846*, 49-51, 80-81, 198-199, in Stokes, "Public Affairs in Arkansas," 321-322; Bolton, *Arkansas, 1800-1860*, 60-61.

43. *Randolph County Deed Book B*, 415, 449, and 450, and *Deed Book C*, 23, 26, 36, 38, 39, 41, and 64. The loan from Mary is referred to in an 1850 deed transferring a substantial amount of land to Mary to repay the debt.

44. John W. Weeks to Margaret Bennett Barringer, 1921, in the possession of the author.

45. Peggy Jacoway, *First Ladies of Arkansas* (Little Rock: Southern Publishers, 1941), 82.

46. Daniel Walker Howe, *What Hath God Wrought: The Transformation of America, 1815-1848* (New York: Oxford University Press, 2007), 628, 635; Paul E. Johnson, *The Early American Republic, 1789-1829* (New York: Oxford University Press, 2007), 69.

47. Margaret Ross, *Arkansas Gazette*, 193-197.

48. Thomas Stevenson Drew to William Black, Little Rock, October 1, 1846, Robert W. Trimble manuscript collection, Arkansas Archives, Little Rock, Arkansas. The word "principle," which appears three times in this letter, also appears twice in Drew's 1844 Message to the Arkansas Legislature.

49. Thomas Stevenson Drew to E.H. Fletcher, August 22, 1846, Fletcher manuscript collection, Arkansas Archives, Little Rock, Arkansas.

50. Margaret Ross, *Arkansas Gazette*, 231-241.

51. Ibid., 243-249; Roberts, "Thomas Stevenson Drew," 15.

52. Dalton, *History of Randolph County*, 49.

53. Roberts, "Thomas Stevenson Drew," 15.

54. Brown, *A Life of Albert Pike*, 247-249.

55. Ibid., 284.

56. Ibid., 291.

57. *Randolph County Deed Book 3*, 67.

58. Donald McNeilly, *The Old South Frontier: Cotton Plantations and the Formation of Arkansas Society, 1819-1861* (Little Rock: The University of Arkansas Press, 2000), 132, Table 5.2.

59. Ibid., 136.

60. Ibid., 121.

61. *Arkansas Mortality Schedule*, 1850, compiled by Dr. Ronald Vern Jackson (Bountiful: Accelerated Indexing Systems, Inc.), Arkansas Archives.

62. *Desha County Deed Book D*, 120.

63. Dalton, *History of Randolph County*, 51.

64. Alvin M. Josephy Jr., *The Civil War in the American West* (New York: Random House,1991), 17-18.

65. T. J. Stiles, "The Filibuster King: The Strange Career of William Walker, the Most Dangerous International Criminal of the Nineteenth Century," accessed May 25, 2018, mrtomecko.weebly.com/uploads/1/3/2/9/13292665/walker.pdf.

66. Obituary of Ranson Drew, Prescott, Arizona, newspaper, April 16, 1913. The obituary was probably written by his youngest brother Joseph Drew, who had only reconnected with him near the end of his life, when he was very ill, and had brought him to Joseph's home in Arizona.

Notes to Chapter 25, Border Worlds

1. See William G. McLoughlin, *After the Trail of Tears: The Cherokees' Struggle for Sovereignty, 1839-1880* (Chapel Hill: University of North Carolina Press, 1993), 98-110, for details of some of the resulting policy shifts.

2. Thomas S. Drew to commissioner of Indian Affairs George Manypenny, March 24, 1854, United States National Archives microfilm roll M-234, 833-0249.

3. A thorough and detailed account of this history, from a point of view sympathetic to the Ross party, can be found in McLoughlin, *After the Trail of Tears*. A briefer and more dramatic version, rich in human interest and told from a point of view sympathetic to the Treaty Party, can be found in John Ehle, *Trail of Tears: the Rise and Fall of the Cherokee Nation* (New York: Anchor Books, 1988).

4. McLoughlin, *After the Trail of Tears*, 112-113, 102-109.

5. Ibid., 86-97.

6. John Ross to Thomas S. Drew, September 26, 1853, in Gary E. Moulton, ed, *The Papers of Chief John Ross*, Vol. 2 (Norman: University of Oklahoma Press, 1985), 384.

7. Thomas S. Drew to George Manypenny, February 22, 1854, United States National Archives microfilm roll M-234, 96-0576; Thomas S. Drew to George Butler, quoted in Drew to Manypenny, February 16, 1855, roll M-234, 97-0160.

8. Superintendent's Report, Southern Superintendency, addendum to United States Office of Indian Affairs, annual report of the commissioner of Indian Affairs for the year 1854, United States National Archives, accessed April 14, 2014, digicoll. library.wisc.edu/cgi-bin/History/History-idx?type=browse&scope=HISTORY. COMMREP.

9. McLoughlin, *After the Trail of Tears*, 92.

10. All reports attached to United States Office of Indian Affairs, annual report of the commissioner of Indian Affairs for the year 1854, United States National Archives, accessed April 17,2014, digicoll.library.wisc.edu/cgi-bin/History/History-idx?type=browse&scope=HISTORY.COMMREP.

11. Superintendent's Report, Southern Superintendency, addendum to United States Office of Indian Affairs, annual report of the commissioner of Indian Affairs for the year 1853, United States National Archives, accessed October 10, 2017, digicoll.library.wisc.edu/cgi-bin/History/History-idx?type=browse&scope=HISTORY.COMMREP.

12. Ibid., 136.

13. United States Office of Indian Affairs, annual report of the commissioner of Indian Affairs for the year 1853, United States National Archives, accessed April 17, 2014, digicoll.library.wisc.edu/cgi-bin/History/History-idx?type=browse&scope=HISTORY.COMREP, 13-16,

14. McLoughlin, *After the Trail of Tears*, 117-119.

15. United States Office of Indian Affairs, annual report of the commissioner of Indian Affairs for the year 1854, United States National Archives, accessed October 10, 2017, digicoll.library.wisc.edu/cgi-bin/History/History-idx?type=browse&scope=HISTORY.COMMREP, 116.

16. Daniel F. Littlefield Jr., and Mary Ann Littlefield, "The Beams Family: Free Blacks in Indian Territory," *The Journal of Negro History* (January 1976), 17-35, accessed October 11, 2017, freepages.genealogy.rootsweb.ancestry.com/~texlance/my/beams/beamsfamily.htm. The reader is advised to come prepared with a scorecard to keep track of the players.

17. The Littlefield article states that the Drew family was still living in southeastern Arkansas. However, in April of the same year Drew had notified commissioner Manypenny that he would be absent from his office for the month of May, while visiting his family in Pocahontas: Drew to Manypenny, March 24, 1854, United States National Archives microfilm roll M-234, 833-249.

18. George Manypenny to US Interior Secretary McClelland, December 14, 1854, United States National Archives microfilm roll M-348, 8-201.

19. George Manypenny to Interior Secretary McClelland, February 2, 1855, United States National Archives microfilm roll M-348, 8-303.

20. A lengthy draft of a brief for the defense in a murder trial, United States v. Ruby and Jennings, in which the defendants were white men who were citizens of the Cherokee Nation by virtue of their marriages to Cherokee women, was among the documents found in the green folder in my attic. The surnames of two men peripherally involved in the case, Scales and Vann, are those of close associates of Ross or their relatives. The original document was subsequently donated to the Arkansas Archives.

21. 1850 federal census for Johnson County, Arkansas (Overton Alston, Ranson Bettis, Civility Bettis Patterson, Elijah Bettis); 1850 federal census for Franklin County, Arkansas (R.D. Alston).

22. Dewey A. Stokes, "Public Affairs in Arkansas, 1836-1850"(PhD diss., University of Texas, 1966), 158, citing *Arkansas Gazette,* December 2, 9, and 23, 1840.

23. Frank Parkhurst Brackett, *History of Pomona Valley, California, with biographical sketches of the leading men and women of the valley who have been identified with its growth from the early days to the present* (Los Angeles Historic Record Company, 1923), 79.

24. *Arkansas Mortality Schedule, 1860,* compiled by Dr. Ronald Vern Jackson (Bountiful: Accelerated Indexing Systems, Inc.), Arkansas Archives, Little Rock.

Notes to Chapter 26, Worlds Destroyed

1. Bobby Roberts, "Thomas Stevenson Drew," in Donovan and Gatewood, eds., *The Governors of Arkansas: Essays in Political Biography* (Fayetteville: The University of Arkansas Press, 1981), 15.

2. Walter Lee Brown, *A Life of Albert Pike* (Fayetteville: The University of Arkansas Press, 1997), 321-328.

3. Thomas S. Drew to His Excellency H. M. Rector and the Honorable B. C. Felton, Military Board for the State of Arkansas, Little Rock, Arkansas, August 28, 1861, Arkansas Archives.

4. A draft of this letter, subsequently donated to the Arkansas Archives, was among the scraps of Drew papers found in my attic. Because the first two pages are missing, the date and recipient cannot be determined.

5. Nicole Etcheson, *Bleeding Kansas: Contested Liberty in the Civil War Era* (University Press of Kansas, 2004), 26.

6. Ibid., 62.

7. In the concluding paragraph of the letter he also describes Douglas as "Napoleonic," suggesting that the fact that Douglas, like Napoleon, John Ross—and Drew himself— was a man of unusually short stature, may have contributed to his sympathy.

8. Brown, *A Life of Albert Pike* (Fayetteville: The University of Arkansas Press, 1997), 351; Donald McNeilly, *The Old South Frontier: Cotton Plantations and the Formation of Arkansas Society, 1819-1861* (Fayetteville: The University of Arkansas Press, 2000), 188.

9. Etcheson, *Bleeding Kansas,* 189.

10. Thomas A. DeBlack, *With Fire and Sword: Arkansas, 1861-1874* (Fayetteville: The University of Arkansas Press, 2003), 18.

11. Thomas S. Drew to His Excellency H.M. Rector and the Honorable B.C. Felton, Military Board for the State of Arkansas, August 28, 1861, Arkansas Archives.

12. Roll of the Twenty-sixth Regiment, Arkansas Infantry, Company H, accessed May 12, 2014, www.couchgenweb.com/civilwar/26thcoh.html, .

13. DeBlack, *With Fire and Sword,* 31.

14. Ibid., 57-58.

15. Thomas S. Drew to Reverend R. W. Trimble, July 30, 1877, copy in the possession of the author. Although the original was donated to the Arkansas Archives, I was unable to find it in their files in 2014.

16. DeBlack, *With Fire and Sword,* 73, 120.

17. Ibid., 120.

18. Pocahontas Civil War River Walk Memorial, text by Gary D. Gazeway, 2014. See also William Monks, *A History Of Southern Missouri And Northern Arkansas: Being An Account Of The Early Settlements, The Civil War, The Ku-Klux, And Times Of Peace,* eds. John F. Bradbury and Lou Wehmer (Fayetteville: The University of Arkansas Press, 2003), 85.

19. George Valentine Massey II, "The Bennett, Drew, Stafford and Westcott Lineages of Margaret (Bennett) Barringer," unpublished report, 1951, in the possession of the author. The story that Bennett was quartered in the Drew house is part of Barringer family oral history.

20. Lawrence Dalton, *History of Randolph County, Arkansas* (Little Rock: Democrat Printing and Lithographing Company,1946-7), 52.

21. *Arkansas Marriages, Early to 1850,* Vol. 2 (Bountiful, Utah: Liahona Research, Inc., 1990), 418, 521.

22. Personal correspondence, Donna Goodwin, a descendant of Joe and Algenora.

23. DeBlack, *With Fire and Sword,* 143.

24. *Pocahontas Star Herald,* November 24, 1916, 3.

25. *Pocahontas Star Herald, Centennial Edition,* September 20, 1956. The date given in this reminiscence must be wrong, since Saidee was already married and living in Illinois in 1866.

26. William G. McLoughlin, *After the Trail of Tears: The Cherokees' Struggle for Sovereignty, 1839-1880* (Chapel Hill: The University of North Carolina Press, 1993), 172-175.

27. Josephy, *The Civil War in the American West,* 330-333; McLoughlin, *After the Trail of Tears,* 191-195.

28. McLoughlin, *After the Trail of Tears,* 198.

29. Ibid., 209-213; Josephy, *The Civil War in the American West,* 370-71, 376-377.

Notes to Chapter 27, The Wilder West

1. Frank Parkhurst Brackett, *History of Pomona Valley, California, with biographical sketches of the leading men and women of the valley who have been identified with its growth, from the early days to the present,* reprint (Los Angeles: Los Angeles Historic Record Company, 1923), 79-80.

2. Horace Bell, *On the Old West Coast: Being further Reminiscences of a Ranger* (New York: William Morrow & Co, 1930), 25; personal communication, Anne Collier, June 29, 2005.

3. Personal communication, Anne Collier, June 29, 2005.

4. Ibid.

5. Bell, *On the Old West Coast,* 21-31

6. Brackett, *History of Pomona Valley,* 85.

7. Bell, *On the Old West Coast,* 12. On page 102 of the same book, Dorsey is identified as the "Register . . . who bit the nose off the US District Attorney." Bell describes him as "a fighter from way back . . . a pistol fighter, a knife fighter, and away up in rough and tumble."

8. Ibid., 102.

9. Brackett, *History of Pomona Valley,* 84.

10. *Legends of America,* "Panamint City, a Hard-Boiled Hellhole," accessed February 1, 2017, www.legendsofamerica.com/ca-panamint.html.

11. The letter, from a Mr. Taylor, was reprinted in the Fayetteville, Arkansas, *Democrat* on July 23, 1923, and was provided to the author by Drew descendant Tony Vagnone. John Coffee Hays was the son of Drew's youngest uncle, Harmon Atkins Hays, who had fought under Andrew Jackson's General John Coffee in the War of 1812. The letter contains at least one mistake: the statement that John Hays was Drew's "Adjutant General" when Drew was Governor. Several online biographies of Hays place him in Texas or Mexico during the entire period of Drew's governorship.

12. Personal communication, Anne Collier, June 29, 2005.

13. Thomas S. Drew to Emma C. Marr, dated February 4, 1875, Arkansas Archives. One of Emma's opponents in these lawsuits was her brother-in-law, Elijah Bettis Marr: *Randolph County Probate Records Book 8,* 343, 353, 402.

14. Letter from Mr. Taylor, reprinted in the Fayetteville, Arkansas, *Democrat* on July 23, 1923.

15. Dee Powell to Tony Vagnone dated March 14, 1982, Arkansas Archives.

16. Unnamed Prescott, Arizona, newspaper, June 2, 1926.

17. John W. Meeks to Margaret Bennett Barringer, 1921, in the possession of the author.

18. Dee Powell, "Arkansas Ex-Governor Lived in Weatherford," Trails West (Parker County Genealogical Society, October 1995).

Notes to Chapter 28, A Free Woman of Color in Jacksonport

1. Deed of W. W. Tunstall to Martha Cooper, *Jackson County Deed Record Book F,* 509.

2. *Jackson County Deed Record Book F,* 512. For comparison prices for similar lots, see sale by W. W. Tunstall to Drew Cooper, *Jackson County Deed Record Book H,* 559, and resale of same lot to Wisdom and Stafford, *Jackson County Deed Record Book I,* 111.

3. Deed of Martha Cooper, December 18, 1855, *Jackson County Deed Record Book F,* 591.

4. Lawrence Dalton, *History of Randolph County, Arkansas* (Little Rock: Democrat Printing and Lithographing Company, 1946-7), 13, 141. The surname Searcy had followed the Bettis and Drew families from North Carolina to Middle Tennessee and on to Arkansas, suggesting a connection that goes back even further.

5. Will of Richard Searcy, dated October 16, 1830, filed January 8, 1833, Independence County, Arkansas, *Arkansas, Wills and Probate Records, 1783-1998,* accessed September 17, 2015, home.ancestry.com/.

6. 1860 federal census, Jackson County Arkansas. Wisdom does not appear as the owner of any slaves.

7. See John Hope Franklin and Loren Schweninger, *In Search of the Promised Land: A Slave Family in the Old South* (New York: Oxford University Press, 2006), 119, 253, and throughout.

8. Arkansas Session Laws, 1840, 87-88 and Session Laws, 1844, 163, cited in Dewey A. Stokes, "Public Affairs in Arkansas, 1836-1850," (PhD diss., University of Texas, 1966), 189, 295.

9. *Jackson County Deed Record Book G*, 18.

10. Since Evalina's name is not included in the lists of enslaved grandchildren bequeathed to the daughters of Elijah Bettis III, she was probably not Mahala's daughter, but perhaps a granddaughter.

11. *Jackson County Deed Record Book G*, 696 and *Book H*, 559.

12. *Jackson County Deed Record Book I*, 111 and 123.

13. Bettie Hurd to Tony Vagnone, July 12, 1976, in possession of Mr. Vagnone.

14. Thomas C. Buchanan, *Black Life on the Mississippi: Slaves, Free Blacks, and the Western Steamboat World* (Chapel Hill: The University of North Carolina Press, 2004), 12.

15. Ibid., 91.

16. Ibid., 93.

17. Ibid., 8, 70.

18. *Jackson County Court Records Book A*, 397 and 414.

19. Personal conversation, Matt Manos, Park interpreter at Jacksonport State Park, Jacksonport, Arkansas, October 9, 2014. The figures for the income of steamboat captains came from the town's founder, T. T. Tunstall, himself the owner of three steamboats.

20. Thomas C. Buchanan, *Black Life on the Mississippi*, 62, 93.

21. Acknowledgment by Charnelsea Bettis of receipt of slaves bequeathed to her under the will of Elijah Bettis, January 12, 1839, *Randolph County Deed Book B*, 106.

22. Tony Vagnone to the author, October 18, 2004.

23. Bettie Hurd to Tony Vagnone, June 30, 1979, in the possession of Mr. Vagnone.

24. Bettie Hurd to Tony Vagnone, September 19, 1976, in the possession of Mr. Vagnone.

25. Acknowledgment by Amy Marr of receipt of slaves bequeathed to her under the will of Elijah Bettis, January 21, 1839, *Randolph County Deed Book B*, 106.

26. Orville W. Taylor, *Negro Slavery in Arkansas* (Durham, NC: Duke University Press, 1958), 247.

27. Ibid., 256, citing "Circular to the People of the State of Arkansas," *Washington Telegraph*, August 4, 1858.

28. Ibid., 257.

29. *Randolph County Deed Book 8*, 336.

30. 1860 and 1870 federal census, Leavenworth County, Kansas.

Notes to Chapter 29, Into the Whirlwind

1. Nicole Etcheson, *Bleeding Kansas: Contested Liberty in the Civil War Era* (University Press of Kansas, 2004), 204.

2. Ibid., 190-195.

3. Ibid., 192, 219.

4. Roger D. Bridges, "The Illinois Black Codes," Illinois Periodicals on Line, accessed June 3, 2014, www.lib.niu.edu/1996/iht329602.html.

5. Henry Clay Bruce, *The New Man: Twenty-Nine Years a Slave. Twenty-Nine Years a Free Man* (York, PA.: Anstadt and Sons, 1895), 74-76.

6. Etcheson, *Bleeding Kansas*, 236.

7. Ibid., 227-228; Thomas Goodrich, *Black Flag: Guerrilla Warfare on the Western Border, 1861-1865* (Bloomington: Indiana University Press, 1995), 7, 11, 26.

8. Goodrich, *Black Flag*, 26.

9. Ibid., 53, 56.

10. Keith Wilson, *Campfires of Freedom: the Camp Life of Black Soldiers During the Civil War* (Ohio, Kent State University Press, 2002), cited in Christian G. Samito, *Becoming American Under Fire: Irish Americans, African Americans, and the Politics of Citizenship During the Civil War Era* (Ithaca: Cornell University Press, 2009), 47.

11. Samito, *Becoming American*, 40.

12. Goodrich, *Black Flag*, 36.

13. Etcheson, *Bleeding Kansas*, 233-234; Goodrich, *Black Flag*, 36.

14. Goodrich, *Black Flag*, 40.

15. Ibid., 76-9; Etcheson, *Bleeding Kansas*, 234.

16. Ibid., 97-100, 160.

17. Ibid., 126

18. Ibid., 132.

19. Ibid., 119.

20. Ibid., 118.

21. Etcheson, *Bleeding Kansas*, 235.

22. Goodrich, *Black Flag*, 113.

23. Jesse A. Hall and Leroy T. Hand, *History of Leavenworth County, Kansas* (Topeka: Historical Publishing Company, 1921)

24. Etcheson, *Bleeding Kansas*, 229.

Notes to Chapter 30, Claiming a Place as Citizens

1. It is possible that the census taker placed the "household number," which was supposed to be entered next to the name of the head of each household, on the wrong line, and that Martha, Drew, and John were actually living together instead of next door to each other.

2. Deed from Edward H. Marsh and Eliza C. Marsh to Martha Cooper, November 27, 1860, Lot #5 in Block #15 in Days' Subdivision, *Leavenworth County Deed Book R*, 94

3. Deed from Drew and Leanna Bettis to Anne Washington, September 7,1881, Lots #1 and 2 of Block 18 in Days' Subdivision. This deed could not be found at the Leavenworth Registry of Deeds and was probably never recorded.

4. Deed from Martha Cooper to Sarah Jane Jackson, January 12, 1867, Lot #5 in Block #15 in Days' Subdivision, *Leavenworth County Deed Book 15, 32.*

5. Kansas state census, 1875.

6. Katie H. Armitage, "'Seeking a Home where He Himself is Free:' African-Americans Build a Community in Douglas County, Kansas," *Kansas History 31* (Autumn 2008), 159-162.

7. Nupur Chaudhuri, "'We All Seem Like Brothers and Sisters': The African-American Community in Manhattan, Kansas, 1865-1940," *Kansas History 14* (Winter 1991/1992), 281-283.

8. Martha Cooper obituary, Leavenworth *Advocate*, November 29, 1890, from Saunders/Felder family tree, ancestry.com, accessed February 1, 2017, /trees. ancestry.com/tree/8842805/person/-730179525/mediax/1?pgnum=1&pg=0&pg-pl=pid%7CpgNum ; Bettie Hurd to Tony Vagnone, September 19, 1976, in the possession of Mr. Vagnone.

9. Martin Bettis obituary, Leavenworth *Advocate*, November 9, 1889.

10. Drew's daughter Mary Jane Bettis, known as Jenny, was in fact named after two of her great-aunts, who appear in Elijah's 1836 deed as Poll and Jenny.

11. Christian G. Samito, *Becoming American Under Fire: Irish Americans, African Americans, and the Politics of Citizenship During the Civil War Era* (Ithaca: Cornell University Press, 2009), 158-161; Nupur Chaudhuri, "'We All Seem Like Brothers and Sisters,'" 283.

12. Samito, *Becoming American*, 72-78, 134, 162, 170, 217, throughout.

13. Henry Clay Bruce, *The New Man: Twenty-Nine Years a Slave. Twenty-Nine Years a Free Man* (York, PA.: Anstadt and Sons, 1895), 156.

14. Bruce, *The New Man*, 157-158.

15. Ibid. 113-114.

16. Ibid., 114-116.

17. *Commonwealth*, Topeka, April 18, 1879, in Charlotte Hinger, *Nicodemus: Post-Reconstruction Politics and Racial Justice in Western Kansas* (Norman: University of Oklahoma Press, 2016), 111-116.

18. Hinger, *Nicodemus,* 125.

19. Ibid., 68.

20. Bruce, *The New Man*, 119.

21. 1880 federal census for Leavenworth County, Kansas; genealogy note on William Kelly submitted byTerry Goode, accessed December 10, 2016, my.ancestry.com/viewer/bfd8abf4-0611-4a13-93ef-737572ee292d/8842805/-723430759.

22. Hinger, *Nicodemus*. Hinger discusses in great detail the careers of two of those men, Abram Thompson Hall Jr., and Edward Preston McCabe.

23. "Nicodemus, a Black Pioneer Town," accessed December 10, 2016, www.legendsofamerica.com/ks-nicodemus2.html.

24. Genealogy note on William Kelly submitted by Terry Goode, accessed December 10, 2016, my.ancestry.com/viewer/ bfd8abf4-0611-4a13-93ef-737572ee292d/8842805/-723430759.

25. *Fremont Eagle*, Fremont (later Moreland), Kansas, November 6, 1889; genealogy note submitted by Terry Goode, accessed December 10, 2016, my.ancestry.com/viewer/ d7ddb9d7-3f69-40c4-b395-9049e6f00b99/8842805/-708526830.

26. Martin Bettis obituary, genealogy note submitted by Terry Goode, accessed December 10, 2016, my.ancestry.com/ viewer/64b362af-f899-4dcf-8f01-0d6d1b4d0316/8842805/-708526830.

27. "Nicodemus, a Black Pioneer Town," accessed December 10, 2016,www.legendsofamerica.com/ks-nicodemus.html.

28. Martha Cooper obituary, Leavenworth *Advocate*, November 29, 1890.

Archives • Collections • Reading Recommendations

Archives, data collections, museums, and documents consulted in the preparation of this book appear below.

Virginia

Library of Virginia, Richmond: Southampton County will and deed books; Isle of Wight will and deed books; personal property tax list 1790 (State Records Collection); Black Creek Church membership list, Antioch Baptist Church Minute Books, 1772 – 1892 (Archives)

William Waller Hening, *The Statutes at Large, Being a Collection of all the Laws of Virginia from the First Session of the Legislature, in the Year 1619*, II, transcribed for the internet by Freddie L. Spradlin, Torrance, California

Index to Virginia Land Office Patents and Grants, Book 20, 280, online at image.lva.virginia.gov/LONN/LO-1/018/201-300.html and Book 24, 620, online at image.lva.virginia.gov/LONN/LO-1/022/601-644.html

"Isle of Wight County VA—Records," *William and Mary College Quarterly* 7 (April, 1899)

Southampton County Court Order books, 1749-1754 and 1754-1759, online at www.brantleyassociation.com/southampton_project/southampton_project_list. htm

Virginia religious petitions, online at www.virginiamemory.com/collections/ petitions

North Carolina

Margaret M. Hoffman, *Abstracts of Deeds Edgecombe Precinct and Edgecombe County as found in Halifax County, NC Deed Books 1-6*

Colonial and State Records of North Carolina

Cumberland County deed books, online at www.ccrodinternet.org/ BookAndPage.asp

North Carolina State Archives, Secretary of State Records Group, Land Office, Cumberland County, online at mars.archives.ncdcr.gov

North Carolina State Archives, Raleigh, NC: Minutes, Cumberland County Court of Pleas and Common Sessions; Records of the Provincial Assembly, Council of Safety

World Vital Records, Revolutionary War Pension Records, online at www. worldvitalrecords.com/SingleIndexIndView.aspx?ix=ft_revwarpensrec&hpp=1&rf=*,z*&qt=i&zdocid=19217694_213_

Weymouth Woods Sandhills Nature Preserve, Southern Pines, North Carolina

Schiele Museum of Natural History, Gastonia, North Carolina

Tennessee

Tennessee State Library and Archives, Nashville: Records of Big Cedar Lick Church, Little Cedar Lick Church, Mill Creek Baptist Church

Historic Mansker's Station, Goodlettsville, Tennessee

Missouri

Cape Girardeau County Archives, Jackson, Missouri: Estate inventory of Elijah Bettis; multiple records of lawsuits involving the extended Bettis family

Tax lists and federal census information for Wayne County, Missouri; Johnson County, Arkansas Territory; Franklin and Crittenden Counties, Arkansas

Missouri State Archives: "Missouri's Early Slave Laws: A History in Documents"

Arkansas

The Arkansas Archives, which has replaced the former Arkansas History Commission, has been expanded, upgraded, and digitized, but as of this writing, its website contains no evidence of any of the documents or newspaper clippings relating to T. S. Drew cited in this book. The Arkansas History Commission collection contained, among other things, letters of T. S. Drew to various recipients; relevant clippings from the *Arkansas Gazette* and other newspapers; and "Letters of Dee Powell, 1982-1985, Concerning Thomas S. Drew, third Governor of Arkansas." Presumably the documents, formerly contained in manila envelopes and file folders, have survived the transition, but their location has not been determined.

Additional articles from the *Arkansas Gazette* previously online at www. arkansasties.com/Social/viewforum.php?f=97, but since removed.

Oppenheimer Library, University of Arkansas at Little Rock: "Proceedings of the Convention Met to Form a Constitution for the State of Arkansas"; Arkansas Constitution, 1836

Dewey A. Stokes, "Public Affairs in Arkansas, 1836-1850," (PhD diss., University of Texas, 1966): Message from Governor Thomas S. Drew to the Arkansas Legislature, Little Rock, Nov 3, 1846, in *Helena Democrat*, November 6, 1846, and *Arkansas Gazette*, November 9, 1846; Session Laws, 1846, 49-51,80-81, 198-199

Desmond Walls Allen and Bobbie Jones McLane, eds., *Arkansas Land Patents*

Randolph County Courthouse, Pocahontas, Arkansas: Deeds, land patents, estate inventories, and cemetery records involving members of the Drew and Bettis families

Obituary of Ranson Drew, Prescott, Arizona, newspaper, April 16, 1913

Gary E. Moulton, ed, *The Papers of Chief John Ross*, II: John Ross to Thomas S. Drew, September 26, 1853

United States National Archives, Washington, D.C.: correspondence of Commissioner of Indian Affairs George Manypenny

United States National Archives, online at digicoll.library.wisc.edu/cgi-bin/ History/History-idx?type=browse&scope=HISTORY.COMMREP: United States Office of Indian Affairs: Annual Report of the Commissioner of Indian Affairs for the year 1853; Annual Report of the Commissioner of Indian Affairs for the year 1854

Martha Bettis Cooper, Arkansas to Kansas

Jacksonport State Park Museum and archives, Newport, Arkansas

Jackson County Courthouse, Newport, Arkansas

Arkansas Wills and Probate Records, 1783-1798, home.ancestry.com/

Federal censuses for Leavenworth, KS, 1860, 1870, 1880; Kansas state censuses for Leavenworth, 1865 and 1875, home.ancestry.com/

The author's personal selection follows of the most interesting and enlightening books on various topics.

General

Ira Berlin, *Slaves Without Masters: The Free Negro in the Antebellum South*

Steven C. Bullock, *Revolutionary Brotherhood: Freemasonry and the Transformation of the American Social Order, 1730-1840* (by far the best treatment I've found)

W. J. Cash, *The Mind of the South* (still relevant and controversial seventy-five years later)

David Hackett Fischer, *Albion's Seed: Four British Folkways in America*. (A sweeping and compelling analysis of four American cultures and the ways in which their differences shaped our nation)

Elizabeth Fox-Genovese, *Within the Plantation Household: Black & White Women of the Old South*

Arthur Herman, *How the Scots Invented the Modern World*

Daniel Walker Howe, *What Hath God Wrought: The Transformation of America, 1815-1848*

Jack Larkin, *The Reshaping of Everyday Life,1790-1840*

Christian G. Samito, *Becoming American Under Fire: Irish Americans, African Americans, and the Politics of Citizenship During the Civil War Era*

Alexis de Tocqueville, *Democracy in America* (well worth re-reading)

Frances Trollope, *Domestic Manners of the Americans* (patronizing and superior but still delightful)

James Webb, *Born Fighting: How the Scots-Irish Shaped America*

Bertram Wyatt-Brown, *Honor and Violence in the Old South*

Norman R. Yetman, ed., *Voices from Slavery: 100 Authentic Slave Narratives*

Virginia

William K. Boyd, ed., *William Byrd's Histories of the Dividing Line betwixt Virginia and North Carolina*

T.H. Breen and Stephen Innes, *"Myne Owne Ground": Race and Freedom on Virginia's Eastern Shore, 1640-1676*

Susan Dunn, *Dominion of Memories: Jefferson, Madison, and the Decline of Virginia* (an unfamiliar but compelling take on two of our most revered founders)

David Hackett Fischer and James C. Kelly, *Bound Away: Virginia and the Westward Movement*

Tim Hashaw, *The Birth of Black America: The First African-Americans and the Pursuit of Freedom in Jamestown* (piracy, international intrigue, drama, achievement, and loss)

Paul Heinegg, *Free African Americans of North Carolina, Virginia, and South Carolina*, fifth edition, online in full at www.freeafricanamericans.com (an indispensable genealogical and historical resource)

Rhys Isaac, *The Transformation of Virginia, 1740-1790* (how the Baptists changed everything)

Edmund S. Morgan, *American Slavery, American Freedom: The Ordeal of Colonial Virginia*

Mechal Sobel, *The World They Made Together: Black and White Values in Eighteenth-Century Virginia* (surprising and fascinating)

North Carolina

Marjoleine Kars, *Breaking Loose Together: The Regulator Rebellion in Pre-Revolutionary North Carolina*

Jack Temple Kirby, *Poquosin: A Study of Rural Landscape and Society*

Ruairidh H. MacLeod, *Flora MacDonald: The Jacobite Heroine in Scotland and North America*

Duane Meyer, *The Highland Scots of North Carolina, 1732-1776*

Kay K. Moss, *Southern Folk Medicine, 1750-1820* and *Journey to the Piedmont Past*

John Ferdinand Dalziel Smyth, *A Tour in the United States of America*, in *Eyewitness Accounts of the American Revolution* (a total fabrication, but a lot of fun to read)

Tennessee to Arkansas

Harriette Simpson Arnow, *Seedtime on the Cumberland* (everyday life on the frontier in meticulous, comprehensive detail, from contemporary sources)

Robert V. Remini, *Andrew Jackson and His Indian Wars*

Missouri

Stephen Aron, *American Confluence*

John James Audubon, *Delineations of American Scenery and Character* (vivid, amusing, and generally a great read)

Thomas C. Buchanan, *Black Life on the Mississippi: Slaves, Free Blacks, and the Western Steamboat World* (fascinating things you never knew)

Carl Ekberg, *Colonial Ste. Genevieve: An Adventure on the Mississippi Frontier*

Rev. Timothy Flint, *Recollections of the Last Ten Years in the Valley of the Mississippi*, 1826, facsimile edition

Walter A. Schroeder, *Opening the Ozarks: A Historical Geography of Missouri's Ste. Genevieve District, 1760-1830* (a vast, detailed, and comprehensive examination of southeastern Missouri in the early years)

Bonnie Stepenoff, *From French Community to Missouri Town: Ste. Genevieve in the Nineteenth Century.*

Arkansas

S. Charles Bolton, *Arkansas, 1800-1860: Remote and Restless*

S. Charles Bolton, *Territorial Ambition: Land and Society in Arkansas 1800-1840*

John Ehle, *Trail of Tears: The Rise and Fall of the Cherokee Nation* (an interesting counterpoint to McLoughlin, below)

Alvin M. Josephy, Jr., *The Civil War in the American West*

William G. McLoughlin, *After the Trail of Tears: The Cherokees' Struggle for Sovereignty, 1839-1880*

Kansas

Nicole Etcheson, *Bleeding Kansas: Contested Liberty in the Civil War Era*

John Hope Franklin and Loren Schweninger, *In Search of the Promised Land: A Slave Family in the Old South* (a brief, compelling narrative of slavery and freedom based on the family's personal papers)

Thomas Goodrich, *Black Flag: Guerrilla Warfare on the Western Border, 1861-1865*

Charlotte Hinger, *Nicodemus: Post-Reconstruction Politics and Racial Justice in Western Kansas*

Carla Barringer Rabinowitz

About the Author

Carla Barringer Rabinowitz was born in Villanova, Pennsylvania, graduated from Radcliffe College and Boston College Law School, and now lives in rural North Central Massachusetts with her husband, Phil. She has been a lawyer, mediator, non-profit executive, school committee member, and founding member of the Athol-Royalston Education Foundation. She has written and spoken on subjects including parent participation in education, what the families of successful learners have in common, and the history of the Barringer Meteorite Crater. Carla and Phil are the parents of two children and the grandparents of five.

Index

Colophon

Text for *Borderers* is set in Adobe Jenson, an old-style serif typeface drawn for Adobe Systems by its chief type designer, Robert Slimbach. Its Roman styles are based on a text face cut by Nicolas Jenson in Venice around 1470, and its italics are based on those created by Ludovico Vicentino degli Arrighi fifty years later.

Jenson is an organic, somewhat idiosyncratic font, with a low x-height and inconsistencies that help differentiate letters. It is considered a highly readable typeface appropriate for large amounts of text and is accordingly often used in book design for body text.

Adobe Jenson was first released in 1996 as a multiple master font. It was created using sophisticated interpolation or multiple-master technology to create a range of weights and optical sizes suitable for different text sizes. This partial automation of font creation was intended to allow a gradual trend in styles from solid, chunky designs for caption-size small print to more graceful and slender designs for headings. It is now sold in the standard OpenType font format under the name Adobe Jenson Pro.

Titles for *Borderers* are set in Stone Sans. Sumner Stone worked together with Bob Ishi of Adobe to create the Stone family fonts, which appeared in 1987. Coincidentally, ishi is the Japanese word for stone, which precluded any squabbling about whose name the font would carry. The family consists of three types of fonts, a serif, a sans-serif and an informal style. The Stone fonts are very legible and make a modern, dynamic impression.

CPSIA information can be obtained
at www.ICGtesting.com
Printed in the USA
FFHW020654191118
49397800-53802FF

9 780998 2735